Culture Worrier

REFLECTIONS ON RACE, POLITICS AND SOCIAL CHANGE

Culture Worrier

REFLECTIONS ON RACE, POLITICS AND SOCIAL CHANGE

SELECTED COLUMNS 1984-2014

CLARENCE PAGE

PULITZER PRIZE WINNER

Foreword by Chris Matthews

BOLDEN

AN AGATE IMPRINT

CHICAGO

Chicago Tribune
Tony W. Hunter, CEO & Publisher
Gerould W. Kern, Senior Vice President, Editor
Bill Adee, Executive Vice President/Digital
Joycelyn Winnecke, Vice President, Associate Editor
Jane Hirt, Vice President, Managing Editor
Peter Kendall, Deputy Managing Editor

Printed in the United States

Library of Congress Cataloging-in-Publication Data

Page, Clarence, 1947-
 [Newspaper columns. Selections]
 Culture worrier : selected columns 1984/2014 : reflections on race, politics and social change / Clarence Page.
    pages cm
 Summary: "The first collection of columns from the Pulitzer Prize-winning and nationally syndicated journalist Clarence Page, touching on politics, social commentary, pop culture, new media, race, and family"-- Provided by publisher.
 Includes index.
 ISBN 978-1-932841-92-3 (pbk.) -- ISBN 1-932841-92-X (pbk.)
 I. Title.
 PN4874.P224A25 2014
 070.4'4--dc23
                          2014017731

10 9 8 7 6 5 4 3 2 1

Bolden is an imprint of Agate Publishing. Agate books are available in bulk at discount prices. For more information visit agatepublishing.com.

To my wife Lisa, whose patience made all of this possible.

CONTENTS

FOREWORD

A great newspaper columnist is a tour guide. He points out what's important, helps interpret what we're seeing, warns us of possible dangers. When he gets the opportunity, he'll jolly up the excursion with a bit of humor.

Always, he will be good company.

Clarence Page meets all these tests with flying colors. His millions of readers look to him for common sense and a fair-mindedness that is, I must confess, rarely found today. Like others in his league—George F. Will, Tom Friedman, Maureen Dowd—Clarence is admired for the way his mind works. More than that, people warm to the steady hum of his conscience.

My colleague knows and respects his readers. It shows in his craft. His decades on a big metropolitan newspaper, the Chicago Tribune, taught him early to write with a wide perspective and forced him to address issues from other viewpoints besides his own.

"Reaching for a broad audience," he argues, "conditions you to be broad-minded."

I first got to know Clarence in the late 1980s when we shared the bench on that early political arena "The McLaughlin Group." We would both wonder when "Dr. John" would send us the high sign that we were going to sub for one of his veteran stars—Jack Germond or Morton Kondracke. I wonder whether he liked throwing us in the game just to keep those big-name guys on their toes.

In recent years, my friend has joined me with great success on "Hardball." I say that because Clarence Page is one of the rare nationally syndicated columnists who speaks on television with the same luminous personality as he does in print. His laugh is contagious, his humor and sensibility reliably generous.

What I like especially is his independence. He doesn't torque his judgments in the direction of the pack. He doesn't score "gaffes" up there with God's judgment on humankind, nor does he build bonfires here on earth to roast those who commit them. This is true particularly when he is dealing in that tricky terrain of race.

Don't mistake his restraint for a lack of passion, however. In his columns or on television, he may smile through the pain, but he sure as hell feels it. I've noted this on those couple of occasions when I've referred to him on-air as "Clarence Thomas." In each instance, it's earned me a smile mixed with just the hint of a wince.

I could excuse, readily enough, this mistaken identification, this confusing he of the august Chicago Tribune with the arch-conservative of the Supreme Court. I could argue that the other Clarence went to Holy Cross, my alma mater, and was thus the more familiar surname. Or I could argue that the two distinguished gentlemen of very different thinking are two of only three Clarences I know, the third being that benign angel in "It's a Wonderful Life" who keeps the depressed Jimmy Stewart character from jumping from that snow-covered bridge.

But I protest too much. Clarence knew the most probable cause of my mistake, the "usual suspect," if you will. I knew it. He knew I knew it. I think we both, in those couple of instances, chalked it up to the American experience we have both lived and know too well, but that also has given both of us what life requires most: hope.

Clarence has been sharp-eyed about such matters when some of us have been too starry-eyed. Consider these words from his column written in the immediate afterglow of the 2008 election: "Race and racism have not evaporated. Nor has the need for diversity to be respected, not just tolerated."

In this and in all that's collected here you'll find what we treasure most: good company. You will encounter here in Clarence Page's writing an American who has seen, if not everything, an awful lot. He's here to be your guide to the interesting plot points of history, those you may have missed, those you may have noticed but failed to register.

In these columns you'll get the benefit not just of what this great journalist has covered but what he's been through as a man. What could be more important? "The life of the law has not been logic," he quotes Oliver Wendell Holmes. "It has been experience."

Same here. When it comes to tour guides, you can't get a better one than Clarence Page. Here you will be in the company of a guy who knows the road, a seasoned grown-up with a sunlit pride in how far this country has come.

Safe travels!

—Chris Matthews
Host of "Hardball with Chris Matthews"

"In response to all the 'culture warriors' I have known and covered, I'm a culture worrier. I worry about those who claim more cultural supremacy than they deserve to claim."
—*Clarence Page*

INTRODUCTION
WHAT? ME WORRY?

When the pioneer media guru Marshall McLuhan visited my university during my student days, he said something that has stuck with me. A student asked what he thought of the "black power" movement that was simmering at the time. "White America is detribalizing," he observed in his characteristically prophetic fashion, "and black America is re-tribalizing."

He said more, but the elegant imagery and symmetry of that statement has stayed on my mind ever since. McLuhan used the term "tribe" a lot. He spoke and wrote about "tribal man" versus "technological man," for whom modern media are extensions of the self. In these and in other ways, he was far more often quoted than understood. But what he was saying made clear sense to me. It was the civil rights era. White America was relaxing its historic customs, institutions and traditions of white privilege. Black America, particularly my young generation—presenting cool but feeling very cautious—was turning inward, rejecting the melting-pot assimilationist values of our elders and reaching back to discover our roots in a place to which we never had been, a romanticized Eden called "Africa"—or in some super-righteous circles, "Afrika."

Fast forward. Were McLuhan around today in the new media age of Twitter, Facebook, Google, Instagram and the cloud—and once he got through with his I-told-you-so's—I believe he would observe something quite the opposite of what he said about racial tribes in the 1960s. He might well observe that African-Americans in the age of Barack Obama have been detribalizing while white Americans in the age of tea party politics are re-tribalizing.

Or maybe he, like the world, would be more complicated than that. In McLuhanesque terms, I have seen all Americans re-tribalize—as in, rearrange ourselves less strictly along lines of race or ethnicity than along lines of shared culture, values, interests and attitudes. Today's tribes are less distinctly racial and ethnic than cultural and political. Such is the new neotribalism that has defined my career as a reporter and my past three decades as a columnist, from which the works in this book were selected. I've written a lot about race and ethnicity, but race only has been the most obvious marker of far more significant cultural and tribal relations in our society. Ambrose Bierce got the point with his dour Industrial Age definition of "the Conservative" as "a statesman who is enamored of existing evils, as distinguished from the Liberal, who wishes to replace them with others."

It is with a similarly fascinated evenhandedness that I have tried as a columnist to track and navigate the vast, tricky terrains of our nation's diverse tribal homelands. Reporting on the streets of Chicago taught me that African-Americans are just one of many ethnic tribes in our American quilt and, on closer examination, hardly a single tribe at that. Chicago taught me a lot about diversity. Southern Ohio, where I grew up and learned journalism, taught me about life in the so-called heartland. Thanks to both aspects of my background, I feel comfortable whether I am covering Al Sharpton or Sarah Palin, Reagan Democrats or Ralph Nader "raiders," Pat Robertson or the Rev. Jeremiah Wright, the MTV generation or the "Greatest Generation," millennials or centenarians.

But I am most thankful to have come up in the world of newspapers before mass media lost their mission to at least try to offer all things to all people. Reaching for a broad audience conditions you to be broadminded. In the age of target marketing, I struggle against the narrow confines of narrowcasting. Don't fence me in.

McLuhan, who died in 1980 at age 69, had an idea of what was ahead. "The tribalizing power of the new electronic media, the way in which they return us to the unified fields of the old oral cultures, to tribal cohesion and pre-individualist patterns of thought, is little understood," he wrote. "Tribalism is the sense of the deep bond of family, the closed society as the norm of community." Had he stuck around long enough to have seen increasingly vast and diverse new political media and vast audiences tuning in not only to their own favorite opinion but also their own favorite version of facts, I suspect he once again would have said, "I told you so."

———————————

A popular myth claims that an old Chinese curse goes, "May you live in interesting times." I learned that it is a myth, thanks to Google, a great arbiter of our interesting times. I was disappointed. Some myths simply sound too good to be inconvenienced by facts. Yet looking back as a journalist, I feel blessed to be tasked with deciphering interesting times.

I have seen "inner city" transformed from a euphemism for "urban ghetto" into a magnet for hipster real estate investors.

I have seen same-sex marriage denounced by some as a threat to the institution of marriage, even as same-sex couples are the only group whose marriage rates in America have been going up.

I have seen African ancestry and a Muslim-sounding name transformed from a political deal-breaker into a marketing advantage among voters seeking "hope" and "change."

I have seen 140 characters emerge as a surprisingly potent format for mass communication. I'm still getting used to that one.

———————————

"Culture" may be the single most surprising word in my career of punditry.

We journalists are drawn to conflict like flies to spilled ice cream— and nothing creates more news-making conflicts than clashes of culture.

Our cultural attitudes are formed by our experiences, which makes topics like race so vexing because all of our experiences are so different.

And even within races we have big cultural differences, as was dramatically put on display by the Clarence Thomas-Anita Hill hearings, where questions of race and class crossed those of gender and political alignments.

Culture lies beneath debates over the "clash of civilizations" behind the Sept. 11 terrorist attacks.

Culture also ironically unifies, in my experience, African-Americans and Southern heritage enthusiasts in clashes over the display of Confederate flags. We argue so passionately because we share so much that few other groups can understand: Southern roots, historical memory of great loss and a belief that, as William Faulkner wrote, "The past is never dead. It's not even past."

And there are the many "gaffe scandals" that stir national tempers and chatter: Culture often marks the awkward, volatile difference between what people say and what their listeners think they hear.

I'm not talking about culture in terms of art criticism. I am talking about culture as the shared values, beliefs, attitudes, customs, practices and expectations of various societies or groups.

While I glory in the power that today's new media give us to hear a diversity of voices and ideas in our rapidly changing world, I worry about how new media also give new power to those who seek to divide us and conquer.

That's why, in response to all the "culture warriors" I have known and covered, I'm a culture worrier. I worry about those who claim more cultural supremacy than they deserve to claim. Some cultural values are better than others, but no culture is perfect. Just as this nation's founders strove toward "a more perfect union," we must always strive toward a perfect common culture while humbly remembering that perfection will always be just out of reach. It is our constant reaching that keeps us on our toes.

These pages represent some of the valuable lessons I've learned about people and media over the past three decades. Among them:

1) Politics is more than a game, yet the pressures that push political journalism to follow the model of sports journalism are relentless.

2) Contrary to all the talk about a post-racial America, nothing lights a spark under news media or politics like race. In much the same way that slavery and post-Civil War politics evolved into a century of legal racial segregation, the civil rights revolution evolved into a new era of racial suspicions. The most talked-about, emotionally charged issues in

the national conversation tend to pivot on questions of racial etiquette or "race card" politics, charges of racism and countercharges of "race baiter." Umbrage itself increasingly has become weaponized into a tool for political leverage and publicity value. Yet race has only been the most visible marker of a much larger and more profound narrative: the post-1950s deindustrialization of America and the creation of a new income divide—defined by education and skill sets much more than by race.

3) New media and targeted marketing have reversed the traditional role of media as a cultural unifier. Do-it-yourself media spawn do-it-yourself demagoguery. Internet fundraising crowds out traditional party organizations. Money, power and audiences flow to the loud, bold and audacious.

4) Political polarization encourages a new moral tribalization. New media and movement politics imbrue the most banal tax-and-spend budgetary issues with life-or-death, good-versus-evil moral urgency. Trouble is, politics and governance thrive on compromise between opposing political factions. How can one compromise with evil?

5) Many of the most talked-about news issues since the 1960s have been what I call "gaffe scandals," or clashes between opposing cultures (racial, ethnic, gender, political, ageist, etc. …) over what some thought they were saying versus the insult that others hear. Many of these episodes are revealing of changing times and America's cultural fault lines. They could be resolved if we took the time to hold the honest conversation that so many people say we need, but those who could benefit the most from such a conversation are the last to engage in it—until they have no other choice. Part of my aim, humbly offered, is to help them to avoid having to make that choice.

—Clarence Page

CHAPTER ONE

BREAKING NEWS

"Nothing concentrates the mind," I like to say, "like a firm deadline." Pressed by time to stop reporting and start writing what I really think, I have written columns under deadline pressure that generated memorably high response from readers, many of whom are still trying to figure out what they think about the events in question, too. Examples in this chapter include the Sept. 11 terrorist attacks, Supreme Court Justice Thurgood Marshall's final news conference, the O.J. Simpson murder trial verdict and President Barack Obama's election victory night.

An old saying that I have long attributed to New York columnist Murray Kempton holds that editorial writers are like soldiers who come down from the hills after the battle is over—and shoot the wounded. The same can be said of columnists. We're the second responders to breaking news, making value judgments, picking winners and losers, and spinning daily events into a larger meaningful narrative. We explain the past and suggest the way to a better future.

Then there are those days when the news breaks so close to deadline that the commentators and reporters are responding at the same time and in real time. Yet the news is too big and important to be put off until another day. Something must be said that won't be rendered obsolete before the next news cycle.

That's what happened, for example, on Sept. 11, 2001. As the Twin Towers collapsed, I watched with the same stunned disbelief and horror as any other American, except I was one of the Americans who had to watch and type at the same time as the clock ticked toward deadline. I had to scrap whatever topic it was that I originally had in mind. But what would I write in its place?

As I recall, I reminded myself of an observation that I have told my wife belongs on my tombstone: "Nothing Concentrates The Mind Like A Firm Deadline."

First I had to get out. I went out onto the streets of the nation's capital to see what a city under siege looked and sounded like.

It was almost empty. I walked a few blocks toward the White House, behind which black smoke billowed from the distant, burning Pentagon.

I talked, listened and took notes. I returned to the office and typed up my impressions, from which observations and even conclusions began to emerge.

Then I pruned and polished my prose as much as I could before the clock told me it was time for my editors to snatch what I had written away from me.

I would not call the end product the best column that I have ever written. But the immediacy of breaking news makes up for shortcomings of style and content. My comments borrow importance from the events I was writing about. "Literature in a hurry," daily journalism has been called. That's more elegant than what I call it: Storytelling on the fly.

The value of that storytelling became apparent on Sept. 12. An unexpected number of letters, phone calls and emails flowed in from readers to express their appreciation for, among other things, my putting into words much of what they were thinking—and feeling.

My Sept. 11 column can be found here, along with several other columns written under pressure and on the fly. Reading them now reminds me more than ever of something else that journalism often has been called: "A rough draft of history."

I also include several similar rough drafts of breaking news events as varied as Thurgood Marshall's final news conference, the O.J. Simpson murder trial verdict and President Barack Obama's election night. Years later, in the cool, stress-free light of a day well past my deadline,

I am struck by how much hope is offered for our future by the resiliency with which we rebounded from times of horrible uncertainties in our past.

SEPTEMBER 12, 2001

THIS TIME IT'S NOT A MOVIE

On TV, two national landmarks—the World Trade Center and the Pentagon—look like the aftermath in the film "Independence Day" or some other end-of-the-world science fiction epic. But this time the footage is real and it's very frightening.

My friend Michele calls from New York before I can call her.

She's OK. She wants to know how I'm doing. She was riding into Manhattan on the last train out of Brooklyn before the subway lines were shut down. As they were crossing the bridge, everyone in her car looked up and saw one World Trade Center tower on fire.

Then the second plane hit.

"We all watched it—a trainload of New Yorkers—in complete silence," she says. "It was like something out of a Hollywood movie. I couldn't believe what I was seeing. Nobody said a word. We just watched the tower fly apart."

Ghastly. Terrorists have accomplished what we Americans hoped we would never see. They have produced a disaster as large in scale as New York City.

Here, in Washington, it looked like a movie, too. Cars and trucks jammed the roads out of town, leaving downtown streets cordoned off near the White House and nearly deserted, except for reporters, lots of reporters and film crews desperately looking for someone to interview.

My 12-year-old son's school calls. He knows my office is near the White House. He is worried about me.

When I ask him how he feels, he says, "Really weird. It's like you see the World Trade Center get bombed in the movies and now it has really happened."

Yes, it has. Terrorists have sent a message, although the meaning of the message is not yet clear. Today's terrorists are too cowardly to claim responsibility for their acts.

Much of the world lives every day with the possibility of being bombed. Compared to them, we Americans have been lucky. Now their war is our war. Someday somebody probably will make a movie about all of this. For now, we're still writing the script.

What, my son asks, can we do now?

Pray for the dead, I answer. And we should try to find the culprits who staged this catastrophe. I assure him that we will find the "bad guys" and I hope events will not make a liar of me.

America will try very hard to find the people responsible for this and mete out some sort of justice. I hope we do it in ways that will not make bad matters worse.

"The resolve of our great nation is being tested," President Bush said. "But make no mistake, we will show the world that we will pass the test."

His statement did not match the poetry of President Franklin D. Roosevelt denouncing Japan's attack on Pearl Harbor as "a date which will live in infamy," but its message was no less ringing and appropriate.

This massive terror attack tests Americans in ways the United States has not been tested before. It tests our ability to rally behind an effective counter-terrorist war. It also tests our ability to avoid turning against each other while we wage it.

This attack on American soil most likely will not be answered in major military assaults like D-Day or Anzio, but in covert intelligence and counter-terrorism measures.

We need to find the culprits and build an effective case to show the world that we have the right suspects. For that, we need effective intelligence work and an absolute certainty of whom we are dealing with before we retaliate against them.

In our haste to avenge Tuesday's deaths and destruction, we also must be careful to go after the right enemy. And, back home, our anger must not lead us to demonize entire ethnic groups for the acts of a few of their distant cousins.

The incarceration of thousands of innocent Japanese-Americans and the detention of innocent Italians and Germans is a lasting stain on America's World War II record. In recent years, Middle East terrorism has led to bigoted attacks against innocent Arab-Americans. If we allow that to happen again, we will have failed the most important test of all, our ability to preserve the values in America that are worth fighting for.

Pearl Harbor shocked Americans, but it also united us as a nation. Our domestic differences begin to subside in the face of a major national security threat from outside.

Even civil-rights leaders at the time decided to put aside their rising movement's agenda and wage a "war on two fronts—against Nazism abroad and racism at home."

That's how we Americans should face the new challenge posed by terrorism. We are a nation comprised of many tribes. But times like these test how truly united we can be behind a common purpose as one American people.

FEBRUARY 5, 2012

TIME TO SHATTER THE BLACK SUICIDE MYTH

The death of Don Cornelius, creator and host of "Soul Train," brought two conflicting memories to mind: the weekly joy of that iconic program as a defining feature of black American pop culture, and the terrible pain inflicted on the surviving family and friends of those who commit suicide.

Like countless other boomers, I grew up with "Soul Train." Today, the old clips look like an amusing period piece, especially to our kids or grandkids who wonder how any of us could have thought those "Saturday Night Fever" fashions were cool.

But in the 1970s and beyond, "Soul Train" defined cutting-edge cool. It became the longest-running syndicated show of its type on TV and, as Cornelius said every week, "The hippest trip in the galaxy."

But the hip trip finally came to an end a few years ago on TV and for Cornelius, amid reports of failing health. Police say he died in his Los Angeles home of a self-inflicted gunshot wound.

That tragedy has special meaning in the African-American community, which has long nourished a dangerous myth that black people don't commit suicide.

It is a point of mythical ethnic pride that our ancestors found ways to persevere despite centuries of slavery, struggle and hardship. Black people created the blues, it is often said, because we didn't have psychotherapists.

Besides, as an old joke goes, we black people don't kill ourselves because you can't kill yourself by jumping out of a basement window. We can only wish that were true. Although whites and Native Americans have the highest suicide rates, according to the Centers for Disease Control and Prevention, the black suicide rate has been high enough in recent years to claim one African-American every 4.5 hours.

No group is immune. By gender, non-Hispanic white and Native American men have the highest suicide rates, of about 25 lives per 100,000. That's more than four times the rate of women in each racial group. It also is more than twice the rate of black and Hispanic men, whose suicide rate of about 11 per 100,000 is five times the rate of black and Hispanic women. Asian-American men have a rate of about 9 per 100,000, slightly more than twice the rate of Asian-American women.

Yet the black suicide myth persists. "As a mental-health advocate, over the years I've heard variations of the 'black people don't commit suicide' meme," wrote Bassey Ikpi on the black-oriented The Root website after Cornelius' death. "Yesterday the chorus was deafening. People went so far as to create elaborate conspiracy theories rather than accept what could be a simple truth—that Cornelius had taken his own life."

I share her sense of frustration. I suddenly became an expert because of a personal tragedy, as many Chicagoans know. Back in May 1984, suicide ended the life and career of Leanita McClain, an award-winning Chicago Tribune columnist and ghetto-to-Gold-Coast success story.

She was also my former wife. She killed herself with an overdose of prescribed pills two years after our divorce. Her upward career trajectory, like our marriage, was stopped only by the furies of her relentless depression.

"Happiness is a private club that will not let me enter," she wrote in her "generic suicide note."

It is not hard, although it is not pain-free either, for me to imagine that Don Cornelius could have written the same message.

Suicides inflict a terrible cruelty on the survivors. Everyone asks "why" and there are no easy answers. I was surprised by how many of my friends came forth to share stories of their own loved ones who had ended their lives or come close to it in their severe depression. I was shocked by how common such illnesses can be, regardless of race or community background.

I also learned about guilt. "People feel guilty if they failed to get help for their lost loved one," a counselor told me, and they feel guilty if they did get help and the loved one killed him or herself anyway. It is best to seek help. Whether you believe it or not, you have too much to lose.

JUNE 30, 1991

THE LEGACY OF THURGOOD MARSHALL

"How do you want to be remembered?" I asked retiring Supreme Court Justice Thurgood Marshall, calling my question over the heads of reporters at his farewell press conference.

Squinting in my direction, the old curmudgeon appeared to be at once amused and irritated as he reflected for a microsecond, then muttered in his gravelly voice: "That he did what he could with what he had." It would make an appropriate epitaph. Whether you loved what he did or hated it, Marshall gave it all he had and dared you to feel neutral about it.

Those who argue that Marshall should be replaced by another African-American miss the more important point: Justice Marshall's value was not in his color; it was in his conscience.

If the web of justice is a great national safety net, Marshall was its last remaining anchor at the end that sympathized most with people too powerless and causes too unpopular for politicians to touch.

He embodied what Oliver Wendell Holmes was talking about when he said, "The life of the law has not been logic; it has been experience." He understood the hard-luck cases because he had been one of them and often had defended them.

Marshall brought to the court his experience as one who had suffered the indignities of second-class citizenship at a time when his skin color kept him out of most restaurants, hotels and the Maryland law school he wanted to attend. He later graduated at the top of his class at Washington's mostly black Howard University.

He also had argued more cases before the Supreme Court than his fellow justices had—32, of which he won 29. He was the only sitting justice to have defended a convict who had been sentenced to death, and he knew the meaning of "rough justice," being the only justice to have found as a defense lawyer that one of his clients had been lynched before Marshall's train arrived in the Texas town where the suspect was to be tried.

As one who successfully argued the landmark Brown v. Board of Education school desegregation case, among other accomplishments, Marshall made his most noteworthy achievements before he came on to the court. Still, he brought to the cloistered chambers of that august body an important peephole into the many exotic ways written laws affect real people.

As the Reagan-Bush court's most unshakably liberal dissenter among increasingly conservative colleagues, Marshall stood for constitutional protections that rankled some but encouraged fair treatment for all, whether they happened to be drug dealers accused of murder, National Security Council officers accused of circumventing Congress or police accused of brutality.

Good for him. A court without vigorous dissenters is unhealthy, whether the prevailing tilt happens to be to the left or to the right.

He was accused of "liberal activism." If so, he leaves behind a court guilty of conservative activism. Reversing four important earlier court decisions the same week Marshall announced his departure, the new court seemed discontent to let a day pass without stripping away another right.

This is a court that allows coerced confessions; random, warrantless searches of bus passengers; censorship of adults-only nude dancers; and the admission of "victim impact" statements to fire up the emotions of juries considering the death penalty.

The danger in these decisions is in the line of thinking they represent. Although Ronald Reagan promised to get government off people's backs, the court he revolutionized is helping state powers expand at the expense of individual rights.

A court that takes a cavalier view of the intimidating nature of uniformed police asking to search without a warrant shows precious little appreciation for why we have warrants in the first place.

A court that justifies a local ban on nude dancing in an adults-only establishment because of the possibility that it might lead to criminal activity might as well confiscate drivers' licenses because they, too, might lead to criminal activity.

A court that allows "victim-impact statements" in their commendable regard for the rights of victims or their survivors who are willing to testify shows a callous disregard for the rights of victims who, for whatever reason, do not testify.

And a court that views some coerced confessions as "harmless error" apparently sees little harm in its encouragement of sloppy police work, like "accidentally" dropping a suspect down a staircase, for example.

Marshall's most powerful parting shot came in an explosive dissent he lobbed into the court's 6-to-3 victim-impact decision on the day of his retirement announcement.

"Power, not reason, is the new currency of this court's decision-making," Marshall thundered.

"Today's decision charts an unmistakable course ... . Cast aside today are those condemned to face society's ultimate penalty. Tomorrow's victims may be minorities, women or the indigent. Inevitably, this campaign to resurrect yesterday's 'spirited dissents' will squander the authority and the legitimacy of this court as a protector of the powerless.

"I dissent."

The ring of Marshall's dissensions shall echo through the halls of justice long after the man has left, a lonely voice that tempered sound legal logic with the warm flesh and blood of human experience.

OCTOBER 21, 1992

HILL-THOMAS: A MISSED OPPORTUNITY FOR BLACK DIALOGUE

Brimming with glee, the little boy rushed into the room.

"Mommy, mommy," he shouted. "He chose a black man! He chose a black man!"

The African-American mother shared his excitement. President Bush had chosen a black man, Judge Clarence Thomas, to replace retiring Justice Thurgood Marshall, the Supreme Court's first and only black justice.

A year later, I am watching her recall the moment in a PBS "Frontline" documentary on the first anniversary of Thomas' hearings that examines how the hearings into Anita Hill's sexual-harassment charges tore America's black community apart.

The mother is more excited by her young son's reaction to the choice than she is by the choice itself. Her son's happiness is all it takes to make Thomas' appointment a worthwhile end in itself. Never mind what his personal beliefs might happen to be, or whether they will be good or harmful to black Americans.

"'Mommy, mommy,'" she repeats, with a satisfied smile, "'He chose a black man!'"

Maybe I am getting jaded, but I am asking myself: Why is this woman so happy with that? After all, I, too, was excited by the selection of a black man back in 1967 when it was a "first." But we've crossed that milestone already, haven't we? Are we so hard up for black heroes that skin color is the only standard we have by which to judge any brother the president hands us, even when he obviously is not the "best qualified" candidate, as the president claims?

At Thurgood Marshall's final press conference he warned us with the ominous, cryptic wisdom of an old African griot that "there's no difference between a black snake and a white snake. They both bite."

But the warning was lost on many of us, judging by opinion polls and a preponderance of anecdotal evidence gathered in living rooms, barber shops and black-oriented talk radio shows.

And a great opportunity also has been lost. As a result, a year after the Thomas-Hill contretemps, blacks have gained nothing from it in comparison to feminists, who channeled their anger into growing political power; or conservatives, who got the impressionable young right-wing justice they wanted; or even liberal Senate Democrats, who looked spineless when they let Hill twist in the wind, but may yet win a Democratic White House at least partly because of it. That's not a bad deal.

Anita Hill also got something: popularity. Recent polls by U.S. News and World Report, Gallup, NBC and the Wall Street Journal show the number of people who believe her has risen sharply in the last year to break even or pull well ahead of Thomas.

So, who lost? Guess.

We could have reached as a community beyond the skin-deep satisfaction of racial symbolism to explore in a meaningful way what kind of person should be Thurgood Marshall's replacement in order to carry on, rather then tear apart, his legacy. Thomas repeatedly warned us that's what he planned to do and, so far, that's what he's done.

Black leaders were caught embarrassingly off-guard by Bush's selection of an eloquent, if woefully underqualified black conservative. By the time they figured out whether to support him or not (most major black groups did not), it had little impact.

Then we were treated to the humiliating sight of white, male Senate inquisitors forcing two of the community's finest young role models and success stories to discuss embarrassing sexual allegations on national television, a sight that might never have happened had the subjects been white.

Black Americans also lost important coalitions with other sympathetic groups, particularly feminists. Along with it, we lost a needed sense of cohesiveness between black men and black women.

One of the more eloquent voices of division, black writer Ishmael Reed, in a Washington Post essay last Sunday blamed the divisions on a conspiracy by "white media feminists" who have "decided to make the lynching of Clarence Thomas an annual event."

Reed is a fine novelist and ardent anti-feminist, which is his right. But his blame game overreaches. It deeply insults black women, since it implies they are too silly, stupid or content to complain without prodding from white women.

Yet, I give Reed credit for believing these issues need to be talked out, not snuffed out by those who abhor washing dirty laundry in public. Unfortunately we tend to avoid meaningful dialogue between those in the black community who thought Thomas should be judged on his conservative views and those who thought he should be confirmed straightaway because any black on the high court is better than not having any black at all.

"Hence," writes black scholar Cornel West in "Race-ing Justice, Engendering Power," a book of essays on the legacy of the hearings, edited by Toni Morrison, "a grand opportunity for substantive discussion and struggle over race and gender was missed in black America and the larger society. And black leadership must share some of the blame."

We all must. Until we speak more candidly with one another and come to grips with the glaring but seldom acknowledged class and gender differences (and resentments) within our own community, we will continue to be vulnerable to manipulation by politicians who may not necessarily have our best interests in mind.

Am I calling for all blacks to think alike? No, not at all. I am merely calling on my fellow black Americans to think.

Otherwise, if "racial reasoning," as Cornel West calls the skin-deep color standard, is the only standard of character judgment we pass on to our children, we should not be surprised if it is the only standard they use.

OCTOBER 4, 1995

ON TRIAL: AMERICANS NEED TO DEAL WITH RACE BEFORE OUR SENSE OF JUSTICE COMPLETELY UNRAVELS

When people ask me what I think of the verdict in the O.J. Simpson trial, I have to ask, "Which one?"

There were two trials here. There was the inside trial that the jurors saw in which Simpson was being judged. And there was the outside trial that the rest of us saw, in which American society, particularly its system of justice, was on trial.

The polls that showed two-thirds of white Americans believed Simpson was guilty while two-thirds of blacks thought he was innocent were polls about the outside trial. As such, they were a measure not so much of faith in O.J. but in the fairness of the criminal justice system.

While whites tend to believe that Simpson would not have been charged if he was not guilty, blacks tend to believe, based on their experience, that Simpson would not have been charged if he was not black.

That's the bigger trial, one that very well may have political repercussions, particularly among conservatives appealing to predominately white constituencies for "more justice for crime victims and less coddling of criminals."

What you will not hear in this attack on criminals is an attack on wealthy criminals who can afford a dream defense team like Simpson's.

Instead I fear you will hear increased cynicism about how much easier it is to put a poor suspect behind bars than a rich one.

As a member of the minority of black Americans who, according to polls, thought O.J. Simpson just might be guilty, I congratulate Johnnie Cochran and the Simpson defense team for giving their client the best defense money could buy.

Did Cochran play the race card? Of course, he did. As he admitted in an unusually candid moment during his press conference afterwards, he would have been liable for legal malpractice had he bypassed that golden opportunity.

First, Cochran did what many good law professors tell their students to do: He served his client the way his client would serve himself if he only knew how. He did an excellent job of summarizing the "points of doubt" which, as he told the jury, are crucially important in a case built on circumstantial evidence like the case against Simpson was. He was right to assert that the prosecution's mountain of evidence becomes "molehills when you look at the facts."

Yet, many of us who have covered criminal trials in the past have seen even less circumstantial evidence lead to the conviction of less well-heeled clients.

So Cochran left nothing to chance. He went completely over the top in an appeal to the predominately black jury's racial suspicions by tossing out a list of racial buzz words, including quotations from Frederick Douglass and Martin Luther King Jr. and claims that made it sound like a vote for acquittal would all but end racism in America the next day.

Obviously, in serving his client, he had to do something to distract the jury away from the holes in Simpson's alibis and in the alternative scenario of a racist police conspiracy that his defense team tried to paint.

It seemed to me that, if I were a member of that jury, I would have been so offended that I would have been moved to vote for conviction, just to send a message that all black people are not so emotional as to forget about evidence.

Part of me also was hoping for a guilty verdict if for no other reason than to disprove the popular and somewhat racist presumption that black jurors would be inclined to let a black man off, guilty or not.

Precious few of those who want to believe the worst about black people will note that the white and Hispanic jury members joined in the unanimous verdict.

Americans who are not too full of themselves have to admit that the Simpson trial attracted worldwide attention in part because it became a stage for long-repressed racial fears, suspicions and resentments across the country.

Simpson owes a great debt to Mark Fuhrman. The police officer's recorded racial venom exposed the popular lie that racism is no longer something white Americans should care about.

Simpson's dream team did not have to prove him innocent under America's system of justice. They only had to raise the shadow of doubt. They did that. Along with it, they raised serious doubts about how well the races are getting along in America.

If we Americans do not deal with the reality of race, our national sense of justice will unravel as swiftly and surely as the case against O.J. Simpson did.

Cochran played more than the race card. He played the whole deck. He did not invent it. Politicians, discriminatory employers, panic peddling real estate dealers and racist cops like Mark Fuhrman have been playing it for years. Cochran only saw his opportunity and took it. I wonder how long it will take for Americans to remove the deck from the table.

NOVEMBER 9, 2008

JACKSON'S ELOQUENT TEARS

Was Rev. Jesse Jackson crying tears of joy at President-elect Barack Obama's victory celebration in Grant Park? Or was the civil rights leader weeping in regret that he might now be out of a job?

Caught by television cameras, Jackson's tears spoke volumes. It is important to remember that Jackson helped to pave the way for Obama. But, like some other old-school leaders, Jackson has been slow to recognize when to step out of the way.

For example, his most memorable contribution to Obama's presidential campaign came when Jackson's whispered wish to "cut his nuts off" was caught by a hot Fox News microphone. Jackson apologized profusely. No problem. His gaffe undoubtedly reassured skeptical whites that Obama was not a Jackson clone.

Much was said about how Obama was opening a "post-racial" era, although "multiracial" is more appropriate. Race and racism have not evaporated. Nor has the need for diversity to be respected, not just tolerated. Jackson's not out of a job yet. But Obama's victory moves our old baseline of racial expectations to a higher and happier level. It's hard to argue that our society is irredeemably racist when our multiracial electorate just elected a man with African roots and an Arabic-sounding name to be commander in chief.

Yes, we did.

No, Obama did not win over a majority of white males, according to exit polls. Neither have the previous five Democratic nominees. But with 41 percent of white men and about half of all white women and independents, Obama outperformed the other five among those groups.

He also did better than John Kerry and Al Gore among Hispanics and all income brackets, including a 5 percent gain since 2004 among those who earn less than $50,000 a year and an 8 percent gain in the over-$100,000-a-year income group, according to the Pew Research Center. Sorry, Joe the Plumber.

Pew also reports that Obama increased voter turnout since 2004 among self-identified Republicans (up 3 percent), moderates (up 6 percent) and conservatives (up 5 percent).

But that doesn't mean that Obama's contest with Sen. John McCain was the "referendum on the goodness of America," that conservative MSNBC commentator Tucker Carlson sarcastically complained that the media portrayed it.

"I just resent the implication that America is a better country if it voted for Barack Obama," he grumped on Election Night. "That's a slur on people who voted against Obama." Agreed. Yet, as one McCain voter who joined the celebration of Obama's victory told me, he was not happy that his man lost but that "our country has won." America is a better country, in other words, not because so many of us voted for Obama but because many more of us have made a place where Obama's victory is possible.

In Kenya, by contrast, Obama's father's minority Luo tribe celebrated, but with a bitter knowledge that it is easier for a Luo to be elected president in America than in Kenya.

"Only in America," Americans said with a new sense of pride. It certainly was better to see folks overseas happily waving our flag instead of burning it.

Back here at home, Pew found the only major group that went the other way, giving fewer votes to this year's Democratic nominee, was voters who were older than 65. Significantly, that generation includes much of our 1960s-era civil rights leadership. When skeptical black political and civil rights leaders questioned Obama's "blackness," Obama persevered, forcing some black leaders, like Jackson, to catch up with the masses whom they were trying to lead.

Obama had an advantage in his quest, I suspect, in his lack of a family ancestry in American slavery, a defining characteristic of most African-Americans. Being raised by his white mother and grandparents in multiracial Hawaii and Indonesia, he was spared the post-slavery traumatic syndrome that for many of us African-Americans has been a cultural crippler. Many of us older folks were conditioned at an early era about our "place" in a white-dominated society in ways that culturally cripple many of our offspring, if the young'uns bother to listen to us at all.

Obama was spared all that, judging by his autobiographies. Although he was born an American, his multiracial view, energized with optimism, is characteristic of immigrants. While others rail relentlessly about America's limitations, he remains resolutely focused on our possibilities. He has enlisted us, his fellow Americans, in his cause and given all of us a good reason to feel like winners.

FEBRUARY 15, 1998

NO QUICK FIX FOR KEEPING KIDS OUT OF TROUBLE

Poor John Dilulio. He gets heard, but not enough.

Get-tough-on-crime legislators eagerly greeted the Princeton sociologist's warnings a few years ago of a rise in violent juvenile "super-predators."

Unfortunately, as he puts it, he has ever since been "more quoted than heeded."

He was quoted widely in the national outrage that erupted over stories of violent preteens like the 11- and 12-year-old boys who dropped 5-year-old Eric Morse to his death from a Chicago public-housing high rise in 1994.

Dilulio has been quoted again after more recent tragedies like the 12-year-old Chicago boy accused of fatally shooting two teens in cold blood earlier this month, reportedly to impress the gang he had just joined.

But so far, he has not been heeded much on Capitol Hill, where Senate Republicans have responded to the rise in so-called super-predators with a juvenile crime bill co-sponsored by Judiciary Committee Chairman Orrin Hatch (R-Utah).

Much of the bill, such as its provisions to improve record-sharing between jurisdictions, should win easy bipartisan support.

But other provisions call for a relaxing of federal restrictions on jailing juveniles with adult felons and would make $1.5 billion in federal aid available only to states that prosecute violent juveniles age 15 or older as adults.

Those proposals have sparked outrage from the Children's Defense Fund, on whose board Hillary Rodham Clinton served before she became first lady, and other liberal and civil libertarian groups that imagine grim scenarios of kids thrown in with adults. Federal law has banned the housing of juveniles within sight, let alone arm's reach, of adults since the early 1970s. But the senators, responding mainly to the needs of rural police whose budgets and facilities are less elaborate than those of their urban counterparts, insist the concerns are overblown.

Dilulio has a more nuanced approach that borrows from both liberals and conservatives, which in itself helps explain why he is only being half-heard in politically polarized Washington.

Liberals love to hear him talk about the devastating impact of poverty and joblessness. Conservatives love to hear him talk about the devastating impact among those poor of out-of-wedlock births and households headed by single parents.

But his prescriptions are harder for both sides to hear. He has long advocated jail as the best response for adult criminals. But for youths, he insists, society must provide prevention at the front end as well as incarceration at the back end.

His warning is particularly worth listening to now that, despite the occasional sensational tragedies like those in Chicago, the rate of violent juvenile crime has been dropping nationally since 1994, when arrests for violent crime among juveniles aged 10 to 17 fell by 2.9 percent.

Since then, the numbers of murders committed by youths younger than 13 fell from 41 in 1994 to 20 in 1996 and the crime rate for juveniles under age 14 has remained steady since 1980.

Over the last two years, Dilulio has been pursuing the kind of responses to crime problems that should warm both liberal and conservative hearts. He has been sharing his time between Princeton and inner-city Philadelphia, where he has been working closely on front-end responses to crime with local clergy and church volunteers, a grass roots alternative to top-down government-funded anti-poverty programs.

From this Dilulio has come up with his "four-M" approach to fighting crime:

"Monitoring" by adult volunteers in Philadelphia's Youth Aid Panel program tailors punishment to fit the crime and the conditions of first-time youth offenders who used to fall between the cracks of the probation system.

"Mentoring" has helped kids who, according to one study, turned out to be 46 percent less likely to initiate drug use, 27 percent less likely to start drinking, a third less likely to commit assault and 50 percent less likely to skip school than their unmentored counterparts.

"Ministering" by clergy working one-on-one with children and families has improved school grades and attendance.

Finally, a sense of "moral obligation" to America's children is needed to transcend conventional politics and get grown-ups involved in the lives of children who need guidance before they hurt others and themselves.

Dilulio has the right idea. Similar approaches are showing positive results in other cities, most dramatically in Boston, where kids with too much time on their hands are getting help from police, prosecutors and community volunteers. The city invested in 42 community centers, summer jobs and on-the-street probation officers. As a result, the city reduced youth homicides to zero for more than two years.

There is some good news happening in America's streets. Legislators should listen and learn, or just leave bad enough alone.

CHAPTER TWO

GAFFES, GOOFS AND GOTCHAS

Looking back, I was surprised by how many of the biggest headline-making, chatter-generating and, in some cases, career-destroying events of post-1960s America were gaffe scandals, especially in race and gender relations. I attribute this to a new post-1960s racial and political etiquette. As racial discrimination receded, racial suspicions increased. Formerly minor controversies of free speech took on new importance. The N-word, for example, became almost as obscene as the F-word.

Racial slights and "microaggressions" took on new power as tripwires of racially "coded" and "dogwhistle" politics by the right or "political correctness" on the left. Umbrage itself became weaponized as each side pressed to shame the other or risk being out-shamed. Examples in this chapter include such big stars as Don Imus, Rush Limbaugh, Al Campanis, Rev. Jesse Jackson, Laura "Dr. Laura" Schlessinger, Michael Richards and, yes, Barack and Michelle Obama.

"A gaffe," Michael Kinsley famously said, "is when a politician tells the truth—some obvious truth he isn't supposed to say." Rep. Barney Frank similarly used "notsaposta" to describe something that a politician is "notsaposta" say in public.

We continue to wrestle with these blunders of etiquette. They appear to be inevitable in our post-'60s age of suspicions as long as we avoid candid talk about the issues of race, gender, power and other differences that we are most persistently suspicious about.

APRIL 12, 1987

GOING TO BAT FOR AFFIRMATIVE ACTION

A lot of theories have been advanced over the years to explain the shortage of blacks in the management ranks of major industries.

Some say black people are not talented enough to be managers. Such people are called racists and, fortunately, there are not very many of them.

Others say a lot of white people will balk at taking orders from black managers. Such people are called dimwits and there are a lot more of them.

Now we have Al Campanis, who was vice president in charge of player personnel for the Los Angeles Dodgers until he appeared on ABC's "Nightline" and advanced his explanation for the shortage of blacks in baseball management.

Black players, he said, had not been turned away because of prejudice; they just didn't need the work.

"I don't believe it's prejudice," he said. "I truly believe that they may not have some of the necessities to be, let's say, a field manager, or perhaps a general manager."

"Nightline" host Ted Koppel expressed disbelief. Campanis dug in deeper. "Well, I don't say that all of them, but they certainly are short. How many quarterbacks do you have? How many pitchers do you have that are black? Why are black men, or black people, not good swimmers? Because they don't have the buoyancy."

Nice. That logic reminds me vaguely of a former Chicago fire chief who, when asked why his department had so few black firefighters, said blacks didn't like smoke.

Predictably, the 70-year-old Campanis was forced to resign after his remarks touched off a firestorm of protest.

Poor Al. I am sure he did not mean to attribute the shortage of minorities in his business to their inability to be good quarterbacks, pitchers and floaters. But that was the way it came out and he had to go.

Ironically, the show was designed to assess how far professional baseball has come since Jackie Robinson broke baseball's color line 40 years ago. If Campanis' views are an indication, baseball management has not come very far at all.

And neither have those who rush to his defense, saying the press and public should have focused on what Campanis meant, not what he said.

He did not mean, they say, that black players did not have what it takes to become major league managers. What he meant, they say, is that black people did not need the work enough to make the necessary sacrifices. The best, brightest ballplayers prefer to run off to some other more promising or lucrative line of work.

It is true that the major league management track is daunting, one that often requires a dues-paying stint in the minor leagues, which means a cut in pay and prestige in bush-league towns for an indeterminate period. You could die of boredom waiting for an opportunity in the majors that might never come. But, rather than defend that system, the bosses of baseball, particularly those who, like Campanis, are involved in personnel, should be trying to change it.

Maybe they should be paying a little more attention to changing their clubby old-boy-network atmosphere into one that encourages rather than discourages minorities—and maybe even someday (Gasp!) women—to attempt to enter the ranks of management.

That is what affirmative action is supposed to be about. It is not supposed to be about quotas, but about developing a system of hiring and promotions that encourages the best of all races and genders to compete, not run away to other industries.

If Campanis meant to say with his awkward remarks that baseball has made little or no effort to encourage minority players to even consider attempting the management track, it is no wonder his bosses thought he had to be sacrificed. He gave away one of the industry's dirty little secrets.

If so, his firing disturbs me, too.

Firing the aging, likable Campanis may make some of the offended feel a little better, but it puts too much attention on him instead of his bonehead remarks and what they say about the world of professional sports.

Instead of dealing with the discriminatory system that lingers in professional sports 40 years after Jackie Robinson's breakthrough, Campanis' dismissal makes it too easy for many to pretend that his remarks reflect an aberration that must be purged, not prevailing attitudes that should be changed.

Perhaps Campanis should not have been forced out so quickly. Perhaps he should have been offered a chance to be educated in the racial realities of his industry and to help teach others.

Maybe, as Bill Cosby has suggested, he should have been offered the opportunity to do some sort of public service work, perhaps with minority athletes.

Organizing a black swimming team would be nice.

SEPTEMBER 2, 1987

COVERING JESSE, A MAN WHO WANTED IT BOTH WAYS

Jesse Jackson is "an American enigma and a difficult man for a reporter to cover," wrote Dan Rather in his introduction to a book about the 1984 presidential campaign. I'll buy that. Reporters accustomed to covering either campaigns or crusades had to adjust to Jackson's odd mixture of both.

But if TV reporters covered Jackson with difficulty in 1984, could they nevertheless cover him with fairness?

No, they could not, concludes a scholarly report, "A Horse of a Different Color; Television's Treatment of Jesse Jackson's 1984 Presidential Campaign," from Washington's highly respected Joint Center for Political Studies, a black-oriented think tank.

After analyzing television coverage of the campaign for 85 pages, author C. Anthony Broh, a Princeton political science lecturer, says that television news did not kill Jackson's campaign, but it helped nail the lid on its coffin.

"In 1984 the United States was not ready to elect a black man as president," Broh writes. "Television news reporters recognized this, and their reports became a self-fulfilling prophecy GUARANTEEING (emphasis Broh's) that the United States was not ready to elect a black man president in 1984."

Maybe. I do not recall any coverage that made it appear as if Jackson had more than a ghost of a chance of winning America's political center.

But if Jackson was not treated like other candidates in this regard, I think he asked for it. Jackson's speeches left no doubt that he was presenting himself not just as a candidate, but as a black candidate.

"The fundamental relationship between blacks and the Democratic Party must be renegotiated," Jackson wrote in an April, 1983, essay in the Washington Post. A few months later he declared his candidacy with that as a theme, making several things obvious: He might increase black voter registration, give voice to black concerns and coalesce with other groups who were willing to sign on to his liberal black agenda, but he was not going to win the nomination by doing battle with his own party.

Jackson also distanced himself from other, more conventional candidates by remaining cozy too long with extremists like Black Muslim Minister Louis Farrakhan, as if he felt the lunatic fringe were more important to his campaign than mainstream America.

Similarly, when his personal off-the-record use of words like "Hymie" to refer to Jews was reported, he might have been more easily forgiven had he not handled it so badly. First he denied it for more than a week, then reluctantly apologized by trying to dismiss it as a "small" thing.

"What disturbs me now is that something so small has become so large," he said. "In part I am to blame and for that I am deeply distressed."

I wonder if Jackson would have considered a racial slur, off the record or on, a "small" thing if one of his opponents had directed it against blacks.

Jackson simply cannot have it both ways. He either presents himself as a representative of a "special interest" group and takes his punches or he presents himself as a candidate for all the people.

This means he must be willing to play by the same rules, written and unwritten, as any other presidential aspirant. Among the unwritten commandments are:

Thou shalt not trash thine own political party.

Thou shalt not anger large portions of the electorate-unless, of course, they are outnumbered by thine own supporters.

Thou shalt not attempt to win the nation's highest office without paying some dues in at least one of the lower ones, or (as in the cases of George Washington, U.S. Grant and Dwight D. Eisenhower) as a hero general in an important war.

The think tank's report does recognize how television actually helped Jackson by giving him an image of legitimacy that helped make up for his lack of experience in elective office.

Even though many blacks had doubts about the viability of a black presidential candidate and many whites had doubts about the desirability of a black presidential candidate, television news was definitive about Jesse Jackson's right to be in the race.

Television coverage enhanced his image as a "spokesman for a large bloc of people," the report notes, and portrayed him as an informed spokesman for President Reagan's "loyal opposition," as well as an "activator" who turned thousands of disaffected youths out to register and vote.

As Jackson conducts his exploratory campaign for a possible 1988 bid, he appears to have learned some valuable lessons. He has broadened his appeal from that of a black leader to that of a populist who cares as much about displaced Iowa farmers as he does about urban welfare mothers.

Jackson appears to be quite willing to behave more like a conventional candidate. It remains to be seen whether the media will cover him like one.

JUNE 17, 1992

BILL CLINTON'S NOTSAPOSTA SAY THAT, IS HE?

Tsk, tsk. There goes Bill Clinton, breaking the rules of "notsaposta" again.

"Notsapostas" are the political taboos too many Democrats live by, according to Rep. Barney Frank, a liberal Massachusetts Democrat.

In his book, "Speaking Frankly: What's Wrong With the Democrats and How To Fix It," Frank defines a "notsaposta" as a truth so troubling that members of a political party cannot acknowledge it without suffering a backlash from fellow party members for giving aid and comfort to their enemies.

For example, liberal officeholders are "notsaposta" denounce the viciousness of violent criminals because, heaven forbid, someone else might use the statement to argue for the death penalty.

Or they're "notsaposta" point out that the United States government is ever in any way morally superior to any other government because, heaven forbid, the statement might be used by some warhawk to argue for more military spending.

The problem with notsapostas, Frank says, is that they automatically surrender high moral ground and, as the Democrats have found to their dismay in five of that last six elections, public respect.

Frank is right, and it doesn't stop there. Judging by Bill Clinton's adventure at a Rainbow Coalition conference in Washington Saturday, Frank might add a new notsaposta to his list: You're notsaposta criticize a young, black, female rap star, even when she spouts inflammatory nonsense.

Clinton broke that rule, with a stony-faced and steaming Rev. Jesse Jackson sitting nearby, by criticizing the organization Jackson founded for giving a forum to controversial rap singer Sister Souljah, who had appeared on an earlier panel.

"Her comments before and after (the) Los Angeles (riots) were filled with a kind of hatred that you do not honor today and tonight," Clinton said.

He went on to quote from an interview Sister Souljah gave the Washington Post after the riots: "If black people kill black people every day, why not have a week and kill white people? ... So if you're a gang member and you would normally be killing somebody, why not kill a white person?"

Racist? Inflammatory? No question in Clinton's mind.

"If you took the words 'white' and 'black' and reversed them, you might think David Duke was giving that speech," said Clinton.

Jackson, who had referred to Souljah with pride minutes earlier, blasted Clinton for showing "very bad judgment."

In other words, Bill, you're notsaposta do that.

But what, I wonder, about Jackson's judgment? Sister Souljah claims she was misquoted. Jackson accepted that, even though Post reporter David Mills tape-recorded his interview with her. Besides, Souljah's hit rap recordings reveal a history of her shooting from the lip.

Her raps, most of which are reasonably intelligent, remind me of the similarly fiery poetry of Nikki Giovanni, when she won national fame in the '60s with lines like, "Nigger, can you kill ... . Can a nigger kill a honkie?"

Like others of our generation, Giovanni grew up and mellowed. I'm sure Souljah, reported to be in her 20s, will, too. But probably not before she has made a few more stabs at glamorizing interracial violence.

"Two wrongs don't make a right," Souljah shouts at the climax of one of her raps. "But they sure do make things even!"

Well, call me an old softie, but I still prefer Mahatma Gandhi's reasoning: "An eye for an eye makes the whole world blind."

Today's young folks could learn a lot from Gandhi's wisdom. It energized Martin Luther King Jr. and Nelson Mandela, among others. It didn't sell hit records, but it got things done.

Nevertheless, say Sister Souljah's defenders, I'm notsaposta say any of this and neither is Clinton.

Ron Walters, chairman of Howard University's political science department and an important Jackson adviser, said as much in a Washington Post opinion-page essay:

"I would be the first to condemn anyone who said and meant that 'Blacks should kill whites,' but I believe that to have been beside the point of Bill Clinton's attack ... (By) attacking Sister Souljah, Bill Clinton's strategists intended to accomplish the objective of having him appear strong and independent by standing up to the 'special interest' of the party, putting blacks 'in their place' and in the process, appealing to the white middle class."

In other words, Sister Souljah doesn't really mean what she sounds like she is saying, so Clinton would be better off just pandering to her fans so he can get their votes instead of scolding them.

Maybe that would be the politically correct thing to do but, unfortunately, Walters' statement presumes only middle-class whites have reason to be outraged by Sister Souljah's excesses.

Further, he infers that otherwise intelligent blacks will run away from Clinton because he criticized the rappings of a young rap star.

It is as if we African-Americans are notsaposta feel offense. Or, if we do, we're notsaposta say so.

We are notsaposta hang our dirty laundry in public, we are told, because it might weaken the movement's ability to resist attacks by political enemies. But what actually happens is almost always the opposite. We end up making the enemy look better.

Bill Clinton has courageously admonished whites in the blue-collar North and the deep South to reach out to blacks. Now he is gambling that we African-Americans, after centuries of abuse, will embrace graciously a similar appeal for harmony with whites.

I know I'm notsaposta think he's right. But I hope he is.

MAY 8, 1985

MALCOLM'S TORCH IS PASSED

By dissolving the organization that was his birthright, Imam W. Deen Muhammad brings to a close an important chapter in the long-running saga of America's black Muslims—just as Louis Farrakhan begins another.

The story began a half-century ago when the Imam's father, the Hon. Elijah Muhammad, built the separatist Nation of Islam, commonly known as Black Muslims, from a storefront church into a turbulent national movement with an estimated half-million followers and $60 million in financial holdings.

Now, 10 years after his father's death, the Imam (Arabic for "minister") proves what he has said all along: He does not want the family business, only the family religion, stripped of its racial rhetoric and pseudo-Arabic symbols that looked less like those of orthodox Islam than the trappings of a Masonic lodge hall.

He announced the move to his followers on April 20 but, because of the spotty coverage afforded to Muslims by the mainstream press, it did not make headlines until last week, on the same day Minister Louis Farrakhan announced that his breakaway effort to restore Elijah's dream is receiving a $5 million interest-free loan from Libyan strongman Moammar Khadafy.

The news brought to mind another coincidence; Malcolm X, the spiritual Big Brother to the Imam and to Farrakhan, was assassinated 20 years ago this year. Had he lived, he would be 60 years old a week after next Sunday, younger than Mayor Washington and a heck of a lot younger than President Reagan. His spirit fired up a generation of blacks in the 1960s. Yet, I wonder how many will observe his birthday?

Twenty years after his death, Malcolm can be seen as the antecedent to Farrakhan as Martin Luther King Jr. was to Jesse Jackson. Malcolm X positioned himself as a tough but reasonable alternative to King's nonviolence. Black nationalism fell out of fashion at some point in the Me Decade but Farrakhan is leading a resurgence, thanks in part to the behavior of the Reagan administration. Now that black gains of the 1960s are being eroded by a president who expresses open hostility to conventional civil rights spokesmen, Farrakhan is drawing big crowds around the nation by playing to the emotional needs of blacks who, once again, feel left out.

The most objectionable part of Farrakhan's behavior is the way he, unlike Malcolm, goes out of his way to criticize the State of Israel and American Jewish leaders. But, of course, Malcolm never got loans from Khadafy, a man whose antics frighten even other Arab leaders.

Farrakhan says his newly formed corporation called People Organized and Working for Economic Rebirth (POWER) will use Khadafy's money for peaceful purposes, the marketing of soap, deodorant and other personal care products in sort of a new twist on Amway or Avon. Perhaps the hip marketing pitch of the 1980s for door-to-door salesmen in the ghetto will be "Farrakhan calling!"

And, why not? It is no secret that most of the dollars earned by America's 22 million blacks are spent making other people rich. Why not funnel some of that money back into the community? Self-help is an easy sell, whether to free-market conservatives or to members of the alienated black underclass, a group that could use a good morale boost these days.

Elijah Muhammad used the same self-help concept to build a financial empire of stores, farms, buildings and even an airplane, all thought to be worth more than $60 million but revealed after his death to be $10 million in the red. Perhaps Farrakhan will be more fortunate.

DECEMBER 26, 1999

OFF HIS ROCKER

The rush is on to marginalize John Rocker.

His sin? The Atlanta Braves' relief pitcher said what he really thinks about people who don't look or sound like he does.

He does not like such people, judging by his response when Sports Illustrated's Jeff Pearlman asked him how he would feel about playing for a New York City team.

What? The Big Apple? Rocker's idea of pure hell.

"I would retire first," he said. "It's the most hectic, nerve-racking city. Imagine having to take the (No.) 7 train to (Shea Stadium) looking like you're (riding through) Beirut next to some kid with purple hair, next to some queer with AIDS, right next to some dude who just got out of jail for the fourth time, right next to some 20-year-old mom with four kids. It's depressing."

Further: "The biggest thing I don't like about New York are the foreigners. I'm not a very big fan of foreigners. You can walk an entire block in Times Square and not hear anybody speaking English. Asians and Koreans and Vietnamese and Indians and Russians and Spanish people and everything up there. How the hell did they get in this country?"

Among other slurs, he also called an overweight teammate of African descent a "fat monkey," according to the magazine. Rocker even delivered the normally obligatory disclaimer about his own prejudices half-heartedly: "I'm not a racist or prejudiced person, but certain people bother me."

Evidently. If Rocker doesn't like New York City I don't think New Yorkers are going to weep. They have too many other people who are quite eager to live there by any means necessary, even though it is best-known as a place where well-educated professionals pay outlandish amounts of money to live in incredibly teeny apartments.

Deep beneath my own annoyance at Rocker's oafishness, I feel sorry for the guy. I always feel sorry for bigots and other narrow-minded people. They miss out on so much in life.

Rocker's mind apparently is too narrow to enable him to appreciate what is, acre-for-acre, the most culturally rich piece of real estate on the planet.

It is culturally rich for the same reasons that it is diverse in ethnicity and lifestyles. People are lured from all over the planet to New York City because of its welcoming culture of tolerance for those who will work hard, make a contribution and get along with their neighbors, even if sometimes quite loudly.

With diversity, there is tension, regardless of what country you live in. We Americans have been able to handle our diversity better than a lot of countries in recent years because racial desegregation has given us more opportunities to know each other as individuals, not just as groups.

In fact, the irony of the Macon, Ga., native's remarks is that they express the sort of ignorant attitudes that feed northern bigotry against Southerners and big-city bigotry against "rubes" and "hicks."

Even Nation of Islam Minister Louis Farrakhan, who seldom has hesitated to play the race or religion card when it helped raise his profile, says he is having a change of heart.

The same day Rocker was issuing his apology, Farrakhan was giving reporters in Chicago a very sincere-sounding sermon in unity and forgiveness among all races and religions. Standing with clergy from the Catholic, Jewish and Muslim faiths, the 66-year-old leader of the Million Man March said that his "near-death experience" with prostate cancer had left him a changed man.

It was a heartwarming sight, even if he didn't issue much of an apology for offenses taken by Jews and others to his past intemperate remarks.

If Farrakhan appears to be seeing this nation's ethnic and religious diversity in a more favorable light, he is following a pattern set by Malcolm X and Elijah Muhammad, the two most famous Nation of Islam leaders who preceded him.

People can change. For that reason, I still hold out hope for John Rocker. He may be facing enough punishment from his own teammates and employers. It is hard to imagine things ever will be the same for him in the locker rooms of a game with so many blacks, Hispanics and "foreigners" in it as today's pro baseball teams have.

Instead of punishing Rocker for saying what he believes, perhaps he should receive some wise counsel. Perhaps Minister Farrakhan could help.

MAY 14, 2000

OLD WORDS STILL HAUNTING FARRAKHAN

Defenders of Nation of Islam Minister like to dismiss his occasional cheap shots against various ethnic groups as "just words." As one who uses words for a living, I take umbrage at their casual dismissal.

Words matter.

Even Farrakhan, in his own roundabout way, is beginning to acknowledge the wisdom of those two words. You can hear it in his nationally televised meeting with Attallah Shabazz, a woman who holds him responsible for the murder of her father. Shabazz is the eldest daughter of Malcolm X, who was gunned down Feb. 21, 1965, by members of the Nation of Islam in front of her eyes in a Harlem ballroom. Her father was 39 years old. She was a mere 6. Three men tied to the Nation of Islam were convicted in the slaying and served prison terms.

Malcolm X's criticism of the Nation's spiritual leader Elijah Muhammad had caused a bitter split in the Nation of Islam in 1964. In the Nation's national newspaper, Muhammad Speaks, a then-31-year-old Louis

X of Boston called Malcolm X a "traitor." "The die is set," he wrote, "and Malcolm shall not escape. ... Such a man as Malcolm is worthy of death."

A few weeks later, Malcolm X survived the firebombing of his home, while the family slept inside unharmed. A week later he died in the Harlem ballroom.

Attallah's mother, Betty Shabazz, who died in 1997, publicly accused Farrakhan of playing a role in the murder. She reconciled with him after another daughter, Qubilah, was charged in 1994 with plotting to hire a hit man to kill Farrakhan. Those charges were later dropped but the family's resentments of Farrakhan still simmer.

So, it is no small deal from the standpoint of history and old grudges that a meeting between Farrakhan and Attallah Shabazz was arranged by "60 Minutes" reporter Mike Wallace for a broadcast that happens to land on Mother's Day. Judging by the review reel CBS sent me, Farrakhan looks remarkably fit for a man who began prostate cancer treatment in 1991 and was reported by a Nation of Islam newspaper to be near death in March of last year.

But he does not look one bit comfortable hearing his own words read back to him while Attallah sits nearby.

When Farrakhan tries to shift attention toward the government, particularly the FBI and the New York Police Department, who had been following Malcolm closely for years, Attallah erupts. Thirty-five years of anguish comes pouring out. "Indeed, the FBI probably had something to do with it," she says. "But we have to say that adult men between the ages of 20 and 40—black faces!—who chose to put a trigger in their hands and unload until [their guns were] empty, have to be culpable. You can't keep pointing the finger because my father was not killed from a grassy knoll," she says, referring to the many conspiracy theories that surround the death of President John F. Kennedy.

With a voice that sounds choked with emotion, she describes the fears of further violence under which she and her sisters—"spun out into this environment as tumbleweeds, unhealed"—grew up. She recounts the pain of hearing Nation of Islam supporters jeer that "the traitor deserved it!" None of this pain came from the government or the police, she points out, but from "tan and brown and black faces" associated with the Nation of Islam.

Hoping for "healing" in the Shabazz family, Farrakhan says, "As I may have been complicit in words that I spoke leading up to Feb. 21 [the assassination date], I acknowledge that and regret that any word that I have said caused the loss of life of a human being."

In other words, while steadfastly maintaining he did not participate in the plot against Malcolm X, Farrakhan now is willing to allow that his words, at least, did play a significant role. Yes, words matter. Words can inspire. Words can move people to action. Words cannot kill by themselves but they can, wittingly or unwittingly, move others to violence, as several tragic rampages by racist gunmen, black and white, have demonstrated over the past couple of years.

During its 70-year history, the Nation of Islam has helped many lost souls redeem lives that have been damaged by drugs, crime, prostitution and other sins. But under Farrakhan's leadership its positive message too often has been corrupted by cheap shots and group libels, particularly against Jews. Cheap shots were what he took against Malcolm X. Now, late in life, maybe Farrakhan detects, as Malcolm used to say, that his chickens are coming home to roost.

AUGUST 13, 2000

"SOFT BIGOTRY" AND THE OTHER KIND

It didn't take long for Vice President Al Gore's choice of Sen. Joseph Lieberman as a running mate for the evil serpent of anti-Semitism to rear its wicked little head.

On the same day Gore announced his choice, Lee Alcorn, president of the Dallas chapter of the National Association for the Advancement of Colored People, reacted on a Dallas radio station with surprising dismay. "We need to be very suspicious of any kind of partnership between the Jews at that kind of level," he said, "because we know that their interest primarily has to do with, you know, with money and these kinds of things."

His crude syntax aside, Alcorn's statement is breathtaking not only as a wrong-headed and dangerous libel against an entire group of people but also as a haunting echo of ignorant and paranoid hate-speak that has plagued Jews for centuries.

Reprimanded by NAACP President Kweisi Mfume for his comments, Alcorn resigned his job as chapter president. Other African-American leaders, including the Rev. Jesse L. Jackson and NAACP Board Chairman Julian Bond joined the chorus denouncing Alcorn's statement.

But despite their quick and decisive responses, Alcorn's remarks reignited an old story about the sometimes stormy relations between blacks and Jews. It also raised concerns about whether blacks would thumb their noses at the Democratic ticket.

Nonsense. If I were Gore or Lieberman, black anti-Semitism would be the least of my worries. Lee Alcorn's comments about the need for blacks to be "very suspicious" show a remarkably shallow view of history and the way blacks view the value of coalitions with like-minded allies to achieve common ground and goals. Blacks and Jews have a long history of working together.

Despite the occasional outrageous outbursts of Minister Louis Farrakhan and some others, you would be hard-pressed to find anywhere in the world two such different ethnic groups that have cooperated as closely as blacks and Jews have.

Examples include the early labor movement, the civil-rights movement and, oh, yes, the founding of the NAACP itself. Doomsayers point to a controversial 1998 Anti-Defamation League poll that found blacks "significantly more likely than white Americans" to hold anti-Jewish beliefs. It found 34 percent of blacks fell into the "most anti-Semitic" category, compared to only 9 percent of whites. Other surveys suggest the ADL survey, which sampled 999 adults, may be too gloomy in its assessment of black-Jewish relations.

Only 7 percent of the 1,000 American Jews surveyed in the American Jewish Committee's latest annual survey characterized most blacks as anti-Jewish, compared to 23 percent for the religious right, 21 percent for Muslims and 12 percent for fundamentalist Protestants.

Two major surveys over the past decade by the National Conference for Community and Justice found "neither blacks nor whites are more anti-Semitic than the other," says Tom Smith, who conducted the two NCCJ surveys of more than 2,500 Americans each. But, Smith, of the National Opinion Research Center at the University of Chicago, adds, "blacks tend to have more economic stereotypes than whites do." In other words, he explains, blacks were more likely to agree with test questions like, "Jews care more about money than they do about people," even while they are less likely than whites to agree with other stereotypes about Jews.

Thus blacks, like members of other races, can have good friends who are Jewish and still carry negative stereotypes about Jews in their head. It is only when those thoughts come out of their mouths that they get into trouble.

Republican presidential candidate George W. Bush speaks of the "soft bigotry of low expectations" that holds low-income and minority children back. We might also speak of the soft bigotry of stereotypes that otherwise well-meaning people carry around in their heads simply because they don't know better.

Soft bigotry, like low expectations, retards everyone's ability to get anything done. Soft bigotry does not excuse the harm it causes but it may begin to explain why a seasoned civil-rights organizer would broadcast a statement as bone-headed as the one Lee Alcorn made.

If so, his gaffe falls into the same sad category as some other famous gaffes. There was Atlanta Braves pitcher John Rocker's recent jeremiad against gays and immigrants. There was former Los Angeles Dodgers executive Al Campanis' statement that black players lacked "the necessities" for management. There was Jimmy "The Greek" Snyder's attributing black running skills to strong thighs bred during slavery.

The good news is that none of these individuals speak for all members of their racial or ethnic groups any more than Alcorn does. The further good news is that each of their offenses appears to have been committed out of ignorance more than malice. That's good, because ignorance can be cured with education.

The first Jewish running mate on a major party's ticket has caused many forms of bigotry to surface on websites and radio call-in shows. But if this candidacy also helps us to understand and eradicate the soft bigotry we Americans still have about each other, Joe Lieberman will have won a great victory even before the ballots are cast.

APRIL 11, 2007

DON IMUS' TRAIL OF WOE
Two-Week Suspension Is Dust-Up's Only Surprise

As she faced the world's television cameras to respond to a gross insult by radio and television showman Don Imus, a member of the Rutgers University women's basketball team spoke volumes with one sentence:

"I'm not a ho," she said Tuesday at the team's first news conference after the incident that history may well remember as the Don Imus "nappy-headed hos" eruption. "I'm a woman and ... I'm somebody's child," she added.

Indeed, she is. So are the rest of Rutgers' Scarlet Knights. And anybody who would make them out to be anything else should be ashamed. Unfortunately, shame is in short supply in the field of shock radio.

Just before the Easter weekend, Imus apparently thought he could get away with a brief apology at the beginning of his program for his racially charged remarks. But by Monday the controversy had percolated to the boiling point. Civil rights activists called for him to be fired. He was apologizing all day long, including on Rev. Al Sharpton's syndicated radio program.

By day's end, his employers, CBS Radio and MSNBC, had suspended Imus for two weeks.

The Imus controversy was not a big surprise to me, although the punishment was. Back in 2001, I led Imus in an on-air pledge in which he promised to avoid humor that relied on inflammatory racial or gender stereotypes, including "simian references to black athletes" and other abuses of which he had been accused.

I had been part of his stable of journalists and commentators who appeared on his show for more than five years. We were invited to the show to offer political views. He took the pledge and we continued with our usual interview, although interestingly I have not been invited back since.

That's probably not surprising. For more than three decades Imus has been one of America's most popular radio personalities, combining some of the shock-jock elements of a Howard Stern, for example, with the irreverent political sense of, say, a Bill O'Reilly.

But when you dance along the edge, you run the risk of slipping. What made the backlash from the Rutgers statement more serious than his previous dust-ups? For one, it was such an obvious cheap shot. The rich and famous, such as Paris Hilton or Whitney Houston, might be fair game, but why pick on a group of college women basketball players?

Second, it was a slow holiday news weekend, which only brought additional attention, spurred by insatiable 24-hour news cycles.

And third, I have a theory, based on the impact of bloggers, YouTube and other Internet-era phenomena, that mass anger of all types has new ways to grow farther, faster and hotter than ever before. After years of surviving controversies that have cost other shock jocks their jobs or at least a month's pay or more, Imus and those who profit from his talents finally found themselves feeling a pinch in their pocketbooks and their reputations.

Now in full damage-control mode, Imus' cleverest move may have been to go immediately to the national confessional that Sharpton's radio show has become for racial transgressors. What could make Imus look more sympathetic than to be berated for an hour or more by a man widely despised by Imus' core audience of mostly white males.

And the ironies don't end there. After all, if Imus offended black folks with his use of words such as "ho" and "nappy head," it was today's black culture that gave him the vocabulary. I understand those who ask whether it is fair to condemn Imus for using language that gets a pass when black rappers use it. Actually I have condemned the demeaning language of rap. So have Sharpton, Rev. Jesse Jackson and innumerable other black commentators.

Still, it is not enough. We must passionately condemn the language of hate, not only when others direct it against us, but also when we direct it against ourselves.

APRIL 15, 2007

DEBATE OVER IMUS ISN'T JUST ABOUT WORDS

And now, as Mick Jagger might say, let's hear a little sympathy for the devil:

Don Imus famously lost his national CBS Radio show, and its simulcast on MSNBC, after describing the Rutgers women's basketball team as "nappy-headed hos."

"Ho," as everyone must know by now, is an Ebonic word for "whore."

He also stirred up the sort of intriguing national argument that this country has had from time to time about hip-hop, free speech, second chances and how men treat women—especially black women.

The most unusual contribution to this spirited debate comes from Margo St. James, who advocates prostitutes' rights and started COYOTE (Call Off Your Old Tired Ethics) in the 1970s. Now 69, St. James, a self-described "sex-positive feminist" who claims to have turned tricks briefly in her youth, caused quite a stir when she raised money and organized to assist San Francisco prostitutes with bail, shelters, health care and legal reforms.

She's also a fan of Imus, she told me in a telephone interview from her home in Washington state on Orcas Island.

She agrees that Imus' words were reprehensible, she said, but also thinks it is "horrible" that "everybody's dealing with the 'nappy' question, not the 'ho' question."

Instead of making Imus a scapegoat for larger sins that the hateful word "ho" represents, St. James says we should do something to reverse the extent to which "drug and prostitution prohibitions institutionalized racism" in America. "We've got to get down to what it does to women to call them whores," she said. "We've got to go after the big problem, not one big mouth!"

In her own way, St. James touches on a major reason why Imus' "ho" comment touched off the biggest firestorm of his 35 years of trash-talk radio. No other word packs so much wallop with so few letters along our society's fault lines of race, sex and privilege.

Imus' defenders argue that he shouldn't be punished while countless rap stars get away with using that word and much worse. That's a pretty feeble diversion from the question of why Imus felt compelled to use it against what he now admits was a thoroughly "inappropriate" target. What many of Imus' defenders do not know is how deeply the word "ho" already divides black America. It's a bum rap to say, as some of my emailers have claimed, that black people haven't protested sexism, racism and gangsterism in rap music.

Students at Spelman College, a historically black liberal arts college for women, forced the rapper Nelly to cancel a charity fundraising visit to the school a few years ago in protest over one of his sexist music videos. Queen Latifah won the 1994 Grammy for best solo rap performance with "U.N.I.T.Y.," in which she tells women, "You got to let him know. ... You ain't a bitch or a ho." The late C. Delores Tucker crusaded for a decade against "gangster rap" pollution, including buying stock in major record companies in order to protest at stockholders meetings.

But positive efforts like that have sadly little impact in the mainstream media or mainstream white culture. As a result, when black listeners, among others, hear the words coming back at them from the lips of a couple of white fellows like Imus and his producer, it's like rubbing salt in our cultural wounds.

As for Imus, reports of the death of his career are undoubtedly exaggerated. He's been fired before. In the late 1970s he returned to Cleveland radio, which he left a few years earlier with a Cleveland Plain Dealer headline reading, "Garbage mouth goes to Gotham." He worked his way back up the food chain at least once and can do it again, perhaps on censor-free satellite radio.

The young Rutgers women have given us all an excellent example of how to stand up for yourself with grace, courage and intelligence.

And Rev. Al Sharpton has promised he will widen his crusade to go after other pollution on the airwaves, including hip-hop pollution. I hope he delivers.

MAY 9, 2007

SATIRE ABOUT OBAMA ISN'T THE SAME AS IMUS' FLUB

Remember when media pundits were asking whether Sen. Barack Obama (D-Ill.) was "black enough" to attract black voters? That was the old media narrative. The new one goes sort of like this: "Maybe he's too black."

Take, for example, his conservative adversaries, such as talk-radio host Rush Limbaugh, who seems to take gleeful delight in reminding everyone of how black Obama is—and even more delight when the rest of us notice.

Back in mid-March, for example, El Rushbo began to air a satirical song titled, "Barack the Magic Negro."

He didn't make up the term. He hijacked it fair and square.

Columnist David Ehrenstein employed the term—which dates to the film industry days before "Negroes" became "black"—in a Los Angeles Times essay to describe Obama's soaring appeal to white voters.

Ehrenstein compared Obama's rapid rise in the public imagination to some of the roles that actors like Sidney Poitier, Morgan Freeman or Will Smith have played: the black hero who arises magically to "assuage white guilt."

Ehrenstein, who is black, described "white guilt" as "the minimal discomfort" that the white film characters feel about the role of slavery and racial segregation in American history.

Limbaugh, in the fashion of our times, chastised liberal "racism" for bringing up race in this fashion, then proceeded to air a song about it. Repeatedly. Sung to the tune of "Puff, the Magic Dragon" by voice impersonator Paul Shanklin, imitating Rev. Al Sharpton, the song goes in part like this:

"Barack the Magic Negro / lives in D.C. / The L.A. Times, they called him that / 'Cause he's not authentic like me ..."

If Limbaugh was looking for something to prove that he's worth caring about, he struck pay dirt.

Predictably, the ever-alert watchdogs at the liberal Media Matters for America website immediately posted an indignant news alert and audio clip about the song. That's the same group that posted radio host Don Imus' "nappy-headed hos" sound bite about the Rutgers women's basketball team that led to the loss of his national radio show within a week.

It probably says something about how isolated Limbaugh may be from the rest of us that the song didn't generate much mainstream media controversy until last week. That was when Obama became the first presidential candidate to qualify for Secret Service protection besides Sen. Hillary Rodham Clinton, who as a former first lady never stopped having it.

It was the earliest assignment of Secret Service protection since another black candidate, Rev. Jesse Jackson, ran for president in 1984 and '88. If anyone still needs evidence as to whether the Illinois Democrat is "black enough," the bigot vote appears to have made up its mind.

Citing the large number of wackos in the world, a lot of people on the Web and on talk radio, particularly listeners to Sharpton's radio show, think Limbaugh should meet the same fate as Imus. I don't.

I may not be in sync with Limbaugh's politics, but the two cases are quite different. As satire, Limbaugh's song passes three critical tests that Imus' offhand comment flunked: (1) it's funny, (2) it took at least half of a brain to think up and (3) it contains a nugget of truth.

The song in question actually mocks Sharpton more than Obama. The flamboyant New York preacher and talk-radio host comes off as a resentful old-school polarizer who doesn't like to be upstaged by an upstart. Obama is portrayed as a rising star who would refuse to let the few things that divide us Americans along lines of race and class get in the way of the many things that we have in common.

Funny thing: As a guy who builds audiences by inflaming political differences, Limbaugh has more in common with Sharpton than with Obama. Birds of a feather mock together.

Imus' targets, by contrast, weren't rich, famous, powerful or political. He's entitled to free-speech rights, but the First Amendment only protects you from government interference, not from losing sponsors or embarrassing your employer.

Limbaugh's target is a wildly popular presidential candidate, which is precisely the sort of political expression that the First Amendment was written to protect. I may not agree with Limbaugh's politics, but he has a right to express them.

Besides, if the potentates of political correctness come after conservative commentators like Limbaugh today, they'll come after liberal commentators tomorrow.

JUNE 25, 2008

DON IMUS' OFFENSIVE DEFENSE

For a guy who makes his living as a professional talker, the topic of race seems to leave Don Imus oddly tongue-tied.

In case you haven't kept up, the pioneer "shock jock" has been broadcasting a new morning show on WABC-AM since last fall, months after he was fired from MSNBC and CBS Radio for proclaiming that the Rutgers University women's basketball team looked like "nappy-headed hos."

He returned to work with profuse on-air apologies and a pledge to foster an open dialogue on race relations on his new show. On Monday he fostered the sort of dialogue he had not counted on.

Or maybe he did. Listening to the on-air chatter that has stirred up another racial eruption, I had to wonder whether it was just another bonehead mistake or a brilliant publicity stunt.

On Monday's show, sportscaster Warner Wolf was talking about how the Dallas Cowboys football player formerly known as Adam "Pacman" Jones no longer wants to be called "Pacman." Jones is turning over a new leaf after having been suspended for a season and arrested six times.

Then Imus inexplicably injected race into the conversation:

"What color is he?" asked Imus.

"He's African-American," said Wolf, sounding a bit bemused.

"Well, there you go," said Imus. "Now we know."

Huh? That's it? You might ask, "Now we know what?" Imus did not say. The omission left the rest of us to wonder whether Imus was expressing some sort of soft bigotry of criminal expectations in regard to black athletes.

It didn't take all day for Rev. Al Sharpton to call the remarks "very disturbing" and say, "We are looking into this." Sharpton led the campaign to have Imus fired last year from his national CBS Radio show and its simulcast on MSNBC.

Jones said he was upset by the remarks and would "pray" for the radio star.

But Imus insisted that those of us who heard something racist in his remarks heard him wrong. He said he actually was defending Jones, whom Imus thought was being picked on because of his race.

On his radio show the next day, Imus said he was trying to "make a sarcastic point" about the unfair treatment of blacks in the criminal justice system but had been misunderstood.

"What people should be outraged about is that they arrest blacks for no reason," Imus said Tuesday. "I mean, there's no reason to arrest this kid six times. Maybe he did something once, but everyone does something once."

Calling the criticism "ridiculous," Imus pointed out how his program's cast is now more diverse than ever. It includes a black producer and two black co-hosts—one male and one female. Still, after his troubles last year, you might think he'd be extra careful about clarifying his sentiments the first time, especially on topics having anything to do with race, instead of letting his insinuations ("well, there you go; now we know") hang heavily in the air.

Instead, he finds himself trying to explain why what he meant to say was different from what we may have heard him say.

If he was looking for attention—and what entertainer isn't?—he could hardly have dreamed up a more slippery way to do it. Even the remarks that he said he intended to say exposed some of our society's deepest racial wounds.

For example, just as it is offensive to imply that blacks are more criminal than whites, it is also offensive to imply that blacks are arrested "for no reason," if you don't back up the assertion. If "there's no reason to arrest this kid six times," that, too, begs for an explanation. Otherwise, Imus seemed to be committing the same offense of which Sharpton is often accused: exploiting serious issues like race, crime and overpampered athletes and shedding more heat than light.

Ironically, if Imus wants to put his edgy humor to the cause of fostering a helpful dialogue on race, he needs to get serious. He could take some valuable tips from George Carlin, a master of the art of humor who died Sunday at age 71. The envelope-pushing Carlin will be sorely missed by those of us who appreciate humor that also makes you think. Whether you agreed with him or not, you knew where Carlin stood. Imus, by contrast, has a self-defeating habit of shooting from the lip—and firing blanks.

AUGUST 25, 2010

SWEARING OFF THE N-WORD

Oh, no, Dr. Laura. Don't go there. That's what crossed my mind when I heard that Laura Schlessinger, better known as the blunt-spoken and socially conservative host of radio's highly rated "The Dr. Laura Show," had dipped herself in hot racial waters.

Her offense: flagrant on-air use of the N-word.

Yes, the "N-word." That's what I call it. In accordance with today's racial etiquette, I avoid trouble with the word's power of offense by simply not using it at all unless I absolutely, positively have to. Those times have become increasingly rare.

There was a time back in the 1960s when, say, Dick Gregory used the unexpurgated N-word to title his best-selling autobiography. In the 1970s, Richard Pryor used it in the title of his breakthrough comedy album, "That (N-word)'s Crazy."

The idea in both cases was to neutralize the word's negative power through overuse. But we're in a different era.

The rapper Nas was refused the right to use the word on a rap album a few years ago, reportedly out of his recording label's fear that Wal-Mart wouldn't sell it. The times they are a changin'—back!

Of course, as a black man I might try to claim the special privilege that our society affords me to use the word. But since Barack Obama's White House win, I've turned over a new leaf. Some folks have become so sensitive about any hint of racial privilege by nonwhites that I am steering clear of the N-word.

For one thing, I want to avoid the confusion into which Schlessinger perilously plunged.

Her problematic N-word episode occurred when a woman called in to talk about "an issue" with her husband. She's black and he's white. She was growing resentful of his friends and family members who had made "racist comments."

"Give me two good examples of racist comments," said Schlessinger. She dismissed the first example, saying a black woman who is married to a white man can't be hypersensitive. Dr. Laura approaches domestic relations in the sound-bite-size way that certain political talk shows reduce international relations to "Nuke 'em!"

When the caller asked, "How about the N-word?" Schlessinger observed that, "Black guys talking to each other seem to think it's OK."

When the caller reminded Schlessinger that the radio host is not black, Schlessinger snapped, "Oh, I see. So a word is restricted to race? Got it. Can't do much about that."

The conversation became more heated as the caller objected to Schlessinger's "spewing" the word repeatedly on-air. This resulted in Schlessinger spewing out a string of N-words like oil gushing out of the Deepwater Horizon.

At best, she was trying to desensitize the caller to the power of the word. That trick's been tried. Even Richard Pryor, among others, eventually backed off, vowing never to use it jokingly in public again.

At worst, Schlessinger's sarcastic tone made her sound like she was enjoying the word with a bit too much glee.

She hinted as much in her on-air apology the next day.

Unfortunately she undermined her show of contrition with her later announcement on "The Larry King Show." There, she expressed the sort of self-pitying characteristics that she usually denounces in her callers: blame-shifting, victimhood and exaggerated entitlement.

She was leaving the airwaves at the end of the year, she said, to "regain my First Amendment rights."

In fact, the First Amendment applies only to rights that the government might try to take away.

They don't protect Schlessinger from the consequences of embarrassing her sponsors or affiliate radio stations.

Here Schlessinger's sense of entitlement was showing. Her ratings actually have thrived off listeners who tune in to hear whom she is going to insult. It was only when her tough-love style trampled on race, one of the rawest nerves in our society, that she felt some serious pushback.

Yet, the point that she was trying to make should not be lost in the wreckage of her fumbling attempt to make it. Racial epithets, like other insulting words, should be treated the same as obscenities. The best way to neutralize them is to avoid using them.

NOVEMBER 26, 2006

SLURS MERIT IRE, NOT LAWS

Until his racist rant at a Los Angeles comedy club threw his faltering stand-up comedy career onto a bonfire of insanity, Michael Richards was best known to millions as The Guy Who Used to Play Cosmo Kramer on "Seinfeld," one of the most popular shows in TV history. Now he's known as the mixed-up weirdo who gave us something besides sports and the midterm elections to talk about over Thanksgiving dinners.

By now you know the story: A raging Richards was caught on video camera spewing the N-word and making obscene lynching references at some black hecklers in the audience.

When the remorseful Richards later apologized ("I'm very, very sorry") on CBS' "The Late Show With David Letterman," even he seemed to disbelieve his own denials of racism. "I'm not a racist, that's what's so insane about this," he said in a rambling satellite interview. "And yet it is said. It comes through, it fires out of me and even now in the passion that's here as I confront myself." His passive voice ("… It is said …") sounded as unconvincing as President Ronald Reagan's saying "mistakes were made" to disassociate himself from the Iran-contra fiasco. Richards sounded like a man trying desperately to disconnect himself from something that he, and only he, stands accountable for.

His apology to "Afro-Americans," a term I have not heard much since the 1960s, revealed a man oddly out of touch with cultural currents, especially for an aspiring stand-up comedian. Yet, if being out of touch on race were a crime, the world would not have enough jails to hold all of the offenders.

With that in mind, one hopes that Richards will not be alone in using this incident as a learning experience, although I am not expecting miracles. The progress we have made from the era of lynchings to the era of racial bridge-builders, like Bill Cosby, Sen. Barack Obama and Oprah Winfrey, fools too many people into thinking our racial divide has been closed—until an ugly surprise like Richards' toxic tirade erupts.

Instead of helping us to learn, celebrities caught in such eruptions tend to do what Richards has done: They hire a spin doctor.

Richards hired Howard Rubinstein, a big-time crisis manager aptly described by the Washington Post's Lisa de Moraes as "The go-to guy for celebrities who have really stepped in it." Rubinstein, in turn, helped arrange apologetic phone calls by Richards to the go-to guys for big-time black rage, the Revs. Jesse Jackson and Al Sharpton.

Jackson has been talking to members of Congress about prohibiting the use of hate language in mass media, according to a WBBM-Ch. 2 news report. If so, let us hope those talks don't get far. It is easy to agree with Jackson that hate speech divides society and can lead to violence, but if we let Congress decide which speech is and isn't hateful, a lot of comedy clubs would be out of business.

And that's not all. Everything offends somebody. Imagine the repercussions for TV shows like BET's "Comic View" or HBO's "Def Comedy Jam" that feature black stand-up comedians. I've heard from readers, for example, who are offended when black comics on TV poke fun at whites, Hispanics or Asians in their audiences. From the black cultural point of view, such a good-natured call-out can defuse racial tensions. But, to some white folks and others viewing at home, it's hate speech.

The same caution should greet the looming legal actions that the two black male targets of Richards' wrath might take. They've hired celebrity attorney Gloria Allred, the go-to woman for newsmakers with an actionable gripe. In a CNN appearance with her clients, Allred said they deserve compensation for the emotional pain they suffered. If so, I shudder to think where that could end. Current hate-crime laws add penalties to assault and other serious crimes if the offender's speech indicates it was motivated by hate. But, if abusive speech without physical damage is grounds for a lawsuit, the biggest laughs will be coming from lawyers.

Richards is living with his own punishment, properly condemned by the court of public opinion. Even his hip and edgy comrades in comedy are acknowledging that there still are lines of decency that none of us should cross.

Among the offended is the real Kenny Kramer, on whom Richards' character was based. "Use some of that 'Seinfeld' money to buy yourself an act!" he advised.

Right. Try some anger-management therapy too.

MARCH 7, 1999

WHEN YOU EXPECT THE WORST IN OTHERS

Expect the worst and you won't be disappointed.

That's been a slogan of mine for as far back as I can remember. Experience tells me I am not alone. Most of us have at least a trace of misanthropy in us. Unfortunately, some of us let it get carried away.

Take, for example, three recent cases of white men who lost their jobs for making statements that offended blacks. Only one was quickly hired back. Each illustrates in strikingly different ways how you can get into trouble these days for expecting the worst in people.

In New Jersey, Gov. Christine Todd Whitman fired Col. Carl Williams as superintendent of the state police because of his assertions in a newspaper interview that certain crimes were associated with certain races. He specifically linked minorities with drug trafficking.

In Washington, D.C., WARW-FM fired nationally known "shock jock" Doug "The Greaseman" Tracht, who after playing a recording by Grammy-winner Lauryn Hill, remarked, "No wonder they drag them behind trucks," a reference to the dragging murder of James Byrd Jr., in Jasper, Texas.

Earlier this year, black District of Columbia Mayor Anthony Williams accepted the resignation of David Howard, a white aide, after some black staffers were offended by Howard's use of the word "niggardly."

The Scandinavian-rooted word really means "miserly" and has no racial meaning at all. Yet Williams apparently thought he could score a few points with black voters, many of whom were still unsure of a black candidate who received more white votes than anyone else on the ballot. The local and national uproar was so great that Williams was embarrassed into inviting Howard back.

Mayor Williams' sin: He expected too little of his city's black voters.

That's nothing compared to the low expectations New Jersey's Col. Williams had about blacks and Latinos. The Garden State's top trooper denied condoning the practice known as "racial profiling" in police stops. But his statement betrayed attitudes far more pernicious in the upper reaches of a department that long has been criticized and occasionally sued by minorities and civil libertarians for enforcing the unwritten crime of DWB, or "driving while black."

Federal figures show that more than 70 percent of the nation's cocaine users are white. Yet it is blacks and Latinos who find themselves fending off the presumption of guilt. A 1996 case, for example, revealed that while 13.5 percent of the motorists on the southern end of the New Jersey Turnpike were black, 46 percent of those stopped by police were black. Horror stories abound of innocent black families and individuals being harassed.

As a result, the colonel committed the ultimate career sin. He embarrassed his boss. Had she not taken drastic action, she would have been perceived as condoning the same attitudes, presuming the worst of blacks and the best of whites.

But narrow-minded as Col. Williams' words may have been, he sounds brilliant compared to the Greaseman, who already was recovering from an earlier offense to decency. In 1986 Tracht was forced off the air briefly for joking that after Martin Luther King Jr.'s birthday became a federal holiday, if somebody "shot four more" maybe "everyone would get a whole week off."

Lost in most of the national buzz about Tracht are the standards, or lack of them, practiced by his bosses. Tracht's broadcasts were delayed by seven seconds and the station positioned a censor on a "dump" button, which would bleep out anything Tracht said that sounded too offensive. Station officials admitted the "dump" button was seldom used.

Apparently no one at the station realized (until their switchboard lit up) that jokingly calling for racial murder was stepping over the line.

Like Howard Stern, Don Imus and other shock jocks, the Greaseman was addicted to the multimillions of dollars he was making by pandering to his listeners' worst feelings. He was more talented than most, but in a show-business world that was willing to give him all the rope he wanted, he eventually hung himself. Twice.

The real test will be whether the Greaseman gets hired again. Chances are remarkably good that, as long as he continues to pull in the ratings, he will find another station as soon as the heat dies down.

All three of these cases offer examples of lessons learned the hard way about today's racial attitudes. It would be nice if more of us could learn our racial lessons the easy way, through easy and honest dialogue, instead of waiting for a crisis.

But cases like those I cite above could make us Americans even less eager to speak honestly and openly about our racial perceptions, prejudices and suspicions. I hope for better than that, although I expect the worst.

JULY 20, 2008

LEFT SPEECHLESS?

When a microphone at Fox News Channel caught Rev. Jesse Jackson's cutting under-his-breath remarks about Barack Obama, it turns out that "nuts" was not the reverend's only troubling N-word.

Besides whispering to another guest on the set that he would like to de-sex the Democratic presidential candidate, Jackson also accused Obama of "talking down to black people ... telling niggers how to behave."

Jackson has since issued two statements of apology for his self-described "trash talking." He also might issue this word of advice: If you want to whisper something that could be damaging if traced back to you, don't whisper it over a microphone.

Am I surprised by Jackson's use of the racial slur? Not really. I was more surprised to hear that so many other people are shocked, especially non-African Americans.

Ethnic etiquette has always given greater latitude to epithets expressed about one's own ethnic group, as long as they are expressed inside of one's ethnic group. That's how people talk within one's family or ethnic group, especially when you regard your ethnic group as affectionately as you regard your nuclear family.

But if we hold Jackson to a higher standard, it is because he has held us to one too. Remember how comedian Michael Richards, the famous Kramer on TV's "Seinfeld," sought forgiveness from Revs. Jackson and Al Sharpton after disgracing himself with an N-word tirade at Los Angeles' Laugh Factory? The club's owner Jamie Masada now fines comics a charitable contribution of $50 for every time they use the word in their act. He wants Jackson to pay the same amount, he says, to the Museum of Tolerance in Los Angeles. Pay up, reverend.

That's just one sign that the N-word etiquette appears to have changed.

For example, the rap star Nas, born Nasir Jones, announced late last year that he was going to release an album with the N-word as its title. But, after months of delays and reports of turmoil inside his record label, the CD has been released untitled.

Which raises an interesting question for pop art historians to consider: Could Richard Pryor have released his hit 1970s album "That Nigger's Crazy" today?

Or how about the white New York disc jockey who later released an answer album called "This Honky's Nuts"? That white disc jockey's name was Don Imus. Yes, he's the same pioneer shock jock whose "nappy-headed hos" remark cost him his CBS Radio and MSNBC shows. He has since returned to the air through a smaller radio syndicate.

Imus pleaded that his language came from the world of black hip hop. This should serve as a warning to white people to always use rap lingo with great caution, unless maybe your name is Eminem.

I was not the only observer who mocked the NAACP for its ceremony to "bury the N-word" at its Detroit convention last year. But maybe the anti-N-word backlash is having an impact. As African-Americans have learned for generations, social change comes after thousands of ordinary citizens change their attitudes and behavior.

Which brings us back to what upset Rev. Jackson in the first place. His claims that Obama was "talking down to black people" and telling us (insert N-word) "how to behave" ring hollow. Obama has not told black people to do anything that Jackson has not also told us to do. Besides, the roaring enthusiasm of Obama's reception at the NAACP annual convention last week indicates the civil rights community does not feel that Obama has talked down to them.

So, is Jackson over the hill? His glory has faded since he scored an impressive 7 million votes in his second presidential run 20 years ago. And black folks are quite comfortable with paying proper respect to more than one leader at a time.

It is us in the mainstream media who keep insisting on acknowledging only one black leader at a time. We need to widen our lens.

OCTOBER 31, 2010

WHY PC IS SUCH A PAIN, NO OFFENSE

Political correctness may be the biggest stealth issue in this political season, partly because people are afraid to talk about it.

For example, a new poll by Rasmussen Reports finds that 74 percent of the Americans surveyed regard political correctness as "a problem"— and 57 percent believe the country has become "too politically correct."

How did the pollsters define "politically correct"? They didn't. The respondents were left to define PC any way they wanted and, whatever that happened to be, most of them didn't like it.

PC is like flu season: Everybody hates it, but it keeps coming back. We try to inoculate ourselves the best we can, hoping we don't get hit by some new, unexpected strains of offense.

Witness, for example, then-Sen. Joe Biden's irritating many African-Americans in 2008 with an unfortunately condescending-sounding use of the words "clean" and "articulate" to compliment then-Sen. Barack Obama. At least Biden wound up with the vice presidency.

Biden's presence came in handy when President Obama found himself offending conservatives by saying the Cambridge, Mass., police behaved "stupidly" in arresting Harvard professor Henry Louis Gates at his home.

Everybody hates PC, it seems, yet everybody seems to have his or her own version of it.

Political correctness generally is defined as a ban, usually unwritten, against language or practices that could offend women, minorities and other legally or socially protected groups.

Personally I prefer to call it by the old-fashioned label that my parents taught me: good manners.

But PC becomes more problematic when it tries to codify what's going to offend people or even violate rights when people and situations can be so different.

Efforts to protect one group sometimes can offend others, as in Grand Rapids, Mich., where state civil rights officials are investigating an unnamed 33-year-old woman for posting an advertisement at her church last July seeking a "Christian roommate."

That violates fair housing laws, the director of the Fair Housing Center of West Michigan told Fox News. "No exemptions."

You don't have to be paranoid to wonder whether cases like that are filed by somebody who deliberately wants to make fair housing laws look bad.

On the other hand, you have cases like Carl Paladino, New York's Republican gubernatorial nominee, who declares, "I'm not politically correct," in ways that make political correctness look good.

He proudly espoused his opposition to PC when asked, for example, about sexually and racially charged emails he had forwarded to friends. One of his missives famously featured a Photoshopped picture of Barack and Michelle Obama as a pimp and hooker. Not too classy.

But, alas, in a democracy, unlike the private sector, voters can decide what's politically correct in their candidates.

Besides, if politics doesn't work out for Paladino, for example, he received an offer from Hustler publisher Larry Flynt to be the porn magazine's executive editor, Politico.com reports.

"It's clear he's better suited to join our team," said Flynt, "than be the governor of the state of New York."

That's why I think PC is a stealth issue in these midterm elections. Although all political sides have their own versions of political correctness, liberal PC further enrages the already-aroused right when they sense, for example, that it protects Obama from criticism.

Tea party movement supporters, for example, don't like to have their nonracial concerns about taxes and government spending dismissed as "racist"—and liberals don't like to have their concerns about health care and job stimulus dismissed as "elitist."

Today's PC battles date back largely to the 1960s. By the end of the decade, traditional partisan differences about how government should be run were recast into a culture war between self-styled forces of good and evil that over time have became even more polarized.

The actor Hal Holbrook once said he hates PC because "it causes us to lie silently instead of saying what we think." We'd be better off discussing what we think openly, candidly and sensibly, if we aren't too afraid to talk.

DECEMBER 27, 2013

DON'T MAKE "DUCK" TOO PC

True confession: I like "Duck Dynasty."

Yes, I know I'm not its target audience, as my big-city liberal, Volvo-driving, chardonnay-sipping, hipster-professional friends are quick to remind me.

Worse, Phil Robertson, the patriarch of the popular A&E reality show's featured family, has run into a buzz saw of political incorrectness.

Why, I am asked, would I watch a reality show about a family of self-described "rednecks" in backwoods Louisiana who love to hunt and hit pay dirt by making and selling high-quality duck calls?

And I answer, "I have eclectic tastes."

Besides, it's a funny show, beginning with the long beards that make Robertson, sons Willie and Jason ("Jase") and brother Si look like try-outs for a ZZ Top tribute band. The Robertsons invite you to laugh with them, not at them.

To me, the show teaches what I think can be most valuable about TV: its ability to show how much, beneath the surface of our vast cultural diversity, we Americans share a lot in common.

Yet things we don't share in common often get in the way. With that in mind, I have had a feeling, especially after last summer's eruption over Southern-style chef Paula Deen's colorful views on race, that Grandpa Robinson's folksy backwoods candor was another cultural train wreck waiting to happen.

The feared collision occurred after Phil Robertson told a GQ magazine interviewer his real thoughts about gay rights and race relations, unfiltered by the popular A&E reality show's producers.

The self-proclaimed "Bible thumper" condemned "homosexual behavior" as a sin and, using imagery too graphic for a family newspaper, equated it with bestiality and promiscuity.

He also offended many African-Americans with praise for those who worked "singing and happy" alongside him in cotton fields during his hardscrabble upbringing, "pre-entitlement, pre-welfare," with "not a word" of complaint about "these doggone white people."

"They were godly," he recalled. "They were happy; no one was singing the blues."

Say what? Since black folks invented the blues, maybe Grandpa Phil was just trying to be funny. Either way, A&E, among others, was not amused. The network put him on "hiatus from filming indefinitely." Those actions predictably drew a widespread backlash from fans and conservative commentators, including such Republicans as U.S. Sen. Ted Cruz of Texas, Louisiana Gov. Bobby Jindal and former vice presidential nominee Sarah Palin.

That's the sort of train wreck I feared was going to happen in this era of culture wars.

Now arguments over free speech and religious freedoms spoil the happy "Duck Dynasty" image. But I'm not mad at Robertson. His remarks are sadly typical of folks from his generation who, like Deen, mistook day-to-day civility in the racially segregated South as black contentment with second-class citizenship.

I'm only upset with people who, when told that their views hurt a lot of people, don't want to understand why.

I don't agree with Grandpa Phil's biblical interpretations or his retrograde cracks about what social conservatives call "the gay lifestyle."

Nor do I believe "free speech" means people can say anything they want at any time without risking consequences from their friends, neighbors or employers. That's why we've seen celebrities as varied as Alec Baldwin, Don Imus and Isaiah Washington lose work because of insults to gays and others.

But I also believe that A&E overreacted in this case. His views may be wrong, in my view, but Robertson never made a secret of his religious conservatism. It is part of the show's appeal, although through the network's editing process.

Robertson says he was only following what he believes the Bible teaches. Yet I was mildly encouraged that he restated his love for "all of humanity." The best answer to objectionable speech is more speech—more honest debate.

Just as I have learned a lot about Robertson's world from watching his family's show, I think he could learn a lot from an honest chat with some of the people whom he has offended.

He even could invite some of them to one of his family's televised dinner prayers. He wouldn't have to televise it, but I'd love to see that show.

CHAPTER THREE

WEAPONIZED UMBRAGE

One of the reasons why our political culture has avoided confronting the absurdity of our gaffe scandals, as explored in the previous chapter, is that so many political people and movements capitalize on them.

In an age of heightened sensitivities, umbrage in itself has value in a new political game known as "playing the victim card."

Umbrage itself became weaponized as each side competed to shame the other—or risk being out-shamed—whether by charges of racially "coded" and "dog whistle" politics on the right or by "race baiting" and "political correctness" on the left.

The new era appears to have been launched most historically by Bill Clinton's definitive use of Sister Souljah to distance his 1992 presidential campaign from Rev. Jesse Jackson—without offending too many in Jackson's base. As I said at the time, Clinton should have sent her a bouquet of thank-you roses. He might have won without her involuntary help, but she unquestionably made it easier—and established a new strategy for political posterity known as "the Sister Souljah moment."

History of a different sort also is memorialized by the other Great Moments in Umbrage in this chapter, including: Rush Limbaugh's "Magic Negro" song, Newt Gingrich blaming "liberal media" for reminding voters of his sordid past, a white District of Columbia mayoral aide hounded for using "niggardly," and President Obama's "beer summit."

OCTOBER 28, 1992

BILL CLINTON'S DEBT TO SISTER SOULJAH

If Bill Clinton wins Tuesday's election, he will owe a lot to Sister Souljah. The most important moment in the 1992 presidential race probably came in early summer when Clinton criticized Jesse Jackson's Rainbow Coalition for giving a forum to the young black rap artist, who had spoken favorably of blacks killing whites instead of one another.

Souljah denied that was what she meant and Jackson criticized Clinton for exploiting the occasion to make a headline. But tracking polls show the incident pretty much marks the upturn in Clinton's popularity that quickly took him from third place behind Ross Perot to first, where he has remained ever since.

She comes up repeatedly in the surveys and focus groups the campaigns conduct to measure the attitudes of white suburban and blue-collar swing voters. They are often called "Reagan Democrats," because many of them would have walked barefoot over broken glass to vote for the Gipper. But, they might as well be called "white-flight Democrats," characterized by fear, wariness or outright resentment of growing influence by blacks and liberal advocates for the welfare poor in the Democratic Party.

After years of complaining that "I didn't leave my party, my party left me," they praise Clinton for standing up to Jackson, for taking a strong stand on welfare reform (after two years of welfare, Clinton would require able-bodied recipients to accept work or job training, along with other supports to prevent working people from falling below the poverty line) and for his unflinching use of the big stick of capital punishment as governor of Arkansas.

Reporters who follow Clinton joke that he tends to jam black community appearances into a day when they will be overshadowed in news coverage by a more significant speech or photo opportunity that he usually schedules for a predominantly white event.

It poses a dilemma for black leaders who are delighted to see Bush fall behind, but dislike the way Clinton has been winning in the polls while distancing himself from Jackson and any special appeal tailored to racial groups. "The damned strategy is working," Rep. Charles Rangel (D-N.Y.) griped in a recent USA Today interview in which he compared Clinton's strategy to a man who says to a woman, "Meet me in the hotel room; I don't want to be seen with you in the lobby." Nothing is more aggravating than to watch your rival succeed.

Nevertheless, Jackson has campaigned vigorously for "the Democratic ticket," although he has noticeably avoided saying the names of Clinton or his running mate, Al Gore. A big reason for Jackson's enthusiasm: A Clinton presidency offers the prospect of District of Columbia statehood and a possible Senate seat for Jackson, which a Bush presidency does not.

Blacks aren't the only minorities who feel miffed. The National Organization of La Raza, perhaps the nation's most prominent Hispanic activist group, recently released a paper titled "Not Invited to the Party," which charges neither party has enough visible Hispanics or has paid enough attention to such issues as immigration reform or civil-rights enforcement.

Still, blacks and Hispanics appear to be supporting Clinton, if only because the alternative, four more years of President Bush, is so much worse. Long before this year's other white Democratic candidates paid much attention to black voters, Clinton was campaigning vigorously in black neighborhoods, skirting around Jesse Jackson, whom whites tend to like the least, to sew alliances with a new generation of elected black officials like Baltimore Mayor Kurt Schmoke, Atlanta Mayor Maynard Jackson and Los Angeles Rep. Maxine Waters.

One expert, David Bositis at Washington's Joint Center for Political and Economic Studies, a black-oriented think tank, says he expects the prospect of better times after years of Republican neglect could spur a record black turnout for Clinton this year.

If Clinton succeeds with his general appeal to people who "work hard and play by the rules," without making specific appeals to minorities, he will have changed the course of American politics. I think it will be for the better.

He will have neutralized the hot-button issues of race and class that have lured whites out of the Democratic Party for more than 30 years. He will have demonstrated, as the party's centrists have maintained all along, that economic opportunity issues are everyone's concern, not just those of "special interests." He will also force leading Republicans to reassess their need to present substance, like Jack Kemp's "empowerment" agenda to improve lives, not just vague symbols like "family values" or flag factories.

So far, Clinton is the first presidential candidate since Robert F. Kennedy, before his assassination in 1968, to bring Southern whites, Northern blue-collar ethnics and inner-city blacks and Hispanics together under the same political banner in great numbers.

But, before it could succeed, he needed a straw pony to attack in the camp of Jesse Jackson. Sister Souljah fit the bill. Clinton may never be able to thank her enough.

FEBRUARY 3, 1999

RACE POLITICS INFLAME ANOTHER "N-WORD"

There's more to some words than meets the eye or the ear. Look, for example, at the eruption that followed a white District of Columbia mayoral aide's use of a word that was misconstrued as a racial slur.

In case you missed the story (vacationing on Mars, perhaps?), the word was an N-word that sounds a lot like the N-word.

In a budget discussion with two co-workers in mid-January, David Howard, ombudsman to newly inaugurated Mayor Anthony Williams, said "I will have to be niggardly with this fund because it's not going to be a lot of money."

Be what?

In fact, "niggardly" is a Scandinavian-rooted word that means "miserly" and has no denotative or connotative racial meaning to a well-known racial slur, other than its similarity in sound.

Still, that similarity was enough, as far as some folks were concerned. Soon Howard was inundated with angry telephone calls in this predominantly black city. When residents heard what Howard actually said, many believed he still had come "too close to the line," as one black lawyer put it, with a phrase inappropriate to the African-Americans with whom he was working.

Howard, a former restaurant manager who ran Williams' volunteer office during his mayoral campaign, offered his resignation to quiet the flap. Williams foolishly accepted it, comparing Howard's judgment to being "caught smoking in a refinery that resulted in an explosion."

With that, the mayor lit a big match of his own, turning a small flap into a racial eruption that quickly exploded and became kindling for the national news media and talk shows. Since Howard was openly homosexual, the gay rights communities rushed to his defense. Williams admitted he had acted too hastily and took steps to reinstate Howard. Good for him.

So goes the political education of Mayor Anthony Williams, a self-described "nerd in a bow tie," who also is a smart, Ivy League-educated, racial coalition builder.

His challenge was illustrated days before the N-word flap erupted, when a local black writer's essay ran in The Washington Post. The lengthy essay's message was summarized in a big, bold headline that asked whether the city's new mayor was "Black enough?"

With that impolite question, the headline writer expressed openly what Washingtonians of all races have been asking each other in whispers. In the political world, black is not just a race. It is an interest group waiting to be reassured that a politician is "on our side."

Williams' predecessor had no problem with that. Mayor Marion Barry was a quintessential race politician. Unfortunately, his most memorable achievements were running the city into financial bankruptcy and getting arrested on camera for smoking crack cocaine. Still, Barry was most popular in the city's poorest, blackest wards, where support for Williams was weakest.

Williams headed the Congress-appointed financial control board that cut jobs to usher Washington, D.C., back to financial solvency. Having made the hard budget-cutting choices that had stymied other mayors, Williams was elected overwhelmingly by a broad interracial coalition. Then, like any other savvy pol, he tried to reach out to those who did not vote for him.

Perhaps it was this quest for a new kind of "blackness" that caused Williams to breathe a sigh of relief when Howard offered to resign. Without doing anything on his own but accepting the resignation, Williams may have figured he would be viewed as a champion of black pride. How simple. How easy. How wrong.

As one whose childhood memories are scarred with the sting of the other N-word uttered by various hateful lips, I, like many other African-Americans, flinch when I hear it and wince when I see it—or anything that sounds or looks like it, like "knickers," "chiggers" and "Niger," the river or the country.

My heightened sensitivity causes me similarly to avoid any words or phrases that might offend other ethnic groups. These include "gyp," "paddy wagon," "Indian giver" and "welsh on a deal." But, horrible or benign as others may find them, I don't view any of these words as a firing offense, especially when they are delivered with good intentions.

Williams would have looked much smarter had he refused to accept his loyal supporter's resignation. He should have held up Howard's experience as an example of how our various racial experiences can clash with others in a pluralistic society. The best leaders bridge differences, instead of exploiting them.

DECEMBER 31, 2008

NO MAGIC IN "MAGIC NEGRO"

Has the party of Abraham Lincoln become the party of Rush Limbaugh? Stay tuned.

Chip Saltsman, a candidate for chairman of the Republican National Committee, brought strange new attention to the race with a compact disc he sent to committee members over the holidays. Quicker than you can say "Grand Old Party," a controversy erupted over one tune in particular, "Barack the Magic Negro."

The song, which first aired on Limbaugh's radio show, is a parody of "Puff the Magic Dragon." The composer, conservative satirist Paul Shanklin, performs the tune with a raspy impersonation of Rev. Al Sharpton that sounds about as black as the two white guys who used to perform as "Amos 'n' Andy" back in the golden age of radio—and the bad old days of racial segregation.

The lyrics start off like this: "Barack the Magic Negro lives in D.C. / The L.A. Times, they called him that / 'Cause he's not authentic like me ..."

Regular readers of my column may recall that I defended Limbaugh's right to air the tune after he first broadcast it in May 2007. Critics were trying to put Rush in the same stew pot as radio host Don Imus, who had been fired for describing the Rutgers University women's basketball team with the brainless slur, "nappy-headed hos."

Imus' slur and Limbaugh's ditty aren't in the same league, I argued. Imus' offhanded remark violated three fundamental rules of comedy: It wasn't funny, it was not in any sense truthful and the targets of the remark were a lot more sympathetic than the man who made it.

The Barack tune, by comparison, is fair comment, whether or not you agree with its slant or tastelessness. "Negro" is unfashionable, but not a slur or it wouldn't be featured so frequently in the speeches of Rev. Martin Luther King Jr., among others. Back in those days, "black" was about as taboo as "Negro" is today.

Context gives words their power, as Mark Twain might have said, like "lightning" compared to "a lightning bug." The real target of the song, in fact, is not Obama but Sharpton and others whose grievance-based approach to politics competes with Obama's coalition-building approach.

I took a little heat from my friends in the left's intolerant wing for defending Limbaugh in this instance, but that's OK. If you can't be politically incorrect from time to time, right or left, what's the fun of being a commentator?

But provoking an audience as a columnist is one thing, winning elections is quite another. In the past two elections, Republicans have lost the White House and both houses of Congress. They virtually gave up on competing for the black vote, leaving African-Americans to give about 95 percent of our vote to Obama, instead of the approximately 90 percent that black voters have given to Democratic presidential candidates since the 1960s.

Hispanic voters, turned off in many cases by the ugly tone of some immigration arguments on the right, also voted 2-1 for Obama.

Post-election maps showed Republicans improved their turnout margins over 2004 in relatively few counties, most of which were in a thin, mostly southern arc of rural mountain districts from the Appalachian regions to the Ozarks.

With so much bad news behind them, it is not surprising that GOP leaders could use a few laughs. But at whose expense?

Party stalwarts who are circling their wagons around Saltsman should think twice. You can win an academic argument over who's in the right but lose the larger battle for the party's future.

That's why Mike Duncan, the RNC's current chairman who is seeking another term, said sensibly that he was "shocked and appalled" that anyone would think Saltsman's CD moves the party in the right direction.

Defenders of Limbaugh's little ditty seem to have forgotten a basic rule of ethnic etiquette: Political incorrectness goes down more easily in comedy and edgy commentary than it does in politics. They've also forgotten how easy it is to win an argument compared to winning elections.

Yet, the controversy actually may have inadvertently helped Saltsman's bid, judging by some other ho-hum reactions. "I had to ask, 'Boy, what's the big deal here?', because there wasn't any," one state chairman told Politico.com. Another was quoted as saying the song "didn't bother me one bit." Maybe not, but to win elections, a party needs to care about what other voters think.

MARCH 8, 2000

WILLIE HORTON 2000: AL SHARPTON'S UNEXPECTED ROLE

At a small restaurant near where I work a young cashier was excited, as if she had just seen a rock star. She told another cashier that she had just seen the Rev. Al Sharpton getting into a limousine. "You know what?" said the other cashier, who sounded less impressed. "It's a shame that we don't have any real leaders any more."

Her friend agreed. Both of them were young, female and black. As I paid for my cup of coffee I wanted to correct the young women. It is not true that we African-Americans don't have any "real leaders" anymore, I was about to say. Unlike the 1960s, we have an abundance of blacks in top management and leading positions in corporations, universities, foundations and other institutions where we could barely have gotten jobs above the shoe-shining and floor-polishing level in the 1960s. We don't need to wait for a black Moses to lead us to the Promised Land. We're already getting there.

But I shut my mouth and put my big ears on. Instead of hearing only what she was saying, I listened to what she meant. She meant to say that it's too bad African-Americans don't have enough leaders who are less problematic than Al Sharpton.

Alfred Charles Sharpton Jr., with his famously processed mullet-style hair draped around his neck, is many things to many people.

To many, he is the black activist who has never apologized for his racially divisive involvement in the case of Tawana Brawley, a teenager from New York who in 1988 told of a gang rape that later proved to be untrue.

Many also remember how he urged Harlem blacks in 1995 to protest against the "white interloper" who owned a clothing store on 125th Street and had threatened to evict a black sub-tenant. Days after one of Sharpton's supporters said, "We are going to see that this cracker suffers," a black man set fire to the store, killing seven employees and himself. Sharpton was not present and denies any responsibility for the tragedy.

To Democratic politicians like presidential candidates Al Gore and Bill Bradley and New York senatorial candidate Hillary Rodham Clinton, Sharpton's "House of Justice" has become an obligatory stop on the campaign trail to build support among black voters. Confronted with Sharpton's mixed record, the candidates insist Sharpton has evolved and matured from his wilder early days.

Yet to leading Republicans, Sharpton is a "wedge issue" that will divide Democratic candidates from mostly white swing voters. Republican presidential candidate John McCain, for example, called Sharpton one of the nation's "agents of intolerance" on the "outer reaches of American politics."

To many rank-and-file black Americans who work hard every day, Sharpton is no Martin Luther King Jr. But when some new offense has been leveled against the race, Sharpton often appears to be the best they are going to get. To see why Bradley, Gore and Hillary Rodham Clinton were reluctant to denounce Sharpton, look at what happened to John McCain after he denounced Pat Robertson and Jerry Falwell. McCain said he wants everyone to be held to a high moral compass, but McCain, in his zeal, violated the 1st Commandment of politics: Thou shalt not divide thy base.

Bill Clinton knows that. He criticized Jesse Jackson's Rainbow Coalition in 1992 for including Sister Souljah as a speaker despite her inflammatory remarks about the Los Angeles riots. With that, Clinton distanced himself from the extremists in his party's base without offending its sensible majority.

McCain tried to do that with Robertson and Falwell but overdid it. His comparison of the two to Sharpton and Nation of Islam leader Louis Farrakhan sparked a backlash even among some of McCain's strongest fans.

Americans of all colors want to see if leaders of both parties can distance themselves from the excesses of their followers or if the leaders will only point fingers at the excesses of their rivals' parties. If so, we may see Sharpton become this year's version of the attack ads that spotlighted former Massachusetts Gov. Michael Dukakis for giving a prison furlough to Willie Horton, a black man who later raped and murdered.

Politics can unite or they can divide. If principled leaders duck and hide, Americans do not have only a black leadership shortage but we have a leadership shortage—period!

When principled leaders fail to rise, no one should be surprised that imperfect leaders fill the gap. Sharpton's no dummy.

JANUARY 25, 2012

THE UMBRAGE CARD TRICK

What do you do when you're a presidential candidate like Newt Gingrich who lugs so much baggage that your baggage has baggage? That's easy. You reach up your sleeve and ... Oh, yes. You play the umbrage card. You fume and fuss with outrage over the question and hope no one demands an answer.

Campaigns bring out the best and worst in candidates. Gingrich at his best is an excellent debater. He thinks on his feet, dazzles with obscure historical fact nuggets and skillfully connects with friendly crowds. At his worst, he's a demagogue, a bully and serial exaggerator, especially when sticky questions put his back up against a wall.

For those avenues to his victory in South Carolina's pivotal Republican primary, Gingrich can thank the mainstream media that he loves to bash. They provided two convenient punching bags: CNN's John King and Fox News' Juan Williams.

Moderator King opened a debate in North Charleston by offering Gingrich a chance to respond to claims by his second wife that he asked for an "open marriage" before they split.

Gingrich responded by ripping into King and "the destructive, vicious, negative nature of much of the news media that makes it harder to govern this country, harder to attract decent people to run for public office." As the crowd roared its approval of Gingrich, a visibly shaken King tried to defend his question. But amid boos from the crowd and angry scolds from the "decent" Gingrich, it was useless.

Funny but I don't recall Gingrich complaining about "negative" news media when ABC's Brian Ross, the reporter who interviewed his ex-wife, broke the Rev. Jeremiah Wright Jr. story four years ago. Nor do I recall his complaining about attracting "decent people" to run for office as he pushed for President Bill Clinton's impeachment during the Monica Lewinsky scandal.

But that's the joy of the umbrage card. If the facts are against you, attack the media. Show enough outrage and nobody calls you on your hypocrisy.

Such was the case a few nights earlier in a Myrtle Beach, S.C., debate, when Juan Williams challenged Gingrich's well-known comments that poor kids should be employed as school janitors, that Obama was a "food stamp president" and that black Americans "should demand paychecks instead of food stamps." Were such statements not "at a minimum insulting?" Williams asked.

Gingrich said no, bringing cheers and applause from the audience as he launched into a lecture about the value of work, about his own daughter Jackie's janitorial work for her first job and his often-repeated claim that "more people have been put on food stamps under Barack Obama than any other president in history." That exchange brought a standing ovation from the crowd and congratulations from at least one woman at a later South Carolina campaign stop "for putting Mr. Juan Williams in his place."

Yet Gingrich's food stamp claim is misleading on several counts. For one, food stamp recipients increased during seven of President George W. Bush's eight years, according to the U.S. Department of Agriculture. The growth came largely because of policy changes that encouraged more participation by eligible Americans. But Gingrich is not about to let details get in the way of a chance to sound offended.

Many in the crowd undoubtedly fantasized with glee that Gingrich might someday do the same to Obama—or as one man told Gingrich during a South Carolina town hall meeting, "bloody Obama's nose."

Gingrich responded, "I don't want to bloody his nose, I want to knock him out." Yes, the man knows his audience.

And that's Mitt Romney's big challenge. The former Massachusetts governor has improved his debate skills, but shows visible discomfort at the attack-dog style at which Gingrich excels. Considering the Grand Old Party's need to win moderate swing voters in November, Romney has to sell a difficult message: Gingrich might be a fun date for now, but they really don't want to marry him.

SEPTEMBER 30, 2007

GIVING SOFT BIGOTRY A BREAK

Does ignorance about race make you a racist? That boiling question bubbles at the heart of the controversy that Fox News star Bill O'Reilly's kicked up with his poorly received compliments of black diners in a New York restaurant. My answer is, no, ignorance about race does not always make you a racist, but it can make you sound like one.

That's O'Reilly's problem. O'Reilly has been vilified recently by the liberal-leaning website Media Matters for America for insinuating how surprised he was to discover how (Gasp!) civilized black folks behaved while dining in Sylvia's, one of (Double gasp!) Harlem's best-known restaurants.

"I couldn't get over the fact that there was no difference between Sylvia's restaurant and any other restaurant in New York City," he marveled. "I mean, it was exactly the same, even though it's run by blacks, primarily black patronship."

Yup, they had knives, forks and everything! Just like white folks!

"It was like going into an Italian restaurant in an all-white suburb in the sense of people [who] were sitting there," he said, "and they were ordering and having fun. And there wasn't any kind of craziness at all."

Nope, no lap dancing, either.

"There wasn't one person in Sylvia's who was screaming, 'M-F-er, I want more iced tea!'" O'Reilly said, sounding almost disappointed.

No, ignorance about race might not make you a racist. It only makes you ignorant. That's why I think O'Reilly deserves a break. When someone is ignorant you should try to teach them. Instead, a lot of otherwise good-hearted, fair-minded and charitable people want to tar and feather O'Reilly.

Peace, people. I know O'Reilly. I've argued with him about various topics on his radio and TV shows. I relish a good "gotcha" moment against inflated egos as much as anyone does. But I also believe that this Sylvia's kerfuffle is a bum rap.

You see, in the context of a later lengthy chat with author Juan Williams, a black National Public Radio reporter and Fox News commentator, O'Reilly wasn't trying to sound racist. Quite the opposite, he actually was criticizing all of those white people who don't personally know many black folks.

What O'Reilly doesn't seem to understand is the weariness black Americans feel over constantly being compared to our community's worst role models.

That's a big reason why it seems curious that O'Reilly, after years of roiling up public outrage against raunchy gangsta rappers and other frightening figures, suddenly expresses what sounds like genuine surprise that some black people are not scary at all. At worst, O'Reilly appears to be afflicted with what President Bush calls "the soft bigotry of low expectations."

But that's OK. How else will O'Reilly, I or anybody else learn anything if we don't make a few boneheaded mistakes once in a while? My greater fear than hearing O'Reilly talk himself into a politically incorrect hole is the silence of those afraid to say anything about race for fear of offending someone. We need more candid talk about race and class, not less.

Besides, look at his upbringing. Through no fault of his own, O'Reilly came from a socially and economically isolated background. He calls himself "working class" in his first book, "The O'Reilly Factor," although compared with my factory laborer dad in Ohio, O'Reilly's family was well-to-do. He grew up in white middle-class Levittown, on New York's Long Island. Like other socially handicapped folks, O'Reilly is a product of his environment. To borrow a line from "West Side Story," "He's depraved on account of he's deprived!" Liberals, of all people, should avoid blaming the victim.

Nevertheless, let's give O'Reilly credit for trying to widen his horizons. It turns out, he was dining that night at Sylvia's with Rev. Al Sharpton, who has made re-educating white folks his life's work.

Does that dinner date surprise you? Who would guess that, after railing against Revs. Sharpton and Jesse Jackson as some sort of race hustlers and poverty pimps, O'Reilly would take the "A Train" up to Harlem to go cattin' around with Rev. Al? Hey, that's show biz. Don't take it personally. Or seriously.

AUGUST 24, 2011

THE ART OF INSULTS

With a presidential contest on the rise, so is the heat of the umbrage wars. That's what I call the endless contest to see which political side can express more outrage about what the other side has to say about it.

Tea party leaders, for example, are taking umbrage at Rep. Maxine Waters, a liberal California Democrat, for the way she expressed her umbrage at the hyperconservative tea party movement while addressing the unemployed at a forum in Inglewood, Calif. "You can't be intimidated," she said. "You can't be frightened. And as far as I'm concerned, the tea party can go straight to hell."

I don't agree with the tea party on much, but here tea partiers have a point. Waters should lay off the name calling. It only reduces her to the level of her opponents—like the tea party.

After all, she's talking about a movement whose supporters waved signs at its early rallies that compared President Barack Obama to, among other figures, Adolf Hitler, Joseph Stalin, the Joker and a jungle witch doctor with a bone through his nose.

Of course, as tea party leaders were quick to point out, snarky left-wingers sometimes depicted President George W. Bush in similar fashion or worse. Like other virtues, civility is easier to praise than to practice. So, true to form, a prominent tea party group's leader fired back at Waters' remarks with a blame storm that by now is familiar enough for me to abbreviate it: ABO—Always Blame Obama.

"We've had Democrats calling American citizens 'terrorists' and 'hostage-takers,' and now an elected Democratic representative says that we can 'go straight to hell,'" the Tea Party Patriots said in a statement. "The president and all leaders of the Democratic Party, who have called for civility in the past, are neglecting to censure their own. ... The president's silence on these latest violations of civility has been deafening, but not surprising."

Deafening? "As someone who's been called a socialist, not born here, taking away freedoms for providing health care," Obama told heckler Ryan Rhodes, a tea party leader in Iowa last week, "I'm all for lowering the rhetoric."

The president also could have mentioned being called a "jackass" by radio host Rush Limbaugh, while replaying the president's debt ceiling speech earlier in August.

He could have mentioned Republican Rep. Doug Lamborn of Colorado saying on another radio show that associating with this president was "like touching a tar baby." Lamborn later apologized when he heard some people find "tar baby" offensive.

Obama also could have mentioned being called "your boy" on MS-NBC by conservative columnist Pat Buchanan, which raised enough eyebrows for him to explain later that he was using boxing lingo and meant no offense.

And that's just in the past month. Robust language always has been a part of politics. Sometimes it can be quite lucrative. Check out the titles of some Ann Coulter best-sellers: "Slander: Liberal Lies About the American Right," "Godless: The Church of Liberalism" and "Treason: Liberal Treachery from the Cold War to the War on Terrorism."

"Treason"? Maybe that's where Texas Gov. Rick Perry got the idea in an Iowa appearance to describe as "treasonous" the possibility that Federal Reserve Chairman Ben Bernanke might take further steps to keep interest rates low. Why would Bernanke, who was appointed by Bush, "play politics," as Perry described it, in this fashion for a Democratic president? Perry did not say.

AUGUST 2, 2009

OBAMA'S BREW-HA-HA
Removing Conflict between the Police and Citizens

President Barack Obama's got his hands full with health care, two wars and the economy. But he put all that aside to have a beer in the Rose Garden with a friend and the cop who arrested the friend in the friend's own home. Out of earshot, journalists focused on Job One: what to call this historic media event.

ABC News offered "The Audacity of Hops." Audacious, indeed.

The Washington Post reported, "Yes, Three Cans," "Menage a Stella Artois," "Beerastroika" and "A Thousand Points of Bud Light."

My Facebook friends offered "Dreams of My Lager," "Fermented Forum," "Draft diplomacy," "Yes We Can—or Bottle," "Brew-ha-ha" and "The Audacity of Cops."

By then my online pals groaned, "I can barley keep from laughing" and "Quit while you're a head."

I'll stop. Obama called the chat-over-brewskis a "teachable moment." I don't know what was taught. Journalists were allowed no closer than 50 feet. But I could guess one thing that Obama had learned: It's OK for a biracial president to talk about race, but don't take sides.

Obama brought trouble on himself when he told reporters he thought Cambridge, Mass., police "acted stupidly" last month when they arrested his friend, Harvard professor Henry Louis "Skip" Gates Jr., for disorderly conduct in his own home.

Faster than you could say O.J. Simpson, Obama's approval ratings slipped, particularly among white, working-class voters, according to polls.

An NBC/Wall Street Journal poll, for example, found 32 percent of whites thought Gates brought the arrest on himself. Only 7 percent thought the arresting officer, Sgt. James Crowley, was more at fault. African-Americans leaned just as sharply the other way: Only 4 percent faulted Gates compared with 30 percent who thought Crowley overdid it.

A Pew Research Center poll found the public disapproved of Obama's comments by a 2-1 ratio, especially among working-class whites. An Obama spokesman said, "the president doesn't spend a whole lot of time focused on polling." That's what presidential spokesmen always say when polls turn bad.

Conservative pundits pounced. Fox News star Glenn Beck said Gates-gate revealed Obama's "deep-seated hatred for white people or the white culture." After being reminded that Obama has numerous white staffers, Beck whipped around in a double-reverse. "I'm not saying that he doesn't like white people," he explained. "I'm saying he has a problem."

Then he said, "This guy is, I believe, a racist."

"Racist," I have noticed, has become the sort of taboo tag to whites that the N-word traditionally has been to blacks. Black leaders partly brought this on themselves. Overusing the R-word robs it of its power and it is easy to overuse. Beck and his like are saying that whites can play that game too, even against the half-white and scrupulously evenhanded Obama.

Judging by my far-right emailers (some of my most faithful readers, thank you very much), Gates is a "racist" for loudly asking police to leave his house after he had established his identity. Having known Gates for about a decade, I think he was simply overly tired from a trip to China.

And I, my conservative critics say, am a racist for writing that Crowley knew all along that his arrest would not stick (which it didn't) and that he had the power to defuse Gates' temper simply by leaving Gates' home. Instead, Crowley apparently chose to teach Gates a lesson for committing an unwritten offense to police etiquette: "contempt of cop."

Can't we all get along? Reports of a "post-racial" America after Obama's election to the White House were greatly exaggerated. If anything, we are a transracial country. As Judge Sonia Sotomayor's U.S. Supreme Court confirmation hearings illustrated, we Americans suspiciously watch one another across racial, ethnic, gender and cultural lines as we uneasily shed our white male supremacist past.

We alert our cultural antennae and react sharply to any signs of preference shown to any group besides the one to which we happen to belong. That's nothing new for women or nonwhites. Men and whites are still getting used to it.

Either way, Americans look to Obama to be an honest broker between the races. The polls reveal a long-standing divide between blacks and whites on police conduct versus law enforcement. Innovations like "community policing" show how the two should not be in conflict. When police and civilians work together, crime goes down. That's the best lesson we can take away from Obama's brew-ha-ha.

And I'll drink to that.

CHAPTER FOUR

BILL COSBY'S CULTURE WAR

Bill Cosby, who I first interviewed as a college journalist in 1968, rates special attention for his cultural milestones during my column-writing career—first with the breakthrough "Cosby Show" and finally as an iconic evangelist for old-school bootstrap conservative self-help values in 2004, ironically helping prepare the way for Barack Obama's meteoric rise in the national spotlight.

He reappeared in my commentaries as a crossover TV superstar in the 1980s, in the early 1990s as a critic of David Duke and as a by-your-bootstraps culture warrior since 2004.

This chapter collects my assessments of him as a "Mid-Racial Man" in the mid-'80s and an outspoken social commentator for the gossip press.

Also included are two interviews I had with him, in-person and by phone, about his frustrations with high-profile black progressives who accused him of casting too much blame on poor people for being trapped in poverty.

DECEMBER 4, 1985

BILL COSBY: MID-RACIAL MAN

What is one to make of the "Bill Cosby Show"?

What can you say about a show that, in its second season, has been No. 1 every week except one, when it was beaten by the World Series?

How do you explain its consistently pulling more than half the households in the nation that have their television sets turned on?

And who would expect his show's success to buoy up "Family Ties," which follows it on Thursday nights, into the No. 2 slot and spur a revival of the domestic comedy as television's leading art form after years of dominance by nighttime soaps?

You cannot just credit Cosby's formidable talent. After all, the man has laid more than a few turkeys in his career. This time he offers something more than comedy; he offers reassurance.

After the evening news tells us about family disintegration, teen-aged rebellion and interracial conflict, Cosby reassures us that life's most nagging problems are solvable, provided you have good sense and a middle-class income.

That's it. It is a message that may not save the world but it will cross cultural and political lines. It can be sold to liberals who need reassurance that the civil rights struggles of the past two decades were worth it. It can be sold to conservatives who need reassurance that the problems blacks suffer as a group are economic, not racial.

And if reassurance sells, Cosby is the man to sell it. Twenty years ago, writer Tom Wolfe wrote of the "Mid-Atlantic Man," a bicultural character who has spent so much time in England and America that he can perform and prosper comfortably in both, jet lag notwithstanding.

Cosby has shown himself to be the ultimate Mid-Racial Man, operating comfortably in that world of gray that television created to span the cultures of black and white.

Cosby is so image-conscious in his quest to appeal to whites and blacks without offending either that he hired Dr. Alvin Poussaint, the noted black Harvard psychologist, as "production consultant." Most creative types would balk at the notion of hiring an in-house censor, but, in his quest for mass acceptability, the Mid-racial Man does not mind yielding to a second opinion.

As a result, the Huxtables are as perfect as a television family can be without losing all ability to amuse. Parental authority reigns supreme in the Huxtable household, which is more than you can say for most TV families. Conflicts are settled in "family meetings." All members get a voice, but parental word rules. When adults disagree, they settle their disputes quietly, away from the children. Tantrums are taboo.

On the Cosby block, everyone gets home on time and pays his own way. There are no street gangs, welfare checks, birth-control clinics or illicit drugs beyond perhaps a crumpled joint of marijuana that turns up in junior's socks one day. The most serious issues the Huxtables are likely to confront consist of who is going to carve the Thanksgiving turkey or where is Sis going to find a date for the prom.

Of course, this describes the American families I know, black or white, about as well as "Father Knows Best" or "Ozzie & Harriet" did in the 1950s. Prime-time televison is seldom about reality.

Nevertheless, I do not want to begrudge a group of black performers their chance to make a buck off the boob tube, as long as the show is just good, clean, sanitized fun.

I just hope all those kids out there who do not have a doctor-father at home realize they can attain that American Dream, too. Maybe someday they will see a television program that shows them how.

MAY 23, 2004

COSBY SOUNDS OFF OVER "DIRTY LAUNDRY"

We usually think of Bill Cosby as the jolly, Jell-O-pitching, Cliff Huxtable father figure who never gets agitated about much. But, even the jolly Jell-O Man feels the need sometimes to liberate his inner grouch.

One such moment occurred as he was being honored at a black-tie bash in Washington's Constitution Hall commemorating the 50th anniversary of the Brown v. Board of Education decision.

According to witnesses, he astonished many at the posh affair by launching into a rant-sermon that mocked the talk, fashion and spending habits of poor black people.

"... People marched and were hit in the face with rocks to get an education, and now we've got these knuckleheads walking around," Cosby grumbled, according to the Washington Post and Associated Press. "The lower economic people are not holding up their end in this deal. These people are not parenting. They are buying things for kids—$500 sneakers for what? And won't spend $200 for 'Hooked on Phonics.'"

Hold on. He was just getting warmed up.

"I can't even talk the way these people talk: 'Why you ain't,' 'Where you is' ... You can't be a doctor with that kind of crap coming out of your mouth!"

And, as for "the incarcerated?" Fuh-gedda-boud-dit.

"These are not political criminals," he said. "These are people going around stealing Coca-Cola. People getting shot in the back of the head over a piece of pound cake and then we run out and we are outraged, saying, 'The cops shouldn't have shot him.' What the hell was he doing with the pound cake in his hand?"

Why is this news? Because Cosby violated what I call "BPC," black political correctness.

We should not hang our dirty laundry out in public, according to BPC, especially in front of white folks—as if white folks didn't already know when our clothes are not clean.

Instead of being candid in our public self-appraisals, BPC tells us to sound like President Bush does on Iraq: If we've made any mistakes, we can't remember what they are.

Conservative talk radio and TV hosts like Fox News Channel's Bill O'Reilly and Sean Hannity used Cosby's remarks to jab liberals who would find anything "politically incorrect" about them. For evidence, they quoted Post reporter Hamil Harris' account of other podium guests—Howard University President H. Patrick Swygert, NAACP President Kweisi Mfume and NAACP Legal Defense Fund head Theodore Shaw—looking "stone-faced" after Cosby finished his little rant.

But Mfume told me later in an interview that he felt anything but "stony-faced" that night. Mfume said he fully agreed with what Cosby was trying to say, even if he would have used different words to say it.

"I just got back from the barber shop an hour ago and the conversation there is probably still going on about how we (as black people) have got to take responsibility for our own lives," he said.

What about the conservatives who say the NAACP cares more about white racism than black self-reliance? "They're not sitting at my speeches," he said. "I am constantly saying that black bigotry is just as cruel and ignorant as white bigotry and that the value of old-fashioned self-reliant values are what have gotten us through so many hard times. But that doesn't get coverage."

No, it is not news when blacks admonish other blacks to work harder. But when anybody from one race accuses or offends somebody of another race, stop the presses!

Cosby's view, by contrast, offers a side of black life that seldom is seen on the news, a self-reliance liberalism. Right-wing ideologues pretend that self-reliance liberalism does not exist. But most successful African-Americans are intimately familiar with it. The message, as Cosby might say, is simple: Those of us who have made it need to help those who have not, but poor black folks need to "hold up their end in this deal," too.

Cosby was saying the same thing backstage when I interviewed him during my college days. It was 1968, but he didn't want to talk about black power, Black Panthers or cultural revolutions. He wanted to complain about why so many young blacks of my generation were wasting the great opportunities that hard-won civil rights victories had brought.

In those politically polarized times, I was disappointed by his traditionalist attitude. But I appreciate its wisdom today with new eyes, the eyes of a parent.

Cosby probably feels liberated these days by a new intellectual honesty that the hip-hop generation has brought to black entertainment. This is, after all, an era in which a bright young black talent like Chris Rock can bluntly declare, "I love black people, but I hate niggas!"—and receive thundering applause from black audiences who understand completely what he is saying.

Here's hoping our new candor can lead us to new action. We need to close the gap between those who have made it and those who haven't. No joke.

MAY 30, 2004

WHAT BILL COSBY MEANT TO SAY

Had Bill Cosby chosen milder, more genteel language for his recent controversial critique of bad habits that keep poor black folks poor, we wouldn't still be talking about it.

Instead, an unusually large number of people, most of them black, have stopped me on the streets and elsewhere with a pronounced sense of urgency just to ask, "What do you think about what Bill Cosby said?"

Of course, what they really want to do is tell me what they think about what Bill Cosby said at the recent Howard University fundraiser in Washington's Constitution Hall to celebrate the 50th anniversary of the Brown v. Board of Education decision.

"The lower economic people are not holding up their end in this deal," Cosby said. "These people are not parenting. They are buying things for kids—$500 sneakers for what? And won't spend $200 for 'Hooked on Phonics.'"

Remarks like that have been reported out of context and misinterpreted so widely that Cosby took the unusual step of releasing a statement to the news media and appearing on Tavis Smiley's PBS program Wednesday night to clarify what he meant.

"The mistake I made was not in clarifying that I wasn't talking about 'all' [poor people]," he said, according to the broadcast transcript on Smiley's website.

Yes, as any preacher or pundit can tell you, that little word "some" enables you to make all sorts of generalities about people. After all, there are "some" people who will fit into just about any category.

But Cosby's speech would not have made news if he had moderated his language with such qualifiers. News breeds on conflict and it is not news in the mainstream media that a black person is admonishing other black people to be more self-reliant.

So, to paraphrase a mayoral press secretary I used to know, don't report what Cosby said; report what he meant.

He is justifiably frustrated. He is an iconic superstar who has used his millions, along with hundreds of hours of donated time, to help black colleges and numerous other self-help causes, including an educational foundation named after his slain son Ennis Cosby, himself a crime victim.

Yet Bill Cosby hasn't received nearly as much publicity for all of that as he has received for his Constitution Hall outburst.

He blamed absentee parenting as the root of alarming black crime and dropout rates and for that he was not apologetic. "You can't just blame white people for this, man. You can't," he told Smiley. "Whether I'm right wing or left, some people are not parenting."

I was particularly delighted to see Cosby dismiss the widely heard concern that he was giving white conservatives ammunition to trash the black liberal agenda: "I don't give me a blank about those right-wing white people," he told Smiley. "They can't do any more to us than they've already started with. ... But by the same token, for God's sake, turn around and let's have some meetings and say, 'Brother, um, let me explain to you. You're the father of so-forth and so-on. Brother, you gotta rein them in, man. You gotta go talk to 'em.'"

Indeed, we do need "some meetings." We also need action. We, who happen to be African-American parents, in particular, need to stop worrying about what white conservative talk-show hosts, for example, think about us and start talking about what we are doing to ourselves.

But then what? What, I hear readers ask, is to be done?

I received one answer on the evening following Cosby's clarifying PBS interview: The year-end ceremonies of a wonderful little 13-year-old volunteer program called College Bound Inc. It pairs underprivileged, but promising, District of Columbia high school students with college-educated adult volunteers who mentor the kids through SAT preparation, scholarship applications and all of the other ins-and-outs of college preparation.

You can find mentoring programs like this in just about every city. We need more. They also need more volunteers. As Kpakpundu Ezeze, board chairman of College Bound, said: "We could serve more kids if we had some more adult volunteers."

That's right. You don't need Cosby's millions to help the next generation grow up with the right values. A little time, attention and advice can go a long way, especially when many of today's kids are not receiving enough of it anyplace else.

I'm glad Cosby realizes that his critics were right about one thing: It is not just the "lower economic people" who are failing to parent their children properly and steer them, as Jesse Jackson says, away from dope and up toward hope.

As the West African proverb says, it takes a village.

MAY 21, 2006

COSBY'S QUEST FOR SOLUTIONS

Bill Cosby can be a very funny guy, but he does not suffer fools gladly.

A heckler found that out the hard way after shouting at the actor-comedian last week during a forum at the University of the District of Columbia, the latest of about 20 cities to host a free "A Call Out with Bill Cosby" symposium for black parents and community leaders.

Two years almost to the day had passed since Cosby caused a national uproar over his blunt statements in this town, on the 50th anniversary of Brown v. Board of Education, about the problems low-income black folks bring upon themselves.

How blunt were his statements? Allow me to refresh your memory:

"We've got these knuckleheads walking around who don't want to learn English."

"In the neighborhoods that most of us grew up in, parenting is not going on ... These people are fighting hard to be ignorant."

"Five and six different children ... Pretty soon you're going to have to have DNA cards so you can tell who you're making love to."

It is no surprise that Cosby's pitch for black self-reliance delighted conservative talk-show hosts. Black Americans expressed a range of reactions as diverse as we are. I, for one, agree with Cosby's general sentiments, as I think most black Americans do, although many of us would have chosen more polite words to express them.

The mostly black crowd at the university last week was on Cosby's side. Through two two-hour sessions, Cosby coaxed poignant stories of violence, abuse, self-reliance and redemption from his panel members, who included educators, family court experts and a mother of adopted children who was named the city's "Foster Parent of the Year."

As I pondered how sad it is that the problems of our communities receive so much more media attention than the solutions, conflict erupted. The heckler, whom news reports called "a self-described community activist," started shouting from the audience. He derided Cosby's "watered-down dialogue" and demanded answers to Michael Eric Dyson's highly publicized book, "Is Bill Cosby Right? (Or Has the Black Middle Class Lost Its Mind?)."

That's when Cosby lost his cool. The 68-year-old former college athlete jumped off the stage, wireless microphone in hand, and raced up the aisle to loom over his somewhat astonished questioner. "I'm sick of you and your Dyson," Cosby declared. "Dyson is not a truthful man."

In a backstage interview with me and another journalist, Cosby scoffed at the "elitist" charge coming from Dyson, a black professor at the ritzy University of Pennsylvania. "And how much does it cost to go there [to Penn]?" taunted Cosby, who attended Philadelphia's less-elite-but-still-proud Temple University on a track-and-field scholarship. "How many black students do they have at Penn?" he continued. If Dyson taught at a school like the University of the District of Columbia that serves mostly lower-income non-whites, Cosby said, "then maybe he could talk."

I don't blame Cosby for feeling steamed. He and his wife, Camille, have given millions to colleges, scholarship funds and worthy individuals. Still, he gets the "elitist" rap.

I, too, might blow my stack.

Still, Dyson must be delighted. As the attacks against "The Da Vinci Code" have shown us, overreaction helps book sales.

That's too bad, since I think Dyson's view of Cosby reveals another curious version of elitism, a version I think is shared too widely in left-progressive intellectual circles. Institutional racism is still a problem, as Dyson repeatedly reminds us, but African-Americans will not defeat it through political agitation and legislation alone. We also need to employ the same basic tools that have brought success to countless black families during far worse racial times than these: education, hard work, strong families and high moral standards.

The debate between black self-help versus outside help is an old one in black America, but it is a false choice. Black America needs to look not for what's right or what's left, but to what works in our drive to liberate those left behind by the civil rights revolution.

Cosby doesn't have all of the answers. He doesn't even have all of the facts. But he's helping the rest of us to find both. That's a good start.

JULY 16, 2006

CRIME MAKES A COMEBACK

The last time I saw Chris Crowder, he was giving Bill Cosby a hard time for allegedly being too tough on poor black folks.

Now Crowder, 44, is dead and I am thinking that Cosby was not hard enough.

Police found Crowder on the morning of July 8, shot multiple times next to the wheelchair he has used since he was shot in the same Washington neighborhood back in 1990, leaving him paralyzed from the waist down.

Back then, Washington, D.C., was the nation's "murder capital" during that era's national crack epidemic. Now Crowder has been killed during a murder epidemic. Police had no immediate motive or suspects in his death, but he was one of 14 homicides in Washington in the first week of July. Last month, the FBI reported that the nation's murder rate spiked upward in 2005 for the first time in five years.

Is crime making a comeback? In some cities it is. Like the District, Milwaukee, Minneapolis and Boston report an upsurge in murder, particularly among juveniles who are not content to merely rob or steal without adding violence.

And adding alarm to newscasters' voices is the way this crime wave in the District, unlike earlier ones, is hitting tourist areas and the neighborhoods of rich people.

Yes, the containment and abandonment of crime problems in poor neighborhoods has long been a dirty little secret of urban life. But when it spills over into other neighborhoods, major media and powerful politicians no longer can ignore the problem.

In D.C., it took the life of a British man in the upscale Georgetown area last week. Four suspects, including a 15-year-old, have been arrested in that slaying. Two days later, Washington Police Chief Charles Ramsey declared a "crime emergency" that allowed him to put more police in troubled areas. Hours later, two groups of tourists were robbed at gunpoint near the Washington Monument on the National Mall, which is patrolled by the U.S. Park Police.

Nevertheless, abandonment by the rich and powerful does not leave less-fortunate residents helpless or hopeless. Churches, block clubs, community organizations and other local residents can step up and give guidance.

That was the message Cosby was preaching back in May as he was taking questions at the University of the District of Columbia during one of the "call-outs" he has hosted around the country for the past two years.

Cosby ruffled a few feathers with his use of blunt, sarcastic humor to criticize parents who shun personal responsibility, blame police for incarcerations and let their children speak improper English. He said what I hear many African-Americans express in our private discussions, if not with the same language.

Nevertheless, Crowder, sitting in his wheelchair near a microphone, yelled to Cosby that he was hosting a "watered-down dialogue," although from my vantage point Cosby seemed to be doing just fine with the rest of the mostly black audience.

The outburst infuriated Cosby, who jumped down from the stage to confront Crowder. "You don't deserve an audience with me," said the star of stage, screen and Jell-O commercials. Fortunately only words, not fists, were thrown. We can all get along.

Outspoken, I have since learned, is the kind of guy Crowder was. A Howard University graduate, he was working his way through law school in 1990 when he was shot in a case of mistaken identity, according to news accounts. During a 1995 interview with CBS' Mike Wallace, Crowder said he was shot by one of three teens who had mistaken him for a police officer.

He became a regular at community meetings, speaking out for affordable houses and programs for young people. Recently, he was running for mayor of Washington. Sadly he now is silenced.

We Americans talk a lot about removing the root causes of terrorism abroad. Crowder's death reminds us of the terrorism too many of us still face on the streets back home, too often at the hands of juveniles. Too many parents have dropped the ball. They are either unwilling or unable to prevent their kids from falling off the social cliff. And too many parents still are children themselves. They have left it up to others to do the child-rearing they should be doing themselves. Some may quarrel with Cosby's language, but they can't fault him for speaking the truth.

AUGUST 9, 2006

COSBY'S CALL FOR UNDERSTANDING

Here's a scoop for you, America: Bill Cosby has a hard time getting his message out.

"The media love to choose what they want to use," he said. "I can't go door-to-door to tell everyone what I really mean."

But William H. Cosby Jr., PhD, did manage to get ahold of your humble scribe on my cellphone during my vacation, scoring some rare cool points for me in the process by saying hi to my teenage son.

Cosby is like my 100-year-old grandmother; you never know what to expect. My heart pounded. Was he calling to praise? To complain? To sue?

As it turned out, he was calling to complain, but not about me. He appreciated my recent column about the national debate he ignited with his now-famous speech on the 50th anniversary of the 1954 Brown v. Board of Education school desegregation decision.

No, Cosby was calling out of frustration, he said, over failure of other media to report what he has been trying to say. The Washington Post, which first reported the uproar over his 2004 speech, and other media have focused too much, in his view, on his sarcastic language. Too little attention has been given to the problems about which he was speaking: crime, violence, school dropouts, out-of-wedlock births and other self-inflicted plagues among black youths who were left behind by civil rights reforms.

"Our children are trying to tell us something [with their self-destructive behavior] and we're not listening," he said.

I listened. He talked. I took notes. The last straw for Cosby appears to have been Michael Eric Dyson, a University of Pennsylvania humanities professor and a Cosby critic. In a July 21 op-ed essay in the Post, Dyson lashed out at what he calls Cosby's "blame-the-poor tour" for ignoring major political and economic forces that continue to reinforce black poverty—such as low wages, outsourcing, urban disinvestment, unemployment and substandard schools.

"None of these can be overcome by the good behavior of poor blacks," Dyson declared.

But, of course, that statement is wrong, dangerously wrong in the disrespect it pays to the value of good behavior. As generations of successful black families can attest, good behavior won't solve all problems, but it beats drugs, crime, abuse, child neglect and other forms of destructive behavior.

Cosby offered two stellar examples, Jachin Leatherman and Wayne Nesbit, who defied the usual young black male stereotypes by graduating at the top of their class from Ballou Senior High School, which has one of Washington's worst crime, poverty and dropout rates. Having survived distractions that included the shooting death of one of Nesbit's football teammates, the two athletes are headed for College of the Holy Cross this fall.

At a July forum in Washington on the state of black men in America, featuring Cosby, Harvard psychiatrist Alvin Poussaint and other experts, Leatherman and Nesbit were asked how they did it. They praised their fathers and their athletic coaches for "staying on top" of them.

(The forum, sponsored by the Post, Harvard University and the Kaiser Family Foundation, can be seen at Kaiser's website, www.kff.org).

"There's the answer right there," Cosby said. "Why won't the media cover that?"

Alas, in newsroom terms, the lads are a heartwarming but play-it-inside-the-news-pages human-interest story. As one cynical mentor told me years ago, "News is what happens when things are not going the way they're supposed to." Want more attention for your honor students? Let them hold up a liquor store.

Some people think Cosby, who has given millions for scholarships and black colleges, has come down too harshly on black parents who shun personal responsibility, blame police for incarcerations and let their children exalt sports and improper dialect over books and proper English.

I suggested in an earlier column that Cosby might not have been harsh enough. For all of the burdens that we African-Americans have to bear from a legacy of historical and institutional racism, we also need to call each other to account for the damage we do to ourselves.

For starters, we could use a lot more fathers like those of the Ballou scholars. Unfortunately, good dads and good moms don't grow on trees, as my own dad used to say about money. If we, as a society, do not do all that we can to help families in crisis and encourage parental responsibility, we will reap the ugly dividends later in our streets.

That's Cosby's message. At least he has what some critics call his "bullying pulpit" to help get his message out—and he's not afraid to use it.

DECEMBER 11, 1991

AND NOW, THE PAT AND DAVID SHOW

Funnyman Bill Cosby recently offered a helpful suggestion to news media covering David Duke: Stop referring to him in every story as a "former Ku Klux Klan leader and neo-Nazi."

In an interview on CNN's "Larry King Live," the Cos observed that, if people didn't know better, they might think Duke's mama had named him "Former KKK Leader" at birth.

How, then, King asked, would you refer to him?

"I'd just call him what he is," said Cosby, "a Republican candidate." If we did, Cosby explained, people would begin to notice something real interesting: "They'd notice he sounds just like Bush!"

Cosby had a point, even if it was more pointed at the time he pointed it out. Bush has since begun to wobble in his conservative convictions, most noticeably by agreeing to sign the civil rights legislation he had decried for two years as "a quota bill."

It's still a "quota bill" to Duke and Buchanan, even though legal experts agree it doesn't differ substantively from the "Republican bill" alternative Bush had been pushing for months. And, as Bush has wobbled leftward, Duke has begun to list starboard about as far as he can without putting his Klan robes back on.

"I think the time has come in America to begin to limit and stop the illegal immigration in our society," Duke said last week as he announced his presidential candidacy. "We've got to begin to protect our values. We've got to begin to realize that we're a Christian society. We're part of Western Christian civilization."

Buchanan has no problem with that. On ABC's "This Week With David Brinkley," he declared, "I think God made all people good, but if we had to take a million immigrants in, say, Zulus, next year, or Englishmen, and put them in Virginia, what group would be easier to assimilate and would cause less problems for the people of Virginia?"

In his own candidacy announcement the following Tuesday, Buchanan bellowed, "Our Judeo-Christian values are going to be preserved and our Western heritage is going to be handed down to future generations and not dumped on some landfill called multiculturalism."

Landfill? If that sounds an awful lot like Duke, that doesn't trouble Buchanan, either. "I'm not going to walk away from views simply because David Duke takes them," Buchanan said on Brinkley's show.

The only significant difference between himself and Duke, says Buchanan, is that Duke "comes out of another tradition, to put it mildly."

True. Buchanan's background as a Roman Catholic would disqualify him by itself. And his resume as a media aide to two presidents, Nixon and Reagan, makes Duke look like what he is, a sweet-talking tub thumper with a nose job, puffed-up hair and a lifelong career as a professional hater.

But, as dissimilar as the pedigrees of these messengers may be, there's hardly a dime's worth of difference between their messages.

A Bart Simpson T-shirt on Buchanan's chest would read, "Intolerant and Proud of It."

Sure, to take one of his issues, it might be easier to assimilate Europeans than Africans or Asians into mainstream American society, but history shows almost all immigrants move to this country intent on becoming Americans and America has drawn strength from its openness to them.

In fact, our historical posture as a nation regarding immigration only illustrates how today's most urgent issue is the economy, since historically we have welcomed immigrants during good times and tried to close off the spigot when times got hard.

And Buchanan's characteristic slur against multiculturalism only shows how Buchanan, much like Duke, draws political strength from demeaning the cultural history of everyone who is not European.

What's wrong with accepting the reality that America is a multicultural society, that everyone's culture is worthy of respect and that we can get along in this country without putting anyone's culture down, whether it be European or non-European?

Liberals should be delighted. By presenting Dukism as an acceptable idea, Buchanan can do for conservatism what Barry Goldwater did for it in 1964, namely run it into the ground.

After years of jeering George McGovern for frightening white, middle-class voters out of the Democratic Party and into Republican arms, Duke and Buchanan can help send them running right back again.

So, maybe the media should take Bill Cosby's suggestion seriously and stop referring to Duke's hateful past. Focus instead on his intolerant present.

Duke would lose his biggest attention-getter, and, most important, his message could be addressed for what it is, a warmed-over sermon of sweetened hate, fed by the politics of resentment.

The rise of demagogues and demagogic politics that prey on resentments of the poor and disenfranchised are another measure of how in hard times, people who are "hurting," as George Bush puts it, turn on each other.

It's time to stop letting David Duke's background make Pat Buchanan look like a moderate.

It's also time to stop helping Buchanan make Duke sound like he's swimming anywhere near America's mainstream.

CHAPTER FIVE

POLITICAL LANGUAGE ARTS

After wallowing in the news that politicians make by stumbling over their language, it is instructive to see masters of political language at work, whether for good or ill, and why, as the words a politician says matter less than the message that his or her listeners hear.

Welcome to the world of spin as we have come to know it since the heyday of the Great Communicator Ronald Reagan and his long-distance students, including Bill Clinton.

Columns in this chapter include an examination of how Shakespeare offers a revealing window—or stethoscope—into why Bill Clinton seemed to do a better job of selling Barack Obama to voters at the 2012 Democratic National Convention than Obama did.

I also look at why Biden's "clean and articulate" compliment of Obama tripped wires in black listeners' ears, why "Hussein" was a burdensome middle name for a presidential candidate and how conservatives like Mike Huckabee could have used better words to express their respect for women.

SEPTEMBER 19, 2012

BUBBA'S VOCABULARY LESSON

Bubba is back. As a word man, I was most impressed at the Democratic National Convention by Bill Clinton's skillful speech, much of it ad-libbed.

Even President Barack Obama seemed to suggest later that the former president did a better job of selling Obama than the current one does.

"Somebody emailed me after his speech; they said, 'You need to appoint him secretary of explaining stuff,'" Obama joked in New Hampshire. "I like that."

In fact, as Seth Meyers observed on "Saturday Night Live," we already have a job for that: It's called "president."

Some presidents are better at that job than others are.

Much of Clinton's success, I believe, comes not so much from the big words that he knows as from the little ones that he uses.

That observation was reinforced by Michael Witmore, director of the Folger Shakespeare Library, a scholarly and theatrical Capitol Hill institution near the Supreme Court and Library of Congress.

Comparing the text of Clinton's prepared remarks and ad-libs with those of Obama's acceptance speech, Witmore told me in an interview that he noticed distinctive linguistic differences in their word choices:

Clinton tended to rely almost solely on the single-syllable, action-oriented words that come from the Germanic Anglo-Saxon roots of English. Obama more often employed longer and more nuanced Latin-rooted words that the French brought to English with the Norman conquest in 1066.

"Today you could say that almost all of our political rhetoric," said Witmore, who earned his doctorate in rhetoric, "comes from two books from the 16th and 17th centuries: the King James Bible and Shakespeare's plays."

As a result, he said, "political speech comes to us in two speeds."

Latin and its derivative, Romance languages (French, Spanish, Italian, etc.) became the English spoken mainly by elites in the law, bureaucracy and intelligentsia. Short action-oriented Anglo-Saxon words with hard consonants ("fighting," "eating," "hiking") became the day-to-day way that common people talk.

That helps to explain why rock 'n' roll lyrics don't tolerate Latinate words, Witmore pointed out. He offered the Rolling Stones refrain "I can't get no sa-tis-fac-tion" as a notable exception. The hard-driving rhythm of that hit breaks the Latinate flow of the word "satisfaction" into Saxon-like bits. Yet the word does not rhyme with anything except, at one point, the memorably inserted "girly action."

Ah, yes, it's only rock 'n' roll, but I like it.

For similar drama in political speech, Witmore said, "you often will hear the speaker launch into a stream of longer impressive Latinate words, then abruptly shut it down with short, Anglo-Saxon words."

One widely quoted example came in Clinton's repudiation of Republican nominee Mitt Romney's charge that Obama cut Medicare's budget to help pay for Obamacare. In fact, Romney's running mate, U.S. Rep. Paul Ryan of Wisconsin, proposed exactly the same cost savings in his own budget plan, Clinton said. Then, in a very Anglo-Saxon ad-lib, Clinton added, "It takes some brass to attack a guy for doing what you did."

His audience erupted with cheers and laughter, perhaps mentally hearing another Anglo-Saxonism that is more often used than "brass" but less suitable for prime time television.

Obama, by contrast, seems more often to mix the Anglo-Saxonisms with the Romance, which is the language of nuance. He even had the audacity to speak a word of French in his acceptance speech: He has never been more hopeful about America, he said, "not because I'm naive about the magnitude of our challenges. I'm hopeful because of you."

As good as he gets, Obama's presentation style tends to speak from a loftier perch of oratory than Clinton's. Bubba's "freestyling"—as hip-hoppers describe his ad-libbing—sounds like he is having a nose-to-nose conversation with you, even when there are 15,000 other people in the room. That's a gift every politician wants.

Gallup found that 43 percent of all respondents rated Obama's speech as "good" or "excellent," compared with 38 percent for Romney's speech. But both fell way short of Clinton's 56 percent—which, ironically, fell just short of Gallup's all-time record of 58 percent, which was achieved by Obama in 2008.

If Obama's post-convention bump was largely a "Clinton bounce," credit the ex-president's ability to make little words mean a lot.

FEBRUARY 7, 2007

BIDEN'S REMARK ARTICULATES A GAP IN UNDERSTANDING

On a scale of 0 to 10, 0 being a minor annoyance and 10 being a complete outrage, the kerfuffle over Sen. Joseph Biden's use of "clean" and "articulate" to describe Senate colleague and fellow presidential hopeful Barack Obama ranks about a 2—although with many black Americans it is a very strong 2.

Having followed Biden for years, I am certain that the Delaware Democrat meant absolutely no harm when he mused to the New York Observer on the day of his presidential campaign announcement about Obama: "I mean, you got the first mainstream African-American who is articulate and bright and clean and a nice-looking guy. I mean, that's a storybook, man."

That glib attempt at a compliment was typical Joe. Those who have seen him unedited on C-SPAN know the dear man doesn't know when to shut up.

Blame Biden's spending too much time in the Senate. Biden was first elected in 1972 when he was a young pup of 29. Senate rules allow members to talk on and on, even when they should be learning how to be better listeners.

This, by the way, should serve as a warning to the young senator from Illinois: Get out of the Senate as soon as humanly possible or you, too, could succumb to its lure of self-important, self-destructive motormouth narcissism.

Obama's two distinctly different responses to his colleague revealed how he, too, has yet to gain his footing in the slippery realm of racial politics.

His first impulse was to play down Biden's statement, rise above it and move on. "I didn't take it personally and I don't think he intended to offend," Obama said when reporters swooped in for a reaction. "But the way he constructed the statement was probably a little unfortunate."

Later in the day Obama realized he needed to defend those black presidential candidates who ran before him. He issued a much stronger statement: "I didn't take Sen. Biden's comments personally, but obviously they were historically inaccurate," he said. "African-American presidential candidates like Jesse Jackson, Shirley Chisholm, Carol Moseley-

Braun and Al Sharpton gave a voice to many important issues through their campaigns, and no one would call them inarticulate."

Every presidential election teaches Americans something about themselves. The rise of America's first truly viable black presidential candidate already has begun to expose racial fault lines that many Americans did not know existed.

One of them is the word "articulate." President Bush certainly meant no offense when he, too, called Obama "articulate" in a Fox News interview. Yet, even when intended as a compliment, the A-word can irritate black Americans like fingernails scratching on a blackboard.

What some black people, like me, hear is: "Oh, you're so articulate—for a black person." It's an irritant that usually has little public consequence, although it can ruin private relationships.

Should white people now be terrified of saying the wrong thing? "Now we can't even say you're articulate?" host Bill O'Reilly asked on his Fox News program. "We can't even give you guys compliments because they may be taken as condescending?"

Let us hope that's not the case. It would be a tragedy for this A-word kerfuffle to lead to fewer candid conversations across racial lines when we need to have more.

I hope Americans take this to be a learning experience, much as I learned from Jewish friends who told me they were annoyed when Gentiles like me feel obliged to fill spaces in conversation with, "Some of my best friends are Jewish."

Or third-generation Asian-American friends who express their annoyance at being asked, "You speak such good English. How long have you been in this country?"

Besides, much of our sensitivity as black Americans to white condescension is rooted in bad experiences with some of our fellow black folks. In my youth, long before the MTV and BET era, some of my peers would denigrate articulate English as an attempt to "put on airs" by "talking proper." Let us thank the patient persistence of many wise black parents for today's articulate black leaders.

In this way, presidential campaigns can be teachable moments in the long saga of American history. We shouldn't be afraid to talk to each other. Just don't forget to listen.

Can you hear me, Joe Biden?

AUGUST 19, 1990

THE TRICK OF GOVERNING IS SEMANTICS

A rose by any other name would smell as sweet, Shakespeare once wrote. Shakespeare obviously didn't work for the government.

America's interruption of Iraqi shipping in the Persian Gulf may look like a blockade, but it is not, says President Bush.

A blockade, which my dictionary defines as "the shutting off of a place, usually by troops or ships," is generally considered in international circles to be an act of war. The president does not want us to think our shutting off of Iraq by troops and ships is the least little bit warlike.

And don't call it a "quarantine," either. That was the word President John F. Kennedy used to avoid using the B-word to describe his own picket line of warships around Cuba during the missile crisis.

No, it is merely an "interdiction," says Bush, a word that, like quarantine, implies a stern but peaceful act of prohibition, proscription, banning or taboo.

It is a game Iraq's Saddam Hussein apparently figures two can play, as his administration refuses to refer to the Americans he has refused to let leave Iraq as "hostages."

"Hostages" is a word we have come to associate with terrorist states. Perish the thought that anyone would think the Iraqi government, which has dropped poison gas on its own citizens and harbors known Palestinian bomb throwers and kidnappers, to be a terrorist state.

No, says Saddam Hussein, the Americans within his borders are "restrictees." They're not captive. They just can't do anything his government doesn't want them to do, like leave.

Man your thesauruses, mates! It's full speed ahead into the rename game, a peculiar but inevitable element of governance in the age of sound-bite diplomacy.

We play it on the domestic front, too. The National Opinion Research Center at the University of Chicago provides a significant measure of the difference words can make in public policy perceptions with polls it has taken since 1973.

Everyone is familiar by now with how much a poll's results can be affected by the wording of its questions, but Tom Smith, a top NORC investigator, says none of the issues on the opinion center's questionnaires produces as much of a difference as words that pertain to government help for the poor.

For example, Americans still share a deep desire to help "the poor," but we don't like "welfare."

The opinion research center found only 24 percent of those surveyed last year thought more money should be spent on "welfare," but 68 percent wanted to spend more on "assistance for the poor."

By contrast, Smith says, we differ very little in our attitudes toward spending on "the military" as opposed to spending on "national defense" or in our attitudes toward "foreign aid" versus "assistance to other countries."

The distinction apparently has not been lost on the federal government. It may help explain why the word "welfare" strangely disappeared when the former Department of Health, Education and Welfare was divided into the Department of Education and the Department of Health and Human Services.

Nor is the distinction lost on Ronald Reagan and other politicians who have put terms like "welfare queens" and "welfare cheats" to good use during political campaigns.

And, after years of growing cynicism about government help, it may help explain why George Bush shows no interest in new poverty initiatives to help make his promise of a "kinder, gentler nation" a reality.

For example, a new anti-poverty thrust recommended by an interagency group of government officials was overridden by the Domestic Policy Council, according to one recent news report, because the council thought it was too expensive or controversial.

Instead, as an unnamed presidential adviser was quoted as saying, we'll "keep playing with the same toys. But let's paint them a little shinier."

That's too bad because, if anything, the negative connotations Americans put on "welfare" reflect widespread dismay over the very toys Bush's people want to "paint a little shinier."

President Bush could leave a lasting legacy if he displayed the courage he has shown in the war against Iraq with a similar commitment to developing new ways to help the estimated 32 million Americans who live below the official poverty line of $12,675 for a family of four.

For example, he could improve and expand government programs like Head Start and the Job Corps that have proved their ability to help break the poverty cycle, but reach only a fraction of the young people who should be eligible.

He could take what innovative states like Massachusetts, Illinois, Wisconsin and California have learned with welfare-to-work and job training programs and help spread their benefits to other states.

He could expand earned income tax credits to help low-paid working families and help welfare recipients avoid losing money and benefits by going to work.

These may not be a perfect set of solutions, but they sure beat another shiny new coat of words.

DECEMBER 17, 2006

WHAT'S IN A MIDDLE NAME?

Did you know that U.S. Sen. Barack Obama's middle name is Hussein? You do now.

Make no mistake: If he decides to run for president, quite a few people will remind you of it. Those people are not his friends.

It's funny how much people don't know about the Illinois Democrat, even as he rides a wave of rapturous news coverage. Santa Claus could hardly have drawn more excited crowds than those who recently turned out for Obama in New Hampshire. Almost no reporter seems to be able get through an Obama story without using the phrase "rock star."

Despite his brief Senate experience, he's the only Democratic hopeful who is waging a serious challenge to U.S. Sen. Hillary Rodham Clinton in the polls. Yet, hardly anyone knows much about him. A hefty 40 percent of the Democrats surveyed in the latest Los Angeles Times/Bloomberg poll said they did not know enough about him to have an opinion on him.

Remarkably, that seems to work in his favor. As with Colin Powell, the last potential black presidential candidate who generated this type of, OK, rock-star excitement, Obama benefits from the Rorschach test factor: People see in him what they want to see in a presidential candidate.

Candidate McDreamy's balloon has left potential foes so little to puncture that some have begun to pick on his middle name. Republican consultant Ed Rogers' frustration showed in the way he emphasized Obama's middle name on MSNBC's "Hardball with Chris Matthews":

"Count me as someone who underestimates Barack Hussein Obama," he said, pronouncing "Barack" in a way that rhymed with "hard rock."

Conservative radio windbag Rush Limbaugh similarly delights in mocking Obama's full name. El Rushbo even posted a caricature on his website of Obama with huge floppy ears and the title "Barack Hussein Odumbo." Cute. Sort of like the class clown taking on the class valedictorian and prom king who also is the captain of the basketball team.

Obama's middle name comes from his Muslim grandfather, a Kenyan farmer, and his father, a Kenyan government economist. To put the anxieties of hyperventilating Islamophobe bloggers to rest, the senator is a member of Chicago's Trinity United Church of Christ. In advertising terms, diversity is his brand.

Nevertheless, the H-bomb is probably a love tap compared to what's in store for him should he decide to run for president. He sees that coming. Obama has been in Chicago long enough to know that politics is not a pillow fight.

So in New Hampshire and in a Thursday meeting with the Tribune's editorial board, Obama joked about the middle-name thing with the right tone: astute, self-deprecating humor. His middle name is no big deal, he says, "when you are already starting with 'Barack Obama.'"

We also know from his autobiography, "Dreams From My Father," that he tried marijuana and cocaine in his wayward youth, unlike President Bush, who dodged probing drug questions as a candidate, and President Bill Clinton, who claimed never to have inhaled.

Obama's candor also has been his best defense against his biggest connection to scandal so far. He acknowledged in the Tribune meeting that "it was stupid" and "boneheaded" of him to purchase a strip of property a year ago that adjoined his $1.65 million home from Antoin "Tony" Rezko, a political insider and fundraiser. Rezko since has pleaded not guilty to charges of trying to extort campaign donations and kickbacks from firms seeking state business.

Obama, who bought the home with his hefty advance for his latest book, is not accused of wrongdoing, just stupidity, as he acknowledged, for letting himself be associated with even the appearance of shadiness.

As Chicago scandals go, that would be small potatoes for Obama were he not the nationally adored embodiment of the audacious hope that the title of his second book touts. As a practical matter, the Rezko flap is not likely to hurt him in a race against Sen. Clinton, who had a questionable land deal called Whitewater. But, if anyone else is looking for attack-ad material, they'll grab whatever mud they can find.

After running successfully for the Senate as "the tall, skinny kid with the funny-sounding name," Obama knows how to turn potential lemons into lemonade. So far, his candor has worked for him. Despite the current holiday-season media hype, though, the 2008 presidential election is still two years away. Political honeymoons end quickly. Soon people want to know what you really believe.

With that in mind, I hope Obama runs. I want to see how candid he will be when it really counts.

CHAPTER SIX

DIVERSITY ANXIETY

"Diversity anxiety" is what I call the hidden side of immigration, multi-culturalism and other hot-button domestic issues: threats, whether real or perceived, that rapidly growing racial, ethnic, gender, religious and attitudinal diversity may pose to the American way of life as we have known it. This chapter examines the issues springing out of the vast demographic changes that caught Mitt Romney, among others, by surprise in his 2012 election loss. The chapter includes what Norwegian mass murderer Anders Breivik learned from anti-diversity Americans; how Elizabeth Warren can properly call herself "part Native American Indian"; what the rapidly diversifying Western world can learn from America's "melting pot" or, as I prefer, "mulligan stew"; how affirmative action goals look too simple because they probably are; how assimilation beats separatist approaches to multiculturalism; and how Pat Buchanan should be left to sink with his irrationally xenophobic message rather than be turned into a martyr of political correctness. I also probe such touchy questions as whether blacks are "more racist" than whites and why a Cosby-like sitcom about a Muslim family is a big hit in Canada, but similar efforts fail to get off the ground in the U.S.

OCTOBER 30, 2011

STILL FIGHTING AN OLD CULTURE WAR

Members of an outraged liberal group have called for MSNBC to fire Pat Buchanan for what they call "white supremacist" views. I'd rather leave Buchanan and his views free to discredit themselves.

Most Americans have pretty much abandoned the idea that racial, ethnic and religious diversity are something to fret about. Yet columnist Buchanan, my long-time colleague on the TV show "The McLaughlin Group," is still trying to pump hot air into that leaky balloon.

In his new book "Suicide of a Superpower: Will America Survive to 2025?" Buchanan views with alarm how "people of European descent from the steppes of Russia to the coast of California have begun to die out, as the Third World treks north to claim the estate."

He sees our nation, "born a Western Christian republic," being "transformed into a multiracial, multicultural, multilingual, multiethnic stew of a nation that has no successful precedent in the history of the world."

"No successful precedent"? That's what people have been saying about our young democratic republic from its very beginning. Yet, despite some big bumps in the road, we have survived and mostly prospered.

Yet, Buchanan is back to retell us that the sky is falling, as if we didn't get his message 10 years ago. That was when, after his second unsuccessful presidential bid, he wrote "The Death of the West: How Dying Populations and Immigrant Invasions Imperil Our Country and Civilization."

Since then, a biracial liberal with an Arabic-sounding name has been elected president and a conservative black man has risen to the top of Republican preferential preference polls.

Indian-Asian Republicans have been elected governors of Louisiana and South Carolina, etc., etc., etc.

Still Buchanan frets. For almost 500 pages he questions whether non-Europeans can be trusted to keep alive the core values that have made this nation of immigrants the envy of the world. In fact, despite Buchanan's best effort to scrounge together evidence of racial-ethnic discord (he even curiously cites Kanye West's ridiculous interruption of Taylor Swift at the 2009 MTV Music Video Awards), I am relieved at the flimsiness of Buchanan's evidence.

Despite some differences here and there, today's immigrants are assimilating into American society in ways not terribly different from previous generations. Instead of simply fretting over what we're trying to do with our unique diversity, I think we have a lot of good things to learn from what we've accomplished.

That's why I do not support the call from Color Of Change, the left-progressives who have launched an online petition drive to have MSNBC fire Buchanan from his gig as an on-air analyst and in-house lightning rod. While I frequently disagree with everything Buchanan says after "Good morning," I also believe talk shows should air a range of views, not muzzle them. People can disagree, as the saying goes, without being disagreeable.

Besides, I believe a big reason why we don't have as much tumult over multiculturalism as some other Western nations do is our refusal to pass restrictive speech codes that might ban Buchanan's book as "hate speech." The best way to resolve our great social conflicts is to talk about them, not put a lid on them. If you can't think of a good argument to back up your opinion, maybe you should re-examine your views or get more information.

Yet, if Buchanan and I agree on anything, it is the need for immigrants, as well as our native-born children, to be encouraged to assimilate into the cultural mainstream. I believe in the melting pot, although I envision more of a mulligan stew. The ingredients don't have to meld in order to share their flavor, which I view as an enriching value of American diversity.

If the younger generations tell us anything, it is how much racial consciousness has relaxed. Buchanan quotes, for example, the late historian Arthur M. Schlesinger Jr., who predicted in his 1991 book "The Disuniting of America: Reflections on a Multicultural Society" that ethnic and racial conflict would replace the Cold War as "the explosive issue of our times." Schlesinger stayed optimistic, however. In that same book, he wrote, "My impression is that the historic forces driving toward 'one people' have not lost their power."

I share that impression.

I hope Pat Buchanan does too.

JULY 27, 2011

BREIVIK'S REAL ENEMY: HIMSELF

Anders Behring Breivik, the far-far-right-wing monster charged in Norway with the biggest mass murder by a single gunman in modern memory, reminds me of how often delusional minds hate others for what they really see in themselves.

"The enemy is clearly delineated: he is a perfect model of malice, a kind of amoral superman," wrote historian Richard Hofstadter in his often-quoted 1964 essay, "The Paranoid Style in American Politics." "(T)his enemy is, on many counts, the projection of the self; both the ideal and the unacceptable aspects of the self are attributed to him."

Thus the Ku Klux Klan, for example, imitated Catholicism to the point of priestly robes, elaborate rituals and elaborate hierarchy, Hofstadter wrote. The John Birch Society, the leading anti-communist zealots at the time, organized its own version of Communist Party cells and quasi-secret "front" groups.

Today we see a similarly sly envy revealed in Breivik's 1,500-page manifesto against Muslims, immigrants, "multiculturalists" and "cultural Marxists," according to news reports. Breivik wrote and released the manifesto on the Internet before he went on his truck-bombing, gun-wielding rampage.

By his warped reasoning, he had to protest the dangers of al-Qaida-style Muslim terrorists by committing al-Qaida-style terror against his fellow Norwegians.

He joined a Knights Templar organization and, judging by his document, thinks he still is engaged in the Christian crusades against Muslims.

His document offers detailed accounts of the crusades, according to reports, and a pronounced sense of historical grievance, plus calls for apocalyptic warfare to defeat the religious and cultural enemy.

Deep down, Breivik's root problem appears to be a mirror-kissing narcissism so fierce and fanatical that it would drive a man to his fellow citizens in order to "save" them, in this case, from immigrants.

In the end, he has achieved quite the opposite of his stated goals. He reveals his delusional anti-immigrant, anti-Muslim and anti-multiculturalism hatreds to be no less of a menace than the Islamic extremists he claims to oppose.

For example, in his truck bomb in Oslo and machine-gun massacre of a nearby youth camp, he single-handedly killed more people than the four Islamist suicide bombers in the July 7, 2005, London attacks did—and for no better purpose.

It should bring us no comfort here in the United States that he found so much of his venom in the blogs of Americans known for their anti-Islam rhetoric and writings. Yet his case also brings attention to what Europeans could learn from America's experiences in navigating their own debates about immigration and multiculturalism.

In fact, both the political left and right have mischaracterized Europe's version of multiculturalism. For one thing, America's version of multiculturalism tends to be geared toward cultural sharing, but on the way to assimilating into our great legendary American "melting pot," which many prefer to call a "salad bowl" or "mulligan stew," depending on how much melting they want to do. Europe, by contrast, tends to view multiculturalism as the recognition of different enclaves of "foreign" cultures within their own cities and borders. The result is a lot less assimilation and more isolation, resentments and suspicions of racism and "reverse racism."

Much has been said and written about Europe's "failed experiment." German Chancellor Angela Merkel, French President Nicolas Sarkozy and British Prime Minister David Cameron have each declared that multiculturalism has failed. But multiculturalism in Europe has been less of an ideology than a weak patchwork of policy initiatives and hopeful-sounding rhetoric aimed at filling labor shortages with as few culture clashes as possible.

Worse, Europe's hate-speech laws criminalize the freewheeling discussions of immigration problems, discussions that we in the U.S. consider to be rather routine, even when infuriating. Such censorship pushes people to more extreme ways to express their thoughts, just as it does in Islamic countries. We can't blame Breivik on hate-speech laws, but such censorship only helps build tensions, not ease them.

AUGUST 15, 2007

DIVERSITY IS DIFFICULT, BUT WORTH THE EFFORT

Robert Putnam's fears have come true. The Harvard political scientist worried that some people would use his latest research to argue against immigration, affirmative action and multiculturalism. Sure enough, at least one favorable commentary has popped up on the website of David Duke, the former Ku Klux Klan leader. But, not to worry. Putnam's findings are valuable for sane people too.

Putnam is best known for the eye-opening "Bowling Alone: The Collapse and Revival of American Community," a 2000 best seller about Americans withdrawing from civic engagement in recent decades.

Now he has a massive new study, based on interviews with nearly 30,000 people across America, that comes up with what he called in a recent Boston Globe interview "an uncomfortable truth."

Contrary to the cherished American notion that our racial and ethnic diversity makes the nation stronger, Putnam has found quite the opposite. The greater the diversity in a community, the less civic engagement it shows. Fewer people vote. Fewer volunteer. They give less to charity. They work together less on community projects.

And they trust each other less, says Putnam, not only across racial and ethnic lines but also within the lines. In other words, residents of the most racially and ethnically mixed neighborhoods show the least trust toward those not only of other races but also of their own race.

Does that mean people are better off living with, as the old racist mantra goes, "their own kind"? Or that we should impose a moratorium on immigration as my column-writing colleague Pat Buchanan suggests in the piece that Duke touts?

Not quite. In fact, Putnam's first paper about his new research, "E Pluribus Unum: Diversity and Community in the 21st Century," makes three points perfectly clear:

(1) "Increased immigration and diversity are not only inevitable" in modern societies, he writes, "but over the long run they are also desirable. Ethnic diversity is, on balance, an important social asset," as America's history demonstrates.

(2) "In the short- to medium-run, however, immigration and ethnic diversity challenge social solidarity and inhibit social capital," he writes.

"Social capital" is the strength of relationships that bond you to people who are like you or connect you to people who are different from you.

(3) "In the medium- to long-run, on the other hand, successful immigrant societies create new forms of social solidarity and dampen the negative effects of diversity by constructing new, more encompassing identities," says Putnam. "Thus, the central challenge for modern, diversifying societies is to create a new, broader sense of 'we.'"

In other words, birds of different feathers do not flock together in the short-run, but it's worth a try. They can benefit in the long run, especially if they develop a larger, more inclusive sense of identity to, say, their community, their country or some other larger sense of purpose.

In that sense, Putnam's "bunker buster," as one headline writer called it, confirms what many of us already know. Living with diversity is a lot like my first days in the Army. It may not be comfortable at first, but you learn to get along.

My platoon at Ft. Dix, N.J., offered a classic Hollywood portrait of young guys plucked by draft boards of every race, region and religion. Many of us came from backgrounds that conditioned us to distrust people who didn't look or talk like us. But, united by a common sense of mission and no-nonsense orders from the top to observe no color but Army green, we learned.

The military, religious institutions and earlier waves of American immigration provide Putnam with good examples of how Americans can learn to live comfortably with diversity. The military offers a particularly quick turnaround after the mid-1960s, when racial tensions on America's streets spilled into military outposts.

In a 1996 book "All That We Can Be: Black Leadership and Racial Integration the Army Way," co-authors Charles Moskos and John Sibley Butler explain how. After years of trying to ignore racial differences, the Pentagon did an about-face. Everyone was ordered to be on the lookout for discrimination and other sources of racial tension or inequality. The military, once a bastion of segregation, became a model of interracial and interethnic cooperation.

Sure, diversity makes a lot of people uncomfortable. Differences cause tensions, at least in the short-run. But history shows we can come out OK, as soon as we learn how much we have in common.

APRIL 19, 2009

RACE GOALS EASIER, NOT BETTER

Here's a quick history quiz for you. Which nationally prominent leader said this:

"Edicts of non-discrimination are not enough. Justice demands that every citizen consciously adopt a personal commitment to affirmative action, which will make equal opportunity a reality."

Was it Rev. Jesse Jackson? Rev. Al Sharpton? Sister Souljah?

No, it was Gov. Ronald Reagan of California in a 1971 executive order. He sounded more liberal, at least on this issue, than the racial-quota fighter who later became president.

Times have changed, but on race not all that much, as far as NAACP Chairman Julian Bond is concerned. Bond whipped out Reagan's old quote during a debate at the Library of Congress last week to argue that what was good for Reagan two generations ago is good enough for America now.

I'm not as certain of that. Sitting in the audience, I was struck by how much America's persistent problems with race have changed, while so many of our leading affirmative action proponents have not.

Yet, I was also struck by how replacing race-based affirmative action with the class-based kind is easier to say than to do. That's one reason why Bond opposed the evening's proposition: "Should affirmative action be based on wealth and class rather than race and ethnicity?"

President Barack Obama thinks it should, and has said so in writing and out loud. "We have to think about affirmative action," he said at a 2008 convention of black, Hispanic, Asian and Native American journalists in Chicago, "and craft it in such a way where some of our children who are advantaged aren't getting more favorable treatment than a poor white kid who has struggled more." It is safe to say that, in the fashion of President Richard Nixon opening doors to China, Obama's position later helped him with white voters and didn't hurt him very much with blacks.

Defending Obama's position in the debate was New York University sociology professor Dalton Conley, an expert on wage and wealth gaps. Past discrimination in jobs and lending has left such a wide wealth gap between the races, he argued, that diversity-minded colleges would end up with a healthier mix by race, ethnicity and class if they focused on household wealth as Obama suggests, instead of race.

Bond's teammate, Lee Bollinger, president of Columbia University, disagreed. Bollinger was president of the University of Michigan during the 2003 Supreme Court cases that upheld and clarified affirmative action at that school. Then and now, he said, "we want both racial diversity and ethnic diversity," plus "diversity based upon income and class." And the most effective way to do that, he said, is to take race into account, as well as class.

Otherwise, "and this has been studied by many people," he said, "if you use only income you will increase the proportion of white students and decrease the proportion of African-American and Hispanic students."

Video of the debate has been posted at the website of its sponsor, the Miller Center of Public Affairs at the University of Virginia (millercenter.org).

The debate's other participant, John McWhorter, a best-selling author and Manhattan Institute senior fellow, was right to point out a more important hidden danger: When diversity policies lower achievement bars the policies can hurt as much as they help.

When he taught at the University of California at Berkeley, McWhorter recalled, it was only after the affirmative action ban "that efforts were actually made to teach black and Latino students throughout the state to qualify for what the admission procedures were." It hadn't happened before that, McWhorter said, and it wasn't going to happen as long as state universities could rely on racial "preferences," a word that proponents hate despite its accuracy.

With that he exposed an eternal truth: If we did the tough job of providing quality educational opportunity to every American kid from preschool on, we would not need special programs to build diverse students bodies. They'd be diverse already.

Even so, I do agree with Bond and Bollinger that too much is made of the argument that affirmative action admissions leave a stigma on black and Hispanic students. People get into colleges for all sorts of reasons—including legacy preferences, athletic scholarships and geographic diversity—without feeling stigmatized.

But in the end, it's not how you got into college that counts; it's how you leave.

MAY 23, 2012

UNEASY "BROWNING" IN STORE FOR U.S.

White babies are no longer a majority of new births, according to the U.S. Census Bureau. America is quietly "browning," it is said, like dinner rolls in a warm oven. Yet such change does not come about without resistance from those who prefer to remain unbaked.

White supremacist groups have been having a "meltdown," says Mark Potok of the Southern Poverty Law Center, which monitors hate groups. In an ABC News report, he called the demographic trend "the single most important driver in the growth of hate groups and extremist groups over the last few years."

To the haters and the racially paranoid, even President Barack Obama's historic election is just one more piece of mounting evidence that whites are losing their majority in America's population. The Census Bureau now expects the nation will have no racial majority in 2042.

Two opposing visions shape our national debate about this demographic development, which largely has been driven by immigration trends. One fears that dramatic cultural change will tear the nation apart. The more hopeful view sees our younger generations, unburdened by historical baggage, leading America to a transformative integrated and post-racial era.

The truth probably lies between those two scenarios. Today's immigrants are assimilating over time in much the same way as earlier generations, driven by the traditional American dream of opportunity and upward mobility. But I don't expect ethno-cultural differences to lose all value.

America's traditional melting pot always has been more of a mulligan stew, balancing respect for ethnic traditions with a sense of common purpose. Our challenge for the future, as in the past, is how we can make that stew work for everybody and keep it from boiling over.

The element of race adds a new complication to assimilation in a country that seldom has undertaken racial change easily. As much as Americans have benefited from a national identity that is based on ideas, not a single racial or ethnic tribe, white supremacy was embedded in law for most of our history. Every naturalization act from 1790 to 1952 included language that reserved citizenship to a "white person," although standards as to who is considered "white" constantly have changed.

Even today, slightly more than half of those who checked "Hispanic" for ethnicity on the 2010 census forms also checked "white" for race. To the census, you are whatever you say you are, even if others see something different when they look at you.

Still, the question of who can melt in today's melting pot rings alarm bells for some who long for a more monocultural past. An unhappy blogger who identifies himself as "Roger" laments in a post on Phyllis Schlafly's Eagle Forum website that "the USA is being transformed by immigrants" who "have high rates of illiteracy, illegitimacy and gang crime, and they will vote Democrat when the Democrats promise them more food stamps."

Roger's narrative runs quite the opposite of historical realities. Most immigrants are known for working long hours in rough conditions for low wages, driven by hope for a better life.

And their social conservatism on issues like abortion, gay marriage, school prayer and capital punishment tends to be closer to Schlafly than Obama. Rising Republican stars like Gov. Bobby Jindal of Louisiana, South Carolina Gov. Nikki Haley and Sen. Marco Rubio of Florida show that immigrant ambitions don't have to lead to the Democratic Party.

But Roger is hardly alone in his discomfort with change—and not all of the uncomfortable folks are white. Former District of Columbia Mayor Marion Barry, now a City Council member, offered a recent example. He apologized for his "admittedly bad choice of words" in suggesting in earlier public remarks that Asian business owners in his ward "ought to go."

Obviously the landscape is changing for us black folks too. As we gain some measure of power in the melting pot, our victim rhetoric must change too. In fact, if anyone should be concerned about helping white Americans adjust to becoming a minority, it is African-Americans. We have lots of experience

MAY 9, 2012

THE "ONE-DROP" RULE

So what if Elizabeth Warren claims to be part Native American? She's entitled, according to historical documents. Besides, Americans never have been all that clear or consistent about what distinguishes one race from another.

Republican Sen. Scott Brown of Massachusetts is calling on his Democratic challenger Warren to clear the air over questions raised by the Boston Herald as to whether she used her ancient and diluted Indian heritage to give herself an unfair employment advantage.

At least she's not lying about her background. Historical records appear to confirm that she has Cherokee ancestors. But is her background Indian enough?

That question looms after researcher Christopher Child at the New England Historic Genealogical Society turned up evidence of her Indian blood. A transcript of an 1894 marriage application shows Warren's great-great-great-grandmother listed herself as Cherokee.

That would make Warren 1/32nd Native American, although it is possible that more recent Indian ancestors could be turned up in further research. Child also found that Warren's great-grandfather, John Houston Crawford, lived in Native American territory but identified himself as white in the 1900 census.

However, Warren's family is not included in the official Dawes Commission rolls, a census of major tribes completed in the early 20th century that Cherokees use to determine tribal citizenship.

Such a tenuous tie to her Indian past has led critics at the Boston Herald, which broke the story, to label her "Fauxcahontas," among other nicknames. Yet, I would ask, how much Indian blood do you need these days to claim Indian heritage?

In other words, whatever happened to the one-drop rule?

That's the rule in America's past, you may recall, that declared anyone who had at least "one drop" of "black blood" to be black. The irony of this rule, invented by slave masters who wanted to have more slaves, is how it has been encouraged in modern times, particularly by black leaders who want to have more blacks in our ranks.

But like other rules of race, this one is not applied uniformly or consistently. George Zimmerman, the man accused of killing Trayvon Martin in Florida, had an Afro-Peruvian great-grandfather on his mother's side, according to his family. That would make him at least one-eighth black, which is a lot more than Warren is Indian. Yet Zimmerman was reported first as "white," then a "white Hispanic." If the old one-drop rule applies, he also could be called a white-Hispanic black.

If taken literally, that would make the killing of Martin, about whose blackness there is no confusion, a black-on-black crime—which, sad to say, attracts a lot less national attention than similar violence that crosses racial lines.

Zimmerman is not likely to be seen as black by many people. But, like the Warren controversy, he illustrates how quickly our old racial narratives are failing to keep up with changing times.

The Herald reported that Warren used to list herself as Native American in law school directories while teaching at several law schools across the country in the 1980s and '90s.

She dropped the reference from her biography after she was hired at Harvard Law School in the 1990s at a time when protesting students and faculty had been pressuring the school to hire more minority female faculty. The law school says it has one faculty member of Native American heritage, according to reports, but won't say which one.

Race is no longer as simple as black and white, but then it never really was. The real issue of what Warren, Zimmerman and the rest of us want to call ourselves has two sides: how we see ourselves and how we are seen by others.

The Warren controversy illustrates how rapidly the one-drop rule and other old rules of race are fading at a time when race is becoming less of a problem than privilege—who has it and who doesn't—regardless of race.

DECEMBER 13, 1998

"NAPPY HAIR" AND WORSE PROBLEMS

Somebody should have warned Ruth Sherman.

She thought she was doing the right thing by offering a cute little book to her 3rd-grade class of black and Latino students in Brooklyn, N.Y.

But some parents, most of whom did not have children in Sherman's classroom, hastily judged the book to be some sort of racial insult based on its title and photocopies of pages from the book.

The book is called "Nappy Hair."

It's a sweet book about a black girl named Brenda whose relatives tease her at a backyard picnic for having curls so tight she has to have "the nappiest hair in the world."

By the end of the book, Brenda learns to feel good about her hair and herself.

Sherman's students, by all accounts, responded enthusiastically to the book. But at a school meeting, those arguments and the fact that Sherman is white and has long, straight blonde hair did little to calm the crowd. Some screamed at Sherman, some threatened her safety. The school defended her, but she requested a transfer anyway, saying she feared for her life and limb.

Too bad. I could have warned her. The roots of black-hair hypersensitivity run deep. I could have warned her in the fatherly way a college buddy cautioned me years ago, "Never speak to a white woman about her hips or a black woman about her hair, even as a compliment."

Even so, I would not have advised Sherman to use another book. She made a good choice. "Nappy Hair," by Carolivia Herron, a black professor, has sold more than 30,000 copies, mostly to black folks. It has been widely acclaimed by educators and major critics. It is been recommended by, among others, the Teachers College of Columbia University and it is on reading lists in schools and libraries around the nation.

As it should. A quintessential part of black life in America is our hair paradox. Having grown up in an African-American household, I vividly recall being brushed, combed and patted relentlessly, usually with a dab of Royal Crown Hair Pomade, all to get rid of those "naps."

That was nothing compared to what the girls in my neighborhood went through. Routinely their hair was "fried" with lye and hot combs in a variety of what seemed to me to be mystifying rituals to straighten out those naps.

The "Black is Beautiful" movement of the late 1960s tried to liberate black Americans from the tyranny of the hot comb, a lasting symbol of our oppressive fealty to European standards of beauty. But the durability of hot combs and other black hair-straightening procedures show black subservience to European standards of beauty remains largely unbroken, especially for James Brown and the Rev. Al Sharpton.

Yes, with all of that in mind, I could have told Ruth Sherman she was stepping into a minefield. But it was a minefield worth stepping into. "Nappy Hair" leaves kids laughing at the black hair paradox, which is better than their being driven crazy by it.

It is disappointing that African- and Hispanic-Americans would be so hypersensitive as to miss the author's point. Fortunately, the kids appear to have gotten it. Sherman's children loved the book, school officials say. It spoke directly to a familiar dilemma and presented a smart, upbeat way to cope with it.

Sounds like those kids have a few things to teach their elders.

Sherman and Herron, the book's author, plan to write a study guide for "Nappy Hair" and other multicultural children's books. I look forward to that. But the controversy may have frightened some educators away from using it. The New York Times says a principal at an intermediate school in the same district as Sherman's PS 75 has turned thumbs down on two other excellent books, apparently out of fear of parental protests.

It is disappointing that anyone would judge a good book so superficially. But it is even more disappointing that the parents at PS 75 were not more active in their children's education before the book flap came along. Buried in Newsweek's account of the book controversy is this interesting item: Only four parents turned out in October for a school meeting on test scores.

Also, the photocopies that set off the protest had been in the child's homework folder for more than two months, apparently unnoticed. "Even after all the commotion," Newsweek reported, "some parents admitted they still hadn't read the book."

Those disclosures shed new light on a fact reported higher up in the story, that the school is under review by the state's Education Department for poor performance.

Gee, do you think the poor performance might have something to do with parents who are too busy to visit their childrens' schools or talk to their kids about their homework?

My parents cared about the hair on top of my head, but they cared a lot more about the education that went into it.

If the parents at PS 75 really want to do their kids a favor, they will, too.

MARCH 27, 2011

NEW BENCHMARKS OF SOCIAL CHANGE

So you think we Americans know ourselves? New census numbers reveal that a lot of our 20th century racial and ethnic assumptions are overdue for an overhaul.

For example, the South is rising again—in terms of mixed-race marriages, one of the most dramatic yardsticks of racial change.

North Carolina's mixed-race population doubled since the 2000 census, according to The New York Times. It grew by more than 80 percent in Georgia and by almost that much in Kentucky and Tennessee. Even Mississippi, infamous in the 1960s for terror killings of civil rights workers, saw a 70 percent increase in mixed-race marriages, matching Indiana, Iowa and South Dakota.

African-Americans also have become less northern and more suburban, the census reports. The percentage of the nation's black population that lives in the South is higher than it's been in 50 years—and higher than ever in suburbs.

Particularly dramatic to many members of my generation is Washington, whose black population was about 70 percent in 1975 when the funk band Parliament's "Chocolate City" became a hit. Washington's black population has since fallen to 50 percent and continues to drop as more blacks move out to colorize what used to be, in the song's lyrics, the "vanilla suburbs."

News media tend to treat these new census findings as if they were a big surprise. In fact, they continue trends that began to appear in the early 1980s, largely as a consequence of seismic changes in anti-discrimination laws, immigration policy and the nation's industrial economy two decades earlier.

Black flight soon followed white flight to suburbs and economic opportunities in the Sun Belt. Economically hard-hit Detroit may be the worst victim of such changes. The Motor City lost a fourth of its population in the past decade alone.

The biggest surprise may be the growth of the Hispanic population, according to a Pew Hispanic Center analysis. If the Hispanic population had not grown in Illinois, Louisiana, Massachusetts, New Jersey, New York and Rhode Island since 2000, Pew says, those states' overall population would not have grown at all.

And non-Hispanic whites make up less than half of the child population in 10 states, says Pew: Mississippi, Georgia, Maryland, Florida, Arizona, Nevada, Texas, California, New Mexico and Hawaii.

Reactions to those demographic changes predictably fall largely along generational lines. We older folks are more prone to diversity anxiety, seeing problems while our children and grandchildren, who will be living in the emerging future, tend to see opportunities.

The hyperventilating I hear from some of today's alarmists reminds me of the immigrant anxiety in past generations of Americans, including young Benjamin Franklin who sounded editorial alarms about immigrants from Germany. He thought they would never make good Americans. But they did.

Today, the rise of Obama-generation Republicans like Cuban-American Sen. Marco Rubio of Florida, New Mexico Gov. Susana Martinez, and Indian-American Govs. Bobby Jindal of Louisiana and Nikki Haley of South Carolina symbolize how well America's melting pot is working.

What keeps it working are families, schools and communities that maintain healthy, achievement-oriented values from one generation to the next. Our challenge today is to help make those values work for everybody. That includes our least-fortunate underachieving households that have been left behind while the more fortunate neighbors moved away.

In that pursuit, we need to pay serious attention to two tough and touchy issues: national immigration reform and long-term poverty, including the one-fourth of black Americans left behind by the exodus of the new black middle class.

Most Americans would rather change the subject than bring either issue up in mixed company. But that only leaves race, poverty and immigration to be exploited by alarmists and opportunists. We owe our kids something better than that.

Bill Cosby in 2004 put his enormous star power to good use, in my view, by calling attention to the role that poor people need to play in taking charge of their own social and economic destinies. But they can't do it alone.

Cosby launched a city-to-city crusade to recharge achievement-oriented values—beginning with hard work, strong families and delayed gratification. His effort received a lot less attention than his tough-love sermon did. But those are values that make the melting pot work.

FEBRUARY 20, 2011

THE WAY TO DO MULTICULTURALISM RIGHT

Among their other headaches, some of Europe's biggest leaders are troubled by the lukewarm state of their countries' melting pots.

As in the United States, a combination of economic recession, terrorism fears and electoral politics has made scapegoats out of immigrants and government multiculturalism policies. Unlike the United States, they don't have a melting-pot tradition. Instead they've tried a brand of multiculturalism that's getting bad reviews.

State multiculturalism has had "disastrous results," says British Prime Minister David Cameron. It has "totally failed," says German Chancellor Angela Merkel. "Clearly, yes, it is a failure," agrees French President Nicolas Sarkozy.

Has "multikulti," as the Germans call it derisively, indeed failed Europe's great leaders? Or are they simply not doing it right?

Multiculturalism means different things to different people. On its best days, it is a salad bowl or mulligan stew alternative to the melting pot. In this country, it means a respect for cultural differences while remembering that, most of all, we're all still Americans, part of a cultural mainstream that is worth assimilating into, even if our leaders sometimes make mistakes.

Cameron, Merkel and Sarkozy, among others, are recognizing that their multiculturalism policies have brought respect for cultural diversity but failed to integrate and assimilate diverse ethnic communities, particularly Muslims, into the mainstream.

When Merkel says Germany's experiment has failed, for example, she is talking about her country's "gastarbeiters" or guest workers of mostly Turkish, Arabic and Kurdish stock. Invited since the early 1960s to fill labor shortages, they have stayed longer and grown larger in population than expected without fully integrating or assimilating.

Now Merkel is facing a tough re-election campaign with voices on the right grumbling about immigrants while German industrialists want even more immigrant workers. As a result, Merkel took pains to say that all immigrants are still welcome, but also asks, among other requests, that they please try to learn some German.

Cameron called for a "more active, more muscular liberalism" in a recent Munich speech to counter the current "doctrine of state multiculturalism" that has led to alienation and even jihadism among young British Muslims. Cameron also called for the active promotion of democratic values, the rule of law, freedom of speech and equal rights.

That begins to sound like the American model. Our debate has centered in various ways on how cultural differences can be respected without causing our melting pot to boil over.

Sometimes we have panicky outbursts of xenophobia like Arizona's recent legislation to outlaw ethnic studies. The state's new attorney general, Tom Horne, wrote the law when he was the state's superintendent of schools. He thought the Mexican-American studies classes offered in Tucson's schools encouraged too much separatism and resentment toward mainstream American culture. Unfortunately, his remedy probably alienates immigrant communities even more.

So does Oklahoma's referendum issue that voters approved in November to outlaw Shariah law, even though there was no known effort to impose the Islamic legal code in their state. At least a dozen other states are reported to be considering similar legislation, despite its distinct aroma of Islamophobia.

In short, there's a thin line between efforts that encourage full participation in mainstream American culture and those that punish one particular culture. We can oppose arranged marriages, animal sacrifices, speech censorship and other cultural practices that conflict with American law and freedoms without disrespecting the home cultures of those who sincerely want to be Americans.

Doing multiculturalism right calls for striking a balance between a respect for diverse cultures and respect for the common culture we all share. Regardless of their origin, immigrants to this country tend to be driven by a desire to find opportunity and stir themselves into our melting pot. Even if the first generation resists, their children tend to embrace the America of "Sesame Street" and Big Macs with great enthusiasm.

By contrast, Europe has allowed large communities of immigrants to grow in ethnic enclaves that endure from one generation to the next with remarkably little assimilation.

Don't blame multiculturalism for that failure. Blame people. People will have to fix it.

MAY 6, 1992

RODNEY KING'S POIGNANT PLEA

Rodney King, who shall be known for the rest of his life as the black motorist whose beating by Los Angeles police officers touched off riots, made more sense than all of television's mighty pundits when he called for calm amid the chaos.

"People, I just want to say," he stammered, nervously choking on the words, "you know, can we all get along? Can we get along? Can we stop making it, making it horrible for the older people and the kids?"

King's trembling voice expressed the key question facing America on a day newscasters and commentators were calling a defining moment for America. We've been through urban riots before. We tried, as a nation, to fool ourselves into believing we could make the threat go away by putting a lid on it. When will it boil over again? Can we make progress in the simple task of behaving decently with each other? Can we get along?

Getting along seemed far from the minds of media-selected spokespersons parading across my television screen while riot ashes cooled.

Representing black America, I saw firebrands like Al Sharpton and rappers Chuck D., KRS-One and Sister Souljah. All of them were angry at whites for victimizing blacks.

Representing white opinion, I saw firebrands like presidential candidate Patrick J. Buchanan. He was angry at blacks for victimizing whites.

I also heard the voices of one or two (since their identities were concealed, it was hard to tell if they were the same woman) members of the jury that exonerated the police officers in the videotaped King beating.

The jurors sounded fearful and confused, the sort of folks who fled to the suburbs to escape the threat to life and limb a big black man like Rodney King who wouldn't lay down while police shouted, hit and kicked must represent to them.

Can we get along?

Media tend to put the most incendiary voices of both sides into the spotlight, but I like to think most Americans are somewhere in the middle, yearning for protection and willing to work against crime, while looking sincerely to Washington for leadership in salvaging our long-ignored and disinvested inner cities.

Eventually we have to ask the same question Rodney King asks: Can we all get along?

After all, the middle-class whites and blacks who fled to the suburbs after the riots of the '60s don't have a lot of escape routes left.

"Please, we can get along here," King pleaded. "I mean, we're all stuck here for a while. Let's try to work it out. Let's try to beat it. Let's try to work it out."

Working it out wasn't on the minds of politicians who stood over the ashes of mayhem and pointed fingers of blame at the other party.

Presidential spokesman Marlin Fitzwater tried to blame the riots on the liberal social programs of Presidents Lyndon Johnson and Jimmy Carter in the '60s and '70s. But when reporters pressed him to name one or two, he couldn't.

"I don't have a list with me," he said.

Fitzwater correctly listed good Bush-sponsored initiatives the Democrat-dominated Congress has ignored: home ownership for the disadvantaged, creation of urban enterprise zones, and public housing rehabilitation, just to name a few.

Fitz is right. There's plenty of blame to go around. The dirty little Democratic secret is that they would rather kill a good idea than let a Republican president get credit for helping the poor. No wonder Americans are fed up with Washington.

Can we get along? Can't we do what black conservative Robert Woodson, director of Washington's Center for Neighborhood Enterprise, has suggested, judge ideas not by what's Right or what's Left but by what works?

Maybe there's hope. Spurred by the riots, President Bush has rescued Housing Secretary Jack Kemp, the only Cabinet member who has a sense of common ground with grass-roots black leaders, from political Siberia. Together, if Bush wishes, they can use the riots as an opportunity to embarrass the Democrats into going along with what Kemp calls a "conservative war on poverty."

After earlier wars against poverty, inflation and drugs, I'm getting a little weary of combat metaphors. But it's worth a try.

The King video and "not guilty" verdict snapped Americans into a new awareness of what blacks had been saying all along about police power run wild and white indifference to it. The subsequent riots, particularly the televised sight of black mobs ruthlessly beating a couple of innocent white men, was the great white American revenge nightmare come to life: blacks doing to whites what whites historically did to blacks.

After all this, can we get along?

It was encouraging to see a rainbow of volunteers working together to clean up the wreckage and put their community together again. Maybe the rest of the country can learn something from those final images of interracial cooperation in the ashes of chaos. Maybe we can regain a sense of common ground and common purpose.

I hope so. After all, as Rodney King says, we're all stuck here for a while.

APRIL 8, 2007

THIS COLUMN GETS "SO GHETTO"

Somebody should have warned Newt Gingrich to stay away from the "ghetto."

The word, I mean. If so, the former speaker of the House, who is weighing a presidential bid, could have avoided the embarrassment for which he is apologizing.

In a video statement on YouTube that's read in Spanish and subtitled in English, the Georgia Republican says his "word choice was poor" when he equated bilingual education with "the language of living in a ghetto" in a recent speech.

What he meant to say, he says, is that, "In the United States it is important to speak the English language well in order to advance and have success."

Alas, poor Newt. As a journalist who has had the G-word stricken from my copy by cautious editors, I could have warned him. "Ghetto" means so many things to so many different people that it is best avoided as a metaphor in mixed company unless you're trying to be, say, Grand Master Newt, the rap artist.

Gingrich fell into an unexpected culture gap similar to the one that Sen. Joe Biden opened up by referring to Sen. Barack Obama as "clean" and "articulate." On the bright side, such political gaffes offer rare opportunities for the rest of us to see how different cultures can draw vastly different meanings from the same words.

Gingrich didn't know it, but his G-bomb stepped into the middle of a bubbling controversy in the black community that has boiled over into mainstream American culture.

"Ghetto" originally referred to the areas of Rome, Warsaw and some other European cities into which Jews once were confined. Black activists in 1960s America embraced the word to label impoverished urban areas into which blacks had long been segregated.

But in recent years, the word increasingly has come to mean simply "low class," sometimes with irony, sometimes not.

Gingrich's gaffe coincides with the publication of a book he would have found helpful: "Ghettonation: A Journey into the Land of Bling and the Home of the Shameless" by Cora Daniels, a contributing writer for Essence, Fortune, The New York Times and O: The Oprah Magazine, among others.

She was moved to write, Daniels says, by the sight of Paris Hilton remarking on the reality TV show "The Simple Life," that "this truck is so ghetto," as she tried in vain to start up an old, rusted pickup truck. At that moment, Daniels says, she realized that "ghetto" is no longer a "black thing," but "an American thing."

Martha Stewart helped confirm that when Daniels saw her boast on TV that she can "get ghetto" when she needs to. Not a good thing, Martha.

Daniels is not radical chic. She comes courageously to vilify "ghetto," not to praise it.

With wit and wisdom, she explores and exposes the ghetto "mind-set" that demeans women ("hos," "bee-yatches"), devalues education ("acting white"), ridicules proper English ("talking white"), celebrates criminality ("gangsta love"), discards traditional parenthood ("babydad-dies," etc.) and celebrates tacky fashion and behavior ("ghettofabulous").

She knew things had gone off the rails when, shopping for Halloween, she found "pimp" and "ho" costumes in preschool sizes.

Or when she discovered that more than 1,200 babies were named Lexus in 2006.

Yet, Daniels writes with an undertone of love. She softens the inevitable "elitist" label that some critics have pinned on Bill Cosby by spreading the blame. Cosby famously chastised poor people three years ago for "not holding up their end in this deal." Daniels quite properly includes black middle-class Americans, like her and me, in her critique, too.

Daniels fails to pin down the precise moment when the most self-destructive values took hold, if there is one. I would put it at the point when, as black novelist-journalist Jill Nelson tells Daniels, "We lost hope." Our generation saw Martin Luther King Jr., Malcolm X, Robert

F. Kennedy and other great leaders rise, only to be violently snatched away from us. Then, Nelson recalls, we "smothered our kids in material stuff to insulate them from the pain."

We also saw the poorest of the black poor becoming increasingly isolated in the economic ghettos from which their more fortunate neighbors escaped. Like impoverished societies everywhere, our black poor created new music and fashions from the resources they had. These, in turn, were ironically exploited by entertainment executives when they found big profits to be made, often in white suburbia.

At a time of great national argument over who is to blame for poverty, racism or bad habits, Daniels reveals that society can be blamed.

JUNE 21, 1998

ELIMINATING "BALKANIZED" COLLEGE PROGRAMS

Ward Connerly, the Sacramento crusader against affirmative action, has turned his sights on a new target: Ethnic studies.

And that's not all. He's also suspicious of women's studies, gay and lesbian studies, "Black Welcome Week," Latino orientation day, separate graduation ceremonies, ethnic "theme houses" in some of the dorms and everything else he sees as "Balkanizing" life on the campuses of California's state universities.

He admitted to me in a telephone interview that he doesn't know much about gay, ethnic or women's studies, to name just three issues. He also insisted for the record that he does not, "repeat, not," plan to crusade against them as a University of California regent the way he led the successful Proposition 209 campaign.

But he does plan to visit classes and talk to faculty over the next couple of months to conduct his own "private" investigation. He may come away convinced, he says, although he admits "I do have my biases."

Connerly, who is African-American, raised eyebrows when he told an Associated Press reporter last week that he suspects Hispanic, African-American, Asian-American, Native American and other ethnic studies programs are promoting "self-imposed segregation" at the state's colleges. If so, he said, he wants to put a stop to it.

It was the rise of a recent student movement to form a gay and lesbian studies department at the University of California at Davis campus that was the last straw, Connerly told me. He questioned whether the purpose of the classes was truly academic or whether they were exercises in racial, ethnic and gender cheerleading.

He questioned whether ethnic studies was "something people can learn from their parents, at home, without the taxpayers paying for it."

When I pointed out that many students have enrolled in studies about groups to which they do not personally belong—white and Latino students in black studies, for example, and men in women's studies—he said he was impressed, but added, "that has not been my experience" during campus visits.

Too bad. But Connerly's idea intrigues me. What if he's right? If we get rid of those divisive ethnic studies, which hardly existed before the late 1960s, can we can get back to the togetherness we had before?

Ah, yes, whatever happened to those halcyon days of old, those days of unity, those days before those Balkanizing ethnic studies came along?

Whatever happened to those jolly days of housing covenants, legal job discrimination, segregated lunch counters and other aspects of American togetherness?

How united we were when the only people who really counted in history and literature classes were white and, for that matter, male. How light-hearted our students could be, unburdened by any obligation to learn about anybody else.

But, why, I wondered, stop with studies about women, gays and ethnics?

As long as we're going after academic special interests, how about European studies?

After all, if studies of the history and culture of one particular group are Balkanizing, why exempt the part of the world that gave "Balkanize" its name?

Do we really need all those classes in Socrates, Milton, Shakespeare, Mozart and Chopin? Are they going to get you a job in today's global economy?

Or are they merely exercises in ethnic cheerleading? Are they "something people can learn from their parents, at home, without the taxpayers paying for it."

Hey, didn't your mom always keep a copy of Plato's "The Republic" within easy reach, right next to Dr. Spock and Betty Crocker?

You want unity? Take my word for it: Announce to America's college students that they no longer will have to learn European history and you're going to see a lot of students from every race, creed and color dancing in the streets.

Closer to home, how about Civil War studies?

Talk about Balkanizing. The farther you go south of, say, Ohio, the more you run into people who don't question who won the Civil War or, as they may prefer to call it, the "War Between the States" or, my personal favorite, "The War of Northern Aggression."

And what about all those foreign language studies classes? What can be more divisive and self-segregating than to have a bunch of people on campus practicing how to talk to each other in languages only a few other students can understand?

I'm not saying this is what we should do. I'm only raising questions, just like Connerly is.

Let's not think small. Why not pull everyone together by eliminating courses that don't teach everybody the same basic stuff?

That's a good way to make everybody the same, together and equal.

Equally ignorant.

DECEMBER 14, 2011

ALL-AMERICAN MUSLIM BASHERS

A conservative Christian group has launched a boycott against "All-American Muslim." The TLC cable TV reality show about Muslim families in America fails to live down to the group's narrow-minded stereotypes. Their gripe, in my view, makes about as much sense as boycotting "The Cosby Show" back in the day because it didn't mention black street gangs.

The Christian group's boycott made national headlines this week when the home-improvement giant Lowe's pulled its ads from the program. If the North Carolina-based company was hoping to dodge controversy, it failed. The move touched off protests joined by music mogul Russell Simmons and actor Kal Penn, among other celebrities, and a second boycott campaign—against Lowe's.

The company apologized to everyone who is offended, citing its "strong commitment to diversity and inclusion." But it stuck by its decision, explaining the show became a "lightning rod for people to voice complaints from a variety of perspectives—political, social and otherwise."

Blame the Tampa-based Florida Family Association, which launched the boycott.

When I clicked on the association's website, a notice from David Caton, the group's executive director, said it was shut down because of "extremely mean-spirited" hacker attacks. "In a country that supposedly embraces free speech," a posted statement said without a hint of irony, "those that oppose our position have no qualms about destroying our free speech." Right. No more qualms than the association feels about silencing "All-American Muslim."

Nevertheless, if the association's protest actually helps to boost the show's ratings as people tune in to judge for themselves, I think it will have performed a valuable public service.

The show premiered in November on TLC, which previously made news with "Sarah Palin's Alaska," a reality show that I imagine the Tampa group found more to its liking. "All-American Muslim" follows the daily lives of five Lebanese families in Dearborn, Mich., a suburban Detroit city with one of the nation's highest concentrations of Arabs. In a format mercifully free of self-congratulatory piety or eat-your-broccoli earnestness, its middle-class subjects offer entertaining yet also enlightening evidence that America's multiethnic, multicultural melting pot still works, despite occasional bumps in the road.

Yet, the Tampa group and its allied fearmongers complain about what the show leaves out: The violence that Muslim fanatics have committed in the name of Islam.

"The show profiles only Muslims that appear to be ordinary folks," the Florida group asserts in a letter to TLC advertisers, "while excluding many Islamic believers whose agenda poses a clear and present danger to the liberties and traditional values that the majority of Americans cherish." Is it not enough for the critics that images of such violence appear on TV news almost every day? Most of the violence occurs overseas and, by the way, kills mostly fellow Muslims. Yet, the Florida Family Association insists that we judge Muslim Americans by their worst actors overseas, not as families who live in much the same way other middle-class Americans do.

I am reminded of the black intellectual critics who complained in the 1980s that "The Cosby Show" was too sentimental and far-removed, with its upper-class professional African-American family, from the lives that most black people lived. Yet, Bill Cosby's show broke TV audience records during a time when race relations were less relaxed than they are today. Viewers across racial lines quickly connected with its subtle subtext: The American dream is not for whites only.

That's why I suggested a few months ago that, as Muslims seem to have replaced African-Americans at the bottom of America's totem pole of ignorance-based stereotypes, all Americans would benefit from a Muslim version of Cosby's Huxtable family.

Some of my readers scoffed, but Canadian TV has aired five seasons of the popular "Little Mosque on the Prairie," a comedy about a Muslim family and their interactions with non-Muslims, since January 2007. U.S. networks have produced pilots for similar sitcoms here but the occasionally funny moments in "All-American Muslim" are the closest that a Muslim family comedy has come to broadcast. We Americans are justly proud of our land of opportunity and fair play, but we're behind Canada this time.

Maybe our networks still think Islamaphobia is still too raw in our minds for Americans to laugh about. Perhaps "All-American Muslim" can help to ease those tensions, even if some of its critics hope that it doesn't.

JULY 10, 2013

ARE BLACKS MORE RACIST THAN WHITES?

A new poll suggests that Americans, including black Americans, tend to think blacks are more racist than whites or Hispanics. I don't think we are. We only sound like it sometimes.

The poll by the conservative-leaning Rasmussen Reports finds a larger minority of Americans, 37 percent, think most black Americans are racist compared with the 15 percent of the respondents who think most white Americans are racist and the 18 percent who think that about Hispanic-Americans.

I expected the numbers to fall heavily along racial and partisan lines, and they do. For example, 49 percent of conservatives consider most blacks to be racist compared with21 percent of liberals. Considering how many of today's conservatives tend to hear any racial grievance as "playing the race card," I'm not surprised.

What defies the usual stereotypes is the sizable minority of blacks, 31 percent, who agreed with the 38 percent of whites in the poll who think most blacks are racist. That's higher than the 24 percent of blacks (and 10 percent of whites) who think most whites are racist.

That stereotype-shattering result might suggest that we black folks have some work to do in cleaning up our own prejudices. Understood. But what? The poll offers not a clue.

For starters, it doesn't define "racist," even though there is hardly a more abused, misused and overused word in the English language than the R-word.

Two major misunderstandings make a mess of today's race debates. One, our racial attitudes are based on our personal experiences and all of our experiences are very different. Two, everybody carries different definitions in their heads of what racism is.

Merriam-Webster's online dictionary lists two definitions. One is "a belief that race is the primary determinant of human traits and capacities and that racial differences produce an inherent superiority of a particular race." The other is simply "racial prejudice or discrimination."

But there's at least one other definition, widely believed among black folks, that touched off an uproar after filmmaker Spike Lee expressed it in a July 1991 Playboy magazine interview: "Black people can't be racist, he said. "Racism is an institution."

Although "black people can be prejudiced," Lee allowed, we "don't have the power" to enforce the sweeping institutional racism that perpetuates social, economic and political inequality. Maybe not, I say, but we're moving up.

Lee's argument was easier to make before African-Americans gained as much institutional power and influence as some of us are beginning to achieve, all the way up to the White House.

As we aspire to full equality, I believe we need to hold ourselves as accountable as we hold Paula Deen, Don Imus, Michael "Kramer" Richards and every other racial gaffe-maker.

But that's not always easy. What we say can be quite culturally different from what other people want to hear.

Remember, for example, the blowback last year after President Barack Obama framed the fatal shooting of Trayvon Martin in personal terms by saying, "If I had a son, he'd look like Trayvon."

"Disgraceful," fumed Republican presidential hopeful Newt Gingrich. "We should all be horrified no matter what the ethnic background." Of course. Obviously the president didn't mean to say otherwise.

But, when even Obama gets slammed for an innocent tribute after all of his years of diligently playing by the rules of today's racial etiquette, it is no wonder so many people think black folks are racist.

Yet, as the poll results hint, it is no secret that the black community has to contend with its own internal racism too.

I recall, for example, how one of my son's black high school classmates responded when I asked whether he detected any racism in today's youths. Yes, he said, "The black girls get mad when they see you dancing with a white girl." Ah, yes. Race, like sex, is complicated, children.

Considering today's tragic shortage of marriageable black males, I can't help but sympathize with those girls. They didn't create this world. They're probably just imitating us, their elders.

FEBRUARY 25, 2004

HERE'S WHY THERE IS NO "WHITE HISTORY MONTH"

Black History Month was never intended to make people uncomfortable—unless maybe they ought to be.

Nevertheless, despite the best of intentions, a misunderstanding of what the month is all about can lead sometimes to a whopper of an embarrassment.

That's sort of what happened recently at Connecticut's Suffield High School when a group of sociology students decided to hang posters around the school to promote April as "White History Month."

Shortly after they were nabbed, the five students explained to their upset principal, Thomas Jones, that, alas, it was all a misunderstanding, according to The Hartford Courant. The students had been assigned to "explore the effect of rumors." They decided the posters would be a real nifty way to do that. Needless to say, their experiment triggered a lot of rumors, especially in the school's small but understandably alarmed black student population.

The principal scolded the white students for their insensitivity and turned them over to a teacher who reportedly specializes in civil rights and cultural sensitivity issues. In this way, the school at large was able to turn the incident into what one school board official called a "teachable moment," an opportunity to educate both offenders and the offended about differences in how the world looks through each other's eyes.

Good for them. No long-term harm done, I hope. This particular high school poster flap is the most embarrassing incident related to Black History Month that I can recall since early 2001. That was when then-Virginia Gov. Jim Gilmore revoked a proclamation declaring May to be "European Heritage and History Month." The governor had learned to his deep dismay that the request for the commemoration had come from a white separatist group headed by former Ku Klux Klan leader David Duke. Such an embarrassment.

But you don't need to be a klansman, past or present, to ask "Why don't we have a White History Month?" I've heard that question quite a few times over the years. So have other black people I know. Some of us have come up with a list of appropriate responses to it, such as:

1. "Because every month is white history month."

2. "Because white history has not been lost, stolen or suppressed over the years as much as black history has."

3. "Yo' mama!"

4. "History is taught so poorly in our schools these days that maybe we should have a white history month."

5. "That's right. I said, 'Yo' mama'!!!"

Now, now. We should all try to manage our anger at such moments. Such encounters reveal precisely what Black History Month was intended to remedy: an ignorance about history—black and otherwise. That's why I oppose so-called "political correctness." We need more dialogue, not less.

For example, when someone asks "Why is there a Black Entertainment Television network? Wouldn't all hell break loose if somebody started a White Entertainment Television?," simply respond, "There is. It is called ABC, NBC, CBS, Fox ..."

Such questions can be a departure point for cross-racial, cross-cultural dialogue—a teachable moment, in modern education-speak. After all, when the late black scholar Carter G. Woodson dreamed up what was then called Negro History Week in 1926, he too dreamed of the day when it no longer would be needed.

He imagined a day when every student's education would include such African-American figures as Crispus Attucks, who died in the

Boston Massacre; Matthew A. Henson, who co-discovered the North Pole with Robert Peary, and Benjamin Banneker, the pioneer scientist who helped conduct the first survey of Washington.

It was important, Woodson felt, that African-Americans understand that we had more to our history than our victimization. In fact, there was a much greater all-American story to be told in how mightily many of our ancestors had triumphed despite adversity.

Woodson imagined a day when the contributions of people from various races, ethnicities and, for that matter, genders would be taught fairly and properly. Then Americans might move more swiftly toward a society where such differences would no longer matter.

Unfortunately, history seems to be given such a low priority in today's schools that I sometimes wonder whether Woodson's dream day is slipping further away.

As a parent of a 14-year-old, it seems to me that the schools are teaching quite more black history than they did back when I was a kid, but they're teaching less overall history. The result is a deficit of knowledge about where we all have come from as Americans.

And, as the old saying goes, if you don't know where you came from, you're going to have a hard time figuring out where you're going.

SEPTEMBER 8, 1999

PREACHING HATE: SUNSET FOR FANATICS

What do Pat Buchanan and Khallid Abdul Muhammad have in common? Each demonstrates in his own way that these are hard times for demagogues.

Each has played his usual tunes of fear, suspicion and resentment in recent weeks but failed to gain much of what political consultants call "traction."

Buchanan's pitch assails free trade, affirmative action, welfare recipients, international involvements and immigration—or, at least, the immigration that has occurred since his family arrived here.

All of this played remarkably well to the angry mood of voters in the recession of 1992 and the anti-Clinton fervor of 1996.

But this year, despite Buchanan's oratorical gifts, his reception in the political polls and elsewhere has been so lackluster that he appears poised to leave the Republican Party and mount a third-party bid, perhaps, if they will have him, in the Reform Party of businessman Ross Perot and Minnesota Gov. Jesse "The Body" Ventura.

If Buchanan's star is fading at the moment, he is not unlike Khallid Muhammad, whose "Million Youth March" bombed last week like a well-promoted Broadway flop.

Muhammad won permission from New York City and the courts to close six blocks of Malcolm X Boulevard in Harlem. But when the big day finally came he attracted barely enough of a crowd to clog one block, according to witnesses.

Muhammad's best publicity came from New York City Mayor Rudolph Giuliani, who lost court fights to deny Muhammad a parade permit for two consecutive years. The more a figure like Giuliani (who is very unpopular among black voters) attacks Muhammad, the more Muhammad's appeal is enhanced.

Muhammad, a former aide to Nation of Islam Minister Louis Farrakhan, broke away from Farrakhan several years ago to take his own act on the road after discovering one of the keys to modern demagoguery: You're nobody until somebody hates you. The effective demagogue must have enemies to use as scapegoats.

And, if nobody hates you, offend someone until someone does hate you. Muhammad was a nobody in the national spotlight until he made some crude remarks about Jews and others, including several prominent black leaders, a few years ago on a New Jersey campus.

Farrakhan achieved national fame the same way. He was well-known among African-Americans, but not well-known elsewhere until he made some hateful remarks about Jews, Israel and Zionism during Jesse Jackson's 1984 presidential campaign.

Muhammad's supporters try to blame this year's low Million Youth March turnout on negative media coverage and various other conspiracies. But the media coverage, boosted by Giuliani's ham-handed attempts at censorship, probably did more to increase attendance at the march than reduce it.

More effective in cooling Muhammad's turnout was the heated criticism he received from respected black leaders like Harlem Rep. Charles Rangel (D-N.Y.), who managed to criticize Muhammad without appearing to side with Giuliani.

But Muhammad's worst publicity was himself. At last year's event and at this one he did not march, did not draw a million and had little to say about youths.

Instead he ranted on about various white enemies, black sell-outs and Jewish "impostors." It is black people, Muhammad claimed, who are the "true Jews." Spouting nonsense like that, Muhammad doesn't need any outside attackers. He destroys his own credibility.

The same is true of Buchanan, who seems to relish in what columnist Charles Krauthammer, one of Buchanan's fellow Washington conservatives, recently called "subliminal appeals to prejudice."

In one of his columns shortly before he declared his latest presidential bid, for example, Buchanan called for quotas to end the underrepresentation of "non-Jewish whites" in Ivy League universities. Cute.

Back in 1992, the Anti-Defamation League charged him with "a 30-year record of intolerance unmatched by any other mainstream political figure" and "a disregard or hostility toward those not like him and a consequent displeasure with the exercise of freedom by these others." Buchanan has toned down his red-meat rhetoric since then, but not by much.

Fortunately, in these flush economic times with the conservative agenda for lower taxes, more jobs, lower crime, welfare reform and a balanced budget largely won—and with the help of Democrats, no less—Buchanan's politics of fear, suspicion and resentment have a hard time gaining much of a foothold, even with conservatives.

For now, at least, the shoot-from-the-lip hatefulness of Buchanan and Muhammad seems to have played out. That's a tough break for them and great news for the rest of us.

CHAPTER SEVEN

PROFILING: THE ACCEPTABLE PREJUDICE

My column-writing decades have seen the focus of racial profiling as a political issue shift from black and Latino drivers to Arabs and Muslims at airport security, anyone who "looks like an immigrant" in Arizona and the fear of Shariah law in states that have very few Muslims. Among other topics, I look at how blacks in one poll favored the profiling of Arabs and Muslims more than whites did and how NPR overreacted to Juan Williams' anxieties about "Muslim garb" in airports—and handed a propaganda coup to Fox News.

OCTOBER 3, 2001

MY, OH, MY, LOOK WHO'S PROFILING NOW

If you think, as some social commentators have opined, that the age of irony ended with the recent terrorist attacks, consider this:

Two major polls find that African-Americans are more likely than other racial groups to favor profiling and extra-thorough airport checks for Arabs and Arab-Americans.

Since it was black Americans like me whose criticisms of the criminal-justice system gave rise to such phrases as "racial profiling" and "DWB (driving while black)," I was surprised by that polling result, but, sadly, I was not shocked.

We're not proud of it but black people profile, too. We are no less prone than many others to judge by appearances, as long as the person being judged is not us.

In cities where blacks live with or near substantial Arab populations like Chicago, Detroit and New York, I have seen many unfortunate tensions as well as warm friendships arise between members of both groups.

As one black professional woman I know responded to the polls, "Arab taxi drivers have passed me by too many times for me to feel much sympathy for them. Let them find out how it feels to be profiled."

She's far from alone in her feelings. The Boston Globe reports that 71 percent of black respondents to a Gallup poll said they would favor special, more intensive security checks for Arabs, including those who are U.S. citizens, before boarding airplanes.

A smaller majority of whites, 57 percent, said they would favor such a policy and, while there was no specific category for Hispanics and Asians, 63 percent of non-whites said they, too, would favor the policy.

A Zogby International poll revealed similar results, although with a narrower margin between the races. It found 54 percent of blacks favored singling out Arab-Americans for special scrutiny at airport check-ins while 63 percent of Hispanics and 53 percent of whites opposed it.

Even more disturbing in the Gallup poll was the 64 percent of blacks and 56 percent of other non-whites who favored requiring Arabs, including those who are U.S. citizens, to carry special identification as a means of preventing terrorist attacks. Forty-eight percent of whites opposed such a drastic move.

Say, didn't a lot of us Americans recently criticize the Taliban for requiring Afghanistan's Hindus to wear yellow ribbons on their chests (a charge denied by the Taliban)? Didn't it remind a lot of us of Nazi Germany's treatment of Jews? Americans haven't gone nearly that far in profiling Arabs, but watch out. The slope is slippery.

Fortunately, all of the news is not bad on this front. Many black Americans have joined others in letting their Arab and Muslim neighbors know they do not stand alone in this time of international crisis.

A recent Congressional Black Caucus seminar, attended by James Zogby, who heads the Arab American Institute and is the brother of the pollster, denounced discrimination of all sorts against Arabs and Muslims. So have President Bush, Atty. Gen. John Ashcroft and numerous governors and mayors.

"That poll actually contradicts my experience," said my friend Ray Hanania, a Chicago author, public relations executive and child of Palestinian Arabs. "I hear more sympathy from blacks than I do from whites." He can use it. He self-published a witty 1996 memoir about his experiences on being profiled titled, "I'm Glad I Look Like A Terrorist: Growing Up Arab in America."

Still he does not oppose all profiling. "Hey, I don't want to get hijacked, either," he said, "whether it's by an Arab or anyone else."

Me, either. But there's smart profiling and stupid profiling. Smart profiling looks at more than just ethnic or racial features, especially when we know the Sept. 11 terrorists were instructed to look as inconspicuously "American" as possible.

If airlines and the U.S. government want to make passengers feel safer, they should install proper security measures in airports and on planes, not take the cheap route of racial profiling.

Hanania doesn't think black Americans who favor profiling "have really thought it through." Neither do I. The first casualty of war is often rational thinking.

Stupid profiling can alienate entire communities when their cooperation is needed for effective law enforcement. If anyone should know that lesson, it is black Americans. It is not going to be easy for us to argue against the unfair profiling of blacks if most of us favor the unfair profiling of Arabs.

It also helps terrorists like Osama bin Laden sell the lie that America is waging war against Arabs and Muslims, not just terrorists. Let's prove him wrong.

AUGUST 11, 2002

DUMMYING UP: FOR FEAR OF READING A BOOK ABOUT THE KORAN

I'll say this for Bill O'Reilly. Unlike some other windbags of radio and TV, he's not afraid to invite guests on his Fox News Channel program who, even if he's not listening, show the rest of the world just how wrong he can be.

One recent example involved a book that has put a burr under O'Reilly's saddle. It is a book about the Koran, the holy book of Islam, that the University of North Carolina is requiring incoming freshmen to read over the summer.

If they don't want to read the book, titled "Approaching the Qur'an: The Early Revelations," by Michael A. Sells, a professor of comparative religion at Haverford College, they have to write a 300-word essay explaining why.

That's less than one single-spaced typewritten page, not exactly heavy lifting for a student at a respected university.

The important thing, as Robert Kirkpatrick, the professor who chose the book, explained on "The O'Reilly Factor" TV show is this: First-year students need to know that "as a member of an academic community they have to learn to think and to read and to write and to defend their opinions."

That's right. Start pushing a book on college freshmen and, who knows? They might try reading another one.

That's what college is supposed to be about. It is not just a time for learning but a time to arouse curiosity in preparation for a lifetime of learning.

That process begins when you learn not only to have opinions but also how to express and defend them.

"And defending the right not to read the book is something that will be very interesting to read," the professor said.

Indeed, it should be at least as interesting as listening to showman-journalist O'Reilly explain why he will not read the book. According to a Fox transcript, he called UNC's assignment "unbelievable," compared it to assigning "Mein Kampf" during World War II and asked why should freshmen be required to study "our enemy's religion."

Yes, there is a lot more to Islam than Osama bin Laden and his violent brethren, but apparently not in O'Reilly's mind.

"I mean, I wouldn't give people a book during World War II on [how] the emperor is God in Japan. Would you?"

"Sure," Kirkpatrick said. "Why not? Wouldn't that have explained kamikaze pilots?"

That's a sensible answer, not that sensibleness gets you anywhere on high-energy cable TV news-talk shows these days or, for that matter, in politics—especially religious politics.

Since O'Reilly's outrage was broadcast, UNC has come under fire from politicians and religious activists. A Virginia-based Christian group called the Family Policy Network has filed suit against the university, charging that it is unconstitutional for a publicly funded university to require students to study a specific religion.

And a North Carolina state legislative committee voted to pull public funds from the reading assignment unless other religions get equal time.

Perhaps that will please the druids, just for starters. But not to worry, folks. Part of the assignment is to discuss the book in the fall within the context of other religions.

Still, North Carolina's Republican State Rep. Sam Ellis said quite bluntly on a campus radio show that students should not be "required to study this evil." No? Maybe they just stumble blindly into the world, guided by their own blind rage?

What needs equal time is a sane response to those who generalize all of Islam as "evil" just because a few fanatical factions insist on taking scriptures out of context to wage holy war. That's no more fair than those who denounce Christianity because fanatics during the Inquisition, the Crusades and similar tragic moments in history used the Book of Joshua and other scriptures to torture and slaughter non-Christians in God's name.

"Like some Christians who may see themselves as new Joshuas, some Muslims portray the West as equivalent to those who attacked Muhammad and his followers and call for jihad [holy war]," author Sells wrote in

Thursday's Washington Post. "But we can only identify and counter them if we avoid assuming all Muslims interpret the Koran in the same way."

Quite right. I deeply regret that we have not given our children a more peaceful world to inherit, but they're a bright bunch. They'll figure out that they need to be reading more books, not fewer.

NOVEMBER 24, 1996

THE INJUSTICE OF FITTING THE "PROFILE"

My friend Ray Hanania has a problem that is indicative of our times.

He looks like a terrorist.

His accent is pure Chicago, which is where he was born and raised. But his parents were Palestinian and they passed on to him looks that tend to make some of his fellow airline passengers nervous—dark eyes, dark complexion, prominent nose, long hair and bushy mustache.

In modern security parlance, Hanania, 43, "fits the profile." This sometimes causes inconveniences.

"When I walk through airports, people look at me funny," he says, with a sardonic chuckle. "I don't get mad. I don't hate 'em. I know I look like one of those guys. What can you do?

"There's an alert out at airports now for the people who take bags at curbside check-in. They're supposed to send anyone inside who fits the profile. But, once they decide you're okay, you get first-class treatment. Once they find out who you aren't, you get to go right inside, ahead of the line."

It really annoyed him when immigration agents pulled him out of a long line at Miami International Airport as he returned with his family from a vacation outside the country. But, once they cleared him, they allowed him to proceed to the exit, ahead of the crowd.

"I don't know what's worse. Suffering through the long line or suffering through the indignity of being pulled out of line and having the guy go through my new brand new huaraches only to tell me to go ahead of everyone else who is in line."

Fortunately, Ray has been able to keep his sense of humor about his predicament. Perhaps his years as a political reporter for the Chicago Sun-Times have given him a keen sense of the absurd. Freelancing from his home, he decided to write the story of his life and publish it himself. Its title: "I'm Glad I Look Like A Terrorist: Growing Up Arab in America."

Its cover features a close-up of his passport photo which makes him look a convict, the way most passport photos make their subjects look like criminals.

"It gets double takes from passport checkers," he recalls. "They look at the picture. Then they suddenly look up at me. Then back to the picture. Then back at me. This can go on for a while."

After Ray sent me a copy of his book, I showed it to a few friends around Washington to get their responses. The most interesting came from Linda Chavez, conservative commentator, founder of the Center for Economic Opportunity and former Reagan administration aide.

"Me, too," she said. "I look like a terrorist, too."

I was astonished. Linda looks tanned, dark-eyed, Latin and classy. I have often described her as the Republican Party's best sex symbol since Clare Boothe Luce.

"You look too prosperous to be a terrorist," I said. "You worked for Reagan, for Pete's sake."

"Just don't stand behind me in an airport line," she said. "You'll be kept waiting all day while they check out my ID and luggage."

So it goes. Although it is fashionable to denounce racial and ethnic stereotyping in this seemingly enlightened era, our society actually is becoming more stereotype-dependent.

The most feared creature on urban American streets today, for example, is the young black male. It is not because most of them are criminal. Most are not. But, for the many white people who know nothing about black people other than what they see on the evening news, any young black male in gym shoes "fits the profile."

"Fit the profile" has become a new national mantra. Even Christopher Darden, the O.J. Simpson prosecutor, complains in his autobiography of being stopped repeatedly by California police for the crime of "driving while black."

What is a security-conscious society to do? We rationalize that it is better to be safe than sorry, that it is better to be too careful about terrorists or muggers than to fail to be careful enough.

But I wonder sometimes just how effective the "profiles" are. In a suit against the Maryland State Police, for example, the American Civil Liberties Union found that 73 percent of the cars police were stopping on Interstate 95 between Baltimore and Delaware since January of last year were operated by blacks, even though only 17 percent of the drivers on the busy 44-mile stretch were black.

Yet, while many more blacks were stopped than whites, proportionately, a slightly higher percentage of the whites who were stopped (28.8 percent of the whites versus 28.4 percent of blacks) were found to be carrying drugs, according to the department's own figures.

Since more than 70 percent of the stops were not carrying drugs, as one ACLU lawyer put it, it looks like the state police might have done just as well with completely random searches as they have been doing with their "profile."

Sometimes stereotypes are useful. Other times, they're just a pain in the neck, especially for those whose necks happen to be darker than other necks.

OCTOBER 24, 2010

PUNISHED FOR BEING TOO HONEST

Juan Williams' unfortunate firing by National Public Radio raises a question: Can we admit to having our own prejudices while arguing against other people's?

Speaking last week on "The O'Reilly Factor" at Fox News, where he also was a paid commentator, Williams said people in "Muslim garb" on planes make him "worried" and "nervous." For that, NPR released Williams from his job as a senior news analyst, saying the Fox News remarks "were inconsistent with our editorial standards."

Roger Ailes, Fox News' chief executive, happily jumped at the chance to make the network appear to be more fair-minded than NPR. As first reported by the Tribune Washington Bureau, Ailes handed Williams a new three-year contract worth almost $2 million — which, I should not have to tell you, is way more than the usual pay for pundits.

Before I offer my view of this dust-up, some disclaimers: I have personal connections to all of the parties. I have been a paid NPR commentator, an unpaid repeat-guest on O'Reilly's program (although I have not been invited back since President Barack Obama's election) and a longtime friend and neighbor of Williams'. For several years we even attended the same church. Alas, media are a small world, especially in Washington.

That's why I was sorry to see NPR let him go, although I was not surprised. He might have gotten off with a warning, except that he had been warned in the past about expressing stronger views on Fox than NPR would find acceptable on its own air. Conservative critics accuse NPR of liberal bias, although it's no more biased in my view than the other mainstream media channels that conservatives call "liberal," which is almost all of mainstream media except Fox.

Whatever your view, Williams' firing is not a First Amendment issue as Fox contributor Sarah Palin and other conservatives have suggested. It is more of a conventional policy and personnel management decision. In the news business, the dividing line between "commentary," which is what Williams did at Fox, and "news analysis," his job description at NPR, never has been crystal clear. Further blurring the line, NPR and Fox have about as much in common as a symphony orchestra and Lady Gaga.

I have a different defense of Williams' remarks. I hate to see yet another valuable opportunity for candid discussion and debate suddenly blown away in a whirlwind of scandal. When I heard Williams confess to feeling a shiver of nervousness since the Sept. 11 terrorist attacks when he sees people in "Muslim garb" on an airplane, my initial thought was, heck, who doesn't? We all have prejudices. Everybody "profiles" somebody or other. What matters is how well we put irrational prejudices aside in favor of good sense.

It is a sad, unfortunate fact of life that everybody profiles others to some degree, including those of their own race, religion or ethnicity. I interviewed Muslim- and Arab-Americans in the early days following Sept. 11, for example, who freely admitted that they, too, looked at other Arabs or Muslims in a new way at airports. As one of my Palestinian-American friends said, "I don't want my family to get hijacked, either."

But Williams' nervousness about "Muslim garb" unfortunately sounded about as welcome to many ears as a white man complaining that he gets nervous when he sees young black males on a dark street at night.

If it is doubtful that Fox would have embraced quite as enthusiastically a white man who was fired for speaking that view, it is only because prejudice against Muslims has become more socially acceptable than prejudice against blacks. It shouldn't be.

After listening to his remarks in context, I think that's the point Williams was trying to make. He actually was arguing against those who want to blame all Muslims for the tragedy of Sept. 11, which was caused by a fanatical minority. But as political spin doctor Frank Luntz often says, it's not what you say that matters, it's what others hear.

The list of newsmakers caught in racial, ethnic or gender gaffes runs long. Instead of trying to put the lid on these episodes—or blowing them up into another battle of good versus evil in the nation's long-running post-1960s culture wars—we should be finding ways to build bridges of understanding with serious thoughtful discussions. We who work in the news media have a great platform on which to start those conversations, if we're not too afraid of being punished.

JULY 24, 2011

JUAN WILLIAMS' PAYBACK TIME

Revenge is a dish that is best served cold, a saying goes. Juan Williams, the Fox News political analyst who was famously fired last fall from NPR, serves up a generous platter of the cold dish in his latest book, if only as an appetizer.

"Muzzled: The Assault on Honest Debate," offers his own account of his firing and his later hiring by Fox CEO Roger Ailes with a contract reported elsewhere to be worth somewhere north of $2 million. Williams does not confirm that figure, other than to say Ailes promised him more dollars than he was making before. I'm so sure.

That saga takes up the first 31 pages. The rest of the book is a grand attempt to explain what Williams was really trying to say about how "political correctness" is stifling "honest debate" in America when his attempt in the feverish chatter of Bill O'Reilly's show on Fox's cost him his NPR job.

After 11 years at the public radio network, NPR ended Williams' contract two days after he said on "The O'Reilly Factor" that, "...when I get on the plane, I got to tell you, if I see people who are in Muslim garb and I think, you know, they are identifying themselves first and foremost as Muslims, I get worried. I get nervous."

To many ears, especially out of context, Williams was justifying the profiling of Muslims as terrorists. In fact, his burst of candor about his personal feelings came during a discussion in which he was trying to argue against such stereotyping.

Nevertheless, Ellen Weiss, NPR's senior vice president for news, fired him over the telephone without a fair hearing. She was backed up by NPR's CEO Vivian Schiller. "As a reporter, as a host, as a news analyst, you do not comment on stories," Schiller said, trying to draw the line against news staffers getting too personal about big issues. Both women have since left the network, partly because of fallout from Juan-gate.

Fox's chief was not the only soul to use this episode to crow about liberal bias at NPR. House Republicans used the dust-up to argue for cutting NPR's funding. A measure passed by the Republican-controlled House in March would have cut $50 million from the Corporation for Public Broadcasting, which supports NPR and PBS. The funding cuts died in the Senate and in the final budget deal NPR kept most of its funding. As with similar attacks at NPR in the 1990s, the listeners came to the rescue.

Yet Williams, although he remains a fan of NPR, calls for an end to federal funding of the network. Its journalism, he says, "has come to embody elitism, arrogance and the resentments of its highly educated, upper-income manager and funders." Yet he does not offer specific examples of how this bias has shown up on NPR's airwaves, except in his absence from it.

Instead, Williams gives a higher purpose to his narrative by using it to spotlight what he sees as a growing crisis of political correctness in political discourse. This is not a new complaint on the left or the right. By now the definition of PC has been bent and stretched by the right and the left so much that it means, in essence, "any view that disagrees with mine."

Williams devotes several thought-provoking chapters to such impediments to honest debate as political polarization, a reluctance to call terrorists "terrorists" and a blindness to the political middle ground on touchy issues like abortion and immigration.

But if there is any area on which he does not devote enough attention, it is the fundamental question of why people find certain statements or images offensive and how much deference we should pay to them, regardless of whose side we happen to be on.

We do need to have honest, candid debate in our diverse nation. That requires a mutual respect not only for each other's views but also for the unpredictable ways, based on different experiences, that different people may respond to the same words.

NOVEMBER 14, 2010

FIGHTING A LEGAL MIRAGE

I was happy to see President Barack Obama continue his outreach to the world's Muslims during his Asia trip last week. It's important for Muslims overseas to hear that Americans are waging war against terrorists, not Muslims, even though some Americans have a hard time telling the difference.

A good example of such bad thinking occurred in the midterm elections. Oklahoma voters decided in a 70 percent landslide to amend their constitution to ban Shariah law, Islamic law based on the teachings of the Prophet Muhammad. Take that, Taliban, although I doubt they're going to react to Oklahoma's measure with anything but laughter.

In a state whose Muslim population numbers only 15,000, Oklahoma's Shariah law ban is a solution in search of a problem. Even its author, Republican Rep. Rex Duncan, acknowledged that the Sooner State has not had any cases of Shariah law and does not expect to see any, but "why wait until it's in the courts?"

Now it's in the courts anyway. Federal Judge Vicki Miles-LaGrange granted a temporary restraining order to Muneer Awad, executive director of the Oklahoma chapter of the Council on American-Islamic Relations, who sees the measure as a threat to his rights. It sounds to me as though he has a good case. The boundaries of religious freedom are a never-ending argument in this country, but it is safe to say that the First Amendment frowns on laws that single out religions, whether for penalties or preferences.

Yet this case is nationally significant because, as its backers have said, more than a dozen states are preparing to place similar initiatives before voters in 2012. The notion that Shariah law is invading America has been boiling up in conservative circles for the past year. Former House Speaker Newt Gingrich, a potential 2012 Republican presidential candidate, stated at the Values Voters summit in September that, "We should have a federal law that says Shariah law cannot be recognized by any court in the United States."

And, before Nevada Republican Sharron Angle lost her campaign for the U.S. Senate, she told an audience incorrectly that Shariah law had been allowed to "take hold" in Dearborn, Mich., and Frankford, Texas, which turns out to have been annexed by Dallas in 1975. As for

Dearborn, which has a large Arab and Muslim population, its mayor, John O'Reilly, said Angle "doesn't know what she's talking about."

That's appropriate. Facts have had a lot less to do with the current dust-up over Shariah law than fear—a fear not so much of Muslim law as of Muslim terrorism which, as I mentioned, a lot of people seem to think is the same thing.

Frankly, if all I knew about Shariah law was the part that gets the most attention—the subjugation of women, cutting off hands for petty theft, stoning for adultery and other horrendous acts in its name—I'd be angrily opposed to Shariah law too. Instead we should be angry at the fanatical extremists. Judging Shariah law by the Taliban's interpretations is like judging Christianity by the Christian Ugandan officials who want to punish those who engage in homosexual sex with the death penalty. Every religion has its fanatics.

Gingrich, among others, cites debates going on in the United Kingdom about allowing Islamic courts to arbitrate deals and disputes over marriage, real estate and other business matters, in tandem with the conventional royal government. But the U.K. and the United States have long recognized the authority of rabbinic law courts, the Beth Din, to oversee similar matters between consenting adults in Orthodox Jewish communities. In the United States, which unlike the U.K. has a more strict separation of church and state, the religious courts' decisions can be appealed to conventional courts all the way up to the U.S. Supreme Court.

That makes Oklahoma's move not only unconstitutional in singling out a single religion's courts but also unnecessary. The U.S. Constitution would have the final word.

The new Oklahoma amendment also includes a ban against international law in its courtrooms. That could create havoc, some observers have pointed out, in conventional relations with Native American Indian tribal governments. The state has the nation's second largest Indian population.

In short, the so-called threat of Shariah law in America is a legal and political mirage. Even as a feel-good measure in today's post-Sept. 11 world, the anti-Shariah amendment and the hysteria that created it should only make us feel bad. We need to wage war on terrorists, not on Islam, even when terrorists commit horrible acts in its name.

CHAPTER EIGHT

GIANTS WORTH REMEMBERING

Obituaries are the most underappreciated part of the paper, until they report the death of someone you care about. This chapter collects my views of how some of the newsmakers who are worth remembering should be remembered.

They include Justice Thurgood Marshall, Sen. Daniel Patrick Moynihan, James Brown, Coretta Scott King, Bill Raspberry, Christopher Hitchens, Hunter S. Thompson, Michael Jackson and, among memorable non-human entities, the era of Hugh Hefner's iconic Playboy image as we once knew it.

JANUARY 27, 1993

JUSTICE MARSHALL'S LEGACY IS NOT ONLY FOR AFRICAN-AMERICANS

Justice Thurgood Marshall was a delightful grump. He did not suffer fools gladly and could scold the naive like a tough schoolmarm.

So I watched with delight as he attempted to re-educate the crowd of mostly young and mostly white reporters who had gathered to cover his farewell press conference in 1991.

"Justice Marshall, do you think black people are better off as a result of your serving on the court?" asked one young male reporter who looked barely old enough to shave.

"I am not a black people," the justice snapped, wheezing badly. "I am an Afro-American!"

After the reporter struggled to rephrase his question, the retiring justice fumed: "That is a question that has absolutely no relevance whatsoever. So are the whites! They, too, are better off!"

He was right, and you didn't have to be a liberal to think so. In a recent Stanford Law Review, Marshall received unusual tributes from two white Reagan-era appointees to the current Supreme Court.

Justice Sandra Day O'Connor wrote that Marshall's ability to draw powerful messages from his own life experiences "reminded us ... that judges, as safeguarders of the Constitution, must constantly strive to narrow the gap between the idea of equal justice and the reality of social inequality ... . No one could help but be moved by Justice Thurgood Marshall's spirit; no one could avoid being touched by his soul."

She recalled how one of his anecdotes about a miscarriage of justice due to racial prejudice in a long-ago death penalty case he had handled as a trial lawyer "made clear what legal briefs often obscure: the impact of legal rules on human lives."

Justice Anthony Kennedy acknowledged, like Justice O'Connor did, that he and Justice Marshall often disagreed.

Nonetheless, he wrote, Justice Marshall's opinions "show a willingness to raise the moral issues which all decent societies must explore and attempt to resolve, whether through the courts or some other means."

Yes, whites, too, are better off. All Americans are better off because of Thurgood Marshall's work. His critics try to disparage him as too liberal, too radical or too racially embittered. Yet, he came not to overthrow the Constitution but to fulfill its highest ideals.

Marshall knew that when the Framers of the Constitution wrote about the rights of minorities, they were not as concerned about the rights of the disadvantaged as they were worried about their own ability as a privileged minority to stand up against a propertyless majority.

That's why their originally ratified document was able to allow slavery, disallow the right of women or Native Americans to vote and completely omit a Bill of Rights.

But Marshall was deeply impressed with the Constitution's built-in capacity to be revised. With that and his gift for passionate and persuasive argument, he used the keen sword of this nation's most cherished traditions to cut through the bindings of its most shameful traditions.

Marshall's life experiences as an advocate for minority rights, sometimes up against lynch mobs, were unique on a court composed overwhelmingly of the same sort of privileged white males who wrote the Constitution.

But it was those experiences that gave him his liberal tilt on capital punishment, civil rights, reproductive rights, search and seizure and the rights of the accused.

When he used the court to bypass legislative processes in such volatile issues as abortion or capital punishment, he was accused of "judicial activism" because he didn't allow popularly elected legislatures to make such delicate decisions.

Guilty.

But sometimes it has taken court activism to force the public and legislatures to take a position, one way or another, on controversial issues they would just as soon avoid.

It was called "judicial activism," for example, when the Supreme Court overturned school segregation in its landmark 1954 Brown v. Board of Education case, which a young Thurgood Marshall argued as chief lawyer for the NAACP Legal Defense and Educational Fund.

Yet, it helped launch the civil-rights revolution that resulted in the Civil Rights Act of 1964 and the Voting Rights Act of 1965, both legislated by a popularly elected Congress.

Similarly, the "activism" of justices like Marshall on a wide range of other issues has helped make America's beacon of light and liberty shine a little brighter.

When political winds tilted the high court to the right, Marshall would ask prospective law clerks, "How do you like writing dissents?" He gave those he hired plenty of dissents to write. Justice Marshall was too big a grump to be a consensus builder. More important, he had seen too much to allow him to compromise very much on principles he viewed as fundamental, and he seemed to view almost all of his principles as fundamental.

So he wrote dissents as if they mattered, as indeed they do. They matter to lower courts and future courts that are looking for the unique perspective only a Thurgood Marshall could bring. They matter to legislatures, governors and presidents who are looking, as Martin Luther King Jr. once preached, "with divine dissatisfaction" on the way things are and search with hope for an enlightened vision of the way things could be.

Justice Thurgood Marshall died Sunday of heart failure. As someone once said of another civil-rights hero, Mississippi's Fannie Lou Hamer, it was the only time his heart ever failed him.

MARCH 30, 2003

REMEMBERING MOYNIHAN'S MIND

I knew, as an African-American Baby Boomer, that I was not supposed to like Daniel Patrick Moynihan.

After all, he wrote that inflammatory work "The Negro Family: The Case for National Action," that singled out the breakup of black families as a major impediment to black advancement.

Liberal academics and black activists savaged the book and Moynihan, calling the book and the man "racist" and other impolite epithets.

As a college freshman, I, too, thought the book's generalities were a bit too sweeping. Sure, we had a poverty problem in black America, but civil rights reforms were opening new opportunities that would drive black poverty down to about 30 percent from more than 60 percent over the next two decades. I defy you to name any other major racial group on the planet that progressed so far, so fast.

Family breakdown seemed to be too simplistic of an explanation for black poverty. On the other hand, poverty certainly makes it harder to keep a family together.

Nevertheless, I appreciated Moynihan for bringing up the issue. I didn't always agree with what he thought, but he always gave me something to think about.

Moynihan, who died Wednesday at age 76, eagerly invited criticism. Not the name-calling sort of criticism that you hear sometimes on radio call-in shows, but the genuinely constructive criticism that advances ideas, not just arguments.

He was, among other distinctions, one of the most important and controversial minds and voices on the front lines of racial, ethnic and social policy in post-World War II America.

He shifted the debate on race, one year after passage of the landmark Civil Rights Act of 1964, from a debate about rights to the role of family in predicting a lifetime of poverty.

In 1963, he co-authored "Beyond the Melting Pot." The book exposed the durability of ethnic identity in the United States despite widespread assimilation and set the stage for today's "celebrate diversity" movement.

A few years later, as an aide to Richard Nixon, he persuaded the Republican president to give a speech advocating a downright radical idea, the Family Assistance Plan. To stop fathers from leaving home so their families could qualify for welfare, the plan would provide guaranteed income to the unemployed and supplements to the working poor.

Nixon made the speech, sent the legislation to Capitol Hill, astonished Democrats by appearing to snatch a key issue away from them, then, he let it die, with the impoverished still waiting for aid.

"I didn't wander into politics," Moynihan said. "I wandered into academics having been defeated in politics."

Nevertheless, Moynihan's concepts would lead years later to the Earned Income Tax Credit and the welfare-reform legislation of 1996, which, characteristically, Moynihan, as a fourth-term senator from New York, strongly opposed on principle, despite its being promoted by Democratic President Bill Clinton, because it imposed time limits on job-seeking welfare recipients.

News of Moynihan's death saddened me because it brought his inquiring mind to a halt just as he was pursuing more research into the relationship between marriage and poverty.

Perhaps the fact that he made a success of himself the hard way after being abandoned by his dad and reared by a single mom during the Depression gave him special sympathies for the subject.

But during two interviews with him over the past two years, he sounded just as puzzled as ever over the relationship between family breakdown and poverty and what other factors might lead to each.

The alarms he sounded when 26 percent of black children were being born out of wedlock are now being sounded over white out-of-wedlock birth rates, which are higher than 26 percent and getting higher while the black rate has leveled off at 69 percent. Yet, curiously, no one that I know of refers to the problem as "pathological" among whites the way Moynihan did when he was studying blacks.

Out-of-wedlock birth rates are climbing throughout the industrialized world, he also found. But they are not always accompanied by growth in poverty. In Scandinavia, for example, more than half of all births are to unmarried mothers, but a much higher percentage of them live with the man who fathered their child in a stable relationship. Generous government family-support programs, even more generous than those Moynihan proposed, appear to be replacing the traditional breadwinner role of fathers.

When I presented these paradoxes to Moynihan, he did not argue. He nodded and, with a twinkling smile, admitted that the topic cried out for more study. Pat Moynihan didn't always have the answers, but he seldom failed to raise the right questions.

"And now goodbye," he told Nixon's White House staff when he left in 1970. "It really has been good to know you."

You, too, Pat.

DECEMBER 27, 2006

GODFATHER OF SOUL, AND OF OUR GOAL

Can James Brown really be gone? Are we sure? After all, no one could stage a false exit better than the Godfather of Soul.

He'd be singing "Please, Please, Please" down on one knee at the foot of the stage, his face gleaming with sweat, his pompadour gleaming with pomade, after two hours of sweet pulse-pounding soul stirrings. Then his dapper assistant would appear and drape a bright satin cape over Brown's shoulder's and Soul Brother No. 1 would slowly stand up and turn around slowly and step rhythmically offstage as the band and

backup singers, moaned "Please, please don't go-oh-oh..." and...the...
crowd...would...go...wild!

And Brown would stop, shake off the cape, which the dapper aide
would catch in the nick of time, and dance back to center stage for an
encore! And another! And another!

It was pure cornball show biz, but we, the James Brown Baby Boomers, loved it because Brown did it with so much, ah, yes, soul!

In fact, he defined "soul" in the 1960s and forevermore as much
as Sam Cooke or Aretha Franklin or Ray Charles or the Supremes or
Jackie Wilson or Marvin Gaye or anybody else in the rhythm-and-blues
pantheon. His 1962 "Live at the Apollo" hit album set the mood for
countless "blue-light" parties in our parents' basements. His eye-defying,
quick-shuffling, rubber-legged dance moves were widely imitated but
never quite duplicated. Others like Joe Tex or Jackie Wilson or Al Green
might be able to drop the mike, spin around, drop into a split and catch
the mike before it hit the stage floor, but never with the same level of
style, flair and all-out screaming passion as Brown.

Ever wonder where Rev. Al Sharpton found his exotic hairstyles?
Blame Brown.

J.B. befriended Sharpton, then a prodigious teen preacher and
youth leader who became Brown's road manager in the 1970s. When
Sharpton married show business and civil rights activism, he learned
from the master.

Ever wonder why Mick Jagger started dancing like a madman on
stage? Blame Brown.

As a singer, Jagger was a remarkably calm-looking chap until the
Rolling Stones were booked to follow Brown in the Santa Monica
Civic Auditorium in 1965. As "The T.A.M.I. Show" (Teen-Age Music
International) video documentary reveals, "The Hardest Working Man
in Show Business" whipped those California kids into such a frenzy
that a nervous young Jagger decided to explode onto the stage with an
improvised chicken walk dance that soon became his trademark. Jagger
has hardly stopped moving onstage since.

And after surviving the Motown wave and the British invasion,
Brown proceeded not only to "go political," as many performers did
in the 1960s, but write the anthem for a new sociopolitical consciousness: "Say It Loud, I'm Black and I'm Proud." No one drove the nail

into the coffins of "colored" and "Negro" as acceptable labels as much as Brown's song did.

Yet, as music and message, I prefer the less known anthem with a mouthful of a title that says it all: "I Don't Want Nobody to Give Me Nothing (Open Up the Door, I'll Get It Myself)."

Musically, the song's compelling beat displays to full effect Brown's distinctive emphasis on "the ones" (the one and the three, instead of the two and the four) in his rhythms. Its message offers an important response to the many people who were asking in the midst of urban riots and a rising black power movement in the late 1960s, "What do black people want?"

If Brown's answer is what it sounds like in his songs, "We want equal opportunity, not guaranteed results," it should come as no surprise that he endorsed Richard M. Nixon in 1972 for president. After all, it was Nixon, not John F. Kennedy or Lyndon B. Johnson, who actually signed the first affirmative action executive order into law.

Looking back, it is easier to appreciate the message Brown was trying to give. "Black power" rose in 1966 in the wake of the civil rights movement as a slogan in desperate search of a program. Brown, a 7th-grade dropout, suddenly became the least academic but most influential voice to give a little intellectual meat to the new movement.

As an impressionable student, I was changed forever by Brown's recounting in an interview in the late 1960s about his own struggles against childhood poverty. "I used to shine shoes on the front steps of an Augusta, Ga., radio station," he said. "Now I own that radio station." So could we all, he was telling our generation, if we took full advantage of the doors that were opening to us.

Unfortunately, Brown took great advantage of those open doors only to lead a life of maddening swings between wealth and ruin, artistic genius and spouse abuse, amazing fitness and drug abuse. Yet he kept coming back for encores and honors. The curtain has come down on his turbulent life. This time his exit is for real. But we still have his music, his memories and his messages, still taking encores for many years to come.

MAY 18, 2005

SYMPATHY FOR GEEZER ROCK STARS
Old Rockers Like the Rolling Stones Are Touring Again.
But Youth Will Be Served, and Rock May Not Be in Their Future

On the culture front, it is encouraging for an aging Baby Boomer like me to learn that the hottest act on this summer's rock concert circuit happens to be a group of senior citizens.

Yes, roll out the black denim, my dear, and pack up the extra-strength painkillers. The Rolling Stones are leaving their English homes to come back and kick boo-tay on tour yet again, some 40 years after Mick Jagger couldn't "get no satisfaction" in their first invasion.

Sometime back in the 1970s, if memory serves, Mick Jagger scoffed at the notion that he still would be dancing around stage to "Jumpin' Jack Flash" by the time he turned 40. Right. Now Sir Mick—he's been knighted—is 61.

Yet, as he performed a few numbers with the band at their recent news conference, he looked not only fit but physically pumped and buffed, more muscular than the scrawny Kid Mick we used to know.

Still, there was an ironic message to the occasion. The ability of geezer Stones to roll in as this summer's hottest-selling rock concert ticket is a testament not only to their resilient talents but also to how much rock 'n' roll is ailing as a vital, edgy soul-capturing engine of youth culture.

The summer of the Stones follows a winter of rock's discontent. "Rock Radio No Longer Rolling," blared a headline in the March 24 Rolling Stone magazine (no relation to the band). In the previous seven months, no fewer than five major-market rock radio stalwarts (Philadelphia's WPLY, Washington, D.C.'s WHFS, Miami's WZTA, San Jose's KSJO and Houston's KLOL) switched to other formats.

The sounds of "urban," the radio industry's artful term for hip-hop, or "hurban," short for "Hispanic urban," are the new engines of creativity and sales, outside the easy listening "cool jazz" or golden-oldie rock stations.

CD sales show a similar trend. All 10 of the top performers on the Billboard music sales charts were black artists in October 2003, for the first time in the 50-year-history of the charts. Nine were rappers and the other was a song by R&B singer Beyonce and reggae star Sean Paul.

If young black artists are emerging at music's new cutting edge, history is only repeating itself. Like countless other rockers, the Stones (who got their name from the Muddy Waters blues song "Rollin' Stone") reverently embraced the low-down, fundamental Mississippi-Memphis-Chicago blues axis, dropping in on Chicago and Memphis clubs to jam with Buddy Guy, B.B. King and others and recording an instrumental track titled "2120 S. Michigan Avenue," the address of blues-giant Chess Records' studio in Chicago.

And now, years after studying the lords of ancient blues arts, the Stones themselves have become elder statesmen of rock, a role to which the media are unaccustomed. In an interview on NBC's "Today" show, Jagger and lead guitarist Keith Richards, also 61, hinted at a curious "inverse racism," as co-host Matt Lauer put it, in the way reporters always seem to ask white seniors like the Stones why they're still touring while black artists keep touring no matter what age they are and hardly anybody asks them why they still do it.

"We're just musicians," Richards said. "I mean, it's other people's bags that we get put in, and, I mean—right, because we're white. Oh, 'You— you made a lot of money, why the hell would you want to do that?' Because we love it. It's as simple as that."

Still, it doesn't speak much for the state of new rock artists that the old guys seem to make a bigger noise than the new ones.

I suspect that rock as we have known it is over. Been there, heard that, bought the T-shirts. Maybe rock died as a cutting-edge force with the 1994 suicide of Nirvana leader Kurt Cobain, the king of grunge, the Seattle-born music of youth-despair that became rock's first and last Big Thing of the 1990s.

Maybe some new Beatles, Stones, Sex Pistols, Nirvana, Jimi Hendrix or some other Messianic Big Thing is coming around the corner to save rock once again. But, if history is our guide, I predict that rock will fade after a half-century of vitality into a pastime of aficionados in the way of jazz, the blues, bluegrass and other once-prominent genres.

The new nurseries of music creativity are much the same as the old ones: black culture, Latino culture, working-class whites, angst-ridden suburban kids and the fast-rising global multicultural techno-reggae pulse of "world music." Who knows? As the world's young people live increasingly in the fast-paced, planet-shrinking paths of cyberspace, the next musical rage may not be so easy to pin down by geography.

In the meantime, as we boomer geezers fill our iPods with memories and gather in amphitheaters to hear soulful rock survivors perform what's left of our music and the selves that we once knew, indulge us, children. These days we hear a new message in the Stones' refrain, "... This could be the last time. May-be the last time, I don't kno-o-ow." Oh, no.

JUNE 28, 2009

JACKSON'S CREATIVE SELF-DESTRUCTION

Which was your favorite Michael Jackson? Not your favorite Michael Jackson song, but your favorite Michael? There were so many of him.

News that the "King of Pop" had died at age 50 might well have felt more shocking had he not shocked us so often in the past.

He shocked the world in a good way back when he was a kid. Fronting for his older brothers in the Jackson 5, he thrilled a lot of us when we were kids—decades before we would find ourselves trying to explain him to our own kids.

Even at age 11, when the group scored its first No. 1 hit, Michael's own versions of Jackie Wilson's and James Brown's stagecraft lifted the J5's bubble-gum soul from a Gary novelty act to international stardom.

In the late 1970s, he shocked us again, this time with how much he had grown as an all-around musician and dance artist. He teamed up with producer Quincy Jones to enrich the last days of disco with "Off the Wall," which many critics call Jackson's best album. I'm partial to "Thriller," the biggest-selling record of all time and one of the most influential.

Jackson's 13-minute "Thriller" video became a classic and encouraged the young and timid MTV to air more black musicians. It also led to Jackson's next shock. He began turning white.

Questions began to grow around Jackson. Was he getting plastic surgery? (Gee, do ya think?) Skin peels? What else was he changing? Why didn't he have any girlfriends?

Even in the music world, where gossip is at least the second favorite leisure activity, questions about Jackson took center stage. It was a tribute to his prodigious talent that we even cared.

Jackson seemed to relish feeding our speculation. His friends ranged from Elizabeth Taylor to Bubbles the chimp. Or was he just being weird?

He built an estate in central California, complete with amusement park rides, and called it Neverland Ranch, after the place where Peter

Pan, the boy who never grew up, lived with Tinkerbell and the Lost Boys. Hey, it was his money, right?

But it also revealed a sad, lonely and confused side of the gifted star, a side that seemed to be confirmed by our next shock. In a 1993 sit-down with Oprah Winfrey, Jackson claimed to have vitiligo, a skin disorder that can leave its victims without skin color.

He revealed heart-rending accounts of crying from loneliness as a child. He said he was abused so badly by his father, Joseph Jackson, that he sometimes would get sick and start to vomit when he saw the elder Jackson's face.

After Michael Jackson's death, those stories give new meaning to his songs about the "Man in the Mirror" and how "it don't matter if you're black or white." Was he trying to convince us or himself?

The man that the aging Jackson saw in the mirror increasingly resembled his father, according to Jackson biographer J. Randy Taraborrelli. He seemed increasingly determined to change his face.

Sad.

Yet the same troubled-childhood stories that elicited so much public sympathy were turned against Jackson when he was charged with seven counts of child molestation and two of intoxicating a minor. He was acquitted of all charges, but questions remain, fed by his many eccentricities, that stain his legacy and enrich his mystique.

Michael Levine, a publicist who represented Jackson in the early 1990s, called him a "disciple of P.T. Barnum," who was "much more cunning and shrewd about the industry than anyone knew," according to The Associated Press. "There's a sucker born every minute," said the circus master Barnum, who promoted newsmaking hoaxes from time to time. Even when the hoax was exposed, Barnum reasoned, any publicity was good publicity.

Stoking gossip helped Jackson's ticket and music sales too. But controversy ceased to be much fun when his fame morphed into infamy and threatened his freedom.

I don't know whether Jackson was guilty as charged. I don't know what it is like to be surrounded by people who are telling you how wonderful you are, after a childhood of being told that you're not. But it is not hard to understand how, after living so long with his fantasies, he might have lost sight of what's acceptable behavior in the real world.

Mourning his death pulls us back through a kaleidoscopic montage of the many Michaels we have come to know over the years. He leaves behind more questions than we can ever answer. But his electrifying music and moonwalks never seem to get old. Preserved in music and videos, we can continue to appreciate his art and the childhood he sacrificed in order to create it.

JULY 18, 2012

FAREWELL TO A RARE VOICE OF REASON

He called himself a "solutionist." It's not what's "right" or "left" that counts, he would say; it's what works.

Such evenhanded open-mindedness made William Raspberry something of a throwback in our raucous age—and that's why I miss his work.

His columns offered an island of calm, sober and often witty reflection amid the rising tide of polarized punditry on talk radio, cable television, blogs and the "belligerent brutopia," as Australian social critic Clive Hamilton described the vulgarities of Internet comment strings.

William James Raspberry died Tuesday at his home in Washington at age 76. He had prostate cancer, said his wife, Sondra Raspberry.

Many remember him as a Pulitzer Prize-winning syndicated columnist for the Washington Post. I knew him as a trailblazer.

When he began writing a local column for the Post in 1966, the only nationally syndicated black columnist in the general press was Carl T. Rowan. That was a big deal at the time, as urban riots sparked an informal affirmative action push for black reporters and photographers.

In fact, Raspberry broke out of the Post's Metro desk, where he was one of the newspaper's first black reporters in that "Mad Men" era, by an assignment in 1965 to cover riots in the Watts section of Los Angeles. A year later he was a columnist.

Two years after that he was covering the riots in Washington after the assassination of the Rev. Martin Luther King Jr. Two years after that, his column moved to the paper's op-ed page and to syndication in hundreds of other newspapers.

Readers who sought predictable iron-willed ideological cheerleading for the political, cultural or economic left or right were disappointed by Raspberry. He kept us guessing. You actually had to read his column to find out how he felt. Some complainers sounded annoyed by that. I, coming along into the pundit trade in the 1980s, was energized by it.

He demonstrated how a writer who expresses his or her honest views can withstand charges of "racist" or "socialist" from some and "sellout" or "Uncle Tom" from others—sometimes for the very same column. Speak clearly and honestly, without wishy-washiness, and even those who don't always agree with you will appreciate knowing where you stand.

As a result, Raspberry was quoted by newsmakers on the right and the left as an honest broker looking for answers that would liberate us from endless arguments, even if it poked the sacred cows of his own biggest fans.

Amid clashes over urban gentrification 2001, he memorably pointed to the supreme irony: how we blacks get upset when white people move out—and when they move back in.

"If whites abandon our neighborhoods, we say they are segregationists who want us confined to a ghetto," he wrote. "If they move in, we say they're taking over. What's a poor white guy to do?"

He angered some readers when he expressed grudging respect for the polarizing Nation of Islam Minister Louis Farrakhan, organizer of the Million Man March—and he angered others when he criticized the "gratuitous anti-Semitism" of Farrakhan and some of his supporters.

"Is it too much to suggest," Raspberry wrote, "that those who demand sensitivity have a duty to practice it?"

He died less than a month after he was honored at a roast and celebration for him at the Post that raised money for BabySteps, a childhood education foundation for low-income parents and children. He founded it in his hometown of Okolona, Miss., after he retired from writing in 2005, and funded it from his own pocket.

He was the child of schoolteachers, who believed education was "the one best hope black Americans have for a decent future."

He also lamented that "the civil rights leadership, for all its emphasis on desegregating schools, has done very little to improve them."

In the end he decided to put his time and money where his ideas had been, promoting smarter kids and better parenting. I appreciate his decision. But I miss his voice of reason.

FEBRUARY 23, 2005

GONZO'S FINAL DISPATCH

Just as nearly every woman has a little Aretha Franklin in her, as I once heard someone say, I believe that every journalist has a little bit of Hunter S. Thompson inside, raging to be heard.

Now he lives only within us, his readers. Thompson was found dead Sunday at age 67 from a self-inflicted gunshot wound in his famously "fortified compound" in Woody Creek, outside Aspen, Colo.

Thompson made journalism look like fun because he was so much fun to read—too much fun for us to ruin it by worrying about whether all of his facts were actually factual or whether the dark shadows of personal danger that lurked sharklike beneath the dazzling waves of his rants, revelations and screeds might someday drag him under.

"Political writing has become too timid in this spin-doctor age," said Abe Peck, chair of Northwestern University's magazine program. "But Hunter's hyper-reality changed how we look at political business as usual. And I'd give a lot to have his 'Hell's Angels' and 'Fear and Loathing' books on my resume."

"You were always glad to see him [on the campaign bus] because you knew things would lighten up," Bruce Morton, the veteran CNN reporter, recalled on the air Monday. Thompson's peers admired and envied him for doing what the rest of us "journos" wanted to do, if we had an ounce of heart and soul still beating within us: He was free to report not merely what he saw and heard, but also what he felt.

"When the going gets weird, the weird turn pro," Thompson once wrote. He was weird but he made it work. A lesser reporting talent who took Thompson's liberties with facts and invective would be fired and forgotten, but Dr. Gonzo, a nickname he picked up from a fan, was blessed with a gift for producing richly detailed, colorfully written, darkly amusing journeys into American subcultures that became instant classics. His books sold millions. Books and movies about his books sell millions. Just about anything with his name on it sells millions. He achieved today's ultimate commercial status: He is a brand.

But all envy now evaporates. His fabulous high-wire act has come crashing down before our eyes, despite the glimmers of hope he occasionally showed that he might take charge of his inner lunacies before they took charge of him.

Even in his 1971 drug-crazed classic "Fear and Loathing in Las Vegas," originally serialized in Rolling Stone, he reaches some profoundly unflattering conclusions about the biggest scam of the 1960s, the notion that hallucinogenic drugs would fling open our doors of perception.

In a sober and prophetic sermon-rant in his book's final chapters, he writes: "We are all wired into a survival trip now. No more of the speed that fueled the '60s. That was the fatal flaw in [LSD guru] Tim Leary's trip. He crashed around America selling 'consciousness expansion' without ever giving a thought to the grim meat-hook realities that were lying in wait for all the people who took him seriously. ... All those pathetically eager acid freaks who thought they could buy Peace and Understanding for three bucks a hit. But their loss and failure is ours too. What Leary took down with him was the central illusion of a whole lifestyle that he helped to create ... a generation of permanent cripples, failed seekers, who never understood the essential old-mystic fallacy of the Acid Culture: The desperate assumption that somebody ... or at least some force—is tending the light at the end of the tunnel."

Three-and-a-half decades later, Thompson's self-destruction tells us that maybe he should have taken that "desperate assumption" of a "force" at the end of the tunnel a bit more seriously. Belief in a higher power has saved countless other souls from the miserable hopelessness that feeds their own self-destruction. I wish it could have reached Hunter Thompson in time.

Both the book and the Johnny Depp movie version of "Fear and Loathing" begin with an epigraph from poet and essayist Samuel Johnson about the perils of alcohol: "He who makes a beast of himself gets rid of the pain of being a man." By choosing that stunning quote, Dr. Gonzo shows a better understanding of his obsessions than of his limits.

His addictions were not only to booze and drugs, but also to politics ("Better than sex," he said of politics, an obsession I share, if not to that extent) and to journalism. His obsessions made him more interesting to us. Now they only seem tragic.

His death has the last word now. No matter how much joy we seem to be bringing to the party, Thompson's suicide tells us, we cannot simply mask our personal pain. We must dig deeper and find the faith to help us drive out that beast.

DECEMBER 18, 2011

REQUIEM FOR A CONTRARIAN

Only once since my foolish adolescence do I recall actually feeling fortunate to be a smoker, a truly insidious addiction that I have since kicked. It was the slightly chilly Washington evening on which I was joined during a smoke break at a friend's birthday party by Christopher Hitchens, one of the few people who can be called a journalist-intellectual without it sounding like a punch line.

How ironic that memory now seems upon hearing the news Thursday that the simultaneously celebrated and vilified curmudgeon had died at 62 after a long, highly publicized bout with esophageal cancer, an ailment that his smoking certainly didn't help. Yet, how like Hitch it was for the famous self-described contrarian to remain a symbolic last-man-standing, even against clean air.

This was the author, after all, of numerous books and essays, most recently for Slate, Vanity Fair and the Atlantic Monthly, taking on such varied targets as Henry Kissinger, Princess Diana, Bill and Hillary Clinton, Michael Moore and even—Gasp!—Mother Teresa.

Yet, while admitting he brought it upon himself, he was constantly irritated by those who mentioned those high-value targets without noting what he criticized them for. For example, he went after Mother Teresa for among other things, "her warm endorsement of the Duvalier regime in Haiti." Even so, Vanity Fair editor Graydon Carter told NPR that the magazine received hundreds of complaints and subscription cancellations, including from some members of his staff.

Although I frequently disagreed with Hitchens I admired his courage, his exhaustive research and his relentless logic. As much as you will read elsewhere about his addiction to against-the-current, in-your-face arguments and polemical put-downs, he was quite the opposite in my brief encounter with him.

And he was full of surprises. It seemed at first that he had refused or forgotten the host's request to bring, instead of gifts, a poem to read at the party. But when his turn came, he smoothly recited a touchingly appropriate work by William Butler Yeats without hesitation or a hint of uncertainty. This brought applause and a request for an encore, which he granted without the blink of an eye. He seemed to have a library of literature in his head.

A mutual friend who had been one of his editors later told me that "Hitch" had a photographic memory. He also had a talent for doing remarkable things without sleep.

Such was his legend. He was admired by fellow Washington scriveners in the way that other raconteurs like Hunter Thompson were admired, although fortunately without the same streak for self-destruction.

Yet Hitchens also was vilified. He parted company with the liberal The Nation magazine after expressing support for President George W. Bush's invasion of Afghanistan, and the later invasion of Iraq.

He refused to be a lackey for the left or the right, despite concerted efforts by both sides. Unlike the abundance of popular commentators who predictably take one ideological side or the other, he courageously surprised everyone with his eloquent independence, even when it cost him friends.

How did he respond to criticism, some of it quite inaccurate? "The brief answer is that I have become inured without becoming indifferent," he wrote in "Letters to a Young Contrarian," a 2001 book. "I attack and criticize people myself; I have no right to expect lenience in return."

That's good because he didn't get it, especially when he took on the almighty himself with his atheist polemic, "God is not great." Many people asked him, he said, whether he was having second thoughts about God and the possibilities of an afterlife after hearing that his own life was about to end. Did he feel, as the old joke goes, like he was all dressed up with no place to go?

No, he dismissed such a possibility that personal emotions might overwhelm his rational side. He remained consistent, working hard and turning out more provocative prose until his end, including some poignantly brilliant insights into such symbolism-rich developments as the loss of his speaking voice. He never lost his spirit, as far as I could tell, as he turned out prose that stands as a lasting gift to those he leaves behind.

OCTOBER 18, 1992

PLAYBOY NO. 1 RETURNS TO HIS ROOTS

At first I didn't recognize him.

He darted out of the buffet line, balancing his plate, squinting through thick eyeglasses and scurrying across the room like a mouse caught in the beam of the television camera's light that was eagerly following him.

Only the video camera gave away the importance of this graying little man in the cream-colored suit.

He was Hugh Marston Hefner, founder of all that the name Playboy has come to mean.

"Hef" had returned to his hometown for the first time in seven years to premiere at the Chicago International Film Festival a David ("Twin Peaks") Lynch/Mark Frost documentary he had commissioned about his life, a prelude to his reported 800-page autobiography in progress.

At 66 and deep into his anecdotage, he is eager to shape history's memory of his pivotal role in the making of popular culture in the last half of the 20th Century.

"There goes my hero," I said to nobody in particular as I marveled at how the world's most famous playboy has changed in age, if not in temperament or charisma. The power center of the room still heaves and moves along with him wherever he moves. Perhaps that's why he scurries to his seat, just so the room will settle down a bit.

No, he's not my hero of today, but he is still idolized, I suppose, by the 14-year-old boy who still dwells somewhere within me. How many of us once dreamed of the Good Life of cars, penthouses and babes, before we wound up in sedate suburban domesticity?

Don't snicker, young 'uns. Hefner was to yesterday's 14-year-old boys what Madonna is to today's 11-year-old girls. Think about it. Both are arbiters of style, creators of attractive fantasies and impresarios of sex as a marketable commodity.

Each outrages extremists of the religious Right and the feminist Left with equal and opposite ferocity. And they do it with wit. Anybody who can pull that off can't be all bad.

Once there was a time when Hefner's vision, a product of working-class fantasies, embodied a new postwar cosmopolitan sophistication that helped make Chicago a cultural mecca for innumerable working stiffs. All they needed was a club key, and the world of glitz could be theirs. If Pat Buchanan wonders whatever happened to the sedate, rigidly conformist, white-male-dominated values of the '50s, which seems to be his favorite decade, he can start at the steps of Hefner's old mansion, where the entry plaque read in Latin, "If you don't swing, don't ring."

For those who really did read the magazine for its articles, it also offered a platform for controversial artists and ideologues as varied as Vladimir Nabokov and Malcolm X to express their visions and move the great debates of our times.

Perhaps most important, both Hefner and Madonna appeal to every young generation's obligation to torment and outrage its parents, which becomes a surprisingly dominant theme in his documentary.

Narrated with God-like tones by James Coburn, the documentary, which might as well be called "The Gospel of the Last Half of the 20th Century According to Hugh M. Hefner," presents the Big Bunny's entire career as one long rebellion against the values of his conservative parents on Chicago's Northwest Side, parents who loved their two sons but, in the view of the boys today, probably didn't hug them enough.

Hefner's odyssey ends back where it started, with the traditional values embodied by his second marriage, this time to Kimberly Conrad, 30, Miss January of 1988, and by life with their sons, age 2 and 1. His daughter, Christie, from his first marriage, took over the financially troubled empire in the '80s.

After a frightening stroke, Hefner shed his trademark pipe, gave up his dexedrine-driven workaholism and replaced his ever-present Pepsi with the caffeine-free version. He has become, at last, a very wealthy version of what he once rebelled against.

So, as Hefner returns to his Midwestern roots for a comfy little visit with old friends and his old neighborhood and to inspect the new scaled-down offices that no longer paint Playboy's name across Chicago's skyline in giant letters, the occasion invites those of us who remember the fantasy's glory days to reflect a bit, as Hefner has, on what it all meant—and means.

"How does Chicago look to you this time around?" I asked him. "A lot better," he shouts gleefully. "I got a proclamation from the mayor today. That never would have happened 20 years ago." Quite right. When Hefner moved to Los Angeles, the late uptight machine boss Richard J. Daley behaved as if the stain he thought Playboy's name put on the city's magnificent lakefront skyline was barely worth the revenue and international publicity the empire brought in. His son, today's mayor, has a different appreciation. What his father saw as a lemon, the son treats as lemonade.

The Hefner vision came just in time to be a handbook (or one-hand book, in writer Tom Wolfe's assessment) for the mod era of JFK, Camelot, the Pepperment Twist and John Profumo's sex scandal.

It peaked out when its cavalier rebellion against today's puritan roundheads began to look surprisingly tame for some and too unforgivably male-chauvinist for others. Now Hefner's life itself has gone tame. He speaks glowingly of the traditional values he once trashed.

Yet he's not apologetic, not even to those whose lives might have been ruined by taking his old Playboy fantasies to extremes. After all, he warned us against excesses in his "Playboy Philosophy," his long-running series of intelligent essays. If you didn't get that message, Hef seems to be saying, maybe you weren't really reading the magazine for the articles after all.

FEBRUARY 1, 2006

A LITANY OF HER TRIUMPHS
Let Us Remember Coretta Scott King for the Earlier Triumphs of Her Life and Not So Much for Her Family's Later Controversies

Let us remember the love, courage and tenacity of a woman who worked, by all accounts, as a full partner with her husband, Rev. Martin Luther King Jr., even when his traditionalism kept him from letting her show the extent of that partnership in public.

Let us remember the stirring speech she gave in her own political coming-out, a month after her husband's assassination in 1968, when she called on "black women, white women, brown women and red women—all women of this nation—[to join] in a campaign of conscience."

Let us remember how courageously she persevered, even when their house in Montgomery was bombed in 1956, while Mrs. King was at home with their first-born baby, Yolanda. Let us remember her courage, along with her husband's, in telling angry black residents who had marched to the house with guns in their hands and retaliation on their minds to go home in peace.

Let us remember those times when she quietly moved history in the right direction, such as her persuading John F. Kennedy, then a presidential candidate, when he called her during her husband's jail sentence in Georgia in 1960, to intercede on Dr. King's behalf. Although the move undoubtedly cost Kennedy votes in the South, it helped him win a majority of votes by blacks that may have made the difference in his presidential victory.

Let us remember her successful crusade for a national holiday in her husband's name and to preserve his legacy in the Martin Luther King Jr. Center for Nonviolent Social Change, an Atlanta complex that houses her husband's tomb, archives and exhibits.

And, finally, let us pray that the beloved memory of Mrs. King, whose death at age 78 was announced by her family Tuesday, will help bind together her children into sensibly resolving the controversies that have proved so embarrassing to the family's legacy in recent years.

For example, the King Center has become one of Atlanta's most popular tourist attractions. Unfortunately, it also has become the focus of an ugly family fight, dividing the four King children, with Dexter and Yolanda pushing to sell it to the National Park Service over the objections of Martin III and Bernice. Although the National Park Service does a fine job of managing other national landmarks, the objection seems to center around speculation over whether the late civil rights leader should have his legacy managed by the government he often protested against. But if that's what it takes to keep the center going, so be it. Instead of viewing it as King's legacy selling out, view it as the federal government buying in.

Then there are the speeches. We used to believe great historic speeches belong to the ages. Dr. King's family has treated his speeches as marketable commodities. The result has been such odd paradoxes as the sale of his historic "I Have a Dream" speech for use in cell-phone commercials while suing serious scholars and journalists who dare to use King's speeches without paying a fee.

USA Today was forced to pay $1,700 plus legal fees after the newspaper published the text of the "I Have a Dream" speech, and CBS was sued for selling a video documentary of King and the 1963 March on Washington, even though it used the network's own film footage. A similar dispute over Henry Hampton's widely praised PBS documentary, "Eyes on the Prize," was settled out of court for an undisclosed sum.

I don't want to be begrudge the King family its ability to earn royalties from the late civil rights leader's work, particularly if those royalties are going to help keep his legacy alive. But when the drive for royalties makes it difficult for new generations to appreciate Dr. King's stirring oratory and charismatic presence, history is cheated.

So is the history of his widow, who worked so tirelessly to be the caretaker of her late husband's legacy. She also wanted to be known as more than just the "widow of the slain civil rights leader," even though we in the media persistently labeled her as such.

"Sometimes, I am also identified as a civil rights leader or a human rights activist," she once observed. "I would also like to be thought of as a complex, three-dimensional, flesh-and-blood human being with a rich storehouse of experiences, much like everyone else, yet unique in my own way, much like everyone else."

Indeed she was. Let us remember her storehouse of experiences for all of its richness.

FEBRUARY 12, 2006

WHEN A PULPIT TURNS TO POLITICS
Are We in Need of Pointers on How to Behave at a Funeral?

Conservatives pride themselves, accurately or not, on grounding their arguments in fact, not emotion. Yet, some comments at Coretta Scott King's nationally televised funeral that were critical of President Bush, as he and First Lady Laura Bush sat silently at center stage, made some of our country's most prominent right-of-center voices turn passionate to the point of silliness.

Rush Limbaugh called the Democratic Party "funeral crashers" at the services. With breathtaking clairvoyance, he opined during an appearance on the Fox News Channel, "... I think Coretta Scott King and Martin Luther King Jr., if there was to be any anger from above looking down at that, it would be from them."

Frankly, if there was to be any anger from above, I think it might come from the Kings, God rest their souls, at having Limbaugh presume to be their spokesman.

At least, Bill O'Reilly, spoke only for himself on his own Fox News program. "When I die," he said, "I don't want my demise to be used as a political rally, and that's what happened ... to Coretta Scott King." Fine. I don't necessarily want O'Reilly's demise to turn into a political rally either, since there's a better-than-even chance that I would not agree with all of the politics that were being rallied.

The fuss is all about two or three remarks that were made by President Jimmy Carter and Rev. Joseph Lowery, former president of the Southern Christian Leadership Conference, which Rev. Martin Luther King Jr. once led.

Without mentioning the current president by name, enthusiastic applause underscored Carter's mention of the "forgotten" of Hurricane Katrina, which was Bush's biggest setback in public opinion. More applause punctuated his mention of the "secret government wiretapping" that harassed the Kings, echoing the controversy over Bush's authorization of eavesdropping on suspected terrorist phone calls and emails without court permission.

Lowery read a light-hearted poem that turned prickly, igniting a standing ovation with this line about Mrs. King's anti-war views: "Coretta knew, and we knew, there were no weapons of mass destruction over there but there were weapons of misdirection right down here."

Angry messages about how "rude" or "inappropriate" it was to turn the funeral political have poured into my in-boxes and those at the Chicago Tribune.

Yet, we heard few, if any, such discouraging words when President Ronald Reagan's funeral resembled a political rally. As Media Matters for America, an excellent liberal-leaning media-watching website, recounts, the speaker lineup for the Reagan funeral included President Bush, who was running for re-election at the time, but no Democrats. Not even former President Bill Clinton, who delivered a surprisingly moving tribute to Richard M. Nixon at that former president's funeral.

Whether people find politics appropriate in church rises or falls heavily on whether they agree with the politics. Remember Princess Diana's funeral in 1997? When her obviously angry brother Charles Spencer strongly criticized the press in his eulogy and indirectly criticized the royal family for their treatment of her, the guests burst into applause, defying centuries of tradition in the normally staid Westminster Abbey. Few observers objected.

Having grown up in the Southern, African-American church tradition, I was amused when I first heard that one did not clap during funerals. In most of the black church funerals I have known, you are likely to hear not only hand-clapping but toe-tapping, shouting and a host of other joyful noises.

My point: Different groups of people have different styles of worship and different roles for their churches to play. In the tradition of progressive black churches, politics and social action are as much a part of the church as gospel music. Even during slavery, black churches were sanctuaries for abolitionist forms of liberation theology. Over time, many black churches have continued to be centers of political planning, organizing and rallying.

Because Mrs. King, like her late husband, was consistently anti-war, anti-poverty and anti-wiretap during the presidential administrations of both parties, no one should have been surprised that those issues were addressed at her funeral. "We weren't burying a rap artist [or] a famous cook," Lowery said in a National Public Radio interview. "We were burying a woman who gave her life to world peace, racial justice, human dignity. ... What did they expect us to talk about?"

What, indeed?

FEBRUARY 10, 2002

"MANCHILD" AUTHOR LEAVES US WITH A LASTING MESSAGE

"...I ran. There was a bullet in me trying to take my life, all 13 years of it."

With those startling words in its opening page, Claude Brown's "Manchild in the Promised Land" opens a rare and riveting window into his dangerous journey from theft, drugs and juvenile detention on the streets of mid-20th Century Harlem to eventual redemption and education at Howard University and Rutgers University Law School.

As one of the many who was tantalized and ultimately inspired by this racy but also redemptive work as a teen in the 1960s, I felt as though I had lost an old friend when I heard Brown died on Feb. 5 at age 64 from a lung condition in Manhattan.

If you have only one good idea in life, it is said, make it a really good one. Brown did in 1965. He wrote only one best seller and it was a doozy. Imagine a black Huck Finn or Holden Caulfield growing up amid street crime, jail and heroin and you'll get an idea of the book's flavor.

Maybe Brown couldn't match the literary artistry of Ralph Ellison, James Baldwin or Richard Wright. But it didn't matter.

No one could beat his ability to make you feel the intense joy and pain faced by low-income and no-income black urban kids after the great black migration from the rural South to "the promised land" in the urban North.

As author Tom Wolfe wrote in The New York Herald Tribune, "Claude Brown makes James Baldwin and all that Rock of Ages rhetoric sound like some kind of Moral Rearmament tourist from Toronto come to visit the poor." Right you are, Tom.

In the late '60s, when everybody seemed to be trying to understand black people—including a lot of us black people—Brown was obligatory reading for many of us, right along with "The Autobiography of Malcolm X."

My generation loved it because it captured our language and attitude. Older folks embraced it because they were trying to figure out us younger folks.

During those times of urban riots, the federal "War on Poverty" and rising "supergangs" like Chicago's Blackstone Rangers, "Manchild" helped to shape the social debate on how to save America's poor inner-city kids.

With that in mind, it was particularly dismaying to read Brown's lamentations in the 1980s over how life for poor black kids had actually gotten worse 20 years after the civil-rights reforms of the 1960s.

"In the New York City teenage gang fights of the 1940s and '50s we used homemade guns, zip guns and knives," he wrote in the Los Angeles Times in 1988. "Now America's inner cities have become the spawning grounds for adolescents who bear increasingly appalling resemblances to rabid, homicidal maniacs."

The new crack-cocaine generation was filling jails with kids who made Brown's generation look like cream puffs. He visited many of these new offenders in prison, but never finished the book he intended to write about this new generation of manchildren.

That's our loss. Yet looking back at "Manchild," I think it offers ingredients for success for today's hip-hop generation as much as it offered to ours.

Brown dedicated his book to the Wiltwyck School for Boys in upstate New York. That no-nonsense juvenile facility helped him to turn his life around, simply by offering him some older mentors and role models who cared enough to give Brown and his buddies the father figures and tough love they had not received anywhere else. Brown later lamented the demise of such schools for troubled youths "when they were most needed."

No, schools like the Wiltwyck are rare for the kids who need them most, but there are other ways that we, the elders of our various communities, can help fill the gap.

Across the nation today, you can see numerous successful programs for troubled kids that provide the mentoring, ministering, motivation and monitoring our kids need.

Some of them are novel partnerships between the public, the private and the preacher sectors. Boston's Ten-Point Coalition provided one of the more dramatic examples in the 1990s. Led by black ministers like its founder, the Rev. Eugene Rivers, the Ten-Point program brought police, preachers, politicians and parole officers together to help bring troubled kids back from the brink of disaster. Programs like theirs helped reduce Boston's teen homicide rate to zero for almost three years in the mid-1990s.

Much has been written since Claude Brown's heyday about teen supergangs and "superpredators" of all races. But, as one tough Chicago cop once told me, "Yeah, they act tough. But take them away from their gangs and most of them are just kids like any other kids."

That's Brown's lasting message for us.

Today's manchild—and womanchild—still is a kid searching for the promised land. More than ever, it is up to us, their elders, to help them find it.

CHAPTER NINE

CRIME AND CURES?

Columns in this chapter mark milestones in the evolution of crime as a major issue from the crack cocaine wars and "superpredators" alarm in the 1980s, to the more recent right-left moves to reduced or alternative sentences for nonviolent offenders.

The columns also include a look at how the Duke lacrosse fiasco showed racial profiling in reverse and why Chicago's gang violence soared even as a Chicagoan ironically sits in the Oval Office.

JANUARY 5, 1994

MESSAGE TO JACKSON: THE WORD IS CRIME, NOT BLACK CRIMINALS

"There is nothing more painful to me at this stage in my life than to walk down the street and hear footsteps and start thinking about robbery. Then look around and see someone white and feel relieved."

—Rev. Jesse L. Jackson Sr.

Jesse Jackson was looking very much like a has-been as recently as two months ago.

After building up hopes, then ducking out of running for mayor of the District of Columbia, his stellar career as a tree-shaker and headline grabber seemed to slide to the brink of oblivion.

After two unsuccessful campaigns for president, his campaign for District of Columbia statehood, a stillborn issue that he single-handedly reignited, was going nowhere fast. His opposition to NAFTA left his image almost as battered as Ross Perot's opposition left his. Jackson was marching tirelessly for various causes, but was anyone listening?

Well, don't count him out, I cautioned detractors. Jackson was already playing the "Comeback Kid" when Bill Clinton was still smoking without inhaling at Oxford.

Since America is addressing its great questions of race and poverty as poorly as ever, I expected it would only be a matter of time before another crisis of race and poverty would come along that only a Jesse Jackson could address and he would be back in the headlines, strong as ever.

Now, a few months later (surprise, surprise!) Jackson has found his issue: black criminals.

Or, as he puts it, the BBB—"Big Black Brother." In one of his strongest statements, he has admitted, "There is nothing more painful to me at this stage in my life than to walk down the street and hear footsteps and start thinking about robbery. Then look around and see someone white and feel relieved."

To stop the BBB, Jackson has been urging black teenagers not only to behave but also to break their "code of silence" and turn in classmates who are carrying guns or using drugs. I don't know how many will do it, but it's good to hear Jackson say it.

A Ronald Reagan or Dan Quayle saying that would be crucified as a latent or blatant racist. But, with the moral authority that comes with black skin and decades of bashing white power elites, Jackson has won widespread praise and a new wave of media attention.

Riding the wave, Jackson's Washington-based National Rainbow Coalition has teamed with a longtime pal, Bill Cosby, to host a three-day, star-studded "National Black Leadership Conference on Youth Violence and Black on Black Crime" Thursday through Saturday in Washington.

Among the big names: Spike Lee, Salt-n-Pepa, Mary Frances Berry, Roger Wilkins, Marian Wright Edelman, the Rev. Al Sharpton, Atty. Gen. Janet Reno, Detroit Mayor Dennis Archer and Sen. Carol Moseley-Braun. (No word from Sister Souljah.)

Will Jackson's anti-violence campaign do any good? No question that it has done a great deal of good for his public image. With fear of violent crime suddenly soaring as a concern in opinion polls, many who disagree with Jackson on other issues are pulling for him to succeed with this one.

Jackson's stance also has given President Clinton, whose political centrism often has been at odds with Jackson's left-progressivism, to take on black-on-black crime and black-on-black responsibility in his highly publicized November sermon in a black Memphis church.

The real change here is not so much with Jackson as with the way he gets covered. He and most other black groups, particularly at the neighborhood level, have always opposed the terrible toll crime takes on black communities. But major media tend to ignore such self-help efforts in favor of sound bites that, at worst, "Blame Whitey" or, at best, urge more attention to the root causes of crime, like poverty, joblessness and poor education.

If Jackson has helped liberate the airwaves to discuss the toll of black-on-black crime more honestly, he has performed a great service. The most recent FBI statistics show 94 percent of blacks killed are killed by other blacks. As a threat to black life, the Ku Klux Klan doesn't even come close.

But the less happy side of Jackson's bold new stance is that it risks encouraging unhealthy stereotypes by putting a black face on crime, as if blacks, not crime, were the problem. Richard Cohen, the liberal Washington Post columnist (and a friend of mine), who received nationwide criticism from some blacks-including me-a few years ago for sympathizing with jewelry store owners who refused to buzz young black males in past their electronic door openers, said he now feels vindicated by Jackson's statements.

At last, he wrote, maybe we can speak candidly about black crime across racial lines without name calling.

Maybe, but again let's remember: The problem is crime, not blacks.

It is important to note, for example, that the FBI says white crime has increased 250 percent since 1965. Similarly disturbing statistics recently reported by conservative author Charles Murray ("Losing Ground") show a growing "underclass" of long-term poor whites in America, along with growing pathologies among poor whites that the media usually associate with poor blacks.

No, America's crime problems will not be solved simply by locking up blacks. Nothing quick or cheap will solve our problems with crime, race and poverty. Quick fixes only put a lid on our problems for a little while, until the next crisis erupts-and Jackson once again answers the call to action.

JANUARY 27, 2008

IN ABORTION, CRIME STATS, WE SEE WHAT WE WISH
Volatile Issues Defy Predictions

If legalized abortion led to the dramatic 1990s decline in crime, as some people think, will a decline in abortion lead to a crime surge?

That question came to mind as activists last week marked the 35th anniversary of the Supreme Court's Roe v. Wade decision that legalized abortions.

Although the "pro-life" and "pro-choice" groups don't agree on much, both found something to celebrate in the big news of the day: U.S. abortion rates have fallen to a 30-year low.

The New York-based Guttmacher Institute, whose research is cited by both sides in the superheated abortion debate, reported that abortions fell to 1.2 million in 2005 from a peak of 1.6 million in 1990. That's a decline to 19.4 abortions per 1,000 women and girls of reproductive age in 2005 from 27.4 in 1990.

Both sides of the debate applauded the numbers, even as they argued over who should claim the most credit for the decline, which included abortions by pills as well as surgery.

Either way, the numbers served to vindicate Bill Clinton's centrist policy early in his presidency to make abortion "safe, legal and rare." Whether his critics like what he did or not, the trend lines under his watch moved in a direction that can satisfy the largest number of people in this highly contentious issue.

But every silver lining has its cloud. Although abortion declined in the 1990s, crime dropped even faster. Some folks see a connection. The most controversial hypothesis as to why crime dropped in the 1990s attributes the decline to the emergence of legal abortions two decades earlier.

Preventing the birth of many unwanted babies meant fewer teens and young adults who would be most likely to commit crimes in the 1990s, according to the theory famously proposed by the economists Steven Levitt and John Donohue, and later popularized in Levitt's 2005 best seller, "Freakonomics."

Just before the Jan. 22 anniversary of the Roe decision, Levitt took a new look at the numbers and mused in his New York Times blog on how the recent decline in abortions might predict future crime patterns.

The answer?

It depends on why abortion rates are falling, he writes, "and I'm not sure we know the answer to that question."

I appreciate his humility. Although I stand firmly on the pro-Roe side of the abortion debate, I have always been troubled by theorists who try to make too much of the decision's long-term benefits.

Supporting that view is Franklin E. Zimring, a criminologist at the University of California at Berkeley who reviewed the data and found: "The crime decline of the 1990s was a classic example of multiple causation with none of the many contributing causes playing a dominant role."

American women already were reducing their birth rates a decade before Roe through birth control pills and other measures, Zimring points out in his book, "The Great American Crime Decline." Also, Canada experienced a crime decline that paralleled the one in this country without a Roe v. Wade decision to go along with it.

That's what crime and abortions have in common: Everybody wants crime and abortions to decline and everyone claims credit when they do. Yet, the experts have done a better job of explaining crime and abortion trends than predicting them.

In the early 1990s, experts predicted that a new generation of young "superpredators" would make crime shoot through the roof. Instead, crime rates fell through the floor.

The noted social scholar James Q. Wilson of Pepperdine University, for example, predicted that the first decade of the next century will see "30,000 more young muggers, killers and thieves than we have now. Get ready." But a few years later Wilson admitted to a New York Times reporter, "So far, it clearly hasn't happened" and that "This is a good indication of what little all of us know about criminology."

Recent surges in violent crime in cities like Philadelphia and Los Angeles reflect the constantly changing, yet highly local, nature of such problems. In a world of rapidly changing science and social attitudes, the same is true of a sensitive and highly individualized issue like abortion. The best lesson for us to remember in dealing with the future is to remember what worked in the past. Then keep doing it.

JANUARY 9, 2013

TREAT CITY'S HOMICIDE SURGE AS AN EPIDEMIC

For once, Chicago has beaten New York in a competition that the Windy City had no desire to win. Chicago ended 2012 with more homicides than New York. No one cheers for that.

Chicago, with only a third of New York's population, ended 2012 with 506 slayings, compared with 418 in New York. Even Charles Dickens would be taken aback by this tale of two cities.

It's the first time Chicago topped 500 homicides since 2008, when Barack Obama's election to the White House brought renewed national attention to his hometown's crime statistics.

Gun lovers, for example, can barely suppress their glee as they see Chicago's bad fortune with firearms as a rebuke to gun control and other policies pushed by President Obama and Mayor Rahm Emanuel, Obama's former chief of staff. If only the issue were that simple.

In fact, as New York Mayor Michael Bloomberg recently pointed out, New York state has some of the toughest gun control laws in the nation. But illegal guns will keep finding their way into the wrong hands as long as people can go to the suburbs or another state for weapons.

Pardon the pun, but there is no simple magic bullet solution to big-city crime woes, although everyone has their favorites. Here's mine:

Chicago's latest homicide surge calls for a shift in how we view crime fighting. Too much of our thinking about homicide waves and other urban crime is based on outdated models. Instead of waging "war" against homicides, we need to treat such reoccurring waves as an epidemic.

Gone are the huge street gangs and illegal drug networks I used to cover as a young Chicago reporter in the 1970s and '80s. Large street gangs have been broken up, much like Tony Soprano's mob under pressure from federal RICO (Racketeer Influenced and Corrupt Organizations Act) laws.

Instead, academics and law enforcement experts agree that violent crime has gone in the direction that today's newspaper planning editors like to call "hyperlocal."

The old "supergangs" who fought deadly turf wars over lucrative street-corner drug markets have become fragmented and dispersed into hundreds of harder-to-track street "cliques" using firearms to settle petty beefs.

The old metaphors of military intelligence and assault work fine in waging war against well-organized gangs with known networks and hierarchies. Violence by hundreds of small street-corner cronies is frustratingly random and hard to anticipate without close-up knowledge and personal associations with the community.

The epidemic metaphor is often associated with experts like Dr. Gary Slutkin, a University of Illinois at Chicago epidemiologist who, after battling the spread of diseases in Africa, applied his knowledge to the virus of violence in Chicago streets. His work led to the creation of CeaseFire, an organization now known as Cure Violence, which puts "violence interrupters" into neighborhood "hot spots" to interrupt violence that feeds more violence.

Among other differences with New York, Chicago demolished its high-crime, low-income public housing high-rises—including Robert Taylor Homes, the nation's biggest. Getting rid of what many called "high-rise ghettos" of concentrated poverty, gangs and crime was beneficial, but it displaced thousands of residents into neighborhoods that are now experiencing the greatest rise in homicides.

"Much of that violence from the high-rises has spilled out into the neighborhoods, where it attracts more attention by the rest of the city," said Alex Kotlowitz, author of "There Are No Children Here" and co-producer of an award-winning PBS "Frontline" documentary, "The Interrupters." "They've eliminated those high-rise pockets of extreme crime, yet there are still places in the neighborhoods where the knowledge of violence feels very oppressive, even to those who have not experienced it directly."

Chicago police Superintendent Garry McCarthy, among other ideas, has called for stiffer penalties for crimes committed with a gun. Even the National Rifle Association, the politically powerful lobby that seldom sees a new anti-gun law that it likes, has supported such moves that don't penalize lawful gun owners.

But more work also needs to be done on the ground by police, street workers, churches and other community leaders to deal with the environment that generates the virus of violence—before it spreads.

NOVEMBER 7, 2001

LESSONS FROM THE 'HOOD ABOUT LIVING WITH TERROR

As America struggles to adjust to terrorism, I turned to some voices of experience for advice.

They are unfortunately easy to find.

In a country where one in six children still live in poverty, despite some gains in the prosperous 1990s, many families have learned to live with the terror that the entire country is beginning to share.

In neighborhoods where parents routinely fear for themselves and their children as they go about their daily lives, the "new normalcy," as Vice President Dick Cheney called it, is not much different from the old normalcy.

Kerron Weston knows. In 1993, the Washington, D.C., woman's 28-year-old brother, Gary, was shot to death in a quarrel in a District of Columbia alley.

Six months later, she, too, was shot. She was hit in the neck by a bullet during a shootout near the Environmental Protection Agency office where she works as a program analyst.

The bullet barely missed a major blood vessel, but she dismisses the suggestion that she is lucky to be alive.

"Luck is for people who believe in the lottery and scratch tickets," she told me. "I don't believe in luck. I believe in God!"

A few months later, in 1994, her faith was tested further when her nephew, Leroy, was shot and killed for a jacket he was wearing.

How does she cope?

"Tragedy helped draw our family that much closer," she said. "We try to help each other understand what love and life is about, control our anger and figure out what to do with it."

She "threw" herself into community work. She volunteered to counsel other survivors of violence at a community center at Hunter Pines, a Section 8 apartment development.

She also helped organize Survivors of Homicide Inc., a support group to help people through their grief.

"The community work I do came out of that experience of teaching the value of life, of conflict reaction and of not reacting with violence to every negative word," she said. "That's kind of what I do to try to heal."

Her story echoes three themes I have heard repeatedly from those who have experienced neighborhood violence: faith, family and community.

"Make the best of a bad situation," said Tyrone Parker, of the Alliance of Concerned Men.

After his son was shot to death in 1991, Parker helped organize the alliance in Washington, D.C. In 1997, it mediated a truce in a "war" between two gangs in the district's Benning Terrace housing development, a war that had claimed nine lives and terrorized the neighborhood in the pervious two years.

Acting as mentors, alliance members, some of whom were reformed ex-offenders, helped some youths quit their gangs and find jobs. The development's homicide rate was reduced to zero in 1999.

"Americans should be encouraged by the stories of those who have had troubles yet still march on," Parker said.

Yes, they should. Since Sept. 11, the entire country has begun to learn what terror feels like. Terror attacks and anthrax scares have made the future feel less certain, more fragile, more threatening.

In neighborhoods where violence is not new, residents turn to whatever resources they have at hand, beginning with family, friends, churches and other neighborhood networks.

"Ground zero is happening every day for the grass-roots people we work with in violent neighborhoods," said Robert Woodson, head of the Washington-based National Center for Neighborhood Enterprise, which helps neighborhood-based community groups. "Every day is their version of Afghanistan."

"They have a choice. They either become apathetic or they fight against it. They either become apathetic or they organize and they reach out to help save their community and themselves."

That pretty well describes the task that lies before us Americans today.

Many Americans have made a habit of avoiding neighborhoods plagued by crime and violence. But they may have a lot to teach us.

Today we are faced with outsiders who want to kill us for no other reason than the fact that we are American.

The world has become a dangerous neighborhood. We can't run away from it. We can only try to improve it—with faith, family and sense of community that tries to embrace all of us.

SEPTEMBER 30, 2009

VIOLENCE VIDEOS SPUR BAD POLITICS

Americans are shocked by youth violence—again. What a difference videos make.

The fatal beating of a South Side teenager shocks the world, as it should. Yet the real tragedy differs little from a trail of similar kid-on-kid violence, except that it was caught on video.

We easily become benumbed after years of tragic headlines about youth violence. Then we get jerked alert by the horrific video images of youths fatally beating 16-year-old Derrion Albert, an honor roll student at Fenger High School.

In our horror it is natural for us to look for someone to blame besides the suspects that police have rounded up with the help of the video that the Internet beams around the planet.

It just happens to be the bad fortune of President Barack Obama and Chicago Mayor Richard M. Daley that this tragedy coincides with their efforts to woo the International Olympic Committee, which decides Friday whether Chicago will beat out Rio de Janiero, Tokyo and Madrid to host the 2016 Olympics.

As Richard Nixon once said of presidential campaigns, there are no silver medals in this race. The competition for the games is intense and so is the opposition in Chicago. Chicagoans were about evenly split on hosting the games, according to a recent Chicago Tribune poll. The Internet crackles with critics of the Olympics, Daley, Obama or all three. Some raise the death of Derrion Albert and other young victims of school or street violence to argue Chicago might be too unsafe, too corrupt or too indifferent to the plight of its poor to host the Olympics.

Unsafe? Compared to ... Rio?

Here's an Associated Press account of life in Rio during a week in early September: A police shootout "stopped a commuter train and sent passengers fleeing for cover." Officers conducted a drug raid on a slum, "keeping 2,000 children out of school." Police gun battles "killed more than a dozen suspected traffickers." Yet that was the same week that the IOC released a report that gave high praise to Rio's bid for the 2016 Games.

The sad fact is that most of the violence that plagues metropolises like Rio or Chicago occurs in parts of town to which tourists do not usually go. Tragically, this makes the pain of poverty and violence too easily ignored by those who could do something about it. Yet video and the Web have the power to break down the emotional walls that separate communities from one another, even when they transmit a misleading message.

For example, those who are moved by video to judge Chicago's liveability are no more ridiculous than Rush Limbaugh's recent rant after Matt Drudge's Drudge Report website posted another video of youth violence: a school bus security camera in downstate Illinois captured a black kid pounding on a white kid in the next seat.

Police reported, but then discounted the possibility, that the incident was a hate crime. But Limbaugh was not deterred by a mere lack of evidence. "Greetings, my friends. It's Obama's America, is it not?" he bellowed. "Obama's America—white kids getting beat up on school buses now. I mean, you put your kids on a school bus, you expect safety, but in Obama's America, the white kids now get beat up with the black kids cheering, 'Yeah, right on, right on, right on!'"

Note to Rush: Most black youths have not exclaimed "right on" since the days when you and I were young.

The truth is that race has little to do with youth violence compared to the impact of poverty and the disconnection from hope. There is good news happening in some violence-plagued neighborhoods, even if it occurs too quietly to get as much media attention as the violence does.

A variety of neighborhood-based programs have shown real success in reducing youth violence. One leading example is the "violence-free zones" that police and school officials in Milwaukee, Baltimore, Atlanta, Dallas and Richmond, Va., have organized with assistance from the Washington-based Center for Neighborhood Enterprise.

"The Chicago tragedy is part of a plague sweeping the country," said Robert Woodson, the center's founder and president. "Kids are targeted not for being in a gang but for coming from a different neighborhood."

The key to a "violence-free zone," as Woodson explains it, is adult "youth advisers" who have enough local connections and street savvy to win the trust of teens, yet who also can pass rigorous background checks. Effective "advisers" build enough trust to serve as "antibodies" in a toxic atmosphere, so kids will alert them to looming troubles without fear of being stigmatized as a "snitch."

In other words, before we waste our breath spouting off about what our kids need, it pays to listen to the kids.

SEPTEMBER 5, 2010

COPS TO STREET GANGS: WAGE PEACE OR LOSE YOUR STUFF

When gang leaders go out of their way to tell the media that the latest police crackdown tactic isn't going to work, the tactic already may be working.

That was the hidden message in the rambling, poorly focused news conference that current and former gang members held Thursday in Chicago. The city has been associated famously with gangsters more than once, although the gangs usually don't hold news conferences.

Chicago Police Supt. Jody Weis is not playing fair, they said, with the secret "gang summit" he held in mid-August with other street gang leaders.

Join the queue, gentlemen. That controversial event has given some folks on both sides of the city's war against street violence something to hate, which means the superintendent probably is doing something right. Cities faced with similar crime problems are watching to see if he is.

At first, the invitees to the so-called summit were told it would be a routine parole meeting. They expected perhaps a sermon about keeping themselves on the straight-and-narrow. Instead, the city's chief cop appeared with a message to deliver: If gangs don't stop the killings, police will go after their leaders—and the leaders' assets.

"I told them a word they ought to get used to is RICO," Weis later told a reporter.

RICO, short for the 40-year-old Racketeer Influenced and Corrupt Organizations Act, strikes fear into the hearts of organized criminals. RICO can enable federal authorities to target an entire gang as a criminal enterprise, which can lead to arrest and forfeiture of one's cars, house, money, jewelry and other assets.

In other words, stop the killing or we'll take your stuff. Bye-bye, bling! No wonder the veteran gangbangers at the news conference were howling. It is not fair to hold leaders responsible for everything members do, they said. It was not possible, argued a Vice Lords member, "for one person to micromanage a group."

Ah, there's nothing like the prospect of indictment and loss of property to make gang leaders brag about how little power they have.

Yet, Weis is taking heat from the other side just for meeting with "urban terrorists," as one alderman called the parolees. "The top cop should never be negotiating with gang leaders," the alderman said. "Period."

Fortunately for Weis, Mayor Richard M. Daley, who faces re-election in February, backed up his police superintendent. In this war, he said, "We'll negotiate with anyone to have peace."

It is important to note that Weis did not offer the gangbangers a negotiation. He offered an ultimatum: Wage peace or lose your freedom and maybe all of your stuff.

While gang leaders complain, they'll be wise to spread the word as best they can for fear of any new violence that could blow back against them.

The bigger question is whether Weis' RICO threats will work. Some anti-violence specialists have their doubts. Gang leaders can be like kids, they note, digging their heels a little deeper with every threat.

"It's like threatening a kamikaze pilot with death," said Bob Woodson, founder of the National Center for Neighborhood Enterprise, which has helped community groups establish "Violence Free Zones" in a half-dozen cities that have measurably reduced school violence. "You can threaten and threaten until they get to a breaking point where they don't care anymore."

A "holistic approach" works better, says Torrey Barrett, founder of the KLEO Community Family Life Center on Chicago's South Side.

That means inviting police to work more closely with churches, school administrators and community organizations to build after-school activities and "life skills" programs. To dodge gang life, low-income youths need something to do besides steal cars for a joy ride to a police record.

For now, Chicago's holistic approach will have to include the threat of RICO. Although the mayor can point to statistics that show Chicago's homicide rate following national trends, the city has been cursed with a surge in particularly shocking killings, including innocent teens and three police officers killed in two months earlier this summer. The public wants to see some action now. Gangs don't cause all of the city's murders, but if the RICO threat can push them to be part of the solution, use it.

APRIL 25, 2010

STOP KIDS FROM KILLING KIDS

What might the highly publicized suicide of a Massachusetts girl tormented by cyber-bullying have in common with the fatal videotaped beating of a teenage boy in Chicago? Other students apparently knew trouble was brewing, but no one managed to step in and stop it.

Bullying by other teens is alleged to have driven Phoebe Prince, a 15-year-old immigrant from Ireland, to end her life in Massachusetts in January. Six students now face criminal charges, including violation of civil rights and statutory rape.

Four months earlier the world watched Derrion Albert, 16, beaten to death near his high school on Chicago's South Side. Three youths were charged. Students told police that youths from rival neighborhoods had been attacking each other for more than a month. Didn't any adults know? Did anyone know what to do?

Sadly, as anyone who has raised a teenager should know, they give up inside information about what's going on in their world about as easily as CIA agents give up nuclear secrets.

Yet studies of teen violence show that almost every school fight—or worse—is preceded by a "buzz," gossip that may go on for days without adults getting a clue. The key is to gain the confidence of young people in a culture that ranks "snitching" or anything that resembles it to be the height of uncoolness.

Fortunately some old schools are learning new tricks. One that recently impressed me was Forest Park High School in Baltimore, a school that turned the corner on student violence and disorder in ways that sound like a movie just waiting to be discovered by Hollywood.

There's the idealistic principal, Thomas Hill, a former Chicago and Ann Arbor, Mich., resident who is white and therefore, he says, "not expected to last past Christmas" at the all-black school. That was in 2008. He's still there.

So far this year, the school has reduced fights, attacks and suspensions by about 55 percent compared with last year, according to Baltimore public school figures, and reduced expulsions by 70 percent. "And so far this year, no dropouts," said Hill, resisting the temptation to knock on wood.

Part of the credit goes to another character, an idealistic ex-con church leader who would be hard to make up if he didn't already exist: Minister Billy H. Stanfield, a former drug kingpin who says he found the Lord after surviving a botched execution. Yeah. That would work for me, too.

Stanfield's New Vision Youth Services provides youth advisers as mentors from the local community, available 24/7 to help youngsters work out problems ranging from academics to anger issues.

And, yes, there are the kids. Fifteen group homes feed into this one high school where almost 30 percent of the students are classified as having "special needs."

Several spoke to me with poignant candor about how the program helped them turn their lives around enough for them to help mentor other students. "I used to be angry all the time," said one senior. "I just wanted to fight. I'm still angry. But I'm learning to stay cool about the fighting."

Another key player in this "movie" is the outside facilitator, Robert Woodson, a John D. and Catherine T. MacArthur "genius grant" recipient who founded the Washington-based Center for Neighborhood Enterprise to help organizations like New Vision develop market-oriented solutions to big social problems that government programs couldn't solve.

Since the center initiated its Violence Free Zones program five years ago, it has set up similar programs to Baltimore's in schools in Milwaukee, Atlanta, Dallas and Richmond, Va.

Chicago school officials are considering it, too, encouraged by a Baylor University study of the Violence Free Zone program in Milwaukee.

It found not only reductions in violence similar to Baltimore but also reductions in other crimes like auto thefts near targeted schools.

What a difference better communications make. The key is the youth advisers, said Woodson, who compares them to "antibodies" helping the body fight off diseases. Advisers who are ex-offenders, as some of them are, should not be excluded, since they often know the streets and empathize best with youths as troubled as they once were. But the program does screen them with "FBI standards," Woodson says. That's essential. Everyone knows the reputation of the program could be destroyed by one scandal.

I asked Hill what advice he had for other schools. He suggested tips like: "Honestly, look at where you are now" and "Hire the best people." They don't have to have big academic credentials, he said. Sometimes they just have to care about kids and know how to show it.

JANUARY 10, 2007

IN DUKE CASE, EMOTIONS OVER RACE TRAMPLE FACTS

It's hard to say which is unraveling faster: the sexual-assault case against three former Duke University lacrosse players or the public's interest in it. Too many facts can ruin a good story for folks who already have made up their minds.

The Duke players should be prosecuted "whether it happened or not," a student at North Carolina Central University, a mostly black college, told Newsweek a few weeks after the March incident. "It would be justice for things that happened in the past."

No, it wouldn't. It would be racial reparations run amok and morphed into mob justice.

As with earlier media-fueled eruptions over race, sex, politics, celebrity and class privilege, the Duke case in many minds is about feelings, not facts. It is not about the accused lacrosse players or the accusing woman. It is about the personal pain that this drama represents to the rest of us.

As a feast of familiar stereotypes, the Duke story has it all: rich white boys allegedly gone wild; a struggling single black mom and college student who reportedly turned to stripping to make ends meet; an outspoken white prosecutor who needed black votes in a tough re-election bid; and a publicity-savvy "dream team" for the defense.

After promising black voters that he would not let the Duke case drop against the players he called "hooligans," Mike Nifong, the district attorney for North Carolina's Durham County, indicted two of the players two weeks before the election. He narrowly won the three-way district attorney's race.

But just before Christmas the accuser said she could not say for sure whether she was raped, and Nifong had to throw out the rape charges. Yet, he left the charges of sexual assault and kidnapping still pending against the three defendants.

So much for his declarations on MSNBC in March: "I am convinced that there was a rape, yes sir." He also cited an emergency-room nurse's report to a local radio station that indicated "some type of sexual assault did, in fact, take place." That was before DNA tests failed to match the alleged assailants to the accuser.

As Nifong's case fizzles, he's beginning to resemble the worst descriptions of President Bush's Iraq policy, stuck with a lost cause and not much of an exit strategy, yet refusing to pull out.

Meanwhile, Duke President Richard Brodhead has invited the two players who were suspended (one already graduated) back to school. Brodhead also has called for the district attorney to step aside and give control of the case to an independent party "who can restore confidence in the fairness of the process." That's asking a lot.

And lost in the furor are the people who have to live with the aftermath.

However the Duke case plays out, it offers some valuable lessons about rushing to judgment. Nifong's questionable statements and actions should remind law-and-order hardliners that prosecutors are not always right.

Our long history of injustices has made black Americans particularly sensitive to the rights of the accused black, but we also can't forget the rights of suspects who are not black. After all, if institutional racism still holds any power at all, then rights that are denied to whites today can just as easily be denied to blacks tomorrow.

And, while the accuser's media image doesn't look very sympathetic these days, she too has rights. We can still feel for her. What we don't know is all of the facts.

CHAPTER TEN

PRISON PIPELINES, REVERSING THE FLOW

After crime, we look at punishment. This chapter's columns look at how even the NAACP and tea party Republicans found surprising common ground in the incarceration-reduction movement for different reasons: Sensible sentencing also saves money. Among other topics, libertarians like Rand Paul turn out to be way more progressive than President Obama on marijuana legalization.

SEPTEMBER 1, 2002

WHEN PRISONS LURE MORE THAN COLLEGES

Here's a late-summer news item that made me feel about as sick as a crow with West Nile virus:

There are now more black men behind bars in America than in its colleges and universities.

So says the Justice Policy Institute, a Washington-based research center, which found a black inmate population explosion over the past two decades, an era of booming prison construction and get-tough-anti-crime legislation.

In 1980 there were three times more black men enrolled in colleges and universities (463,700) than in prisons (143,000), the study said. By 2000, black male numbers grew to 791,600 in prison, but only to 603,032 on campus.

Although the two groups are not directly comparable, since the college figures count a narrower student-age population, the numbers do dramatize a disturbing trend. Despite the progress African-Americans have made, too many young black males are slipping back into becoming tax consumers in prison instead of taxpayers.

The Justice Policy Institute favors alternatives to incarceration when such alternatives are appropriate. So do I. I also favor alternatives to the leading cause of incarceration, which is crime. Young people do not naturally fall into lives of crime unless their elders fail to steer them toward better choices.

I once met with a group of ex-convicts, almost all of whom happened to be black like me, at the Safer Foundation, a remarkably effective post-prison rehabilitation program based in Chicago. I asked each of them to think back to when they were kids and tell me what they wanted to be.

"A lawyer," said one.

"A carpenter," said another.

"A railroad engineer," said another.

None of them said they had wanted to be gangsters.

It's the same with kids today. Ask them what they want to be when they grow up and you probably are not going to hear, "I want to be a thug."

Yet after meeting with the adult ex-offenders in Safer's headquarters, I encountered another group of male ex-offenders, all teenagers. Unlike their elders, they were adopting the properly defiant cool-tough pose as they strutted single-file down the hall. Seldom have I seen the tendency of kids to rise—or fall—to society's expectations demonstrated so dramatically.

Criminologists speak of the "labeling effect," in which police and others label kids as outlaws and, in a self-fulfilling prophecy, the labeling encourages the youths to act out that identity.

As the father of a 13-year-old manchild, I am acutely aware of how young black males appear to be particularly vulnerable to the lure of "thug life" and all of its trappings, compared to the lure of campus life. This imbalance helps to explain why black women have been earning college degrees at twice the rate of black men in recent years, according to federal Department of Education statistics.

Women outnumber men on campus nationally for the first time, but the gap is particularly striking among blacks. Whereas women now comprise about 55 percent of overall undergraduate enrollment, black women outnumber black men by about two to one.

An achievement gap appears as early as elementary school. When girls appear to be more cooperative and studious, many of us grownups tend to lower our expectations of boys. As a result, we often give them less attention at a time when we should be giving them more.

It would be nice if all of the boys who do not go to college found gainful employment elsewhere, but quite the opposite tends to happen. Disproportionately larger numbers of them are chronically jobless and involved in criminal activity. Even those who work are more vulnerable to layoffs and other economic disruptions if they don't get some education or training beyond high school.

Locking up bad guys is important but it is also expensive. In today's tightened economy, governors increasingly are faced with tough spending choices. More prisons or more universities? Which would you choose?

More attention needs to be given to the supply-side end of our criminal population.

Distressed neighborhoods need more police on the street, but they also need more youth-intervention programs and volunteers to bring youths and older citizens together. It is nice that some of us leave our daily work worlds to drop in for an occasional "career day" at a local school, but it is not enough. We also need to involve ourselves whenever possible in the daily lives of young people, if only to show them that, no matter who they are, they have alternatives in life. They just need help in making the right choices.

AUGUST 14, 2013

PUT SOME SENSE BACK INTO SENTENCING

Up against the wall, Mr. Mayor! Sometimes law enforcers need to be stopped, questioned and frisked, too.

I am referring, of course, to New York City Mayor Michael Bloomberg. The usually likable Mayor Mike unfortunately hasn't done enough in the eyes of U.S. District Judge Shira Scheindlin to flush racial and ethnic profiling out of his city's stop-and-frisk police policies.

Her ruling came coincidentally on the same day that Attorney General Eric Holder announced a new policy to reduce the use of "draconian mandatory minimum sentences" against low-level, nonviolent drug offenders.

Both moves illustrate a sea change in the nation's attitudes toward crime, the drug war and the outlandish cost in tax dollars and ruined lives of what both political sides criticize as "the prison-industrial complex."

Ironically Holder, in a Democratic administration, is rolling back tough-sentencing policies that originally were pushed by Democratic lawmakers who didn't want to look soft on crime in President Ronald Reagan's 1980s.

But now? What a difference a generation, smarter community policing and a mid-1990s plunge in crime rates make.

Even in today's polarized politics, the bipartisan coalition that escalated the war on crime is being emulated by a bipartisan coalition to replace costly mass incarceration with smarter alternative sentences.

"With nearly every state budget strained by the economic crisis," Americans for Tax Reform president Grover Norquist wrote in the conservative National Review, "it is critical that conservatives begin to stand up for criminal-justice policies that ensure the public's safety in a cost-effective manner."

Norquist and other big-name conservatives such as former House Speaker Newt Gingrich, former Florida Gov. Jeb Bush and former drug czar William Bennett have signed on to the Texas-based Right on Crime, a leader in seeking cost-effective alternatives to mass incarceration for nonviolent offenders.

In a statement on behalf of Right on Crime, Marc Levin, of the Texas Public Policy Foundation, said, "It's good to see the (Obama) administration following the lead of conservative states such as Texas, South Carolina and Georgia that have proven it's possible to reduce crime while also reducing criminal justice spending."

Stop and frisk and mandatory minimum prison sentences are emblematic of the "tough-on-crime" drug-war politics that began in the era of President Richard Nixon and reached a fever pitch during the Reagan years.

Yet, as Holder said, too many small-time or first-time offenders were sentenced to too much time for too little of a crime. Today, he said, the system has 40 percent more prisoners than it was designed to hold—with almost half doing time for drug offenses.

The big remaining question amid these new attitudes is whether Congress, especially in the Republican-controlled and perpetually locked-in-gridlock House, will respond with bipartisan alternatives for those who already have been incarcerated. Bipartisan bills have been introduced in both chambers to ease mandatory minimums, but they're awaiting hearings. Sensible leadership needs to give them a nudge.

On the stop-and-frisk front, there have been too many stops, especially among young black and Hispanic males, and too few arrests.

Of the 4.4 million times that New Yorkers were stopped and frisked between 2004 and 2012, according to the New York Civil Liberties Union, 88 percent of the stops failed to turn up evidence of a crime—and 80 percent of those detained were black or Hispanic.

Yet, Judge Scheindlin did not overturn the stop-and-frisk policing policy. It remains in her eyes an important tool of law enforcement that, as the mayor says, has widespread support—even in crime-plagued neighborhoods that produce most of the complaints about its abuse.

But as it has been practiced on the street, Scheindlin's ruling called it "indirect racial profiling."

To remedy that situation, she ordered a new independent police monitor and some police will have to wear cameras while on the beat. That would help to make sure, among other things, that the stop-and-frisk stops meet the "reasonable suspicion" standard set by U.S. Supreme Court precedents.

That's not too much to ask in the continuing struggle to find a sensible balance between liberty, privacy and crime fighting.

MAY 29, 2011

BRING BACK THE 20 STINGING LASHES?

When Peter Moskos' new book landed on my desk, I wasn't sure if it was going to be a treatise on crime and punishment or some sort of kinky sex manual.

Its title: "In Defense of Flogging."

You rascal, I thought. Moskos, a former Baltimore cop who teaches law at John Jay College of Criminal Justice, knows how to catch our attention.

It's not giving away too much to say that Moskos doesn't really want to bring back flogging. But he doesn't like our correctional system, either. And as long as we insist on fooling ourselves with well-meaning fantasies like the "war on drugs," he says, nothing is going to get better.

There already are about 14 gazillion other books that will tell you that. So Moskos uses the horror of flogging to focus our minds on the greater horrors that have resulted from the prisons that were invented to replace the lash.

He builds his argument on a simple question: If you were convicted of a felony and had a choice between "five years or 10 lashes" as dealt in Singapore and Malaysia, which would you choose?

Yes, flogging is brutal. It breaks skin and requires days to heal. Many call it barbaric. But what does it say about us and the brutality in our prisons, Moskos argues, that more than a few small-time offenders would probably prefer the lash to incarceration?

The U.S. Supreme Court expressed similar sentiments in a 5-to-4 decision last week that ordered California to transfer or release more than 30,000 inmates from its overcrowded prisons over the next two years.

Justice Anthony M. Kennedy, writing for the majority, described in lurid detail a prison system that houses suicidal inmates in "telephone-booth-sized cages without toilets" and produces "needless suffering and death."

Across the nation, shrinking state budgets, tea party politics and bulging prison populations have forced states and the courts to take a new look at sentencing alternatives.

Forty states cut spending on their corrections programs in 2009 and 2010, according to the National Governors Association Center for Best Practices. Vermont, Alabama and many other states are enacting new programs to reduce repeat offenders and find alternative penalties for nonviolent offenses.

State spending on corrections has quadrupled during the past two decades to $52 billion a year, according to an April study by the Pew Center on the States. That's a burden surpassed only by Medicaid as the fastest-growing item in state budgets.

And the concern crosses partisan lines. In April, I wrote about an unusual coalition of the very liberal NAACP with cost-conscious conservatives, including former House Speaker Newt Gingrich and Grover Norquist, head of Americans for Tax Reform, calling for more efficient alternatives to our increasingly expensive and questionably effective emphasis on incarceration.

Against that backdrop, Moskos' startling invitation to reconsider the whip, cane and cat-o'-nine-tails doesn't sound so preposterous. At least it gets us thinking.

Yet the lock-'em-up mentality remains strong. In his spirited dissent, Justice Antonin Scalia ridicules the high court's order to downsize California's prison population as "absurd," "outrageous" and "the most radical ever issued by the court."

That's appropriate rhetoric for a talk-show host, perhaps, but out of touch with the changing realities faced by governors wrestling with overcrowded jails and prisons.

No one denies the need for some people to be locked up. But neither California Gov. Jerry Brown nor any other governor intends to release dangerous "happy-go-lucky felons fortunate enough to be selected," as Scalia described them in a statement from the bench.

Brown already has a plan to move tens of thousands of low-level offenders from state prisons to county jails or to other states, if California's famously feisty Legislature approves the funds. But that's for the state to work out. Scalia understandably opposes micromanagement of state affairs by federal courts. But his argument undervalues the Supreme Court's fundamental role as a protector of individual rights from abuses by government.

I wonder how he feels about flogging.

APRIL 13, 2011

NAACP, RIGHT-WING FOES GET FRIENDLY

Can prominent right wingers like Newt Gingrich and Grover Norquist get along with the very liberal NAACP? Yes, they can, at least on the high cost of prisons.

I'm talking about the recent dance toward common ground taken by some prominent conservatives and the National Association for the Advancement of Colored People.

Paragons of conservatism such as Gingrich, a 2012 Republican presidential hopeful, Norquist, head of Americans for Tax Reform and David A. Keene, former chairman of the American Conservative Union, have endorsed a new NAACP report, "Misplaced Priorities: Over Incarcerate, Under Educate."

Although the trio do not all agree with the NAACP's call for more spending on public education, they found common ground on this much: Americans are spending too much on prisons.

Over the last two decades, the report finds, state spending on prisons grew at six times the rate of state spending on higher education.

Even during the 2009 recession, public funding for public schools and colleges declined while 33 states increased their spending on prisons.

Of the nation's 2.3 million inmates, the report finds, more than 500,000 were convicted of a nonviolent drug offense. This has resulted largely from various "wars" on drugs over the past 40 years. Drug crackdowns led to more police stops, more arrests and more mandatory minimum sentences that judges have to impose, regardless of individual circumstances.

According to the NAACP's report, more than half of all inmates on the local, state and federal level have mental health or drug problems. Many of their situations could be handled at lower cost outside of prison.

An emerging and impressive roster of prominent conservatives agrees. One new cost-conscious group called Right on Crime includes Norquist, Gingrich, former Attorney General Edwin Meese and former drug czar William Bennett.

As some prisons are overcrowded and others stand empty because states can't afford to operate them, some states are increasingly becoming interested in alternative sentencing like home confinement, probation, ankle bracelets and reduced-sentence incentives for education and drug rehabilitation.

Even in notoriously tough-on-crime Texas, boasted NAACP President Benjamin Jealous during a PBS "NewsHour" report, "You have tea party activists and NAACP activists pushing the same (incarceration reform) bills." That's not bad for two groups that last summer were hurling charges of racism at each other.

"I'm delighted to work with the NAACP on this," Norquist told me, putting a new spin on his famous wish to shrink government "down to the size where we can drown it in the bathtub."

Although he's no softy on crime, Norquist points out, costs have been driven up by lawmakers granting prosecutors what they want in budgets without taking a cost-benefit analysis. "Just spending money on something and calling it crime prevention doesn't make it so," he said. "You need to do a cost-benefit analysis of what works and what doesn't work."

What can be done? Disabuse yourself, first of all, of any belief in single, magic-bullet remedies for a problem this complex. Letting too many people skirt prison terms makes no more sense than locking too many people up.

But each level of government needs to take a fresh look at old assumptions about incarceration, many of which were developed in the heat of the super-predator crime fears and crack cocaine tragedies in the 1980s. States are learning new lessons about the benefits of alternative sentencing.

Significantly, while an emerging left-right coalition agrees on the need to find better uses of our prison money, they predictably disagree on what should be done with the savings. At a time when some states spend as much per inmate as a year's tuition to Harvard, the NAACP understandably wants the savings to be redirected to public education. Norquist would just as soon return it to the taxpayers. Hey, they can't agree on everything.

But "we can have that conversation another time," Norquist says. Indeed, despite his firm beliefs, Norquist has long promoted a fundamental rule of political organizing: Don't let the issues on which you disagree get in the way of the issues on which you agree.

MARCH 27, 2013

OBAMA SHOULD LISTEN TO PAUL ON POT FRONT

As the nation's capital prepares to open its first legal medicinal marijuana dispensary and Sen. Rand Paul's call for legalization basks in bipartisan praise, it's time for President Barack Obama to clear the air around his own passive-aggressive position.

Until now, the president has been remarkably adept at taking positions that seemed to be ahead of their time—and getting ahead of them.

For example, when he declared his full support for the right of same-sex couples to marry nationwide, there were fears even among his supporters that he would lose important votes before his re-election campaign, particularly among black churchgoers. Those fears proved to be exaggerated.

But four years after his Justice Department announced the feds will no longer crack down on medicinal marijuana sellers who follow state laws, the president's pot position continues to be dangerously vague and confusing.

In California, where voters approved medicinal marijuana use in 1996, the law was so vaguely worded that about 1,000 dispensaries mushroomed in Los Angeles County alone. Yet busts continued, partly over disputes as to whether the law allowed only nonprofit businesses.

At the other extreme, November ballots in Colorado and Washington state legalized marijuana for recreational use, and the District of Columbia's first dispensary, Capital City Care, has its website up and plans to open in April.

On another front, Sen. Paul, a famously libertarian Kentucky Republican, has introduced a bill with Democratic Sen. Patrick Leahy of Vermont to give judges greater flexibility in sentencing for drug crimes.

In a recent TV interview with Fox News' Chris Wallace that even Think Progress praised as "uncharacteristically sensible," the left-progressive website's equivalent of a four-star review for the Kentucky conservative, Paul got to the heart of the current tragedy: ruined lives.

"Our prisons are full of nonviolent criminals," Paul said. "I don't want to encourage people to do it. I think even marijuana is a bad thing to do. ... But I also don't want to put people in jail who make a mistake."

He spoke forcefully of the many young nonviolent offenders like Obama, who has written about his teen drug indiscretions, and possibly former President George W. Bush, who has politely refused to confirm or deny drug use during the years before he found sobriety.

"Look, the last two presidents could conceivably have been put in jail for their drug use and I really think, you know, look what would have happened," Paul said. "They got lucky, but a lot of poor kids. particularly in the inner city, they don't get lucky, they don't have good attorneys, and they go to jail for these things, and I think it's a big mistake."

On that note, Paul strikes a nerve with me and numerous other African-Americans and civil rights advocates. As Michelle Alexander, an Ohio State University associate law professor, writes in her best-seller, "The New Jim Crow: Mass Incarceration in the Age of Colorblindness," statistics show a majority of African-American men in urban areas to be in jail, on probation, otherwise "under correctional control" or "saddled with criminal records for the rest of their lives."

The result is a new form of second-class citizenship that traps them in "a parallel social universe, denied basic civil and human rights." That includes the right to vote, to serve on juries and to be free of legal discrimination in employment, housing, access to education and other public benefits.

And the financial cost on top of the social cost of the failed "war on drugs" has caused such big conservative names as anti-tax lobbyist Grover Norquist, former House Speaker Newt Gingrich and former Attorney General Edwin Meese to join others in Right On Crime, an organization aimed at promoting less costly and more productive alternatives to incarceration, like drug treatment and community service for nonviolent offenders.

With the trends moving in such a productive direction, I'm hardly alone in wondering what Obama is waiting for. As with the issue of same-sex marriage, his support could get ahead of the trend and help move it along. He can even claim it was his idea all along.

JUNE 15, 2011

DUMP THE WAR ON DRUGS

When David Simon, creator of HBO's late dramatic crime series "The Wire," heard that Attorney General Eric Holder wanted to see the series return for a sixth season, he offered the nation's top prosecutor a deal.

He'll start working on a sequel season, Simon responded in an email to the Times of London, "if the Department of Justice is equally ready to reconsider and address its continuing prosecution of our misguided, destructive and dehumanizing drug prohibition."

Holder was not available for comment, but it's a safe bet Simon's deal asks too much of the Obama administration. Despite declarations to the contrary, Team Obama appears to be stuck in the 40-year-old rut better known as the "war on drugs."

That's how long it has been since President Richard Nixon on June 17, 1971, announced $155 million in new anti-drug funding that he would later call "the war on drugs." A third of the funds would go after drug traffickers and two-thirds of it would be aimed at treatment and rehabilitation. That's called a balanced approach, but it didn't last long.

The lock-'em-up side surged with the mandatory-minimum sentencing under the Anti-Drug Abuse Act of 1986, largely in reaction to the rise of a crack cocaine epidemic and related street violence.

Among the results, a 100-to-one sentencing disparity between crack cocaine and powder cocaine offenses that boosted incarceration rates, particularly of African-Americans—producing statistics that Michelle Alexander, an Ohio State University legal scholar, calls "The New Jim Crow" in her well-researched book with that title.

I come not to praise drug use. I condemn it. But some drug fights work better than others.

A new report by the Global Commission on Drug Policy, which includes former United Nations Secretary General Kofi Annan, President Ronald Reagan's secretary of state, George Shultz, former Federal Reserve Chairman Paul Volcker and the former presidents of Mexico, Brazil and Colombia, calls the global war on drugs a costly failure "with devastating consequences for individuals and societies around the world."

They urged the Obama administration and other governments to try new ways of legalizing and regulating drugs, especially marijuana, to deny profits to drug cartels and focus law enforcement on violent offenders. The White House immediately responded: No way.

So did the government of Mexico, which is allied with the U.S. in a war against drug cartels that have killed more than 38,000 people in Mexico in the last five years.

Obama's drug office fired back with statistics that claimed huge declines in drug use since the peak of the late 1970s. But correlations between those declines and the drug war are highly disputed. What's indisputable is the increased incarceration of millions of Americans, many for simple possession.

To his credit, Holder has called for the U.S. Sentencing Commission to release some of the 12,000 federal prisoners who were sentenced or arrested for crack cocaine before Congress changed the sentencing law last year to reduce the disparity between crack and cocaine. Holder recommended early release for 5,500 prisoners whose crimes did not involve the use of weapons and who did not have long criminal histories. The releases, which could begin this year, would be a good start.

But why, we should reasonably ask, should people be subject to prison terms if their only offense is their use of illegal substances?

"Drug addiction should be handled as a health issue," says Neill Franklin, executive director of Law Enforcement Against Prohibition. The organization released a report Tuesday that finds the Obama administration carrying on the drug war as usual. That includes Drug Enforcement Administration raids of legal medical marijuana clinics at a higher rate than the George W. Bush administration did, despite pronouncements that states would be allowed to govern themselves on that issue.

LEAP favors drug legalization and strict regulation. That means arrest the sellers and send users to treatment. "It's easier to beat a drug addiction," Franklin observed, "than to beat the devastating impact of a prison sentence."

CHAPTER ELEVEN

HEAT-SEEKING MEDIA

(OR IF YOU CAN'T SAY ANYTHING NICE, HOST A TALK SHOW)

If media criticism is America's second-favorite leisure activity, as George Will once observed, today's heat-seeking media offer plenty to chew on. I include former FCC Chairman Newton Minow's 50-year follow-up to his historic "vast wasteland" speech, how Twitter and Stephen Colbert's humor clashed, how right-wing bloggers destroyed ACORN through shoddy pseudo-journalism, how some of Rev. Martin Luther King Jr.'s children sell his legacy to highest bidders, and the value of taking occasional "news fasts" to calm our nerves.

MAY 11, 2011

A PLEA FOR BETTER JUNK ON TELEVISION

Fifty years ago this week, then-Federal Communications Commission Chairman Newton N. Minow famously skewered the nation's daily television programming as "a vast wasteland." Today, it is still largely a wasteland, in my view, because that's mostly what people want.

I have tried to avoid getting too excited about that over the years. After all, bad TV has its good qualities. It provides me with much less of a distraction from life's more useful and rewarding activities—like reading.

But every so often a smart visionary like Minow comes along to remind me that, hey, the public airwaves do belong to the public. That's us. Broadcasters make truckloads of money through our good graces. We let the broadcasters use our airwaves at no cost. For that, we deserve to have a little more than the TV that architect Frank Lloyd Wright described as "chewing gum for the eyes."

In fact, as Minow, now a spry 85, reminded his audience at a commemorative event at the National Press Club, "public service" was the two-word phrase that he had intended the world to remember from his May 9, 1961, speech to the National Association of Broadcasters.

They were not amused. In one subtle sign of grumpy disrespect, Minow recalls, a Hollywood producer named the sinking boat on "Gilligan's Island," the "SS Minnow," camouflaging Minow's name with the additional "N."

But some 4,000 letters mostly applauded Minow's critique, the current FCC Chairman Julius Genachowski recalled at the press club event. Minow cheerfully remembered his favorite: A viewer who wanted to know "What time does 'The Vast Wasteland' go on?"

Alas, a half-century later the metaphor of the vast wasteland remains too vivid—and too appropriate—to be easily forgotten.

You could hear that in the audience laughter as former CNN anchor Frank Sesno, now director of the School of Media and Public Affairs at The George Washington University, read excerpts from Minow's speech. In an average viewing day, it said, "... You will see a procession of game shows, formula comedies about totally unbelievable families, blood and thunder, mayhem, violence, sadism, murder, western bad men, western good men, private eyes, gangsters, more violence, and cartoons. ..."

"What's changed?" Sesno asked, sparking more laughs. That's a good question, Frank.

It's easy to knock today's abundance of unreal "reality TV" shows like "Jersey Shore" or "Keeping Up with the Kardashians" or new-wave versions of old game shows and talent shows like "Celebrity Apprentice" and "American Idol." And it is easy to knock those of us who knock such self-consciously low-brainpower shows as elitists.

Let the marketplace decide, goes the modern argument, especially now that there are so many channels available in the cable TV universe, plus the Internet and other new technologies. Those arguments have merit. The abundance of channels today would have been hard to imagine 50 years ago when, Minow reminds us, there were only three networks and almost no cities had what we now call "public television."

Even so, I often surf around the channels with a Bruce Springsteen song on my mind: "57 Channels (And Nothin' On)." The marketplace practices an elitism of its own. Network programmers race to the bottom of public tastes in order to come out on top of the ratings. The best shows are often on cable channels, which don't use public airwaves but cost extra.

The marketplace in broadcasting tends to reflect the tastes of only a slice of the public, the slice that advertisers view as the most impressionable consumers, especially young people who have money to spend and respond most quickly to whatever TV happens to be selling.

MARCH 12, 2006

TRADING RACES DRAMA
Can We Ever Get Out of the Skin We Were Born In?

Compared to its obvious inspiration, "Black Like Me," it is easy to knock "Black.White.," the new reality TV experiment on race relations on FX—and many people do.

"Nonsense masquerading as substance," scoffs USA Today critic Robert Blanco. Maybe it is. Or maybe it's a rare injection of substance into TV's usual nonsense.

Maybe, wrapped in its unreal "reality-show" grab for drama, suspense and easy laughs, it might actually help us Americans learn something about how we get along or don't get along in our ethnic stir-fry.

In a twist on the TV show "Trading Spouses: Meet Your New Mommy," FX offers what might be called "Trading Races: Meet Your New Angst." Through the magic of modern Hollywood makeup, "Black. White." allows the black Sparks family of Atlanta and the white Wurgel/ Marcotulli family of Santa Monica, Calif., to trade races in suburban Los Angeles.

Racial and ethnic passing are old themes in America, a land of ambitious border crossers:

• Gregory Peck played a journalist who passed for Jewish in the 1947 film "Gentleman's Agreement," to expose everyday anti-Semitism.

• The real-life writer John Howard Griffin turned himself black with a doctor's help to tour the segregated South in 1959 for "Black Like Me." Griffin's racial tourism offered few laughs. It was a relentlessly humiliating and ultimately death-defying experiment. Afterward, he endured death threats for having challenged the South's racial apartheid.

• Years later, Griffin's racial tourism compares to the 1986 movie "Soul Man," in much the same way that lightning is like a lightning bug. A spoof of the "Black Like Me" theme, "Soul Man" offers a white youth who passes for black to get an affirmative-action scholarship to Harvard. Although he eventually learns in typical Hollywood fashion that it's harder out here for a black dude than he thought, "Soul Man" squanders a great opportunity to get substantive for the sake of cheap laughs.

It might be easy for some to say the same about "Black.White." The participants obviously have a tougher time in this, the era of Oprah Winfrey, Barack Obama, etc., to find exciting video of racial conflict. The pilot episode, the only one I have seen, reaches for stereotypes while supposedly trying to break through them. Black father Brian Sparks, for example, is steered as a "white" man to observe life in a "redneck bar" (Note the lingering shot of a bald, burly and tattooed biker guy) and a golf course. White teen Rose Wurgel is steered as a "black" girl to a black poetry slam group. The show's idea of "authentic" white and black experiences obviously leans toward the bold and visual.

And one cannot help but wonder how desperately some of the participants are looking for evidence to fulfill their personal agendas. Brian Sparks, for example, seems hypersensitive to racial slights at times. Even when some white people move aside to let him and artificially black Bruno Marcotulli walk by on the sidewalk, the whites are suspect in

Brian's eyes. Bruno sees common courtesy in their moving aside. Brian suspects bias because he doesn't like "the way they did it."

Bruno bubbles with an irritatingly cheerful sense of liberal white-guy entitlement. A teacher, he seems overly eager to treat black people like his students, preaching the virtues of hard work, proper attitude and high tolerance for racial slurs.

In fact, Bruno, in and out of his blackface, seems to relish throwing around slurs like "honkie" and "nigger," even when they make others wince.

How many episodes, one wonders, before we see a Brian-versus-Bruno smackdown? Hey, suspense is good for ratings, right?

If anything rises up as rays of hope in the pilot episode, it is the teenagers. Rose bubbles with adventurous excitement at the prospect of becoming black for a while. Nick, the Sparks' son, unintentionally upsets his mother by failing to object while he is "white" when a white kid uses the N-word in a conversation.

The youths, typical of a generation that can't even remember when Michael Jackson didn't have a nose job, are a lot more relaxed than their elders about the old racial rules. In the age of white rappers like Eminem or black golfers like Tiger Woods, it's not as big of a deal as it used to be for today's teenagers to cross racial boundaries. Some of them are doing it every day.

APRIL 26, 2006

COURT OF PUBLIC OPINION GOES LOCO

As big news stories go, the Duke University lacrosse team's rape scandal already feels like old news even as new news breaks.

That's because the defendants are being tried in two courts: the criminal justice system and the COPO, the Court of Public Opinion.

A prosecutor has indicted two members of the team for the alleged rape of one of two young women hired to perform what is delicately called "exotic dance" at an off-campus team party-gone-wild.

If that's all there was to it, this would be a local story, although a sad one for everybody involved.

But add the juicy elements of race (the suspects are white, the alleged victim black), class (the lacrosse guys come from money, the dancer is a working-class single mother who attends the historically black North Carolina Central University) and celebrity (Duke is to universities what Tom Cruise and Katie Holmes are to People magazine), and you have our biggest media racial eruption since, say, that fateful night when Kobe Bryant called for room service in Colorado.

In the COPO, old wounds are ripped open along lines of race and class, struggle and privilege, titillation and exploitation. Old fears, resentments and suspicions bloom again that a black woman or white man or (fill in your grievance group) cannot get a fair shake in the (take your pick) "racist," "sexist" or "politically correct" media or court system. These are the elements that draw a circus of cable TV-news gabbers and talk-radio yakkers, unfettered in their drive to fill air time by anything so trivial as, oh yes, an absence of facts.

If Rev. Jesse Jackson or Rev. Al Sharpton do not parachute in on their own, they will be invited. Rush Limbaugh, for one, openly taunted them to come to town as he called the victim a "ho," a remark for which he later apologized. (He was "running on fumes" that day, he said. OK, Rush, but what's your excuse on other days?)

MSNBC talk-show host Tucker Carlson challenged the credibility of a "crypto-hooker" who "hires herself out to dance naked" in front of strangers, as if the strangers who hire that dancer are not equally suspect. Ah, what a tangled web tough-on-crime conservatives weave when they try to defend rowdy jocks.

The first casualty of a media circus is the truth. Everything we are hearing about evidence and personal reputations is secondhand, highly selective and carefully spun by high-powered lawyers on both sides.

For example, none of the DNA samples from the team connected any of the players to an attack on the woman, but most rape convictions are made without any DNA match, legal experts say. It is we, the public, who have exaggerated the importance of DNA after watching, say, too many episodes of "CSI."

Besides, nurses said the woman's injuries are consistent with rape, but the athletes claim someone else must have raped her. Leaked photos suggest that the woman was injured before she went to the party, but other photos suggest she received new injuries while she was there.

Outsiders say race had nothing to do with it, but other accounts differ. For example, a neighbor outside the March 13 party at the Durham,

N.C., house rented by three of the four captains of the Duke lacrosse team, says he heard one partygoer yell, "Thank your grandpa for my nice cotton shirt."

And on and on. "Pick your fact," writes Dahlia Lithwick, legal expert for the online magazine Slate, after going over the known evidence. "Each of them can, it seems, be spun both ways." That is, pick your facts to match your prejudices or whatever grievance on which you want this case to stand.

Small wonder that a lot of people lose faith in the ability of the courts to bring justice, let alone satisfaction, in such disputes. Think back, for example, to Clarence Thomas and Anita Hill, Tawana Brawley, or the trials of O.J. Simpson and Michael Jackson. How satisfying were those outcomes?

Don't expect much satisfaction in this case, either. Once the opposing sides are dug in around a racial eruption, their heels stay dug in.

But I don't blame the regular courts. I blame the Court of Public Opinion, energized the media. When the COPO goes loco, genuine news turns into a form of pornography and it becomes harder for both the accused and the alleged victims to find justice.

APRIL 2, 2014

COLBERT SATIRE AND TWITTER A BAD MIX

One of the first unwritten but widely respected rules of satire is that somehow, somewhere, someone simply isn't going to get the joke.

And if they don't get the joke, you get taken seriously about something you don't really believe.

That makes Stephen Colbert, who has turned a satirical version of himself into a Comedy Central superstar of fake news, one of the bravest people on television.

It is therefore appropriate that he has found himself caught up in a real-time example of a new hazard of the digital age: Satire and Twitter go together like drunks and driving.

"Who would have thought," he lamented Monday night, "that a means of communication limited to 140 characters would ever create misunderstandings?"

No kidding. Or maybe he was. It's sometimes hard to tell when the real Colbert dives deeply into his self-described role as Stephen Colbert, the "willfully ignorant" right-wing pundit.

He was responding in this instance to last week's angry Twitter eruptions over a segment in which he satirized Washington Redskins owner Dan Snyder's new nonprofit. Aimed at helping Native Americans, it is called, yes, the Washington Redskins Original Americans Foundation.

Colbert heard irony in Snyder's use of a racial slur to name a foundation that was created to perfume the slur that many, including me, hear in the pro football team's name.

So fake-conservative Stephen Colbert responded by announcing his own group: the Ching Chong Ding Dong Foundation for Sensitivity to Orientals or Whatever.

Edgy? Uncomfortable? Yes. But satire is supposed to make you at least a little uncomfortable. In his show's context, the joke worked. The audience laughed with Colbert and groaned at Snyder's tone-deaf—or tone-indifferent—cluelessness.

Trouble came later, Colbert explained this week, when "a Web editor I've never met" tweeted his Ching Chong punch line without its setup or even posting a link to any mention of Snyder's foundation.

Among those who were outraged by that naked tweet was Suey Park, a 23-year-old freelance writer and hashtag activist. To the uninitiated, that means she raises issues by attaching a hashtag (#) to her written viewpoints in the hope that they will get virally retweeted on Twitter.

Park rocketed to Twitter stardom in December with #NotYourAsianSidekick, a provocative invitation to a much-needed debate about Asian-American stereotypes that trended for several days.

She since has been named one of The Guardian's top 30 young people in digital media, garnering international fame that would make Andy Warhol smile.

Her new cause, #CancelColbert, outdid her previous campaigns, triggering frontlash and backlash in every direction. Critics blasted Colbert and were blasted back by Colbert fans, political correctness opponents and a broad zoo of general-purpose haters.

Genuine right-wingers in some cases used #CancelColbert as a golden opportunity to vent their long-held outrage at Colbert's fake conservatism. Snyder's R-word controversy was lost in the Twitter storm.

To his credit, fake Colbert asked people to stop attacking Park. "She's just speaking her mind," he said. "That's what Twitter is for, as well as ruining the ending of every show I haven't seen yet."

Quite right. For that, I give what the fake Colbert would call a "Tip of the Hat" to the real Colbert and a "Wag of the Finger" to the haters. We can disagree without being disagreeable, as President Barack Obama likes to say, although you wouldn't know it from some of his critics either.

Satire is not dead, as some grumps have tweeted in response to this dust-up. But Colbert demonstrates that good satire requires a tad more than a birdbath's depth of thinking to create or appreciate.

It requires context to be provided by the satirist and understood by the audience. Context, more often than not, exceeds the capacity of a Twitter tweet, unless it includes a link to something longer than 140 characters.

Park has said in interviews that she usually likes Colbert's show but hates the ways in which Asian-Americans too often become a go-to group for comedians to ridicule.

As an American, not just an African-American, I sympathize. When your only way to talk back is offered by social networks, every problem becomes a potential tweet.

Just keep it short, please. And if you're joking, let us know it.

AUGUST 16, 2009

A RACE CARD FROM THE RIGHT WING

I thought slavery reparations was a dead issue. Glenn Beck set me straight.

The radio talk-show host and Fox News Channel star says President Barack Obama's proposed health-care overhaul is really "stealth reparations," a form of racial payback in Beck's words.

I am not making this up. On his radio program last month and in a video floating around the Web, Beck argues that Obama's announced opposition to reparations is only a smoke screen for his "stealth" support of reparations.

How does Beck know? Through his own tortured logic, he takes Obama's argument for color-blind alternatives to color-conscious concepts like reparations and affirmative action and turns the argument on its head. He is happy that Obama opposes reparations, Beck says, but he dislikes Obama's reasons for opposing it.

Try to follow Beck's logic here. It's not easy.

When asked about reparations and affirmative action during his presidential campaign, Obama said he preferred programs that targeted poverty, education and other social problems based on need, not color. Beck correctly quotes Obama as saying programs like "universal health care ... will disproportionately affect people of color because they are disproportionately uninsured."

The same is true for programs aimed at improving education, housing and job opportunities. Obama's reasoning is hardly in dispute. Polls and the November election show that Obama's belief in helping those most in need, regardless of race, creed or color, is the sort of common-sense social policy that most Americans support across political party lines.

In fact, since low-income whites outnumber low-income blacks overall, even though a higher percentage of blacks are in poverty, more whites would receive help than would other Americans.

Yet, Beck insists Obama is pushing "universal health care, universal college, green jobs as stealth reparations." Why would Obama do that? Because, says Beck, "It's a much less obvious route to reparations."

Less obvious? You've got me there, Glenn. Your conspiracy theory makes about as much sense as the 98-pound boxer who hopes to beat Mike Tyson by tiring him out.

Yet, Beck is not alone in his twisted logic. Rush Limbaugh, the Big Kahuna of conservative radio talkers, declared in a June broadcast that Obama's "entire economic program is reparations," although Limbaugh did not explain why he thinks that way. The mere mention of the R-word is enough in Limbaugh's logic to condemn Obama's "wealth redistribution."

Do such not-so-subtle race cards have an effect? One example may be Richie Drake, a disabled sheet-rock installer in Bristol, Va. He was unemployed and his children were on Medicaid, yet he told a National Public Radio reporter last month that he wants no part of the Obama overhaul. "Minorities are going to get more attention than the whites and stuff like that," he said. "That's the way I take it from what the news was talking about."

Add to Drake's misimpressions the rising prominence of the "birthers," who insist against all evidence that Obama may not be a natural-born citizen. Add the "tea-party" protesters who appear to have re-emerged to help disrupt town hall health-care meetings.

Amid the headline-making mayhem, one can be forgiven for thinking Obama's lofty vision of a post-racial, post-partisan presidency in "not red state or blue state but the United States of America" seems to have gone the way of twice-a-day mail delivery.

Still, I am an optimist. Just beneath the noise of town hall protesters there's a real health-care debate going on. It's just hard to separate the folks who have legitimate questions from those refighting last year's presidential election campaign.

In the meantime, if there is any justice regarding the broadcast demagogues, it could be in the reported departure of about a dozen companies that have withdrawn their commercials from Beck's Fox News program. The mass exodus reportedly came after he said last month that Obama was a racist with a "deep-seated hatred for white people or the white culture."

It is encouraging to see confirmation of my parents' warning: If you keep throwing mud, some of it is going to splash back on you.

SEPTEMBER 27, 2009

HOW ACORN HELPED ITS ENEMIES

Never underestimate the power of a 20-year-old woman in hot pants.

Just hook her up with an apple-cheeked young man dressed as a sort of preppy pimp, add a video camera and send them off for a chat with some dimwitted neighborhood financial counselors for ACORN. Stir in enough chutzpah to make Borat look like a shrinking violet and you've got one heckuva scandal.

Young conservative activists James O'Keefe and Hannah Giles hardened up their fresh-faced looks just enough to pose as a pimp and prostitute seeking advice at ACORN offices on setting up a brothel. Their hidden-camera videos have provided a bonanza of what President Barack Obama characterizes as "catnip" for commentators and late-night comedians.

They've also spurred Washington's usually sluggish funding gears to spin into warp drive. The Democratic Congress and Washington's bureaucracy have cut off funds to ACORN.

Suddenly an activist organization that used to beg for media attention to the issues for which it campaigned is receiving an abundance of the sort of attention that nobody wants. Of course, you'd never guess that from the hyperventilated claims of conservative talk show hosts who regard ACORN, the Association of Community Organizations for Reform Now, to be a bigger menace than the swine flu.

Most of the right's recent obsession with ACORN, founded in 1970 in Arkansas as an organization for poor people, does not grow out of concern for poor people. It grows largely out of a faint hope that bringing down ACORN will help them to bring down Obama. Back in 1995, young Harvard Law grad Barack Obama helped ACORN and a team of Chicago attorneys—along with the U. S. Department of Justice—win a lawsuit forcing the state of Illinois to implement the federal "motor-voter" bill. The organization and the former community organizer have not had much contact since, other than connections that have been alleged or exaggerated by conservative media.

Yet mere mention of ACORN can transform Fox News' Glenn Beck into Howard Beale, the deranged commentator in the movie "Network" who leads the nation in shouting, "I'm mad as hell and I'm not going to take it anymore."

"Right now, get off the couch," Beck demanded in a recent broadcast. "While I'm talking, you pick up the phone. You call the newspaper." If ACORN isn't a top priority with your newspaper, he said, "then what the hell are they good for?"

Yet, conservatives underestimate their successes in framing this debate long before Hannah put on her hot pants. Most ACORN coverage in major media has been overwhelmingly negative, according to a recently released study by Peter Dreier, a professor of politics at Occidental College, and Christopher R. Martin, a professor of journalism at University of Northern Iowa. Of the 647 newspaper and broadcast news stories about ACORN that they found in 2007 and 2008, most were on allegations of massive voter registration fraud against the organization.

Some of the names included "Mickey Mouse" and other questionable celebrities. Yet more than 80 percent of those stories failed to mention that there is no record, for example, of Mister "Mouse" actually casting a vote and almost all of the other allegations proved to be unfounded, too.

You may recall, in fact, that failure to find cases of voter fraud to prosecute led to the controversial firing of some U.S. attorneys under pressure from President George Bush's political czar Karl Rove. That does not excuse the stupid, immoral and possibly criminal assistance that several

ACORN staffers were caught on video offering to the young pimp-and-ho duo. But it does offer a valuable lesson: When people are out to get you, try not to hand them more ammunition.

It is somewhat reassuring that the video pranksters reportedly were turned away at some offices, including two that actually reported the phony clients to the police. It is also comforting to know that ACORN immediately fired the offending employees and has since hired Scott Harshbarger, a former Massachusetts attorney general, to conduct what he calls a "robust, no-holds-barred" and transparent review—even if it resembles closing the barn door after the pimp and prostitute have run away.

Nevertheless, ACORN activists brought most of their troubles on themselves long before conservatives piled on. The group's enormous growth since its humble start around a kitchen table in 1970 has brought scandal, financial calamity and internal rifts over charges of bad management. ACORN was an inviting target for political adversaries. The invitation was cheerfully accepted. Now ACORN's big embarrassment sends to the world the worst possible picture of low-income Americans, the very people whom ACORN is supposed to help.

APRIL 1, 2001

MLK'S MEMORY IS PITCHING THE UNEXPECTED

In one of his final speeches, Martin Luther King Jr. said he wanted to be remembered simply as a "drum major for justice." Recent TV viewers may remember him in quite a different role: corporate pitchman.

Perhaps you have seen the recent TV commercial that features the slain civil rights leader delivering his historic "I Have a Dream" speech.

Except, something doesn't look quite right. As the camera orbits around him on the steps of the Lincoln Memorial, and he throws his head back in his full oratorical glory, there are no people. King preaches to an empty landscape, except for a trio of birds soaring across the distant sky.

"Before you can inspire, before you can touch, you must first connect," an announcer's voice says. "And the company that connects more of the world is Alcatel, a leader in communications networks."

Or maybe you have heard King's voice in another recent commercial for the cell phone service Cingular Wireless.

At the end of a montage of voices that include Kermit the Frog and William Shakespeare, you hear King deliver a line from his "I Have a Dream" speech.

Then, after a brief dramatic pause, you hear the doofus voice of Fox TV's animated star Homer Simpson exclaim, "Doh!"

As I sat peacefully watching TV at home, I was jerked alert by both of these commercials.

"The King family has done it again," I moaned.

In recent years the King family has sharply restricted journalists, researchers and academicians in their use of King's words and likenesses, while selling the same to commercial interests for use in ads.

The Martin Luther King Jr. Center for Non-violent Social Change, founded by his widow Coretta Scott King and chaired by their second son Dexter Scott King, closely guards the copyrights, licensing fees and other rights over the slain civil rights leader's speeches and writings.

In 1997 they struck a multimillion-dollar deal with AOL Time Warner Inc. to produce recordings and books of his speeches and writings.

Earlier they settled a lawsuit against USA Today out of court after the newspaper reprinted the entire text of the "I Have a Dream" speech without permission.

All of this protectiveness serves a good cause, the King family assures us. Proceeds go to help support the King center, they say. Besides, they insist, the family can help King's message reach a larger audience.

How wide? Well, in 1999 they approved the use by Apple Computer of magazine ads and billboards featuring King as part of its "Think Different" ad campaign, which also included likenesses of Picasso, Gandhi, Einstein and Amelia Earhart.

Alcatel, a French company that builds voice and data networks, hired George Lucas' Industrial Light + Magic wizards to recreate King's best-known moment.

And, why not? All icons are vulnerable to commercialization. Look at the way Presidents' Day has become synonymous with post-Christmas clearance sales. Look at the way Christmas and Easter have become occasions for feverish shopping and buying.

Many of my fellow Baby Boomers went ballistic when Nike leased the rights to John Lennon's "Revolution" from Michael Jackson and used the Beatle's song for athletic shoe commercials in the late 1980s. Hardly a peep of protest has been heard more recently as the sounds of Jimi Hendrix and other '60s rockers are used to sell cars and other products.

It is not that hard to imagine King's most famous sound bites similarly morphed into future ad campaigns. How about:

"'I have a dream' of a brand new convertible...!"

"'All should be judged, not by the color of their skin, but by the content' of their cold medicine!"

"'Justice will roll down like waters and righteousness like' the all-new cola sensation!"

"'Free at last ...' with store discount ..."

Anything is possible when King is sold on a new auction block—and by no less than his own kinfolk.

JUNE 29, 1988

MORT DOWNEY JR.: IS THIS GUY ZANY? LEMME TELL YA, PAL!

The Morton Downey Jr. show came along at the right time. Downey, a former singer, politician, lobbyist and, more than once, down-and-outer who has become a screaming, smoking, snarling and cursing right-wing television talk show host, went into national syndication with his gabfest just as the summer political and television doldrums were setting in. Neither television nor, perhaps, political issues will ever be the same.

Mort does not pose issues. He slaps you and his guests in the face with them. This is "The McLaughlin Group" for low-brows, "Oprah" for Archie Bunkers.

Facts? Complexities? Hey, LEMME TELL YA, PAL (as Mort would say), save it for "60 Minutes" or some other PABLUM-PUKING program if you wanna be some SCUMBALL who's trying to RUN DOWN AMERICA! Yeah! You don't like it? Well, just ZIP IT, PAL. We've had ENOUGH!

Theater of the absurd? You got it, pal, complete with props! When he had a guest from Iran, a furious Mort draped a huge American flag around his own rear and invited the guest to "Kiss my flag!" On another show, his nostrils flaring and his neatly capped teeth bared, Mort shook a giant noose at the camera and demanded that all drug pushers be hanged "by their testicles!"

Perfect. Just as the politics of passion was giving way to the sleep—inducing dominance of George Bush and Michael Dukakis, along comes Mort, the freshest-and-zaniest-thing a lot of local television stations have to offer in a summer of reruns made all the more deadly by the never-ending writers' strike.

He may not last until fall, but these days he is being talked about vigorously even among those who don't watch him. Everyone, it seems, has something to say about Mort and what his success is saying about American values.

Does this program and other successful "tabloid television" shows, like those of Phil Donahue, Oprah Winfrey and Geraldo Rivera and others that prosper with I-ate-my-offspring topics, or the more raucous "shock TV" shows (Downey soon will be joined by "Liddy," a syndicated gabfest featuring, yes, Watergate figure G. Gordon Liddy) signal the downfall of television or even (Gasp!) the decline of Western civilization? Stay tuned.

In a way, Mort's show reminds me of "Two Minutes Hate," a forced daily ritual in George Orwell's "1984" in which everybody works themselves into a screaming, frothing frenzy by watching a couple of minutes of TV each day.

The broadcast featured a political attack "so exaggerated and perverse that a child should have been able to see through it," Orwell wrote. "And yet just plausible enough to fill one with an alarmed feeling that other people, less level-headed than oneself, might be taken in by it."

How does that compare to Mort's audience? In less enlightened times, these are the folks who, watching Christians being fed to the lions, would have cheered for the lions. Drawn largely from the bungalow belt around Secaucus, N.J., the show's home, and as male as Phil Donahue's is female, his audience constantly screams "Yaaaaaahhhh...!", howls and snarls like wild dogs and slaps high-fives with Mort when he prances triumphantly in their midst.

But I think we are dealing with a fad here. Viewers tend to tire of screamer shows in the long haul.

Besides, sometimes some real honest-to-gosh information does ooze out. One recent show, which began with Mort asking if Shakespeare was right when he wrote that we should kill all the lawyers, featured Alan Dershowitz, the distinguished Harvard law professor, and, among other attorneys, representatives from the American Civil Liberties Union and the Washington Legal Foundation.

Downey began by tossing each of the books the lawyers had come to promote over his shoulder and noting that he does not allow book promotions on his show. He won my heart right away with that one.

Then, with his audience backing him all the way, he forced the lawyers to cut through their legalese and confront each other and regular folk who had been burned by lawyers and to deal with such issues as why rich folks get fancy lawyers and poor folks get legal aid but the working stiff in between only gets the shaft. Within minutes, Harvard talk went out the window. Everyone was shouting at each other. It was great! "Nightline" may deal with the subtleties of these issues, but Mort gets down to the nitty-gritty.

Besides, in my book, any show that makes Dershowitz and some of the other pompous ideologues and intellectuals we see all too often on more sedate programs sweat some real honest sweat can't be all bad. Maybe this Mort isn't so bad, after all. Now, if only he could get a few other pompous twits on the hot seat, like maybe George Will or Pat "Bullethead" Buchanan. Hmmmm... "The horrible thing about the Two Minutes Hate was not that one was obliged to act a part," Orwell wrote, "but that it was impossible to avoid joining in."

Yah! Yah! Yah!

APRIL 29, 1998

SPRINGER SHOW DEBASES US ALL

Quite a number of people are outraged over allegations that the fights between guests on "The Jerry Springer Show" are staged.

This is a big deal, since the brawls on Jerry's shows have tied or topped the shows of America's sweetheart, Oprah Winfrey, since the February sweeps. According to Nielsen Media Research, Oprah has dominated daytime TV for almost 15 years.

Although this once again confirms H.L. Mencken's dictum that no one ever went broke underestimating the tastes of the American public, count me out among those who have their shorts all tied up in a knot now that it has been revealed that Jerry's fights may be staged.

I'm not angry. I'm relieved. What a relief it is to hear that people are not really as crazy, maniacal or idiotic as "The Jerry Springer Show" would have us believe.

Rather, it appears that they are merely naive. They apparently are naive enough to believe their fighting, cursing, spitting and hair pullings over family dysfunctions, unusual dating habits, extramarital love affairs and betrayals of friendships are going to enhance their self-esteem, once they are "interviewed" on national television for all the world to witness.

The syndicated news-magazine show "Extra" aired charges last week by 16 former Springer guests that a producer had urged them to tell fake stories and stage fights.

"Dateline NBC" took the story a step further by reporting that the "Extra" guests have hired a lawyer to sell their story, which suggests they may be guided by something more than just journalistic ethics.

In a cover story, the current Rolling Stone (May 14) contains an eye-witness account by writer Erik Hedegaard who describes Melinda Chait, a Springer producer, enthusiastically encouraging guests to get angry to the point of visible violence.

Backstage before the show, the producer is talking to a guest named Keith from Arkansas, who is "sickened unto death" that that his ex-wife, Brenda, 32, is about to marry his 19-year-old son, Bryan, who happens to be her stepson. They are to be married on the show, but not if Keith can help it.

Lathered up, Keith threatens to stuff his sock into the mouth of Brenda's girlfriend, Tabitha, who also is on the show's lineup.

To this, Chait says, according to Hedegaard, "If that's what you're going to do, do it fast, because security will try to stop you."

She encourages "moving objects. Moving objects are what get the attention of the audience ..."

Later, she says, "I want you up out of your chair, but not slugging ... . Stand up. Show me. You're here to make sure your ex-wife doesn't marry your teenage son, period."

Well, guess what? During the show, a brawl breaks out before the ceremony can begin. A security guard gets the wedding cake pushed into his chest.

Finally, Brenda's real son from some other marriage comes on stage and tearfully voices his own objection to the wedding. Apparently surprised and saddened by this, Brenda and Bryan call off the wedding.

Springer has denied the charges of staging and launched an internal investigation. If any staffers have encouraged guests to lie, they'll be punished, Springer promises.

But Springer apparently doesn't need credibility in the traditional journalistic sense. All he needs is audience. He quickly reminds reporters that the show is "entertainment," not "Meet the Press," so, hey, there's nothing wrong with encouraging people to visibly express themselves.

Under pressure from Studios USA, the show's distributor, the show reportedly is taking steps to reduce the fighting. Chairs have been moved farther apart and extra security has been posted.

But Springer's show without fighting is about as easy to imagine as a war without anybody getting shot. Now that he has ratcheted the craven appetites of his audience up to such a feverish pitch, don't hold your breath waiting for him to ratchet them back down to the level of civil discussion. More likely, the show will soar up and flame out soon—although not soon enough for my tastes—like the old Morton Downey show and other zany predecessors. Audiences that are quickly excited also quickly lose interest.

Meanwhile, since all television is educational, it is instructive to note the message Springer's scufflefests are sending, particularly to young people who are wondering how to deal with their emotions. If you have a family problem or other domestic conflict, the message here is to talk, but only after you have screamed and slapped and wrestled somebody to the ground.

That's entertainment, Springer-style. It is all done for laughs.

I have only one question: Why are we laughing?

JULY 9, 1997

WHEN "NO NEWS" IS ... A RELIEF

Don Imus, syndicated radio and cable TV talk show host, invited me to appear on his morning radio program recently. Then he admitted on the air that he didn't know what to talk about.

"I just came back from a two-week vacation," he said. "I took a news fast."

News fast?

Yes, said Imus, it is a term used by the popular self-help book author Andrew Weil. Weil recommends taking a break from the news every so often in order to soothe your mental and physical health.

My first reaction was of sheer horror. He was talking about fasting from an industry known in my house as "Daddy's meal ticket." As a big-city sewer administrator once said to me, "It may be sludge to you, but it's our bread and butter." Still, I have to be honest with you, dear reader. When I go on vacation, I take news fasts, too.

I take fasts from pagers and cell phones and fax machines, too.

And, you know what? I am amazed to discover how well the world gets along without my assistance.

When I get news back into view, I can feel my stress level soaring again. I attribute that higher stress partly to work and partly to the news, which, in my case, are the same thing.

News is stressful when it is about things that aren't very pleasant, which is almost always. Television news, in particular, has become so violent and PG-13, in my view, that I do not want my 8-year-old son to watch it. It causes him to come up with too many questions that I would prefer not to answer.

For example, one day when he was 4 he asked, "Da-a-ad, why did they arrest Michael Jackson?"

Every time I hear him say "Da-a-ad," I brace myself.

Lately he has become obsessed with a well-to-do county official in suburban Maryland. She is on trial for allegedly trying to kill her husband by adding poison to his dinner.

"Da-a-ad, why did she want to kill her husband?"

I had a brilliant answer to that one. "Ask your mother," I said.

Even my friends who work in television news tell me that they do not let their young children watch the stories they perform for a living.

It's a good thing, too. News distorts and TV news distorts absolutely. TV makes America look far more violent, corrupt and oversexed and crime-ridden place than it really is, simply because it devote so much time and hyperventilation to it.

Crime news gobbles up 29.3 percent of broadcast news time, according to a study of local news in eight cities (New York, Los Angeles, Chicago, Miami, Syracuse, Indianapolis, Eugene, Ore., and Austin, Texas) by eight universities (Northwestern, Columbia, Syracuse and

Ball State Universities and the Universities of Texas, Miami, Oregon and Southern California.)

That compares to only 2 percent of news time for education and 1.2 percent for race relations, just to name two other important areas.

Local TV news even conditions us to seeing things that aren't there. For example, even when news reports make no reference to a suspect, 42 percent later say they recall having seen a perpetrator, according to a recent UCLA study.

And, in two-thirds of those cases, they recalled the non-existent perpetrator as black.

Crime gets lots of airtime because it draws big audiences, which can be sold to advertisers. Crime also is easy to cover and requires little or no analysis or follow-up. Small wonder that TV stations are making no reduction in their crime coverage, even though crime rates nationally have been in their sharpest decline in 30 years.

If viewers want to take a fast from that, I don't blame them. Read a book. Read a newspaper.

Sometimes viewer indignation can make a difference. Look what happened when popular Chicago anchor Carol Marin of WMAQ-TV resigned last spring rather than have to introduce the station's newest commentator, Jerry Springer.

Chicago viewers actually surprised the conventional wisdom. They tuned out in droves. The ratings of WMAQ-TV's news programs actually went down. Springer's career as a Chicago commentator lasted less than a week.

I was proud of those viewers. Television needs more like them.

Think fast.

FEBRUARY 22, 2009

AT LEAST THE "CHIMP" CARTOON GOT US TALKING

When you have to explain a joke, it's not funny. That's the core problem in the dust-up over a New York Post editorial cartoon, a peculiar and confusing creation that strikes many as linking President Barack Obama to a raging chimpanzee.

Cartoonist Sean Delonas depicts a dead chimp on a sidewalk with a couple of bullet holes in its chest while police officers standing nearby with a smoking gun say, "They'll have to find someone else to write the next stimulus bill."

The drawing is a timely reference to Travis the chimp, an ape-gone-wild that was shot to death by Stamford, Conn., police last week after it mauled a friend of its owner. Still, the cartoon leaves one muttering—"Huh?"

Was the chimp supposed to be Obama? The Democratic Congress? Does the Post view firearms as an appropriate way to settle the economic debate?

No and no, say Delonas and the newspaper, although it is hard to tell what the cartoon is about. Even animal lovers have taken offense at its depiction of cruelty to apes.

We've seen controversial scenarios like this before: A publication infuriates a prominent minority group. Protest leaders demand apologies. They also may demand that someone be fired. If the publication's owner also is a broadcaster, licenses are threatened, as Rev. Al Sharpton threatened the newspaper's owner, Rupert Murdoch, while leading pickets outside the Post.

The scenario continues: Defenders of the publication cry foul. They cite "free-speech" rights and accuse grievance leaders like Sharpton of inflaming racial tensions for personal gain. "You've got a black president," one reader wrote to a blogger, "What more do black people want?"

We saw a similar harangue-and-flagellate scenario happen last year with The New Yorker's cartoon controversy. Its cover depicted Obama in Islamic dress and his wife Michelle as a Black Panther militant. Now that the two have moved into the White House, is it safe to laugh? Don't ask.

The Post's editorial board tried to weather this storm. They lasted two days before posting an apology on the newspaper's website while pickets marched outside their offices and politicians called for investigations or, at least, better taste in political artwork.

The Post's apology sounded half-hearted, as if it were forced from a schoolyard bully by a bigger bully. The cartoon, explained the Post, "was meant to mock an ineptly written federal stimulus bill. Period."

They apologized to "those who were offended by the image," but not to "some in the media and in public life who have had differences with the Post in the past" and "see the incident as an opportunity for payback."

Surely they were not talking about me. I like the Post. Whether I agree with the paper's editorials or not, I have long been entertained by its elevation of Page 1 headline writing to a high art.

Among its greatest hits: "Axis of weasel" (2003), "Marla: 'Best sex I ever had'" (1990), "Kiss your asteroid goodbye!" (meteor misses Earth, 1998) and the all-time champ in my record book, "Headless body in topless bar" (1982). Ah, the memories.

The same day that the Post cartoon appeared, a Black History Month speech by Eric Holder, the nation's first black attorney general, sparked another controversy with the way that he called for the very thing his speech stirred up: More talk about race.

Holder called our country "a nation of cowards" on matters of race, with most Americans avoiding candid talk about racial issues. I have long argued the same point, although I am too cowardly to use the word "cowards."

Reaction to Holder's speech illustrated his point. Rush Limbaugh and other prominent conservatives denounced Holder's notion that Americans, outside the workplace, tend to live racially self-segregated lives. Then his critics, I would wager, returned home to mostly self-segregated neighborhoods.

We need to talk more about race. But what form should that conversation take without turning into a blame storm? As President Bill Clinton's attempt at a national racial dialogue found a decade ago, holding talks for the sake of talk tends to only bring out the open-minded folks who need such dialogues the least.

It is our five-alarm eruptions like the Post's cartoon or Don Imus' "nappy-headed hos" episode that draw the truly angry minds into the arena, even if only to shout at one another. Only then do we see just how widely and deeply race continues to divide us, even in the age of Obama.

CHAPTER TWELVE

OBAMA WORLD VS. PALIN NATION

Pontificating about the 2008 presidential election as it developed was a simultaneously exhilarating and dismaying experience.

Barack Obama's quest for the White House turned out to be what I long predicted the election of the nation's first black president would be: a litmus test right down to states, regions and various demographics of just how willing and able the American people were to be fair.

That is not to say, as some wags complain, that a vote against Obama made you a racist—or that a vote for him cleansed you of all racial guilt. We Americans are more complicated than that.

This chapter offers explorations of that complexity that are worth remembering as benchmarks of how far we have come since the civil rights era and how far we have to go. It includes how Obama has had to walk a tightrope between being too black and not black enough. It also includes Rev. Jesse Jackson's and Rev. Jeremiah Wright's ill-fated efforts to define Obama's blackness and how after his election, Obama ironically found himself less free to talk openly about race than any previous president.

JANUARY 24, 2007

BUMPY RIDE ON WAY TO WHITE HOUSE

"A lie can travel halfway around the world," Mark Twain is said to have exclaimed, "while the truth is putting on its shoes." What an optimist he was. In this age of the Internet, lies go around the globe many times before the truth can even find its shoes.

Just ask Democratic presidential hopeful Barack Obama. Just as Illinois' rising superstar senator announced his White House bid, an anti-Obama smear campaign was percolating in cyberspace and popping up in countless email boxes, including mine.

And by the time Sen. Hillary Rodham Clinton (D-N.Y.) announced her presidential bid Saturday, the Obama rumor had taken on new legs in the mainstream media, thanks to an unfounded accusation linking the rumor to "the Hillary Clinton camp."

The website of the conservative magazine Insight alleged that Democrats "connected" to the New York senator had discovered that Obama had studied at a madrassa, a Muslim religious school, for four years while living in Indonesia as a kid and doesn't want anyone to know about it.

Besides its incendiary implications of anti-Muslim paranoia, the allegation of an Obama coverup and the Clinton outing is simply wrong, wrong and wrong.

First, Obama was not secretly educated in a radical Islamic school when he was growing up in Indonesia. That was confirmed Monday by CNN senior international correspondent John Vause, reporting from Jakarta. With pictures and interviews that include one of young "Barry" (his childhood nickname) Obama's classmates, Vause found that the Besuki School is not and never was a madrassa. It is a secular public school attended mostly by Muslims.

That's not surprising, since Indonesia is the world's largest Muslim country. Yet, about a fourth of the school's enrollment was non-Muslim, like young Barry, as it is now. Children and teachers wear conventional Western dress, not Eastern religious garb, and theology is found only in a weekly class on comparative religions.

Insight also said Obama's political rivals "are seeking to prove" that the school promoted Wahhabism, an austere form of Islam that fuels many Islamic terrorists. But Vause observed on CNN that "I've been to those madrassas in Pakistan ... this school is nothing like that."

Yet, no matter how many facts you dig up, truth has a tough time standing up to a juicy rumor. By the time CNN debunked the unfounded allegations, they had been repeated on Fox News, The New York Post, the Glenn Beck program on CNN Headline News and other outlets. To hear some of the chatter, you would have thought that Clinton's campaign had all but outed Obama as an Al Qaeda agent.

Welcome to the big leagues, senators. Whisper campaigns are a sad reality of politics. Sen. John McCain (R-Ariz.) knows. Vicious rumors that were traced back to the George W. Bush camp helped undo McCain's momentum in South Carolina's critical Republican primary campaign in 2000.

The Internet only deepens the targeted candidate's dilemma: If you deny rumors that are just bubbling around cyberspace, that public denial makes them more newsworthy in the mainstream media. Sen. John Kerry (D-Mass.) learned that in 2004 when his candid denials on Don Imus' radio show of rumored hanky-panky with a young female staffer ("There's nothing to it.") actually helped to spread the unfounded rumors. The rumor was not sufficiently newsworthy for The New York Times and others to report, but Kerry's response to it was.

But if politicians don't respond, they risk the corrosive effect that unanswered charges can have on their campaign. Kerry, again, offered an excellent example by failing to respond to attack ads by Swift Boat Veterans for more than two weeks.

And Hillary Clinton is no political patsy. Although quite a few Democrats sound nervous about her vulnerabilities, one of her strengths as a campaigner is her experience, along with her ex-president husband, at weathering political storms.

Obama's just beginning to learn. Worse is yet to come. If one can be condemned by faint praise, Obama should feel praised so far by faint condemnation. If empty rumors are the worst that his enemies can come up with in their desperate attempts to chip away at his amazingly pristine image, he's doing remarkably well. But, fasten your seat belt, Senator. It's going to be a bumpy ride, to paraphrase Bette Davis in "All About Eve."

And with this much mudslinging a year before the first primary and caucus votes are cast, this presidential contest will be a big test not only for the candidates, but also for the rest of us.

There's a lot of speculation going on about whether we Americans are ready to elect a black or a female president. The real question is whether we are ready to be fair to all candidates, despite the spin doctors, mud-slingers and rumormongers who betray our hopes and play on our fears.

JULY 13, 2008

REV. JACKSON'S "OBAMA TRAUMA"

What did the Rev. Jesse Jackson mean when he accused Barack Obama of "talking down to black people"?

That was the second question on my mind in a telephone interview with Jackson. My first was something like this: "Did you really say you wanted to castrate Obama?"

As the world knows by now, Jackson says he didn't know he was wearing a "hot mic," a turned-on microphone, on the set of a Fox News program when he made what one newspaper headline called, his "cutting remark."

Remember the old saying about how character is what you do when nobody's looking? Jackson's inflammatory whispers suggest a new twist: Character is what you do when you don't know everybody is listening.

Jackson's comments showed the influential civil rights leader at his worst: frustrated and marginalized.

Jackson was smarting over Obama's recent call to expand President Bush's faith-based initiatives. Twice Jackson snapped that Obama has been "talking down to black people." That was in reference, Jackson says, to Obama's Father's Day address at the predominantly black Apostolic Church of God on the South Side. It was a speech in which Obama revealed his inner Bill Cosby, calling for more parental responsibility, whether assisted by government help or not.

"Any fool can have a child," Obama said. "That doesn't make you a father. It's the courage to raise a child that makes you a father."

Jackson, too, has called for parental responsibility. I was part of the national media that gave glowing coverage to his PUSH for Excellence drive in the 1970s. Across the country he preached to black youths that: "You are not a man because you can make a baby. You're only a man if you can raise a baby, protect a baby and provide for a baby."

One can only imagine how Jackson must feel seeing Obama—or Cosby—receive national applause for saying what Jackson has been saying for decades.

The difference between his approach and Obama's, Jackson said, is that Obama was not saying enough about government and private-sector obligations to help the poor, besides self-help. That's a worthwhile debate. In fact, the self-help versus outside-help argument has been going on inside black America for decades.

The enthusiastic response Obama has received from black audiences belies the notion that he is condescending to them. And Jackson had to twist himself into rhetorical knots to explain how that nuance of difference between his rhetoric and Obama's called for Jackson's shocking response. After all, he insisted, his support for Obama's candidacy is "unequivocal," partly because Obama has addressed so many of the issues about which Jackson cares about on other occasions.

No, I suspect Jackson's objection is less to what Obama said than to who was saying it. Jackson misses that national spotlight that he has not held in recent years. Deep down, his anger suggests that Jackson wanted the world—and Obama—to know the depth of his anger.

His objections sent a message that sounds more personal than political: He will not be ignored. He got his wish, although not with the sort of publicity he would like to have had. Even his son Rep. Jesse Jackson Jr., an Obama campaign co-chair, instantly issued a statement that scolded his father with the strongest rebuke that a loving son could give.

Politically, the elder Jackson's scorn comes as an odd gift to Obama. Working-class white voters and others who were put off by video clips of Obama's former minister, the Rev. Jeremiah Wright Jr., may well be oddly reassured that Obama has upset Jackson.

For African-Americans, Jackson exposed to the world a barber-shop and beauty-salon conversation that has been going on for decades among black folks. Rev. Jackson's presidential runs prepared the way for Obama, but so did Bill Cosby. Black folks used to hesitate to be too self-critical in public, for fear of "airing dirty laundry" and the like. But, despite criticisms from some black intellectuals, Cosby's popularity has hardly suffered. Neither, it appears, has Obama's.

That's because they don't talk down to their audiences. They enlist their audiences as partners.

SEPTEMBER 6, 2009

AUDACITY OF THE "OBAMA EFFECT"

After decades of criticizing public schools as places where hardly anybody learns anything, suddenly conservatives are upset that a 15-to-20-minute live Webcast might teach kids too much.

That's because the Webcast is by President Barack Obama. His critics fear he might teach something that they'd rather not have our schoolchildren hear. Seldom has so much power been imagined for a short video presentation that does not carry an X-rating.

The quarrel began after Education Secretary Arne Duncan emailed principals that the president would speak on Tuesday over the Internet, on C-SPAN and via satellite, "directly to the nation's schoolchildren about persisting and succeeding in school."

Somehow that useful message, coming amid the heat of an un-related health-care debate, was immediately interpreted by Obama's conservative critics as a sneaky way to enlist children into promoting his political agenda.

Or, as Jim Greer, chairman of the Florida Republican Party, put it, "As the father of four children, I am absolutely appalled that taxpayer dollars are being used to spread President Obama's socialist ideology."

Mercy. It takes a different planet from the one on which I live to find "persisting and succeeding in school" to be socialist ideology. But conservative pundits were just getting warmed up to the biggest political panic since former Alaska Gov. Sarah Palin accused the House health-care bill of mandating "death panels."

Blogger Michelle Malkin accused schools and teacher unions of using students as "little lobbyists." David Boaz, executive vice president of the libertarian Cato Institute, blogged that the Obama administration is "trying to push its president-worship onto 50 million captive schoolchildren." American Values President Gary Bauer declared, "Tuesday may be a good day to sit in on your child's classes."

The Education Department didn't help matters with the darkly suggestive wording that someone, dare I say stupidly, included in a set of classroom activities posted on the department's website to accompany the speech.

It suggested that students "write letters to themselves about what they can do to help the president." A White House spokesman acknowledged

that the suggestion was "inartfully worded." Translation from government-
mentese: Somebody messed up.

Out went the old wording. The updated version asks students to
"write letters to themselves about how they can achieve their short-term
and long-term education goals." Good. Ask not what you can do for the
president, children; ask what you can do to help your own futures.

Despite the rewrite, the panic took on a life of its own, fanned
like a California forest fire in the hot winds of bloggers and talk-show
commentators. Some schools pulled the plug on the speech. They cited
parents' complaints about what it might say. Some parents said they
would pull their kids out of school.

Though some observers suspect bias in this backlash against the nation's first black president, I don't think race has much to do with it.
Presidents Ronald Reagan in 1988 and George H.W. Bush in 1991 gave
similar televised addresses, amid some criticism from Democrats about
propagandizing on the taxpayers' dime. That's politics.

Besides, values do matter. If conservatives thought Bill Cosby, for
example, was delivering the address, I think they'd be delighted. I cannot guarantee that all of his political views would please conservative
stalwarts. But his five-year-old crusade for self-help and personal responsibility has given voice to values on which both political sides can find
rare agreement: the importance of good parenting.

Here I speak from hard-earned experience. Politics may come and
go, but the day-to-day job of raising kids brings out the conservatism
in us all.

That's why a lot of parents welcome Obama's messages to kids. Many
hope for what some educators have called an "Obama effect," the role
modeling that might help our offspring expand their definition of "cool"
to include academic excellence, family obligations, parental responsibilities and, heaven help us, pulling their pants up to full mast.

And for African-American children, in particular, there's another
important message in Obama's famous unflappability: Don't let racism
or suspicions of racism dim your determination to succeed.

Obama received a huge political boost last year when he espoused the
Cosby-esque values that Americans tend to share across racial and party
lines. Maybe that's what his conservative rivals are really worried about.

APRIL 30, 2008

WRIGHT DOES OBAMA WRONG

For weeks, the Rev. Jeremiah Wright was right to castigate those who used sound bites from his fiery sermons to paint him as "some sort of fanatic." But his latest wounds are self-inflicted.

And, as Sen. Barack Obama's recently retired pastor, Wright is taking the Illinois Democrat's presidential campaign down too.

"I do what I do," Wright said. "He does what politicians do." Wright's right about that. But, as some of his associates have tried in vain to tell him, what he does can help or hurt what Obama is trying to do.

For more than a month the airwaves have been peppered with video snippets of Wright in the pulpit of Trinity United Church of Christ on the South Side. He is seen calling on God to "damn America" for its sins against minorities, the poor and world peace. He is seen accusing the government of flooding black neighborhoods with drugs and HIV/AIDS and declaring "America's chickens are coming home to roost" after the Sept. 11, 2001, terror attacks.

Wright chose to reveal the real Wright to the public only days after Obama's Pennsylvania primary loss to Sen. Hillary Clinton. That primary exposed weaknesses in Obama's ability to connect with white working-class voters—and Wright.

Wright was given a golden opportunity to correct the distorted image portrayed in his sound bites. He could have helped his 20-year former congregant's efforts to win votes in Indiana and North Carolina. But Wright blew it.

At first, we saw Wright's best angels revealed in an hourlong interview he gave to Bill Moyers on PBS' "Bill Moyers Journal." Posted on the program's PBS.org website, it is Wright's first interview since the controversy erupted. He comes off as the thoughtful scholar, a graduate of Howard University and the University of Chicago Divinity School who built his church from 78 members in the early 1970s to more than 8,000 today and gained national respect in theological circles.

In a video package of biographical photos, Moyers reveals that Wright in the 1960s served as a cardiopulmonary technician in the Marines at Bethesda Naval Hospital in Maryland. There he assisted doctors operating on President Lyndon B. Johnson. An old photo shows a young Moyers, then a top aide to Johnson, standing behind Wright in the operating room.

With Moyers, a fellow member of the United Church of Christ and an outspoken advocate of its prophetic witness, Wright explains black liberation theology in terms of black Christian history that are not scary to reasonable white folks.

"The God of the people who are riding on the decks of the slave ship," Wright said, "is not the God of the people who are riding underneath the decks as slaves in chains."

Better late than never, Moyers' program offers a chance to see that, whether you agree with him or not, Wright is not a nut case.

Unfortunately, the good that Wright did for himself on Moyers' show was largely undone by Wright's excessive showboating at his heavily covered news conference Monday in the National Press Club in Washington.

His ego and flair for the theatrical got the better of him in front of a firing squad of news cameras and a dining room populated to the walls with his supporters and fellow religious leaders.

Like the young Muhammad Ali, Wright played to his audience by taunting his conservative critics. But, instead of calming the controversial waters for Obama's benefit as well as his own, Wright pumped up call-and-response applause and cheers from his supporters, giving the news conference the sound and feel of a church revival combined with a political rally.

He defended Nation of Islam Minister Louis Farrakhan's attacks against Zionism. He equated criticisms of himself with an attack on the black church and black Americans as a whole. Instead of backing away from his paranoid accusation that AIDS could be a genocidal government plot, he cited other historic scandals to defend the possibility.

Wright's entitled to his opinions. Nevertheless, as a champion of black advancement, it is hard to believe that he does not see—or doesn't care about—the damage that he is doing to the first African-American to have a realistic shot at being president.

Beware the sin of vanity, Reverend.

MAY 4, 2008

WITH FRIENDS LIKE THESE ...: WRIGHT'S PAST, OBAMA'S FUTURE

After cutting ties with his controversial former pastor, Sen. Barack Obama received a word of sympathy from an unusual source: a Republican.

Former presidential hopeful Mike Huckabee says that Rev. Jeremiah Wright Jr. wants to derail Obama's bid for the White House for a simple tactical reason: Wright does not want Obama to prove that America has made that much racial progress.

"His campaign is not being derailed by his race," Huckabee told reporters following a fundraiser in Montana. "It's being derailed by a person who doesn't want him to prove that we have made great advances in this country."

Huckabee, himself a Baptist minister, added that "Jeremiah Wright needs for Obama to lose so he can justify his anger, his hostile bitterness against the United States of America."

It's hard to imagine that Wright would turn on the rising political star whom he led to Jesus Christ two decades ago at Trinity United Church of Christ on the South Side, when Obama was a community organizer. Yet, Wright has been offering enough evidence to indicate that "Pastor Huck" might have uncovered an awful truth.

Obama's repudiation of Wright came after Wright blew an opportunity at the National Press Club news conference to smooth the nationwide feathers he has ruffled.

In stark contrast with the sedate, almost scholarly discussion Wright gave to Bill Moyers on PBS' "Bill Moyers Journal" the previous weekend, Wright turned up the heat.

He repeated his assertions that the Sept. 11, 2001, attacks were American "chickens coming home to roost" and that the United States had committed "terrorism" against minorities at home and abroad.

He defended the polarizing Minister Louis Farrakhan with enough enthusiasm to cause further damage to Obama's rainbow coalition.

Instead of backing away from his implications in earlier sermons that AIDS was created by the government to kill "people of color," Wright restated his suspicions, saying: "Based on the Tuskegee experiment and based on what has happened to Africans in this country, I believe our government is capable of doing anything."

The Tuskegee experiments were a horrendous episode beginning in the 1930s, when government scientists withheld treatment from African-American syphilis patients in order to study the impact of the disease on their bodies. There hasn't been evidence of similar atrocities since then, except in fringe literature that Wright unfortunately appears to believe.

At a time when Obama's presidential campaign was desperately trying to make up for his soft support among white working-class voters, he didn't need this Wright hook.

Maybe Wright is still bitter, consciously or not, over being asked to withdraw from Obama's presidential announcement ceremonies in Springfield last year.

But a more powerful force may simply be the fundamental differences in the way Wright and Obama view the world. Wright is a man of the past. Obama is a man of the future.

I think Obama got it right in his Philadelphia speech on race when he tried to explain his former pastor's words without condoning them. "The profound mistake of Rev. Wright's sermons is not that he spoke about racism in our society," Obama said. "It's that he spoke as if our society was static; as if no progress had been made; as if this country—a country that has made it possible for one of his own members to run for the highest office in the land and build a coalition of white and black, Latino and Asian, rich and poor, young and old—is still irrevocably bound to a tragic past."

But, as Obama went on to say, we know that America can change—and it has changed. As our elders prophesied to my generation of African-Americans back in the 1960s, opportunities have opened up. It's up to us to prepare ourselves to step inside, rather than stand outside the door complaining about it.

Instead of joining with Obama's call for reconciliation, as Wright has done on other occasions, Wright flamboyantly issued a taunt at the National Press Club. With his finger raised defiantly toward the firing squad of news cameras, he recalled saying to Obama last year, "If you get elected, November the 5th, I'm coming after you, because you'll be representing a government whose policies grind under people."

Oh, really? After all that, I don't imagine that a President Obama would be eager to return Wright's phone calls. Wright may have single-handedly done enough damage to make sure Obama never gets to the Oval Office.

If so, Wright probably will blame the white man for the defeat, but the rest of us will know who helped.

NOVEMBER 4, 2009

RACIAL HOPE FADES DESPITE OBAMA

In my favorite "Star Trek" episode, Capt. James T. Kirk and the crew of the Starship Enterprise encountered humanoids from a planet embroiled in war over an issue as clear as black and white. Literally.

The planet Cheron is locked in a race war. This astonishes earthlings. To us, all Cheronians look alike. Their skin is evenly divided, half black and half white, right down the middle of their faces and bodies.

A perplexed Capt. Kirk asks: "What is the difference that Cheronians are fighting about?"

"Isn't it obvious?" says a Cheronian, who is white on his left side. "All of his people are white on the right side."

The episode, like all good fiction, helps us come to grips with painful realities. It first aired in 1969, at a time when our country's racial differences were erupting in riots and assassinations. The black-white planet was doomed by its inhabitants' inability to deal with the slightest diversity.

Flash-forward 40 years. That old "Star Trek" episode came to mind as I read the latest Gallup Poll on the state of the nation's racial optimism. A year after two-thirds of Americans polled expressed high hopes for a post-racial future, Gallup says, "there is scarcely more hope" for a solution on race than there was before.

If so, I am not surprised. In fact, I am somewhat relieved that we Americans are showing ourselves to be optimistic but also realistic. We know one election is not going to solve our racial challenges.

Since 1963, Gallup has been asking us whether we think relations between blacks and whites "will always be a problem for the U.S., or that a solution will eventually be worked out." The optimistic view that a solution will be worked out surged to an all-time high of 67 percent the day after Obama's White House win. But a year later only 56 percent express that belief. That's statistically the same as the 55 percent who felt that way in December 1963, when Gallup first asked the question.

"In short, despite all that has happened in the intervening decades," Gallup says, "there is scarcely more hope now than there was those many years ago that the nation's race-relations situation will be solved."

But Gallup's forecast shouldn't be so gloomy. Those who took the survey were being realistic. We Americans might want to be post-racial, but I think we know in our hearts that we're not ready yet.

After all, it was not that long ago that Gallup found our racial optimism at an all-time low of 29 percent. That was in October 1995, shortly after O.J. Simpson's acquittal of double murder dramatically revealed the nation's racial divide on national television. Seldom has our state of race looked so bleak. Yet, Tiger Woods was becoming a new cultural hero who crossed racial lines, Oprah Winfrey already was, and Colin Powell was seriously being urged by high-powered fans in both major political parties to run for president. Change was in the air.

It is a sign of our progress that racism has been driven underground, if not eliminated. But racial suspicions rise to fill the gap. For example, it is hard for me to read about church pastors like the Rev. Wiley Drake of Buena Park, Calif., or Pastor Steven Anderson of Tempe, Ariz., who have both proudly prayed for Obama to die soon and not wonder about how race might be a motivating factor in their prayers.

But race is such a touchy topic these days that you can be accused of being a racist just for bringing it up. Obama's thoughts on racial profiling led Fox News star Glenn Beck to call the president "a racist" who "hates white culture." When CBS' Katie Couric later asked Beck, "What is white culture?" he looked surprised. He accused Couric of trying to "trap" him and refused to answer. That's too bad. I, too, would like to know what he means by white culture.

By understanding people who come from other cultures, I hope to gain a better understanding of what I have in common with them—even with Glenn Beck.

CHAPTER THIRTEEN

TEA PARTY CULTURE WARS

Every action brings a reaction, said Isaac Newton, which helps to summarize this chapter of columns on the rise of the tea party movement on the heels of Obama's election, along with "birthers," Glenn Beck and other "wacko birds," as Sen. John McCain called the far-out crowd.

One column explores the hidden side of the Tea Party: Its ranks are dominated by Evangelical Christians, plus veterans of the Ross Perot budget hawk movement of the 1990s.

Another looks at how Tea Partiers turned rowdy during the 2013 government shutdown, how a culture war erupted over the appearance by rap poet and actor Common in the Obama White House, and what role preachers should play when the pulpit turns to politics.

APRIL 18, 2010

GETTING A HANDLE ON THE TEA PARTIERS

I attended the tea party movement's Tax Day rally near the White House in the way that Mick Jagger in an old Rolling Stones tune "went down to the demonstration to get my fair share of abuse."

"Be careful," warned a liberal friend, sounding as though she feared I would be cursed, spat upon and called the N-word as I was pummeled to the ground.

After all, if you judge the movement by much of its news coverage, I am what the tea partiers are supposed to hate. I am black. I work in what Rush Limbaugh calls the "lame-stream media." I don't think President Barack Obama's health care overhaul is a "government take-over" of health care.

Yet I am happy to report that I was not abused, unless you count the whiny voice of Victoria Jackson, a former "Saturday Night Live" cast member now trying to be the tea party movement's Lady Gaga.

Her anthem, "Communist in the White House," wins no plaudits for understatement. The crowd loved it, especially her "Only Glenn Beck understands me" line. The Fox News star's name brought cheers that briefly drowned out Jackson's voice, which briefly made me unusually grateful for Fox News.

But there were normal people there, too. For example, I met Fred Groat, a retired business executive who lives on Chicago's North Side and is "surrounded by lakefront liberals." He voted for President George W. Bush, but now calls him a "RINO, Republican in Name Only," for running up the deficit and failing to "secure the borders."

He's not alone. Tea parties lack much in the way of formal structure, leadership or agendas because they are an orphan movement. If anything unifies them it is a shared sense of abandonment by Republicans and cluelessness by Democrats, most of whom feel the feeling is mutual.

As much as media portray the tea party as something new, spontaneous political movements have been springing up, making noise for a few years, then fading away since before the founding of the Republic—except this one happened to be ignited by a black president.

That makes it easy to suspect the tea party movement is racist, especially if you have an elastic definition of racism. But polls and conversations with tea partiers confirm my suspicion that race brings a teeny cup to the party.

Looming larger in the lives of tea partiers are issues like money, culture and a leave-us-alone view of government—until, of course, they bump up against an issue on which they can use government's help.

A new CBS/New York Times poll released just before Tax Day found that, contrary to their image as a bunch of poor, ignorant whites, the 18 percent of the public who identified themselves as tea party supporters turned out to be above-average in income and education. They were still more male, white and conservative than the nation's political center, the poll showed. But not too far out of the mainstream to be a force, however unpredictable, in the upcoming midterm elections.

Yet, despite their rightward leanings, the CBS/New York Times poll found tea party supporters were not totally hostile to government. More than 60 percent said they think Social Security and Medicare are worth the cost to taxpayers, most send their children to public schools and most describe the amount they paid in taxes this year as "fair." You wouldn't guess that from what speakers were saying at their rallies.

Maybe that's because 64 percent in the poll said the Obama administration had raised taxes or kept them the same. That's about twice the percentage of Americans overall—and it's wrong. In fact, stimulus legislation resulted in a tax cut on 2009 tax returns, bringing taxes to their lowest levels in 60 years, according to William Gale, co-director of the Tax Policy Center and director of the Retirement Security Project at the Brookings Institution.

No wonder President Obama, when asked about the Tax Day protests, said: "You would think they would be saying, 'Thank you.'" Yes, you would. But it's hard to bring people to the streets in favor of what this administration is doing right.

AUGUST 8, 2012

ONWARD CHRISTIAN TEAVANGELICALS

Despite the tea party's well-known fiscal focus, the anti-tax, budget-slashing movement's most underappreciated energy source may be evangelical Christians.

I suspected as much when I attended a couple of early tea party rallies. News coverage focused on the signs, speeches and slogans that promoted free markets, fiscal responsibility and constitutionally limited government. But my conversations with participants revealed another widely shared agenda: stop abortion rights, same-sex marriage and the other social evils in the eyes of the religious right.

David Brody, Christian Broadcasting Network's Washington-based chief political correspondent, was making similar discoveries. If it often looks as though tea partiers are driven by something resembling religious zeal, you'll understand why after reading his new book "The Teavangelicals: The Inside Story of How the Evangelicals and the Tea Party are Taking Back America."

Along with numerous profiles and interviews, Brody recounts polls, like a 2010 American Values survey, that indicate nearly half of self-identified tea party members say they are part of the "religious right or conservative Christian movement."

For example, the Pew Research Center's Forum on Religion and Public Life found 60 percent of registered voters who agreed with the religious right said they also agreed with the tea party. Some 44 percent of white evangelical Protestants surveyed said they agreed with the movement. Only 8 percent said they didn't. Almost two-thirds of tea party supporters opposed same-sex marriage, and 59 percent said abortion should be illegal in all or most cases.

Whether you agree with their social views or not (I don't), it is fair to say that with attitudes like that, the tea party doesn't sound so new. Its social conservatism sounds much like the religious right of Jerry Falwell's Moral Majority and Pat Robertson's Christian Coalition that backed Ronald Reagan for president in the 1980s.

The tea party emerged mostly from grass-roots libertarianism activism and endures with the help of big dollars from backers like the Washington-based nonprofit FreedomWorks.

But polls indicate their rank-and-file supporters at rallies and elections would be mighty sparse without the robust presence of dedicated evangelicals.

That's OK if your movement is led by a talented coalition builder like Reagan. But sharp differences on social issues, Brody observes, pose a potential threat to the movement's long-term unity.

After all, the movement's more secular tax-fighters tend to lean more live-and-let-live libertarian across the board, including hot-button social issues like abortion rights, same-sex marriage and marijuana legalization, which the religious right so passionately opposes.

So, what holds the coalition together now? Well, there is you-know-who. The guy in the White House.

"Mitt Romney is lucky," Brody told me in an interview. The Republican presidential nominee "has done virtually nothing with the evangelical crowd, but he's got a core group that will come out just to vote against President Barack Obama."

That's a big deal. President George W. Bush was re-elected in 2004 with the help of an unusually high turnout of religious conservatives, including in black churches, heavily encouraged by Karl Rove, Bush's chief political strategist.

Which made me wonder whether Obama or Romney can pull off a similar appeal to religious conservatives this year.

I asked Brody in a later email exchange how he thought teavangelicals would respond if the president resumed a theme he pushed as a candidate in 2008.

In a high-profile speech at a black church, he won big applause with a strong appeal for marriage before parenthood, personal responsibility and responsible parenting.

Sure, the Rev. Jesse Jackson, as many will recall, was irritated enough to threaten Obama's reproductive organs in a sharp sound bite picked up by a Fox News microphone. But Jackson's disapproval appeared only to bring more applause for Obama, even from conservatives.

Brody was intrigued by the suggestion.

"I think if President Obama did a speech like that, it would make teavangelical voters wonder why Romney hasn't done the same," he emailed. While a speech like that wouldn't win a lot of white teavangelicals, it could endear him a bit more with independents and "African-American teavangelical voters" and could "actually make Romney look weaker in this area."

Maybe. It is a speech that may not happen, but I'd like to cover it if it did.

OCTOBER 16, 2013

A VERY SAD WAY TO SALUTE VETERANS

Organizers of the Million Vet March on Washington insist they had nothing to do with interlopers who tried to score political points off their event. But sorry, guys. We are judged by the company we keep.

March organizers are trying to distance themselves from folks who showed up at their protest at the World War II Memorial, tore down barriers put up during the government shutdown, carried them a few blocks to the White House, and piled them up outside the fence. It was a short walk for the men and a giant photo opportunity for publicity seekers.

One man at the megaphone, Larry Klayman, of a conservative group called Freedom Watch, demanded a "peaceful uprising" to impeach the political right's most galvanizing figure, President Barack Obama, whom he called a Muslim. "Demand that this president leave town," he said, "... put the Quran down ... get up off his knees and ... figuratively come out with his hands up." Donations to Klayman's cause are cheerfully accepted, I'm sure.

Another fellow attracted even more news coverage by waving a Confederate flag in front of the White House. Some people saw racism in this gesture. I won't try to read the man's mind. I am more annoyed by the lack of action by the other participants.

I can only imagine, for example, what the world would have said about a similarly racially volatile symbol at the mostly black Million Man March in the 1990s. Instead, no one moved barricades or otherwise misbehaved. The only racially volatile presence was the march's organizer, Nation of Islam Minister Louis Farrakhan, who is quite provocative enough.

No wonder, then, that organizers of the Million Vet March, which fell way short of a million by the way, want you to know they had nothing, nothing to do with all that political foolishness.

"The political agenda put forth by a local organizer in Washington, D.C., yesterday was not in alignment with our message," says a sober statement on the Million Vet March on the Memorials home page. "We feel disheartened that some would seek to hijack the narrative for political gain."

Fine. But trying to take partisan politics out of such protests is like trying to take the bees out of honey.

Before the Million Vet March, Republican senators and congressmen and Republican National Committee Chairman Reince Priebus already had stepped up to make the WWII Memorial a symbol of their efforts to blame Democrats for the government shutdown that Republicans caused. Judging by the polls, those efforts have spectacularly failed.

As a Vietnam-era Army vet who's been observing Washington up close for a couple of decades, I am not shocked to hear about people trying to make politics out of a war memorial during a government shutdown. I am only disgusted by politicians who claim to salute veterans' honor while putting veterans' benefits in jeopardy.

Days before the march, Veterans Affairs Secretary Eric Shinseki told a congressional committee that all public access to the VA's 56 regional offices was suspended when the partial government shutdown began Oct. 1. More than 7,000 VA employees judged "nonessential" were furloughed.

Suspended was the VA's program to reduce the agency's scandalous backlog of disability and pension claims, a backlog that slightly increased after the shutdown, Shinseki said, after falling for months to about 418,500.

And checks would not be issued on Nov. 1 to more than 5 million veterans if the impasse continued, he said. That would include more than 400,000 fully disabled veterans and 360,000 surviving spouses and children of wartime veterans.

If our lawmakers think these expenditures are not necessary, they should say so. They have a right to that opinion, however wrong it is. But instead they line up at the mere mention of the word "veteran" to let everybody know how much they love our retired warriors.

I think that the best way for lawmakers to thank veterans for their service is to stop playing politics with veterans' services.

MAY 15, 2011

AN UN-COMMON CULTURE WAR

How delighted the Chicago-based rapper Common must be to find that someone still views him as controversial.

It's getting harder to shock people in these jaded times, especially for a guy who is becoming less well-known for his edgy rap lyrics than for writing children's books, appearing in Gap ads and co-starring in romantic comedies like "Just Wright" with Queen Latifah.

But, ah, these also are politically polarized times. All that Grammy-winning Common, previously known as Common Sense and originally as Lonnie Rashid Lynn Jr., had to do to regain some street cred was to accept first lady Michelle Obama's invitation to recite some of his poetry in the White House. President Barack Obama's vast community of conservative critics saw a glimmer of an opportunity to paint Common as some sort of a Chicago gangster, and they took it.

They objected, for example, to a couple of lines in a poem called "A Letter to the Law" that he recited on HBO's "Def Poetry Jam." The verses metaphorically protest, among other things, brutal police misconduct and President George W. Bush's invasion of Iraq. Conservative critics interpret his line "Burn a bush cos' for peace he no push no button," for example, as a call to physically attack the president. But it also sounds like a metaphorical play on the biblical burning bush. People often hear what they want to hear in poetry. That's what makes it poetic. But mix it with politics and many hear controversy.

Republicans also objected to the lyrics to "A Song for Assata," in Common's 2000 album, "Like Water for Chocolate." The song gives a shout-out to Joanne Chesimard, a former Black Panther also known as Assata Shakur, who was convicted of killing a New Jersey police officer and now lives under political asylum in Cuba. Does that make Common a "cop killer" or a "thug," as Fox News contributor Karl Rove put it? "The one thing that shouldn't be questioned," said Common in a Facebook message before the poetry event, "is my support for the police officers and troops that protect us every day."

Yet, Fox News host Sean Hannity, for example, insisted, "If this was somebody who used the same type of rhetoric about violence against President Obama I would be against it."

That's nice to hear, except Hannity refused to denounce rock star Ted Nugent after an August 2007 concert in which the frequent Fox News guest called then-Sen. Barack Obama a "piece of (expletive)," a word that rhymes with "fit."

Nugent also urged Obama to "suck on" his machine gun. Nugent also yelled profane sentiments from the stage about then-Sen. Hillary Rodham Clinton that made the Dixie Chicks' controversial remarks on a British stage chiding President George W. Bush sound quite mild by comparison.

But when Democratic strategist Bob Beckel called on Hannity to "disavow this lowlife" Nugent, Hannity said, "No, I like Ted Nugent. He's a friend of mine."

I like Ted Nugent too. I had a very cordial interview with him many years ago, along with his delightful and now deceased mother, Marion "Ma" Nugent. Even if we disagree on the right to bear machine guns, I think Nugent's a good guy. But when I think he's wrong, I will say so. So should Hannity—unless he doesn't think Nugent is wrong.

Hannity's apparent double standard reminds me of another Fox star, Bill O'Reilly, who famously hounded Pepsi into dropping the rap superstar Ludacris as a spokesman in 2002. O'Reilly objected to Ludacris' lyrics glamorizing a "life of guns, violence, drugs and disrespect of women." That's how a lot of people describe Ozzy Osbourne and his band Black Sabbath. Yet, when Pepsi signed Osbourne about three months after dropping Ludacris, O'Reilly said not a peep.

Although O'Reilly and Ludacris ended their feud last year in a chance meeting, my question is this: How many times can you pounce on hip-hop, including "conscious" hip-hop, while giving raunchy rockers a pass? As rap becomes more mainstream, the culture war looks increasingly like a war against black culture.

Fortunately, the White House stuck by its invitation to Common and the event went off without a hitch. That's a relief to those of us who would hate to see future poets vetted closely for hidden political messages in their work.

If anything, the Common episode shows that, for all the complaints we hear from conservatives about political correctness, PC is not just for liberals anymore—if it ever was.

JULY 29, 2009

THE OBAMA HATERS' EXTREME DISORDER

As congressional lawmakers return to their home districts for August recess, they could find a creature from Washington's silly season waiting for them: the "birthers."

That's the nickname given to the odd activists who refuse to believe that President Barack Obama qualifies as a "natural-born citizen."

The birther nickname is half-adapted from the Sept. 11, 2001, "truthers," who hounded the previous administration, blaming shadowy home-grown conspiracies for the Sept. 11 terrorist attacks.

I have my own nickname for both groups: sore losers.

Obama's victory, like that of his predecessor, was too unexpected for some people to wrap their minds around the win, but we always have our imaginations, which in some cases have no limits.

Respect for facts did not help U.S. Rep. Mike Castle when the Delaware Republican's recent town hall meeting was disrupted by a woman who demanded to know why Congress was "ignoring" questions about Obama's birth certificate.

They're ignoring the questions because the questions have been put to rest in most stable people's minds. For example, Dr. Chiyome Fukino director of Hawaii's State Department of Health, has reiterated her earlier declaration that she has seen the "original vital records" of Obama's Hawaii birth with her own eyes, contrary to the birthers' charges of a phony document. Hawaii newspapers also have printed photos of the 1961 announcement of Obama's birth. If there's a coverup, this one has been running for decades.

But when Castle countered that Obama is, in fact, "a citizen of the United States," the crowd didn't like that. Some erupted in boos. The woman took control and led a recitation of the Pledge of Allegiance. Within days, the video went viral, helped along by TV news programs, and threw a chill down the spines of congressmen preparing to face other groups back in their own districts.

The birther leader, Orly Taitz, a California attorney and dentist, has posted the hope on her blog that "each and every decent American comes to town hall meetings with a video camera and demands action." If so, they'll probably do Democrats a big favor. Disrupters of meetings in Democratic districts are likely to be hooted down or thrown out. Congressional Republicans had better be prepared to offer more satisfying answers than Castle gave.

But what? The best they can do is try to change the subject to some of the many more urgent issues facing Americans, like two wars, the economy and the big debate to restructure health care. The Obama birth conspiracy theorists will never be satisfied by something so humble as mere facts.

What's with these suspicious minds? Why is there such an insistence, even after his birth certificate is produced, to have Obama produce even more?

I am hardly alone in my impression that part of the birther movement is a new hood under which racism can hide its ugly face. But, looking at history, I also detect a broader illness: xenophobia, a distrust of people who come from somebody else's crowd.

That's why I call them sore losers. Unable to challenge his vote, they challenge his legitimacy. The birther challenges to Obama remind me of the bad old days of Jim Crow segregation in the South, with "literacy tests" (Sample question: How many bubbles are in a bar of soap?) and other outlandish challenges to black voter eligibility.

But my fellow African-Americans sometimes show more than our share of xenophobic paranoia too. Nation of Islam Minister Louis Farrakhan's claimed an unnamed "witness" saw New Orleans levees blown up on purpose to flood black neighborhoods, exonerating Hurricane Katrina. Polls also showed a widely held belief among black Americans in the 1990s that AIDS was created in a genocidal conspiracy against blacks.

Skepticism is healthy, but I guess I'm old-fashioned in my nagging respect for the weight of evidence over speculation.

It is human, regardless of color, to dream up suspicions that might provide plausible, if not provable, explanations for traumatic events. Some, like African-Americans, can point to real conspiracies that turned out to be true, like the infamous Tuskegee experiments that treated black men like guinea pigs for syphilis research. As the old saying goes, just because you're paranoid doesn't mean that somebody is not out to get you.

But the best response to the endless questions raised by the sore-loser movement is to put the burden of proof back on them. Obama's disbelievers, in my experience, don't really try to win the argument. They only want to arouse suspicion.

SEPTEMBER 1, 2010

BECK-A-PALOOZA

It's so hard to please some people. After pulling off the most spectacular publicity stunt since his fellow Fox News-man Geraldo Rivera opened Al

Capone's vault, Glenn Beck complains that media failed to report what his big rally was really about.

"We knew the reports would ... underestimate (the event's) crowd and we knew the media wouldn't get the message," he said on his Monday TV show. "And they didn't."

That's gratitude for you. All of the major media generously covered Beck's "Restoring Honor" rally at the Lincoln Memorial. NBC's Brian Williams even asked President Barack Obama about it during a weekend interview. (He missed it, the president says, but wished the crowd well. I'm so sure.)

Major media also covered the Rev. Al Sharpton's "Reclaim the Dream" rally, commemorating the Rev. Martin Luther King Jr.'s "I Have a Dream" speech 47 years earlier, but mentioned that Beck's rally was bigger than was Sharpton's.

Still, as far as Beck is concerned, the media didn't get it right and he let us know it—through media, of course. That included the media in which he works: his Fox News cable television program and his syndicated radio show. No one criticizes the media more than those of us who work in it, and Beck is no exception.

"Here's the story the press gave you in the end," he summarized sarcastically. "This was a rally that was non-violent, not racist and not a tea party and 87,000 people showed up."

Yup. As with Minister Louis Farrakhan's historic Million Man March at the other end of the Washington Mall 15 years ago, the biggest news from "Beck-a-palooza," as some hipsters called Beck's big day, was what didn't happen.

Nobody fought, even when Beck and anti-Beck crowds encountered each other at one point during Sharpton's march. Nor did anyone of note sound overtly racist or partisan. And no matter how many people were reported by the widely varying media accounts, organizers of the Beck and Farrakhan events insist to this day that actually there were many, many more in attendance.

And both events had something else in common: If you came expecting to hear calls to political action, you would be disappointed. Each event sounded less like a political rally than a tent revival.

"Every one of you must go back home and join some church, synagogue, temple or mosque that is teaching spiritual and moral uplift,"

Farrakhan preached. "... (W)e've got to be more like Jesus, more like Mohammed, more like Moses."

Beck sounded even less political than Farrakhan, who at least called for voter registration drives. "Something that is beyond man is happening," said Beck, glancing at the sky. "America today begins to turn back to God. For too long, this country has wandered in darkness." Really? Beck had been predicting "miracles" in the run-up to the rally. I was expecting at least a halo, beams of light and a heavenly chorus.

Yet folks who are closer to Beck's wavelength than I am probably heard his message and "miracle" without any help from the "lamestream media," as right-wingers call us.

For example, when he says with the certainty of a faith healer laying on hands that "America today begins to turn back to God," he actually is issuing a call for the faithful to join a national political transformation. So says D. Michael Lindsay, a Rice University sociologist, and author of "Faith in the Halls of Power: How Evangelicals Joined the American Elite."

"To those for whom religion is a core identity," writes Lindsay in a Huffington Post essay after Beck's rally, "this turning back entails a total transformation—until politics flow out of religious convictions, not the other way around."

Some of Beck's fans were disappointed that his rally was less raucous and less anti-Obama than typical tea party rallies. Sure, the tea party movement has mobilized economic conservatives. But Beck was reaching out to another crowd Republicans need, says Lindsay: religious conservatives, who remain as loyal to Republicans as organized labor to Democrats.

If Lindsay is right, Beck's attachment of a holy mission to his politics can help revive the sagging enthusiasm of the religious faithful, who turned out in big numbers for Presidents Ronald Reagan and George W. Bush, among other Republicans. Congressional scandals, economic troubles and Republican disarray turned off the Christian right in 2006 and 2008.

The tea party movement mobilized economic conservatives, but missed many religious conservatives. Pastor Beck could help turn the religious right on again. He doesn't have to run for president, as some speculate. He can just be the sort of player who helps get one elected.

Maybe that's the message Beck thinks the media missed. But, I'm sure his audience heard it.

OCTOBER 18, 2000

NICHE BY NICHE: FIVE YEARS LATER, JUST ANOTHER MARCH

As I joined the Million Family March I could not help but miss the Million Man March that preceded it by five years. Both events were conceived and organized by Nation of Islam Minister Louis Farrakhan, but don't hold that against them.

The aging Farrakhan, deep into what Victorian Prime Minister Benjamin Disraeli would call his "anecdotage," wants you to know that he is a changed man. In Monday's event, as in its predecessor, Farrakhan was on his best behavior. There was not a discouraging word said about Jews or any other ethnic group. After "preaching blackness for 46 years," he says he has broadened his view.

In accordance with that change, Farrakhan devoted much of his two-hour Million Family March sermon to insisting that the races are all equal in the eyes of God after all, although he still didn't sound too keen on interracial marriages.

This was not the black-supremacy rap for which Farrakhan is more famous and it was just as well. This time his crowd, although predominately black, was also quite multiracial in spots, including some interracial marriages of whites, Hispanics, Asians and what have you. Many of the non-blacks were affiliated with the Unification Church of the Rev. Sun Myung Moon, who helped fund and publicize the event. Sun Myung Moon also originated the event that set this march off from the previous one: a mass wedding and renewal of marriage vows.

Yet for all of its kindlier and gentler feelings, the new march did not draw as many people as the earlier march did. The Million Man March filled the space between the Capitol Building and the Washington Monument with black men, most of whom stood patiently and attentively, shoulder-to-shoulder, for hours in the sun.

This time you could see large patches of green between clusters of people who gathered mostly in front of giant video screens. All of this way they came, just to watch the event on television—and serve as animated props for Farrakhan's giant media event.

Both events were huge and historic but the second march lacked the first march's edgy appeal, defiant spirit and sense of purpose. In this way, the second march serves to remind us of how much has changed in America since the first march.

Five years ago the politics of race, crime and economics in America were in the pits. The economic recovery had begun, but not enough that most people were noticing it.

It was a year after the Republican takeover of Congress was fueled by "angry" white males. It was three years after the Los Angeles riots and the televised beatings of Rodney King by white police officers and of Reginald Denny by black thugs. And, oh, yes, days earlier there was the not-guilty verdict in the O.J. Simpson case, which became one of the most racially divided moments in American history.

Every day the news media seemed to be filled with images of black America in crisis, suffering a plague of street gangs, crack-cocaine wars, welfare dependency, broken families and fatherless children.

Many of us who consider ourselves to be responsible black men felt angry that black life and the black male image seemed to be spinning out of control. We felt frustrated over what could be one about it. So, when Farrakhan called for a Million Man March to "atone" and take responsibility for ourselves, our families and our communities, hundreds of thousands of us answered the call. If nothing else, at least we could march. As one participant told me, at least we could "put a positive image of black males on national TV for at least one night."

The Million Man March accomplished at least that much. It may have accomplished more, but that's hard to say. Many black men returned home after the march to energize mentoring programs and other local efforts. Black crime and victimization rates have plummeted since then. It is hard to say how much the march helped, but no one can say that it hurt.

As Martin Luther King Jr. once asked so sagely, where do we go from here?

If Farrakhan leaves no other legacy he will be remembered for pulling off the Million Man March when many doubted that it could be done. But after five years, it should have led us to more than just another march and media event for Farrakhan. It should lead us to a new understanding of what it means to take responsibility for our families, our communities and ourselves. It should lead us to understand that this task extends across lines of race as well as class. Then it should lead us to back home to understand that marching alone will not solve America's problems. Effort will.

AUGUST 28, 1996

FARRAKHAN'S BUDDIES AND BLOOD MONEY

What do you call someone who you invite to your house as a guest only to see him trash the carpet and wet all over your walls?

There are words for such a guest, words that aptly describe Nation of Islam Minister Louis Farrakhan's recent appearance in a Nashville church at the invitation of the nation's largest annual gathering of black journalists.

Speaking at the National Association of Black Journalists convention, Farrakhan thrashed journalists of African descent who work in mainstream newspapers and other media, calling us "slaves" to white media owners.

"White folks did not hire you to really represent what black people are really thinking, and you don't really tell them what you think because you are too afraid," Farrakhan said. "A scared-to-death Negro is a slave, you slave writers, slave media people."

Nobody ever went broke bashing the media and Farrakhan is no exception. After that sound thrashing, at least a few black journalists felt sufficiently intimidated or enthralled to leap to their feet in a standing ovation. If this was an audience of slaves, some of my colleagues appeared to be remarkably eager to leap from the white man's plantation to Farrakhan's.

But not everyone was impressed. Most of my friends, an admittedly older and less easily impressed crew of professionals, sat on their hands. Many of us were annoyed that Farrakhan would stand there and stereotype black journalists as broadly, ignorantly and destructively as any white editor ever has.

Nowhere in the Farrakhan journalism lecture was there a word said about the possibility that one could maybe sometimes disagree with Louis Farrakhan and still be black.

Nowhere was much said about black journalists who have refused to be go-along "slaves" to paychecks or narrow-minded bosses. Nor was any tribute paid to the experiences many outspoken black journalists bring to the news mix, even on those frustrating days when they feel like they are only shouting in a wilderness.

One good example came up the next day after Farrakhan's speech when a black United Church of Christ minister praised Gary Fields, a

black USA Today reporter, for his perseverance earlier this year in reporting on the burning of black churches, keeping the story alive for months
before other major media began to pick it up.

Farrakhan's standards for fairness are about as suspect as the white
editors who, before assigning black reporters to cover Jesse Jackson's
presidential campaigns, asked if the reporters could be "objective" or
"unbiased" about covering a black candidate. Funny but I have yet to
hear of an editor who has asked a white reporter if he or she can be
objective covering Pat Buchanan.

Farrakhan, quite the opposite, beats up the journalists who are most
likely to give a black leader a fair shake, if not a free ride.

Perhaps he was still chafing from the last bold challenge he gave to
black journalists. It came last May when he was asked at the National
Press Club about charges that he was aiding and abetting his friends in
the Islamic government of the Sudan in covering up the enslavement
and selling of non-Muslim blacks, including children, in the nation's
war-torn southern region.

Suddenly the minister's glow-in-the-dark smile vanished. "Where is
the proof?" he exploded. "If slavery exists, why don't you go as a member
of the press, and ... tell the American people what you have found."

Two reporters, one white, one black, for the Baltimore Sun accepted
the challenge and found the purchase of two black boys to be astonish-
ingly easy in the war-torn land. They reported their experience, with
photos, in a three-part series in June. Farrakhan dismissed the report and
the Nation of Islam newspaper, The Final Call, called the Sun a "Zionist
Jewish daily."

Now the plot thickens. The same week Farrakhan was attacking black
journalists, it turns out, he was applying to the Treasury Department for
permission to receive a $1 billion gift from Moammar Gadhafi's Libya, a
nation that at least one State Department report says has received slaves
from the Sudan.

Farrakhan's announced goal was to fund self-help, black-owned
farms, supermarkets and other enterprises. In his quest to win black
hearts here at home, he apparently doesn't care how many blacks it hurts
overseas. One can only wonder how he feels about the few, but significant, African blacks who profited from America's slave trade. Maybe this
is Farrakhan's version of payback.

Before Farrakhan loosely throws around the word "slave" to describe black journalists, he should look up the term "blood money." It refers to money earned with the blood of others.

Then he should ask himself, "Who's enslaving whom?"

CHAPTER FOURTEEN

HOW THE PARTY OF LINCOLN LOST PEOPLE OF COLOR

One of my pet causes has been to restore the genuine competition between the parties for the black vote that I remember from my youth—before divisive white-backlash racial politics surged in the mid-1960s GOP. Mitt Romney's loss left the Grand Old Party divided over how to increase its diversity or whether outreach is worth the effort.

This chapter collects my reflections on Romney's election night surprise, why Republicans lost black voters who used to be as loyal to the Party of Abraham Lincoln as they are to Democrats today, why Rand Paul's earnest outreach went wrong and why today's GOP finds it needs to woo blue-collar white voters back, too. This theme will continue in Chapter Fifteen as I explore conservative ideas that could woo minorities back to the GOP if the party's far-right cultural swing doesn't get in the way.

NOVEMBER 11, 2012

FACTS CATCH UP WITH SPIN

Volumes of political spin bump up against hard facts on election night.

One particularly amusing moment came that evening when Fox News anchor Megyn Kelly interrupted political consultant Karl Rove's wildly optimistic projections for Mitt Romney's chances:

"Is this just math that you do as a Republican to make yourself feel better," she asked, "or is this real?"

Thank you, Ms. Kelly. As the numbers rolled in and one battle-ground state after another fell to President Barack Obama, it was time for despondent conservatives to drop the feel-better projections and start the feel-better rationalizations.

Fox News host Bill O'Reilly got the ball rolling with this memorable explanation: If Obama won, he said as the early numbers came in, it would be because of a rising tide of nonwhites looking for giveaways.

"The white establishment is now the minority," O'Reilly said. "And the voters, many of them, feel that the economic system is stacked against them and they want stuff. ... And who is going to give them things? President Obama. He knows it and he ran on it."

I'm not sure what he means by "white establishment," unless he's talking about white voters who voted for Romney. A majority of white voters, particularly white males, voted for Romney. But a majority of other major demographic groups voted for Obama—and became the most significant trend story of this election.

If Romney had pulled the same percentage of votes among Hispanic voters as President George W. Bush did in 2004, Romney would be our new president. He would have carried Virginia, Florida, Ohio and Colorado, according to The Washington Times, while Nevada would have been too close to call.

Instead, exit polls show Hispanic support for the Grand Old Party's candidate slipped to 27 percent from 45 percent, even as Hispanic participation grew to 10 percent from 8 percent of the electorate.

Obama's support among white voters slipped to 39 percent from the 43 percent he won in 2008. But he made up for that loss with 93 percent of blacks, 71 percent of Hispanics, 73 percent of Asians and 76 percent of gays, lesbians and bisexuals.

Significantly, his percentage slipped a couple of points with blacks but grew among Hispanics. That raises new questions about what went right for Bush, who was advised by Rove, but wrong for Romney.

Rush Limbaugh, who in Republican Party circles makes Jabba the Hutt look like a pipsqueak, sounded a lot like O'Reilly in this rambling post-election rant: "Small things beat big things yesterday," he said. "Conservatism ... did not lose last night ... it is practically impossible to beat Santa Claus. People are not going to vote against Santa Claus, especially if the alternative is being your own Santa Claus."

Folks, here's a suggestion. If you want to win people's votes, stop insulting them.

I don't expect today's industry of political talk show hosts and commentators to follow that advice. Punditry is a profession where nobody goes broke by giving voice to other people's pent-up resentments. The more you sound like Triumph the Insult Comic Dog, the better.

Unfortunately in this era of Anti-Obama Derangement Disorder, the Republican primary debates often sounded like a televised audition for America's Next Top Demagogue.

Who could forget, for example, how Texas Gov. Rick Perry was booed for defending his state's sensible policy of admitting otherwise qualified undocumented students to Texas universities? By contrast, Obama's executive order to stop prosecuting undocumented students was popular enough among legal Hispanic citizens to help make up for his failure to push for comprehensive immigration reform.

Sen. Marco Rubio, a Florida Republican and Cuban-American, floated the possibility in this Congress of a deal on the DREAM Act to help undocumented youths get access to college, but he dropped the effort earlier this year. Neither party has aggressively pushed for a deal to produce the comprehensive immigration reform that the nation needs.

Now as the GOP fears for its presidential future, the long-awaited comprehensive reform is looking a lot more attractive to Republican leaders. So is Rubio. Better late than never.

Republicans need to talk more with the voters they want to reach. More important, they also need to listen.

APRIL 14, 2013

RAND PAUL HAS LOTSA 'SPLAINING TO DO

Within hours after Sen. Rand Paul's news-making speech at historically black Howard University, someone posted this new definition on the user-driven Urban Dictionary website of an awkward-sounding but quite timely verb: "whitesplain":

"The act of a caucasian (sic) person explaining to audiences of color the true nature of racism," says the entry; "a caucasian (sic again) person explaining sociopolitical events and/or history to audiences of color as though they are ignorant children ...."

Whitesplaining appears significantly to be derived from "mansplaining," which first appeared in a thoughtful, hilarious 2008 Los Angeles Times essay by Rebecca Solnit titled "Men Who Explain Things."

Urban Dictionary now defines mansplaining as "condescending, inaccurate explanations delivered with rock-solid confidence of rightness and that slimy certainty that of course he is right, because he is the man in this conversation." I am guessing that a woman wrote that definition. Message received.

Anyway, as an example of how whitesplaining should be used, consider Urban Dictionary: "U.S. Sen. Rand Paul whitesplained to students at Howard University," it says, "that a black Republican founded the NAACP."

Indeed, even Paul looked surprised at Howard when, after he asked if anyone knew that the National Association for the Advancement of Colored People had been founded by Republicans, his audience responded with a resoundingly impatient "Yes!"

"We know our history," one student shouted. Unfortunately, Paul didn't. He had to be prompted from the audience with the name of Massachusetts Republican Edward Brooke, the first African-American to be elected to the U.S. Senate by popular vote—and Paul still mangled it twice as "Edwin Brooks."

Worse, he expounded at length on the historically incorrect narrative that conservatives often give, that blacks left the party of Abraham Lincoln to follow Franklin D. Roosevelt's promise of "unlimited federal assistance," while Republicans only have the "less tangible ... promise of equalizing opportunity through free markets."

Yet, even if you buy that oversimplified view of history, as conservatives with selective memory often do, Paul completely omitted a much more important sea change, the seismic racial realignment that followed President Lyndon B. Johnson's 1964 Civil Rights Act.

In fact, Republican nominees continued to receive sizable black support; 39 percent to Dwight Eisenhower in his 1956 re-election, according to the Joint Center for Political and Economic Studies, and 32 percent to his vice president, Richard Nixon, in 1960.

But after conservatives nominated Sen. Barry Goldwater, who voted against the civil rights bill, to oppose Johnson in 1964, LBJ won 94 percent of the black vote. No Republican presidential candidate has received more than 15 percent of the black vote since.

Widening the divide was the "Southern strategy" with which Republicans mined racial backlash to win white votes, first in the South, then nationwide. Some Republicans, like former party chairmen Ken Mehlman and Michael Steele, have been quite candid and contrite in denouncing such tactics, only to be shouted down by whitesplainers in the Grand Old Party's right wing.

In fact, "rightsplainers" more aptly describes Paul's selective view of GOP history, including his own. When he was questioned about his 2010 interviews with the Louisville Courier-Journal and on Rachel Maddow's MSNBC show in which he criticized part of the 1964 Civil Rights Act, Paul denied the charge. "I've never wavered in my support for civil rights or the Civil Rights Act," he said at Howard.

Yet, as videos posted on various websites show, he wavered a lot. He opposed the part of the act that banned discrimination in restaurants, hotels and other privately owned public accommodations.

True to his libertarian beliefs, Paul used the old argument that the magic of the marketplace would prevent merchants from turning away business. But, as an African-American who is old enough to remember having to sleep in the family car on long trips—in the South and the North—after being turned away repeatedly from hotels and restaurants, I have a sharply different view.

But mere ignorance does not deter the rightsplainers. They just keep on talking.

JANUARY 30, 2013

CAN THE REPUBLICANS ESCAPE THEIR BUBBLE?

Here we go again. Whenever I try to offer a little helpful advice to Republican leaders, I hear from cranky conservatives who blow me off, saying they're "not about to take advice from a liberal like you"—or words to that effect.

To which I am inclined to respond like "Star Wars" Jedi master Yoda: "That is why you fail."

After losing the popular vote in five of the last six presidential elections, the Grand Old Party should be painfully aware of its need to step outside the conservative bubble and talk to people who are not voting for them.

You could hear that message as Louisiana Gov. Bobby Jindal, a rising national political star, told participants at the Republican National Committee's winter meeting that "We must stop being the stupid party."

He also called for fewer "stupid and bizarre" comments. I presume he was talking about such gaffes as failed GOP Senate candidate Todd Akin's campaign-sinking comments about "legitimate rape." If you want to win people's votes, don't insult them.

By now, no one should have to urge Republicans to reach out to Hispanics and other minorities. Mitt Romney's election night surprise makes the case.

Romney won non-Hispanic white voters, no problem. But he lost other major demographic groups. Had he only kept the same 42 percent of the Hispanic vote that President George W. Bush won eight years earlier, for example, Romney's campaign could have set off victory fireworks in Boston. Instead he won only 29 percent and, according to reports, had to hastily cobble together a concession speech he had not expected to give.

With the possibility looming of permanent minority status, Republicans face a predicament: How do they expand their base without alienating the hard-core, change-resistant conservatives?

I think they can take valuable lessons from two examples. One is the Democratic Party's experiences after George McGovern's catastrophic 49-state loss as the deeply divided party's nominee in 1972. Jimmy Carter's Southern centrism won him election in 1976 in the aftermath of Watergate. But it was not until 1992 that the Democratic base was willing to support another Southern centrist, Bill Clinton.

After two losses to Obama, maybe it's time for Republican moderates to reassert themselves. The political center may not be sexy, but it's better than oblivion.

My second example are Republicans at the state and local levels who have won support from blacks and Hispanics the old-fashioned way—by finding out what the voters want and helping them get it.

"The best approach for Republicans to take is not through identity politics," Bob Woodson, founding head of the Center for Neighborhood Enterprise—and a prominent black Republican—told me. "If you believe in conservative principles, as I do, then you must explain to people why those principles will bring a better outcome than the existing liberal programs."

Woodson offered as examples of racial-ethnic crossover success former Los Angeles Mayor Richard Riordan, former Indianapolis Mayor Stephen Goldsmith and former Arkansas Gov. Mike Huckabee.

Years before he ran for mayor, Riordan, a successful businessman, had deep community involvement that included purchasing a new building and raising money for the PUENTE Learning Center in the city's Hispanic community.

Goldsmith worked with local minority communities to make Indianapolis a national model for market-driven urban redevelopment during his two terms in the 1990s. Huckabee's minority outreach was so successful that he was re-elected with 48 percent of the black vote.

"Seek a relationship that can blossom into a partnership," Woodson advised. "You can't just be strongly against something. You must give a vision of what it is possible to accomplish through conservative means."

Could such a relationship produce a new national GOP star? Republicans always have been a resourceful party. If I may paraphrase what Winston Churchill once said about Americans: I believe Republicans will do the right thing, after all the other possibilities have been exhausted.

FEBRUARY 13, 2013

GOP'S CIVIL WAR A STUMBLING MESS

After Mitt Romney's 2012 election shellacking, a predictable blame-storm erupted between Republican pragmatists who want to win elections and the conservative zealots who love to argue.

The big divide is most evident in such events as the Tea Party Express staging its own rebuttal to President Barack Obama's State of the Union address, even though Republicans had booked a tea party favorite, Florida Sen. Marco Rubio, to deliver the party's official response.

Tea Party Express chose Kentucky Sen. Rand Paul, who in the past has described Obama with words like "un-American," to deliver its response—as if Rubio just isn't outraged enough.

Elsewhere you can see the divide in the new Conservative Victory Project, funded by the GOP's biggest donors, according to The New York Times, to recruit candidates who won't frighten swing voters to death.

The Times' Jeff Zeleny reports that the new group, created by American Crossroads, a GOP super PAC that consultant Karl Rove, President George W. Bush's former political adviser, and others built, is "the most robust attempt yet by Republicans to impose a new sense of discipline on the party, particularly in primary races."

In other words, they want to avoid earnest but hopelessly doomed Senate nominees like Christine O'Donnell, who memorably lost her 2010 campaign in Delaware despite running sincere TV ads to assure everyone that she was not a witch.

Or Todd Akin, whose contention that "legitimate rape" rarely causes pregnancy helped sink his 2012 Missouri race.

Or Sharron Angle who lost the 2010 Senate race in Nevada after she invoked, among other nuggets, "Second Amendment remedies" as a check on government decisions that she didn't like.

Although those are the type of GOP opponents who bring Democrats delight, Rove's move has kicked up a backlash among grass-roots tea partiers with a fury that his fellow conservatives usually reserve for Obama.

Rove's an "establishment" guy who raised hundreds of millions of dollars from deep-pocket donors and "had jack to show for it," fumed red state blogger and newly hired Fox News commentator Erick Erickson.

Rove is "a total loser," scoffed Donald Trump, who knows a thing or two about losers.

Town Hall columnist Terry Jeffrey tallied various Bush administration affronts to conservative orthodoxy in a piece titled "Karl Rove is not a conservative." Indeed? If Rove isn't conservative enough for this crowd, moderate GOP presidential hopefuls like New Jersey Gov. Chris Christie don't have a prayer.

For more invective, see the Twitter hashtag, #crushrove.

Welcome to the circular firing squad, the blame-storm that inevitably rolls in after a political party has suffered a big loss. One side says, "We were too extreme" while the other argues, "We weren't extreme enough."

Republican National Committee Chair Reince Priebus has announced plans for "Republican renewal."

Other leading GOP voices express sentiments like those of Louisiana Gov. Bobby Jindal, who said bluntly, "We've got to stop being the stupid party." But the tea partiers seem to want to double down.

To Democrats, the feud may bring to mind the sentiments that former Secretary of State Henry Kissinger is widely said to have expressed during the Iran-Iraq War: What a pity that one of them has to win.

No wonder the biggest fear of the GOP's establishment is that they will stage another big comeback in 2014 midterm elections, as they did in 2010, and learn all of the wrong lessons from it.

Even though the turnout in midterms is typically much smaller, older and more conservative than in presidential elections, as one Republican operative told me recently, the right wing might well "get the wrong message that they don't have to change—and we get clobbered again in 2016."

Nevertheless, this is a soul-searching process that the GOP needs to have—just as Democrats did after their disastrous landslide defeat with presidential nominee George McGovern in 1972.

Until now, attacking Obama was all it took to unify the party's factions. Now the factions are attacking each other. Before Republicans can take their argument about the country's direction to the Democrats, they first need to settle it among themselves.

AUGUST 7, 2013

GOP SEARCHES FOR ITS MISSING WHITE VOTERS TOO

Remember how Republican leaders vowed to improve their outreach to minorities after Mitt Romney's demographic disaster in November? Well, not so fast, amigos. A lot of folks in the Grand Old Party's conservative wing prefer to tap another group that let them down: the "missing white voters."

They're the focus of "The Case of the Missing White Voters, Revisited," a widely discussed four-part series by Sean Trende, senior elections analyst at RealClearPolitics.

"Democrats liked to mock the GOP as the 'Party of White People' after the 2012 elections," Trende wrote. "But from a purely electoral perspective, that's not a terrible thing to be. Even with present population projections, there are likely to be a lot of non-Hispanic whites in this country for a very long time."

Comprehensive immigration reform was named in a postelection "autopsy" by Republican National Committee leaders as essential to patching up frayed relations with Hispanic voters, in particular. But legislation has since run up against a major push-back by House Republicans after passing the Democratic-controlled Senate.

No sweat, Trende says. "(T)he 2012 elections actually weren't about a demographic explosion with nonwhite voters," he writes. "Instead, they were about a large group of white voters not showing up."

Using available exit poll and census data, Trende estimates the actual turnout of blacks, Hispanics and other nonwhites increased about 2 million over four years earlier, a healthy number but considerably less than the 6 million white voters who, he calculates, voted in 2008 but failed to show up in 2012.

That backs up a position advanced by conservatives Phyllis Schlafly and Pat Buchanan and the nonpartisan Center for Immigration Studies. Maybe, they argue, the GOP should focus on the disenchanted among white voters (72 percent of the electorate in 2012) instead of worrying so much about Latinos.

But unless the party wants to confine itself to local, state and regional power, it needs to reach out to all constituencies, argue GOP establishment figures like political consultant Karl Rove. Otherwise the math doesn't add up, he argues in a June op-ed in The Wall Street Journal. Romney, who won 59 percent of white voters, would have needed 62.54 percent to beat President Barack Obama, Rove writes.

"That's a tall order, given that Ronald Reagan received 63 percent of the white vote in his 1984 victory, according to the Congressional Quarterly's analysis of major exit polls," Rove writes. "It's unreasonable to expect Republicans to routinely pull numbers that last occurred in a 49-state sweep."

I don't often agree with Rove, but I think he's right this time. As the "autopsy" report found in polls and focus groups revealed, the GOP has lost touch with a lot of voters across racial and ideological lines, leading to their fifth presidential election out of the last six in which the party failed to win a majority of the popular vote.

What happened to the missing white voters? Democrats asked that same question after 1988, their fifth loss of the previous six national elections. They responded by reconnecting with working-class white "Reagan Democrats" and reoriented their message back to the political center to solve problems, not just present policy arguments.

Those days come to mind in Trende's county-by-county analysis of turnout in the key swing state of Ohio: Romney's worst turnout rates occurred in economically hard-hit rural areas like southeastern Ohio.

It is not unreasonable to see a connection between the missing white voters of 2012 and recent polls that show a widening optimism gap between the races. The new analysis by The Associated Press-NORC Center for Public Affairs Research at the University of Chicago finds that only 46 percent of white Americans say their family has a good chance of improving their living standard, compared with 71 percent of blacks and 73 percent of Hispanics. That's the widest racial gap in optimism that AP-NORC has reported since 1987.

Trende's candid language drew some predictable criticism, but he was not calling for the GOP to ignore minority voters. He mainly argues that the fate of the parties will not turn on a single issue like immigration. He's right. There's no need for the parties to argue over which Americans deserve their attention most. We all do.

NOVEMBER 5, 2012

HIDDEN SIDE OF OBAMA'S RACE GAP

In his 2008 "A More Perfect Union" speech, presidential candidate Barack Obama declared, "Race is an issue that I believe this nation cannot afford to ignore right now." Then he tried his best to ignore it.

At least in public, that is. It says a lot about the trickiness of being the nation's first black or, if you prefer, biracial president that Obama noticeably avoided saying much about race or racism before that speech, which he delivered to calm the furor over his former pastor the Rev. Jeremiah Wright Jr.'s taped "God damn America" remarks.

And Obama has avoided addressing the issue ever since. As author and blogger Ta-Nehisi Coates recently wrote in The Atlantic, citing research by political scientist Daniel Gillion at the University of Pennsylvania, Obama talked less about race in his first two years in office than any Democratic president since 1961.

It is not hard to understand why. Even in his near-silence on matters of race, his critics in conservative blogs and cable TV talk shows often sound like they can't separate Obama from Minister Louis Farrakhan.

That's politics. When your biggest asset is your lack of scariness, your opponents will focus on making you scarier.

That may partially explain why after four years in office, President Obama remains unpopular with white men without college degrees.

Most white male voters, particularly those without degrees, have been turning away from the Democratic Party since the mid-1960s civil rights era.

But polls since midsummer found Obama's white support has sunk from surprisingly high four years ago to historic lows.

A mid-October Washington Post/ABC News tracking poll puts Romney ahead of Obama among white voters by a huge margin, 60 percent to 37 percent. Obama's support among blacks and Hispanics was about the same in 2008, but his support among whites has declined from 43 percent four years ago.

Among men, a poll by Quinnipiac University found Obama attracting just 29 percent of noncollege white men in July, down from 32 percent in Quinnipiac's most recent national survey in April. Similar ABC/ Washington Post surveys had nearly identical results. Romney, by comparison, drew 56 percent in Quinnipiac's poll and 65 percent with ABC/ Washington Post.

A later National Journal study of exit polls found Obama's level of support among white men has fallen lower than any Democratic presidential nominee since Ronald Reagan beat President Jimmy Carter in 1980.

Yet, I believe that those who attribute that race-gender gap to white racism are as dangerously unfair and overly simplistic as those who say black racism is the reason why 95 percent of black voters supported Obama in 2008.

I think Sen. Jim Webb, a Virginia Democrat who retires at the end of the year, makes a good point when he argues that even rural white Southern voters like those who helped him win his seat still can be lured back to "the party of Andrew Jackson." First, he says, Democrats need to get past their "interest-group politics" and appeal to shared cultural values.

Webb pushed that argument in a July 22, 2010, Wall Street Journal op-ed titled, "Diversity and the myth of white privilege."

Advocating for working-class white males, particularly in the South, as the last group to be left out of affirmative action programs, he cited research data that showed those men to be almost as historically underdeveloped educationally and economically as black descendants of slavery.

Republican consultant Mike Murphy, a past adviser to Mitt Romney and Sen. John McCain, offered a similar assessment at a Harvard panel last summer.

"Democrats have a class model for politics," Murphy said. "They don't understand that the real fault line is culture. And we tend to win the cultural questions."

David "Mudcat" Saunders, a prominent Virginia-based Democratic strategist, agreed with Murphy. Democrats could win rural white Southerners again with the right "appeal to the culture," he told me, that lures enough persuadable voters from the Republican column.

Why, my fellow liberals often ask, do working-class voters so often vote for the class that pushes tax cuts for the wealthy? The short answer: Money isn't everything. Nothing connects quite like shared culture to persuade voters that, despite other appearances, you're really on their side.

JUNE 13, 2004

OUR GREAT RACIAL DIVIDE: FROM O.J. TO REAGAN, RACE LOOMS LARGE

It is painfully ironic to me that the death of President Ronald Reagan came so near to the 10th anniversary of the O.J. Simpson murder case. Both tragedies polarized Americans along lines of race, but also demonstrated how much the races still need to learn from each other.

There were not a lot of black faces among the crowds who paid tribute to the nation's 40th president, certainly not when compared to the multihued masses that turned out for the funerals of Presidents Franklin D. Roosevelt, John F. Kennedy and Lyndon B. Johnson.

And 10 years after the June 12, 1994, deaths of Nicole Brown Simpson and Ronald Goldman, a recent NBC News poll found that today 87 percent of whites and only 29 percent of blacks think O.J. Simpson is guilty.

Both tragedies dramatized how differently most black and white Americans still view the world, with Latino, Asian, American and other non-white opinions gravitating toward one pole or the other, depending on the issue.

Simpson's "not guilty" verdict produced shockingly different reactions between the races—cheering blacks and shocked whites—that were caught by television cameras. Suddenly whites and blacks who had been working and socializing in seeming harmony were made aware of the continuing gulf between them.

For the record, I thought Simpson probably was guilty but that the prosecution had not fully proved its case. But nuanced views like that did not get much attention in the media at the time.

The worst consequence of that ugly episode, in my African-American view, was its cost to black innocence. Just as Harper Lee's "To Kill A Mockingbird" classic wins great sympathy for the historical victimization of innocent blacks by all-white juries, the Simpson trial transmitted to many minds an image of a guilty-but-rich black celebrity freed by a nearly all-black jury and a black lawyer who "played the race card."

Some of my black friends, by contrast, told me that they cheered because they were relieved to find a rather perverse form of racial progress in the controversial verdict, that after years of believing that not even money and celebrity status could buy the kind of justice that rich white men usually get, Simpson showed them that it can be bought by wealthy blacks.

A similar racial divide followed Reagan's death. There was no cheering, to the best of my knowledge, in black barbershops or beauty salons, but there also was not a lot of weeping. Many believed that Reagan played the race card himself when he announced his 1980 presidential candidacy in Philadelphia, Miss., where three civil rights workers were slain 40 years ago. Many believed his attacks against "welfare queens," social programs and affirmative action were code words for a halt to black progress.

Although I used a lot of ink criticizing Reagan in the 1980s, I take a more charitable view of his motives. At best, I think his image adviser, Michael Deaver, was right when he said Reagan was "naive" about race.

I could hear that in Reagan's voice when he said during the 1980 GOP convention that his party respected people as "individuals, not groups." As with other issues, Reagan seemed to see only warm, engaging anecdotes, not cold, hard statistics. Black folks, by contrast, have always been discriminated against as a group and made most of their progress as a group. Reagan's view called on blacks to give up an important resource, their community bonds, for no immediate reward.

Yet it is part of Reagan's legacy that he made the world safe for black conservatives like U.S. Supreme Court Justice Clarence Thomas and others who follow the tradition of Booker T. Washington, the pre-eminent black conservative of the early 20th Century.

Washington believed that conservative values like education, hard work and self-reliance could work for blacks as well as anyone else, despite the pain of lynchings, segregation, voter disenfranchisement and other abuses. His views were far more popular with whites than blacks, who gravitated to W.E.B. DuBois and the emerging civil rights movement of the NAACP. Some things have not changed.

Yet today we also hear seemingly conservative values echoing in unusual places, like Bill Cosby's recent bracing and controversial comments about the need for low-income blacks to work harder to help themselves, even as upper-income blacks, like Cosby, try to help them. While many blacks criticized him for sounding like a snob, many others, like me, applaud his candor. Cosby was only expressing in public the frustrations many blacks feel in private about the limits of the traditional liberal agenda.

I hope his candor will lead to a new dialogue among blacks about which liberation strategies will work best in this new century. If it does lead to a new dialogue, history may show this to be another unexpected legacy of the Reagan years: He made conservative values safe for blacks to express in public again.

CHAPTER FIFTEEN

BLACK CONSERVATIVES OFFER REMEDIES, TOO

News, as a wise mentor once told me, is what happens when things are not going the way they are supposed to. Successful efforts by poor people to improve their own lives and communities tend to be buried in newspapers' back pages. From my early column-writing days, I have seen black conservatives and their white allies raise good market-oriented alternatives to government-focused liberal remedies, seen Republican presidents ignore most of these ideas, and watched Bill Clinton and Barack Obama steal some of the best—such as welfare reform, school choice, health care exchanges and an expanded Earned Income Tax Credit. This chapter offers some of my favorite solution-oriented columns about neighborhood-level efforts to fight crime, manage public housing and help poor families to help themselves.

Looking back, I remember this as a period in which black conservatives raised some good ideas for saving our cities under Reagan, George H. W. Bush largely ignored them and Bill Clinton stole them.

JANUARY 27, 1985

A MORE OPEN DIALOGUE AMONG BLACKS

President Reagan observed the anniversary of Martin Luther King Jr.'s birth by ignoring leaders of the civil rights movement. Since he is rarely on speaking terms with them anyway, few people noticed.

Instead, he met with the Council for a Black Economic Agenda. That's a neutral-sounding name for a new group of black professionals who lean toward the conservative side, but swear allegiance to neither.

I like that. That's where I stand—right in the radical middle. Unfortunately, those who stand in the middle of the road get whacked by people going both ways.

Led by Robert L. Woodson, a former fellow with the American Enterprise Institute, the council is too new to get whacked very much, but give it time. Members of the group believe welfare programs of the last 20 years have failed, and that the best way to help the poor is by spurring economic development and educational opportunities in depressed areas.

That sort of reasoning must have brought a big smile to ol' Bonzo's face. Why should he make time for major civil rights groups when he can cultivate his own new black conservative leadership?

The next day, National Urban League leaders called on the President to take steps, no matter how small, to meet with black leaders. Not that the President was not meeting with black leaders already. It's just that he wasn't meeting with the traditional, left-leaning civil rights establishment.

But as if to woo Reagan's right-wing sensibilities, John E. Jacob, National Urban League president, promised that black Americans are placing a "new emphasis" on defining their problems and devising their own solutions.

That translates to mean they are no longer so quick to blame society or "the system" for the plight of all poor people and that they are seeking a new cooperation with the private sector, not just government, to win economic opportunities. History does not record whether Bonzo smiled at that.

I am intrigued by these loosely related events. They appear to be examples of subtle shifts in conventional wisdom among some black professionals and community leaders:

• They are redefining the problem. The Urban League and Delta Sigma Theta sorority, for example, have undertaken major studies of teen pregnancy and the disintegration of black families. They and other blacks are recognizing that this is a problem the government is powerless to do much about without a lot of self-help by blacks.

• They are changing their tactics. Confrontation is taking a back seat to cooperation. The National Conference of Black Mayors last spring endorsed the conservative call for a subminimum wage for teenagers, the worst-off victims of unemployment. That was a no-no among black leaders in the mid-1970s.

• They are grooming new leadership. Evangelical church-centered leadership worked well to rally the masses for earlier stages in the civil rights struggle, but today's world calls for a leadership that understands planning and administration.

This is not to say the old-line leadership has no role. Jesse Jackson and other evangelicals offer priceless talents in rallying blacks to stay in school, hold families together, register to vote and promote other self-help causes. But when it comes to management, as he showed with his inability to account for his PUSH for Excellence Inc. funds, Jackson makes a fine preacher.

This shift in thinking and subsequent rise of a more conservative leadership have come about gradually as many blacks wonder why liberal programs have failed. An unprecedented amount of money was poured into the Great Society programs. Yet welfare rolls have grown to engulf new generations, the teen pregnancy rate has doubled and urban streets have turned into a paranoid's nightmare.

But while some programs may be of questionable value, others clearly do work. Social Security and Medicare, for example, have helped eliminate poverty among most of our elderly. Pre-school programs like Head Start have been shown in independent studies to prevent new generations from being caught in the poverty trap.

And those who blame urban problems of the last two decades on the welfare system tend to ignore a few other significant events: technological change, stagflation, rising unemployment and cultural shifts.

Neither the conservative nor liberal side has all the answers. The most refreshing new development is the way dialogue has opened up within the black community for all opposing views—not just the loudest.

APRIL 17, 1985

TOWARD A NEW BLACK AGENDA

Robert L. Woodson used to be a liberal civil rights organizer. Then he dropped out of the "alms race," as he calls it.

While in Chicago to speak to the right-wing Heritage Foundation, Woodson explained how his attitude changed while he was head of the Westchester, Pa., NAACP, a group of black scientists who had been hired as a result of picketing at a chemical plant immediately turned their backs on the organization and its low-income constituency.

"I realized you cannot apply civil rights solutions to economic problems," he says.

At 47, Woodson ain't marching anymore. Now he speaks of economic development, self-help and positive-sum solutions.

"We have to ask ourselves: Do we want the redistribution of income or the creation of wealth?" he says. "We have to be as concerned with the health of the golden goose as we are with the distribution of the golden eggs."

When Martin Luther King Jr.'s birthday rolled around, President Reagan eagerly met with Woodson's group, the Washington-based Council for a Black Economic Agenda. Because of that access and his attitudes, he is shunned by major civil rights leaders, but says he hasn't lost any sleep over it.

"Civil rights leaders failed to equip themselves for problems we have in the '80s," he said, adding a Mark Twain quote: "If the only tool you have is a hammer, then all problems begin to look like nails."

"We didn't go into the White House to ask for grants or contracts or appointments for individual members or organizations. We weren't there to talk about civil rights or food stamps or to ask for any special black programs," Woodson said.

They did talk about a tax package that would make low-income communities attractive investment opportunities—sort of like enterprise zones but with more tax incentives to help small businesses raise risk capital and provide new jobs.

They also talked about public housing. A large part of Woodson's organization are public housing tenants who took over the management of projects in Boston; New Orleans; St. Louis; Louisville; Jersey City, N.J.; and Washington, D.C. Residents elect "building captains," fire incompetent maintenance personnel, hire fellow residents, organize clean-up crews and enforce sanctions against untidyness and rent default, even if it means helping neighbors find jobs.

"They even reduced teen pregnancy in one project by developing a support system among peers so 'No' became an option once again," Woodson said.

"Boyfriends and husbands also were encouraged to sign leases, get jobs and take care of family obligations.

"In Washington, tenants organized a study group of college-bound youths. They study together, tutor each other and share grades. And when one graduates from college, the whole community gets on buses and goes to the ceremony, like a big extended family."

Woodson's group also includes educators who think public schools would benefit from more competition. "Most people view Marva Collins as an aberration, but there are 250 independent schools started by blacks who were frustrated with inadequate public schools," he said. "Some take only dropouts. In one school, 70 percent of the students are female heads of households."

Woodson is investigating other self-help ideas that appear to be working, like a group of black California professionals he has heard about who "adopt" low-income black families.

Woodson's ideas may not be perfect but they are worth your consideration.

SEPTEMBER 16, 1987

BLACK PROGRESS IN SPITE OF THIS ADMINISTRATION

Supreme Court Justice Thurgood Marshall is right when he says that of all our presidents Ronald Reagan ranks at "the bottom" when it comes to fighting for civil rights. But President Reagan also is correct when he says he has "always been on the side of civil rights." The dispute is over whose civil rights they are talking about.

Speaking in a television interview in Washington, Marshall ranked President Reagan's relations to black Americans "down with (Herbert) Hoover and that group. (Woodrow) Wilson. When we really didn't have a chance."

Marshall said nothing an objective observer of history would dispute. Very few presidents since Abraham Lincoln have been willing to risk their political standing to help racial minorities. Most, in fact, were indifferent, if not hostile.

Harry Truman, who received high marks from Marshall, desegregated the armed forces, something Franklin D. Roosevelt never quite got around to. Not surprisingly, Marshall gave highest marks to his own sponsor, Lyndon B. Johnson, who fought to enact reforms the civil rights movement had sought.

But with the Reagan years we have come from the administration of Jimmy Carter, whose secretary of Health, Education and Welfare called racism the nation's No. 1 problem, to an administration that seldom seems to recognize that racism still exists.

Reagan's defense of his record in response to Marshall's assault was as weak as oatmeal. At first, he tried to shrug it off with a quip: "A young fellow like me is not going to get mad at an old fellow like him." (Reagan, 76, is three years younger than Marshall.) Then, getting serious, he said, "I hope he will be informed that isn't my record, not only in the administration but also as governor of California. In fact, I was raised in a household in which the greatest sin was prejudice. I just wish he had known that. From boyhood on, I have been on the side of civil rights and no discrimination..."

Well, what about the record? Reagan's administration has fought vigorously against extension of the 1965 Voting Rights Act, in favor of tax breaks for colleges that discriminate and against affirmative action hiring and promotion programs.

Reagan has not been willing to take up minority causes except on his own terms. He meets with black leaders, for example, but only with conservative ones.

But one does not have to be a defender of Reagan's policies to suspect that he truly does believe his approach to be free of prejudice or, to use the favored term of his administration, "colorblind."

Unfortunately, many of us who happen to be black or members of other minority groups would rather his administration not be quite so blind to our color, because they also are blind to our cultures and our special problems.

This is why his administration so often refers to white males as sort of a new oppressed class, victims of the civil rights revolution, rather than fellow travelers who should be as interested as anyone else in enforcing laws designed to open to all groups economic opportunities they have been denied for so long.

Nevertheless, I think the Reagan years may be doing more to help black advancement than Justice Marshall cares to recognize, not so much because of Reagan's conservatism as in spite of it.

Legal justice without economic progress is a hollow victory. By holding back the growth of social service programs, Reagan has galvanized black leadership, forcing many to stop bickering among themselves and to start seeking alternatives to what some critics call "the alms race."

Besides, in many ways the Reagan administration only reflects a general decline in the significance of race in comparison to class in our society.

Never before have black Americans done so well and so poorly at the same time. More of us than ever before live in fine suburban houses, have nice corporate jobs and negotiate million-dollar contracts. Culturally, black stars like Bill Cosby and Oprah Winfrey are the hottest names in television.

Yet never before have so many of us appeared to be mired so deeply in an economic underclass as more upwardly mobile blacks follow white flight, leaving the black poor more isolated than ever.

"If racism were to disappear today," asks Robert Woodson of the conservative Washington-based National Center for Neighborhood Enterprise, "would black people be any better off tomorrow?" It is not a new question for black America. But, revived in the 1980s by black conservatives, it may lead us to new answers.

JUNE 3, 1990

WHY "BLACK CAPITALISM" HAS FAILED

When Soviet commentator Vladimer Pozner decided to venture off the beaten path of summit stories to do a bad-news story about the grim side of American life, he didn't have to look far.

Washington's Southeast Side, just behind the Capitol, gave Pozner's crew plenty of poverty, blight, screaming sirens, drug-related deaths and general despair to keep the camera whirring.

Predictably, judging by the footage that was translated and shown to us Americans on ABC's "Nightline," Pozner said nothing about the near-riots over food that were exploding back home in Moscow.

Nevertheless, the ease with which visiting Soviets eager to show how America ain't so hot still can find ample grist for their propaganda mills in our inner cities should give no decent American comfort.

That message seemed particularly piquant in a week when tens of thousands of poor women and children in dozens of states were being dropped from the federal Women, Infants and Children food supplement program because of rising costs, bad budget projections and a reluctance by Congress and the White House to provide emergency aid.

The nagging, if unspoken, question raised by Pozner's report is this: Why has capitalism worked so well for some communities and failed so many others, particularly those of inner-city blacks?

It is hard for the generation that grew up since the '60s to believe that the blighted, boarded-up commercial districts in many of today's black ghettoes once housed thriving black-owned businesses that provided goods, services and jobs to the immediate community.

Such self-contained enclaves of "black capitalism," a term that seems to have fallen out of fashion since the '60s, not only survived in spite of racism much more bold than anything the law allows today but turned it to their own economic advantage, according a new research paper published by the National Center for Neighborhood Enterprise, a Washington-based conservative, black-oriented think tank.

An important model for economic development in neighborhoods even upwardly mobile blacks have left behind is provided by the 40-page monograph, "Entrepreneurial Enclaves in the African American Experience" by sociologists John Sibley Butler of the University of Texas and Kenneth L. Wilson of Florida Atlantic University.

For example, after the 1905 oil boom, the black Greenwood section of Tulsa, Okla., housed a variety of commercial establishments, including nine hotels, 31 groceries and meat markets and two theaters.

The community's boom ended in 1923 when spurious reports of an attempted rape by a black man of a white woman touched off a violent white invasion in which 50 people died, a thousand homes were destroyed and the business district was left in ruins.

A similar enclave that also possessed manufacturing enterprises grew up under segregated conditions in Durham, N.C., in the 1920s, only to be physically devastated by urban renewal and a new highway in the mid-'60s.

"The people were bamboozled," writes Robert L. Woodson, the national center's director, in an introduction to the report. "This time by black politicians."

Chicago, the only Northern city profiled, developed similar strips of black-owned businesses in its predominantly black South Side neighborhoods.

Many old-timers have noted how such black business enclaves thrived best under segregation, but that doesn't mean America's racial apartheid was good. It limited opportunities, imprisoned many in poverty and denied enterprising blacks loans, investment capital, access to white markets or, in general, the "assimilation" process that worked so well for Euro-American immigrants.

Nevertheless, the success of self-contained islands of black entrepreneurship and commerce offers a valuable model for how today's inner-city neighborhoods might be revived, not for the sake of outside "gentrifiers" but for the good of residents who live there now.

Butler and Wilson suggest that we need to look backwards to the conflicting philosophies of Booker T. Washington and W.E.B. DuBois at the beginning of this century as we face the beginning of the next.

Those who took up DuBois' call for full integration into the nation's political, social and economic fabric without simultaneously embracing Washington's call for building basic skills and a strong black community economic base made a poor decision, the authors suggest, concluding that it's not too late to make the right choice.

It's not too late. As the events in Eastern Europe have shown, the success of American capitalism stands as an important beacon of hope to the world. Ultimately we will be judged not by how well we have made American capitalism work but by the speed and determination with which we can make it work for all Americans.

FEBRUARY 19, 1992

AN ELOQUENT LETTER TO JUSTICE THOMAS THAT MISSES ITS MARK

By flouting the usual etiquette of jurisprudence with an unusually stern and blunt open letter to Justice Clarence Thomas, another famous black judge has rattled the legal world's gilded cage.

Good for him. Anything that shakes the legal establishment's lethargy a little bit can't be all bad.

But, excited as I was at the beginning of the lengthy missive A. Leon Higginbotham Jr., chief judge emeritus of the United States Court of Appeals for the Third Circuit, in Philadelphia, dispatched to Thomas, I was disappointed by the end.

Higginbotham eloquently admonishes Thomas to appreciate the mark he now makes on history and the important tradition of Thurgood Marshall, whose seat he fills.

But, in his exposition of the past, he chooses not to deal much with the pressing questions of where we go from here. Instead, he ridicules those who raise them: "I must confess that, other than their own self-advancement, I am at a loss to understand what is it that the so-called black conservatives are so anxious to conserve."

If he were to ask, he might find out. Instead, he lumps black conservatives with David Duke and others among the most reactionary and segregationist of white conservatives, which is sort of like lumping liberals together with the barbarians of Stalinist Russia.

The condescending tone of the letter, which runs 28 pages in the current issue of the University of Pennsylvania Law Review (where Higginbotham, a Yale Law School graduate like Thomas, is a senior fellow), suggests Higginbotham is speaking to a young and naive charge (Thomas is 44) about matters that are above debate.

In other words, "You've got a lot to learn, kid, so shut your yap and be patience and let your elders guide you." Higginbotham then proceeds to bash Thomas' "stunted knowledge of history and an unformed judicial philosophy" evidenced in his past articles, speeches and public utterances which took issue with such laudable liberals as Justice Thurgood Marshall, the court of Justice Earl Warren and various civil-rights organizations.

He goes on to sting Thomas with a comment from Charles Bowser, another distinguished black Philadelphia lawyer: "I'd be willing to bet

... that not one of the senators who voted to confirm Clarence Thomas would hire him as their lawyer." Ouch.

The letter's biggest, barely hidden agenda item may have come when Higginbotham warns that blacks cannot afford to be too impressed by credentials since some of history's best-credentialed justices made "the most wretched decision ever rendered against black people in the past century," Plessy v. Ferguson, which legalized "separate but equal" facilities from 1896 until it was overturned by Brown v. Board of Education in 1954.

Higginbotham's not-too-subtle message: Don't fall under the spell of Justice Antonin Scalia, the court's one true scholar and a wizard at arguing persuasively against affirmative-action programs and everything else he doesn't like.

Higginbotham leans heavily on the weight of legal precedence in an apparent attempt to tug at Thomas' heart strings. That's fair. It should be sobering for Thomas to remember, as Higginbotham reminds him, that he is the only member of the high court ever to have endured the bracing experience of being called "nigger."

But Higginbotham chooses to ignore the most important points Thomas has raised. Thomas never has opposed equal opportunity. He has questioned only those attempts that have been made to bring about equal results.

For example, he never challenged the intent of Brown v. Board of Education. He only questioned some of the arguments made on its behalf that suggested black institutions were, by their very nature, inferior. As the graduates of many a fine black school can tell you, 'tain't necessarily so.

Nevertheless, it has led to constant confusion between "integration," the forcing of races into shared facilities, and "desegregation," the simple removal of barriers to access. As a result, black students sometimes have been taken by bus to integrate white schools that had academic records inferior to the schools the kids were bused from. That may be integration, but it's not progress.

No wonder a significant number of African-Americans, not all of them conservatives, have begun to question integration when it has weakened black institutions and left inner-city communities worse off than they were in the mid-'60s.

Who can blame black conservatives or anyone else for questioning a civil-rights agenda that has resulted in split-level black success, with some of us "making it" handsomely, about a third of us left behind in grinding poverty and a big group languishing in between, only a paycheck away from poverty?

As Bob Woodson, another black conservative and former NAACP organizer who heads the National Center for Neighborhood Enterprise, said recently: "I never marched to be next to white people. I marched so I could have a choice."

What do they want to conserve? Black conservatives I have interviewed are motivated by a variety of interests, some noble, some selfish, just like liberals. But they also espouse a deeply felt desire to conserve those values that have kept us, as a people, strong in spite of economic and legal hardship.

They may not have all the answers, but they give all of us plenty to think about.

MARCH 17, 1985

LET'S HELP THE POOR TO MIGRATE

"I didn't expect anything like this when I moved here," said the woman called "Maw." "Everybody said things would be better up North. It hasn't been better for me."

Maw lives in the West Side's Henry Horner public housing project with seven children and a lot of fear.

On one arm she has a bruise, a souvenir from a recent mugging. The side of her refrigerator has a deep gray dent, left over from a recent random bullet that crashed through her window. Her 7-year-old son has one good eye.

The other was gouged out by a maniac playmate.

Sitting on a rickety chair in her kitchen, I wonder how such a nice person got herself and her well-behaved kids into a mess like this. She tells how she left rural Alabama five years ago hoping for a better life in the North. Instead, she got a cinderblock apartment in the projects, gunshots in the night and street gangs that act like animals. She would like to pack up all the kids and move back, but what if things don't work out?

Countless others, whether welfare mothers or laid-off factory workers, would like to move from old northern industrial cities but feel they can't afford the risk. Our social safety net in Illinois, meager as it may be, is designed to help people survive with the hope that opportunity will come to them. For the forseeable future, that may be a vain hope.

When the poor of past generations ran into tough times, they moved.

"Migration ... is the oldest action against poverty," economist John Kenneth Galbraith once wrote. But today we have made it too easy for the impoverished to stay put, jobs or no jobs.

In "The Changing Economic Landscape," an article in the current Atlantic Monthly that reminds me of Horace Greeley's treatise, "Go west, young man," Washington editor James Fallows examines Chicago's nearly dead steel industry and calls on unemployed workers to do what their fathers and grandfathers did—pack up and move to where the jobs are.

"Why shouldn't we help people rather than places?" Fallows asks. "Why should we decide that the whole national history of migration, adjustment and advancement must now come to an end."

So maybe the best thing the government can do, he says, quoting from a Carter administration study, is to remove barriers to migration and help people move, if they want to, in search of new opportunity.

For the worst hard-luck cases like Maw and her family, one of the biggest barriers to relocation is the welfare system. That's one of the best reasons for us to follow the example of other industrialized nations and federalize welfare.

If the federal government, instead of cities and states, administered the program with direct payments, we could have more consistency of benefits and greater ease of transfer from state to state when recipients want to seek new jobs and better living conditions.

The idea was included in an unsuccessful reform package authored by Daniel P. Moynihan during the Nixon years. Its being revived in some Washington circles now because welfare varies too capriciously from one state to the next. Liberals hold up Mississippi's pitiful payments as an example of how callous government can be, while conservatives hold up generous Pennsylvania, where welfare in some cases exceeds the minimum wage.

And think of the financial bonus local governments could enjoy once the burden of welfare were lifted. Chicago, for example, might have more money for its schools and economic development as a result.

The program would have to make some regional, cost-of-living adjustments but not enough to encourage people to stay in hideously expensive ghettos—like those of Manhattan.

Of course, there are massive financial considerations to be worked out, further complicated by the need to reduce our national deficit.

The biggest opposition is bound to come from states that have the lowest welfare payments now and the fewest poor. Many of these states, particularly in the Sun Belt, have been getting off easily for years, sometimes with economic development subsidies at the expense of the industrial North.

Some of their political leaders even ridicule our "Rust Belt" generosity.

It's time everyone shared the load.

NOVEMBER 13, 1985

HOW TO KEEP APARTHEID ALIVE
(Muzzling Enterprise in the Projects)

If South Africa's government wants to know how to keep apartheid alive in spite of growing black political power, it could learn a lot in America.

I could bring them to a place where blacks have taken over the local government while downtown businesses remain under the control of people who are quite white. South African President P.W. Botha would be hard pressed to design a better scenario for prolonging white dominance over nonwhite minorities.

In other words, I would bring them to Chicago.

Now, before you ask the FBI to put a tap on my phone, let me make one point clear: I am not out to stifle free enterprise; Rather, I want to help more people get in on it.

The apartheid analogy is not original with me. It was used by Robert Woodson, a former Urban League organizer who now heads the National Center for Neighborhood Enterprise, who also wants to help poor minorities get in on the free enterprise system, such as it is.

Woodson used the apartheid analogy to describe Washington, D.C., after that city's black mayor helped pass laws that removed sidewalk vendors, 80 percent of whom were minorities, from downtown streets. Countless millionaires started with nothing more than a push-cart, Woodson notes, yet the City of Washington has taken that entre-preneurial opportunity away from the city's minorities while it beckons Bloomingdale's department store with millions in incentives.

Woodson was in town last week at the invitation of local public housing residents. The street peddler issue is one example Woodson used to show how government can discourage the entrepreneurial spir-it that enabled many blacks to prosper even under racial segregation. Our public housing residents know a lot about segregation, living as they do in an apartheid from whites, as well as better-off blacks.

He has a point. I used to know a woman who ran a modest sewing business in her public housing apartment. Customers went to her thanks to word-of-mouth. But she could not advertise because Chicago Hous-ing Authority rules do not allow residents to run businesses in their units and, of course, no one in the CHA was prepared to help her set up a shop in any of the many abandoned storefronts nearby.

Yet hers was the type of spirit that made Chicago's black business strips, like 47th Street and 63d Street, thrive during America's pre-1960's era of legal apartheid. When blacks were not allowed to stay in downtown hotels or shop with dignity in downtown stores, they opened hotels and stores in their own community that thrived and provided jobs. Today, most of those black businesses are gone and so are the jobs.

"The Americans decided that desegregation meant integration," James Baldwin once wrote, "and, with this one word, smashed every black insti-tution in this country with the sole exception of the black church."

Well, not quite. We also have black fraternal organizations and black community networks, the social grapevine with which neighbors can marshal their meager resources, whether in a neighborhood block club or a public housing tenant management project. It is through all three institutions that Woodson works to help blacks develop a wide range of small businesses.

Coincidentally, Woodson was profiled in last week's Time magazine as one of "a growing number of influential black thinkers who are vigor-ously challenging the liberal notions of their intellectual forebears, the black sociologists who dominated the civil rights era."

But it would be wrong to pigeonhole Woodson as a black conservative. He just wants to help poor people make an honest buck. Only in today's confused political scene would anyone consider that to be a radical notion.

JANUARY 4, 1989

KEMP AT HUD: WILL "PROGRESSIVE" BE THE RIGHT LABEL?

Of all the buzz words politicians find fashionable these days, none can beat the recently broadened parameters for what defines a "progressive."

It used to stand for movements of social protest and economic reforms, particularly those of the far left, I thought.

Nowadays it has become a less abrasive alternative for those who, for whatever reason, are uncomfortable with "left" or even "liberal."

Jesse Jackson has used the term frequently to rally the "progressive wing" of the Democratic Party, and one is hard-pressed to find local politicians in any American city who fail to wrap themselves in the "progressive" mantle.

Even Chicago's Richard M. Daley, as he runs for the seat once occupied by his father, the late Mayor Richard J. Daley, says "I'm a progressive, too," wooing independents even as he benefits from the value of his family name among conservatives who yearn to regress to the days in 1968 when some of those independent voters were being pummeled on or about the head by the senior Daley's police.

But if anyone has shown how broadly the progressive label can be stretched, it is Jack Kemp. As he accepted President-elect George Bush's nomination to be secretary of Housing and Urban Development, he described himself as a "progressive conservative."

Now that truly sounds like an oxymoron, a self-contradiction like "jumbo shrimp," "loyal opposition," "cheerleader scholarship."

But what the heck? If George Bush can promote a "flexible freeze" as his answer to the deficit, why not a "progressive conservative" for housing?

Besides, if anyone fits the label, it is Kemp. These days he is the conservative whom liberals love to like, particularly after eight years of HUD Secretary Samuel Pierce, nicknamed "Silent Sam" because he issued nary a peep of protest as the Reagan administration gutted his programs more severely than those of any other department.

As a result, Pierce probably will be best remembered as the Reagan appointee Reagan almost forgot he had appointed. One day at a celebrated reception for big-city mayors, Reagan mistook Pierce in a receiving line for a mayor. Since Pierce was the Reagan Cabinet's only African-American member, the incident gave rise to a spate of unfortunate they-all-look-alike jokes. Some legacy.

No one expects poverty or the nation's housing ills to roll over and say "uncle" with Kemp as landlord of the nation's housing programs, but he does offer something the post has been lacking: a wealth of ideas and enthusiasm for putting them into effect.

Under Reagan in the White House, defense spending was "in" while the homeless were left out in the cold. Appropriations for new low-income housing were cut in half during the Reagan years, while Reagan dismissed the problem of homelessness as largely the choice of the homeless.

Kemp, by contrast, would have been a hard-core conservative choice had he been picked for the Treasury or some similar financial post that most likely would have been his first choice.

But in urban issues, he has a strong track record as a promoter of enterprise zones, economic development, public housing reforms and public-private partnerships—which has won him remarkable success with key minority and labor leaders.

One of the first voices to praise his nomination, for example, was NAACP President Benjamin Hooks, who referred to Kemp as an "L-word liberal on civil rights."

Is he talking about the same Jack Kemp whose hard-shell conservatism last year wooed the Pat Robertson wing of the GOP, a wing that views the word "progressive" as something not to be used in front of children?

Well, if you view "progressive" not as big spending but as concepts like rent vouchers that use available funds to offer poor people some measure of choice in the housing market, rather than have their choices made for them by bureaucrats in what one Kemp supporter calls "the poverty Pentagon," the label fits Kemp and he's eager to wear it.

The ideas Kemp has embraced have shown remarkably encouraging success in various cities but lacked the big push from Washington that a high-profile figure like Kemp now can provide as head of Housing and Urban Development.

"A kinder, gentler nation doesn't have to be a more expensive one," says Robert Woodson, director of the Washington-based National Center for Neighborhood Enterprise and a black conservative who may become Kemp's deputy.

After eight years of shrinking budgets and interest while the problems of the homeless and the shortage of affordable housing have gotten worse, Kemp offers at least the chance that we will see some long-awaited action.

And who knows? We might even see some progress.

AUGUST 19, 1992

BLACK CONSERVATIVES STILL SEEKING A PLACE AT THE GOP'S TABLE

Black conservatives should be swimming comfortably in the mainstream of the Republican Party by now. Instead, they find themselves stranded in the shallows, orphaned from both parties by the racial politics of the '90s.

Their movement gained a new robustness in the heady days of the Reagan '80s and emerged with impressive polish into the spotlight of the Clarence Thomas hearings. But now, still looking for a place in a party that seems more interested in bashing the poor as looters and "welfare queens" than in using conservative principles to help them become truly independent, black conservatives show signs of weariness, frustration, division and discontent as Republican leaders, pressured from the extreme Right, all but ignore them and their agenda of grass-roots activism.

Credit a recent burst of grandstanding by Alan Keyes, Maryland's Republican nominee for this fall's U.S. Senate race, for drawing badly needed attention to the problem. In a Washington Post story that bore the slightly overblown headline "GOP Hopeful Says Party Is Racist" two days before the Republican National Convention, Keyes accused party officials of treating him like a third-class candidate because he is black.

Without naming names or actually mentioning the R-word, Keyes, a former deputy United Nations ambassador running against popular Sen. Barbara Mikulski, groused that senior Republican officials have committed too few resources to his campaign, actively discouraged potential contributors and dragged their feet on giving him a visible role at the convention.

"They are basically sending the message that beyond a certain level blacks need not apply," Keyes fumed to the Post. "If I can work in the fields, I ought to be allowed to come into the house to dinner."

Keyes didn't back down when we talked on the first day of the convention, although even before the Post story broke convention schedulers booked him to deliver two brief speeches, one in prime time that, as it turned out, was pretty much ignored by the television networks.

"Ten days ago, I didn't have a spot to speak at this convention and I find that impossible to justify," Keyes said, still fuming. "When people speak of a color-blind society, does that mean when I walk into the room they go blind? I don't buy that. I will not be treated like the invisible man."

Republican officials vigorously denied his charges, saying they had given his campaign just as much attention and support as others, regardless of race.

But even if Keyes' complaints are a desperate ploy to breathe life into a lackluster campaign, they express openly a long-simmering complaint of conservative Republicans: They are the party's Rodney Dangerfields— they get lots of tolerance, but no respect.

When I asked another prominent black conservative, Robert L. Woodson, director of the Washington-based National Center for Neighborhood Enterprise and one of the few black leaders with whom President Reagan consistently met, he lashed out at Keyes and the Republicans for playing two sides of the same race card.

He called Keyes' complaints groundless and countercharged Keys with being "morally inconsistent." Using the term Tom Wolfe borrowed from East Africa to describe the way community organizations browbeat liberal government officials to get anti-poverty funds in the '60s, Woodson observed: "I have been very critical of black civil-rights people who mau-mau on the race issue to cover their own personal indiscretions and I think using the race card to mau-mau from the political Right is no better. It erodes the moral foundation of legitimate racial complaints."

Still, Woodson, a close ally of Housing Secretary Jack Kemp, is frustrated that Bill Clinton, the Democratic challenger, is winning support by promoting "empowerment" ideas like enterprise zones, inner-city entrepreneurships and resident management of public housing that Kemp initiated but the visionless Bush neglected, largely on the advice of Budget Director Richard Darman and Treasury Secretary Nicholas Brady.

Blacks, desperate to have a voice in more than one political party, have come to this year's convention in their greatest numbers since Reconstruction, but that's not saying much: 103 delegates and 94 alternates out of a total 2,210 delegates and 2,210 alternates. Judging by polls that show black Americans to hold values that are much more conservative than our liberal voting patterns indicate, there's plenty of potential for more.

But, now that Bush is in deep, uh, trouble with his predominantly white base, he once again has pushed the black agenda to the back burner, which illustrates the short-sighted thinking that got him and the country into this mess in the first place.

Here's the point Bush is missing: The problems of black America are, at bottom, the core problems all Americans face: jobs, housing, education, training, family solidarity, economic growth and financial security, just for starters.

As Keyes would say, these are color-blind problems that cry out for color-blind solutions. So far, the Bush response is simply blind.

AUGUST 14, 1996

RIGHT ON TARGET?
What Will It Take to Bring Blacks Back to the GOP?

After spending some of the best times of their lives in political Siberia, black Republicans are tickled over Bob Dole's choice of Jack Kemp to be his running mate.

And they're not alone. Kemp's nomination is more than a victory for supply siders, although that's important. It's also a victory for conservatives who take more than a passive approach toward protecting minorities and helping the poor.

Kemp catches the irony himself when he jokingly calls himself a "bleeding heart conservative." There are other conservatives who have reached out to work alongside blacks and the poor, but few could match Kemp's enthusiasm and none could match his fame. Both are needed to give prominence to this year's great stealth issues: Race and poverty.

Once there was a time when blacks voted overwhelmingly Republican. The "Party of Lincoln" was an activist party on behalf of black rights in those days and the Democrats were the party in league with segregationists. Those roles began to reverse under Franklin and Eleanor

Roosevelt's New Deal. With the racially polarizing political strategies of Presidents Richard Nixon and Ronald Reagan, black voters in general began to feel increasingly ignored by one party and merely tolerated by the other.

After Bill Clinton won the white swing voters in 1992 by publicly feuding with Jesse Jackson, many black voters began to feel like the tail dog in a sled team—a lot of abuse and few benefits.

Every four years black Republicans could count on one thing at a GOP convention: Being approached by story-hungry reporters asking, "Why are you here?"

Privately some were beginning to wonder about that themselves. That may help explain why, despite the good face put on the convention by retired Gen. Colin Powell's stirring speech, an Associated Press survey revealed there are fewer black and, as long as we are on the subject of diversity, women delegates this year than there were four years ago in Houston.

Many, particularly black Republicans, hope Kemp can help reverse that trend. While other white Republican leaders paid lip service to black outreach, Kemp was doing it. Kemp has steadfastly continued to be a Bobby Kennedy of the Right, speaking out boldly to anyone who would lend him an ear on his party's moral obligation to provide low-income Americans with a Republican alternative path to the American dream.

It is that outspokenness, combined with a willingness to roll up his shirtsleeves and actually work with low-income public housing residents and others who are disadvantaged that has made him something of a nuisance to the party establishment. No one likes to be told to finish their broccoli when they're just beginning to enjoy their dessert.

Yet, the broccoli remains largely untouched. The Republicans' recent draconian welfare reform bill, for example, leaves poor people stranded, in the view of one black Kemp ally, Robert C. Woodson, founder of Washington's conservative grass-roots Center for Neighborhood Enterprise.

"It's sort of like pulling a knife out of somebody's chest, then telling them to get up and walk," he said in a telephone interview from San Diego. "First you have to fix the wound."

Woodson and other black Republicans hope Kemp as vice president will be an even more potent and, if necessary, more irritating voice of guilt in a Dole administration than he was as George Bush's secretary of Housing and Urban Development.

But, as much as Kemp is a unifier, he also represents for the party's white majority an important fault line, a deep philosophical divide that explains why, despite his obvious popularity, Kemp won fewer Republican primary votes in his 1988 presidential bid than television evangelist Pat Robertson did. Kemp exposed the party's dirty little open secret: Too many Republican leaders still translate "urban agenda" as a euphemism for "people we don't particularly care about?"

Powell's message at the GOP convention was clear and unequivocal. The party had reached out to him and he accepted. But there are millions of other black Americans who still are waiting for the call. Kemp knows how to reach out. He should not be left to do it all alone.

CHAPTER SIXTEEN

BIG IDEAS

A PURSUIT OF WHATEVER WORKS

Too much daily journalism, in my view, focuses on social problems with a doomsday attitude, devoid of prescriptions.

This chapter collects an eclectic array of provocative propositions, including: stop spanking children, set up "violence-free zones" in schools and neighborhoods, pay low-income women to avoid pregnancy, implement Nation of Islam security patrols in public housing, mandate DNA testing of criminal suspects, drop race from Census Bureau questionnaires, and liberate "Amos 'n' Andy" from CBS' ban on its broadcast except for academic purposes.

AUGUST 16, 2006

SPARE THE ROD, SAVE THE CHILD

Preschool expulsions? It's not a joke. It's a tragedy.

Harvard's Alvin Poussaint, one of the nation's pre-eminent child psychiatrists, drew audible gasps from an audience when he brought up the topic at a recent Washington forum on the state of young African-American males.

In particular, Poussaint wondered why African-American kids are being expelled from preschool at a much higher rate than other racial or ethnic groups.

Nationally, preschool programs expel children at more than three times the rate of kindergarten-through-12th-grade programs, according to a first-of-its-kind study by Yale University's Edward Zigler Center in Child Development and Social Policy.

African-American children were twice as likely to be expelled from preschool programs as white or Latino children, and five times as likely to be expelled as Asian-American children, the study found.

"Now, what's going on there?" Poussaint, a black man, asked the mostly black crowd at "Paths to Success: A Forum on Young African-American Men," sponsored by the Henry J. Kaiser Family Foundation and the Washington Post.

"Is racial profiling starting at age 3 or 4?" Poussaint asked. "Or is there something going on before preschool that relates to the family and the community that already is making some of these young black males unable to adapt, unable to fit, in a preschool level?"

If you thought he was about to point fingers in knee-jerk fashion at white racism, you'd be wrong. Instead, Poussaint said he believes we all should be asking where that early anger is coming from. He zeroed in on abnormally high levels of child abuse and neglect, particularly in the homes of low-income black families. His principal target was what the forum's featured speaker, Bill Cosby, has called in his own famously blunt terms "parents who are not parenting."

"There's an overuse of beating kids—corporal punishment," Poussaint said. "So that you have 80 percent of black parents believing you should beat them—beat the devil out of them. And research shows the more you beat them, the angrier they get. It is not good discipline."

Abuse also does not have to be physical, he said. Heads in his audience nodded in agreement as he described black parents cursing, shaking or slapping their prekindergarten kids or demeaning them with statements like, "You're no good, just like your father."

As someone who grew up with more than a few "whuppings" from loving parents, I have learned as a parent that other forms of discipline, like "timeouts," work better than physical or verbal abuse. Of course, these non-violent forms of discipline take more patience than some parents are able to muster.

Single parents, usually moms, can easily be overwhelmed by the challenges involved in raising children, especially boys. In the worst cases they pass the consequences of their anger down from one generation to another.

Those consequences can later include social isolation, unruly school behavior and violence. Lacking appreciation at home, kids will often shop for it out on the street.

And once they turn to criminal activity, as panelist Marcellus "Bishop" Allen told the forum, "None of you can stop nothing [they] ... want to do."

Allen knows. The president of Saving OurSelves, an anti-gang-violence organization in Newark, N.J., Allen said he joined the notorious Bloods street gang at age 9.

Spare the rod and save the child? Like a good academic, Poussaint seemed to be more comfortable with raising questions and calling for more study than with making recommendations. "I never recommend," a psychotherapist once told me. "I only try to help my patients find what will work better for them than what they're doing now."

What can be done? The Yale study found that preschools that had psychologists and other support for their teachers had a lower expulsion rate. Back at home, communities may need to provide more resources, whether voluntary or through local social service agencies, to help parents cope. We need to help more parents learn about what works best in raising children—before the problems with their families become our problems.

OCTOBER 14, 1990

SMALL MIRACLES BLOOM IN THE BRONX

"You gotta see what they're doing in the South Bronx," said a friend. She was right, although I must confess I feared for my life.

Like many folks, I had come to associate the words "South Bronx" with high crime, physical blight and moral decay, an image fixed in my mind by Jimmy Carter in 1977 and Ronald Reagan in 1980 when they staged photo opportunities in the burned-out rubble of Charlotte Street in the South Bronx.

Each promised to rebuild our cities, each failed to deliver, and the residents seemed helpless to do anything about it.

The dreary, lawless image was further imbedded by Paul Newman's movie, "Fort Apache: The Bronx," by Tom Wolfe's best-seller, "Bonfire of the Vanities," and by recent news accounts of crime and despair that even had a recent Time magazine cover trumpeting New York City's slide into the swamp of urban violence.

Blame the politicians, banks and other civic leaders whose subtle policy of triage wrote off blighted areas like the South Bronx with a strategy of "planned shrinkage" so that other, slightly better-off communities on the brink might be saved.

"HPD (the city housing and planning department) had plenty of money for demolition, but not for preservation or restoration," recalls Genevieve Brooks, deputy Bronx burrough president and a former Charlotte Street area organizer.

But look at Charlotte Street now. Revived, it displays new single-family suburban-style homes, complete with driveways, flower beds and clean streets.

Rubble, graffiti and broken windows on the blocks in the nearby Longwood neighborhood, where Newman did his filming, have been replaced by a park and refurbished brownstones.

Jose Madrigal, a 20-year resident of nearby Fox Street, which former Mayor John Lindsay once called the world's most dangerous street (one block had 34 murders in one bloody year), proudly shows off the refurbished, re-occupied brownstones on his formerly ferocious block.

These small miracles were initiated not by government but by neighborhood residents who organized into neighborhood groups that have become self-contained community development corporations.

Gennie Brooks' neighbors formed the Mid-Bronx Desperadoes Community Housing Corporation in 1974, she says, "after we got tired of waiting for the government to do everything for us."

Madrigal similarly brags about how his Longwood neighborhood's Banana Kelly Community Improvement Association, where he works, has helped rebuild not only buildings but also a sense of community— and hope.

Neighbors look out for each other again, he said. They keep an eye on wayward children, pick up scraps of paper on the street and keep graffiti off walls, in marked contrast to nearby deterioriating public housing units.

And the organization also operates an innovative "Work Prep" program that puts formerly homeless families together with currently homeless families not only to house but also to help them through sometimes savagely candid discussion sessions to re-organize their lives and avoid the need ever to be homeless again.

As marvelous as their work has been, community development organizations like these do not work their miracles alone.

Both received technical assistance on the in's and out's of financing and planning from organizations like Local Initiatives Support Corp., an 11-year-old not-for-profit that has helped local groups build or rehabilitate more than 5,000 low-income housing units in the South Bronx alone. With its affiliated National Equity Fund, LISC has established partnerships between more than 600 neighborhood groups and another 600 corporations and foundations in cities across the country.

And, since the private market normally shows no interest in building low-rent housing, community development groups have made good use of indirect government assistance in the form of low-income housing tax credits.

Tax credits may be the best way for government to assist the development of low-income housing. Instead of deciding which contractors or neighborhoods will get the government's money to build housing, a process that often hinges less on competence or need than on political connections, low-income housing tax credits provide an incentive where none currently exists for developers and banks to build high-quality, low-cost housing where it is needed most.

The South Bronx, long associated with crime and despair, is now associated in my mind with another word: Hope.

Too bad grass-roots community leaders like Gennie Brooks or Jose Madrigal are a story you don't often see on news media that have become addicted to provocative sound bites and exciting visuals. Pretty houses don't make exciting visuals, I guess.

Yet, for the future of our cities, neighborhood-based development may be the most important story anyone can tell, if only the rest of us will take notice of it.

APRIL 18, 2007

MORE KILLINGS, MORE FEAR

He defied our expectations in the worst ways.

We have a lot to be afraid of in this era of global terrorism and high school shootings. But the young man who took more than 30 lives as well as his own at Virginia Tech did not appear to fit either profile.

Cho Seung Hui, 23, was born in South Korea but was a legal resident of the U.S. He had everything to live for. And yet, he killed.

It was the deadliest killing spree in modern American history.

And once again, we are afraid. Rural Blacksburg, Va., is the type of place many big-city people considered moving to after the terrorist attacks of Sept. 11, 2001. Now a college student with a couple of hand-guns has shattered that illusion.

With that, the focus of media and many others turns to the guns. Reporters ask where Cho got his guns and whether any firearms laws were broken. The questions are now routine. It is easy to blame guns for such violence and pass new laws to control gun violence. But it pays to focus on what works, not what feels good.

As I noted during the first wave of shootings in the 1980s at rural middle schools, country boys have been firing guns since the days long before this country's birth. Yet, only in recent years have we seen them turn those guns on their classmates. Why?

I'm not a big gun-ownership fan, but I do care about finding remedies that work, not just analgesics for temporary relief.

Researchers in the wake of the Columbine High School massacre eight years ago this month in Littleton, Colo., where two teenage gunmen killed 13 people and themselves, have found the problem is in the heads of the shooters.

"The most common element of these events is that the perpetrator typically says something to their peers about their intentions," said Rep. Tom Tancredo (R-Colo.), whose district includes Columbine High School. That also was an important conclusion of the U.S. Secret Service after the Columbine tragedy when agents started interviewing survivors of high school shootings at the request of the Department of Education..

"[Secret Service agents] were looking for a common profile that could let everyone know what to look for in potential high school killers," said Robert Woodson, head of the National Center for Neighborhood Enterprise, who helps coordinate anti-violence programs in schools. "They didn't find a common profile, but they did find that the predators almost always told others what they were going to do before they did it."

Ten years ago, Woodson helped volunteers in the District of Columbia sew up a truce between warring gangs at the Benning Terrace public housing development in Washington. The development had seven homicides in two years but has not had another killing since then. Woodson's organization has since spread the concept of "violence-free zones" to 21 schools in six cities.

Although violence at those schools seem to have been avoided in a few cases by students who tipped off teachers, Woodson said, students are more likely to share useful information with outsiders who serve as "listening posts." In Woodson's program, those listening posts are older volunteers who are "tuned in" to "the same cultural ZIP code" as the students who appear to be the most troubled or serve as confidants of students who are.

That's the sort of early warning system that can be valuable, yet also virtually nonexistent on college campuses, especially big ones like the 26,000-student Virginia Tech. It's too early to say that big, impersonal campuses are to blame for such catastrophes. They only seem to have a larger potential for problems.

"Our schools are like a human body," says Woodson. "The most effective form of protection for the human body is to strengthen its own immune system."

In fact, Virginia Tech's English Department chairwoman said Cho had been referred to counseling because his writings were disturbing.

What our schools need is more people who can serve as antibodies, watching out for troubled students and offering them help. If any sense can come of such senseless killings it may simply be that we have to pay more attention to each other in times of peace, not just terror. Expect the unexpected.

JANUARY 3, 2000

WHEN INNOCENCE ISN'T GOOD ENOUGH

You might think it is a simple matter for prison inmates to walk free when DNA tests prove they are innocent.

You also might think it is easy for them to at least get permission to have the evidence in their cases retested with modern DNA testing techniques.

You might even think prosecutors and the courts are interested, more than anything else, in justice, in finding the actual wrongdoers, not in keeping apparently innocent people locked up.

Maybe you believe in the tooth fairy too. Wrongful conviction, it turns out, is not enough to get you out of jail, even when your innocence is supported by DNA evidence.

Clyde Charles, 46, was one of the lucky ones. He made national news a few days before Christmas when he walked out of the Louisiana State penitentiary at Angola, cleared by DNA evidence, after serving 18 years in jail for a crime he did not commit.

He was lucky because the evidence had not been lost or destroyed as it has been in countless other cases. He was lucky that the Innocence Project at New York's Benjamin N. Cardozo Law School at Yeshiva University successfully sued Louisiana in 1998 to allow Charles to be retested.

Cardozo law professor Barry Scheck, who became famous as O.J. Simpson's DNA attorney, helped free Charles and almost 70 other inmates using DNA testing techniques that were not available when the men were convicted.

Charles was lucky, project attorneys say, that the state did not fight to keep him locked up. Instead, before approving the test, the state required Charles to promise not to sue the state for false imprisonment.

In Texas, Roy Criner has not been as lucky.

Criner, 34, is a burly, baby-faced logger who was sentenced to 99 years in prison for the rape and murder of Deanna Ogg, 16, whose body was found in Montgomery County, Texas, in 1986.

Criner has remained in jail despite two DNA tests in the past three years that refute the testimony that convicted him.

Criner and Charles are two Innocence Project cases being spotlighted in "The Case for Innocence," a "Frontline" documentary scheduled for broadcast Jan. 11 on WTTW-Ch. 11.

When "Frontline" reporters interview Texas state officials, including Judge Sharon Keller, who wrote the appellate court's rejection of Criner's appeal, they simply shrug off the DNA results as compelling, but not compelling enough.

Could he be innocent, an interviewer asks. "Oh, I suppose that's a possibility," says Keller after a slight pause, as if the notion had not occurred to her until that moment. "But he certainly hasn't established it."

So what if all of the arguments made by the prosecution in Criner's case have been refuted? What if, she offers, Criner had an accomplice that the court did not know about.

It is not enough that the state no longer has proof that Criner is guilty. Keller says Criner now must establish that he is "unquestionably innocent."

Such defensiveness on the state's part is all too typical. The sad fact, as one of Criner's defenders puts it, is that "innocence is not a basis for getting out of prison in this country."

Sadder still is the refusal of many prosecutors to reopen cases after DNA evidence shows the wrong person has been jailed.

The path to federal appeals also has been squeezed by new federal laws and Supreme Court decisions limiting one's rights to appeal.

What is to be done? Defenders of the status quo argue taxpayers can't afford to open the floodgates to every inmate who wants a new trial. But taxpayers don't have to. All the states have to do is to pass new laws, rules and procedures that protect prisoners' rights while avoiding frivolous appeals.

A DNA evidence law passed in Illinois two years ago makes a good model. Among its requirements, the conviction must have occurred before DNA testing was used in criminal investigations. The conviction also must have been based almost entirely on identification by a witness and the evidence to be tested has to have been in the custody of a law-enforcement agency since the trial ended.

In the meantime, we, the public, should let our governors and prosecutors know that we want justice for victims and criminals, not just big prison body counts.

One prominent governor, George W. Bush, could make a particularly meaningful contribution by looking into the Roy Criner case.

True, Bush has a lot on his mind these days. But he does call himself a "compassionate conservative."

Talk is cheap. Actions speak.

POSTSCRIPT: After new evidence was presented, in July 2000 state District Court Judge Michael Mayes stated that he could only conclude that Criner was innocent and that he would sign a request for a pardon. In August 2000, the Texas Board of Pardons and Paroles voted unanimously to set Criner free after he had served ten years of a ninety-nine year sentence. Gov. George W. Bush concurred, stating that he agreed "that credible new evidence raises substantial doubt about the guilt of Roy Criner and that he should receive a pardon." As of 2012, Criner had received nearly $204,000 in state compensation, according to the Innocence Project, http://www.innocenceproject.org/.

APRIL 25, 2007

THE 200TH REASON TO TEST DNA

In a statistic that is both gratifying and horrifying, an Army veteran from Chicago is the 200th person to be exonerated by DNA evidence, according to the Innocence Project, a non-profit New York-based legal clinic.

That's gratifying because justice—long denied to innocents like Jerry Miller, 48, and the 199 others who were exonerated before him—finally has been served. But Miller's good news is also horrifying in the questions it raises about flaws in our nation's criminal justice system.

For one thing, only 10 percent of felonies produce any biological evidence that can be tested for DNA, said lawyer Barry Scheck, who co-founded the Innocence Project in 1992 to help prisoners prove their innocence through DNA evidence.

A closer look at the 200 exonerations produces an unsettling view of the mistakes that can made on the way to a conviction. Seventy-seven percent of the convictions resulted from mistaken identity. Almost two-thirds involved faulty scientific evidence. About a fourth involved false confessions or incriminating statements, and 15 percent involved incorrect information from informants.

One type of case most likely to leave DNA evidence is rape, which amounted to 123 of the 200 exonerations. Rape is a crime that also reveals the most evidence of racial bias.

Only 12 percent of sexual assaults are between a victim of one race and an assailant of another, according to Justice Department statistics, yet 64 percent of the 200 exonerated convicts were black males convicted of raping white females.

"The most endangered person to be in America is a black man accused of raping a white woman," Scheck told me in a telephone interview.

Of course, such stereotypes can cut both ways, as revealed in the exoneration of three former Duke University lacrosse players of a rape that apparently never happened. Major media and many of the rest of us, including me, found it all too easy to believe the overzealous prosecutor's scenario of privileged white college boys taking criminal advantage of a poor black woman who was working her way through college as a stripper.

"This entire experience has opened my eyes up to a tragic world of injustice I never knew existed," said Reade Seligmann, one of the cleared Duke students. "If it is possible for law enforcement officials to systematically railroad us with no evidence whatsoever, it is frightening to think what they could do to those who do not have the resources to defend themselves."

So it is. Nothing concentrates the mind around the subject of justice like the prospect of being falsely convicted.

"I am not angry," Jerry Miller told Chicago Tribune reporter Maurice Possley before a Cook County court set aside Miller's conviction Monday. "I'm not swept under the rug anymore."

Unfortunately, too many other cases do get swept under the rug, without the advantages of big money or a blue-ribbon team of defense lawyers.

Gary Dotson was one of the first DNA exonerations in this country, in 1989, when tests showed he had not committed a rape for which he had been convicted in a Cook County court, even though his accuser recanted years earlier. Since then, DNA use has led to other reforms, such as a national federal DNA database, the videotaping of interrogations and changes in lineup procedures to avoid mistaken identifications.

Even so, we still show a troubling tendency to jail innocent people. Any single case of jailing the innocent—and letting the guilty run free —is too many.

Scheck would like to see DNA databases and videotaped interrogations for all felonies, not just murders, which is the case in many states. Too many DNA backlogs also mean evidence sits around too long, allowing culprits to commit more crimes.

At the same time, the national debate is only beginning as to whether too much DNA evidence can be gathered and stored too often. Civil libertarians justifiably fear that too much DNA information will be available to too many people for questionable reasons.

APRIL 23, 1989

D.C.'S BLACK MUSLIM DOPEBUSTERS

In Washington, D.C., where drug wars have turned our national capital into the world's murder capital, the most effective anti-drug unit has turned out to be an unusual bunch of volunteers who call themselves "the dopebusters."

They have no official connection to the police, the FBI or drug czar William Bennett.

They are Black Muslims, members of Minister Louis Farrakhan's controversial Nation of Islam.

Armed with walkie-talkies, they patrol certain apartment buildings and housing developments in characteristic Muslim duds: Conservative suits, bow ties, white shirts and clean-shaven heads.

They began patrolling Mayfair Mansions, an all-black, formerly middle-class apartment development, last year after residents invited them to try their luck against local drug dealers.

The results were immediate and decisive. After a few confrontations with Muslim-style rough justice in Mayfair and the Paradise Manor apartments next door, local drug dealers took their trade elsewhere.

Local crime went down. Drug-related killings stopped. Though the District of Columbia police chief criticized the Muslim patrol as vigilantism at first, the support of some District council members brought cooperation. Residents breathed easier. Children again played outdoors. Senior citizens walked in peace.

Requests for more Muslim aid poured in from neighborhood, civic, tenant and religious groups throughout the Washington area. Just as criminal activity feeds on itself, so does community crime-fighting.

Yet the Muslim success has received little coverage outside the D.C. area. We are reluctant to take the Black Muslims seriously, it appears, even when they are making a serious dent in a serious problem.

By ignoring such grass-roots, community-based efforts, we may be cheating ourselves of information that can lead us to more effective solutions, with Muslims or without.

Like others, I have reservations about the use of Muslims as irregular volunteers in the anti-drug war. Their recent history has been riddled as much with controversy as their earlier days were riddled with bullets.

Take their regard for constitutional rights, for example. When a local television camera crew recorded about 10 Muslims meting out their special brand of rough justice on a man wielding a shotgun, the Muslims beat up the camera operator, too.

Then there are the charges of extortion. One apartment building manager said a Muslim representative told her that the Muslims would appreciate a "donation" of, say, $5,000 in exchange for dopebusters' security work.

Granted, the Muslims' clean-shaven bruisers can seem intimidating. Then again, good security costs. Public demand has outstripped the Muslims' ability to bear all costs themselves. What price safety?

When his men roughed up the TV crew, Dr. Abdul Alim Muhammad, the black physician who heads the Nation of Islam's D.C. mosque, apologized. You have seen us at our worst, he pleaded to news media; now come back and see us at our best. Perhaps we should.

Robert Woodson, the black conservative who heads the Washington-based National Center for Neighborhood Enterprise, is dismayed that, as federal officials call for more police and beefed-up security in public housing, they overlook grass-roots crime-fighting efforts like the Muslim "dopebusters."

"We would rather risk failure with people with whom we are comfortable than risk success with those who hold unorthodox views," Woodson said.

It has become axiomatic among black commentators to wax nostalgic about the old days when those of us who grew up in black neighborhoods (they were not called "ghettos" then) looked out for each other, helped each other through hard times and disciplined each other's children when they misbehaved. Our wealth was in our spirit and our moral network, woven too tight for social decay to eat its way through.

Back then, the Muslims were generally regarded as a quaint, if eccentric, group, selling their newspapers, philosophy and fresh fish door to door. No one would have guessed that now, in an age of unprecedented progress for black Americans, we would be looking to these same Muslims for a semblance of law and order.

Yet, today, with desegregation and upward mobility, our old support network is frayed and tattered, and the black poor find themselves more isolated than ever.

Although whites still outnumber blacks among those whose household income falls below the poverty line, Census Bureau data show most white poor live integrated with better-off whites while almost all black poor live in "poverty areas," the ghettos.

In those areas, we find less to fear from the Ku Klux Klan and other threats of the past than we do from what Woodson calls "the enemy within," a social decay that has mothers trading children for drugs and youngsters wielding Uzis in urban drug wars.

The Muslims are trying to tell us something. Maybe we should listen.

MAY 5, 2013

HOW TO UPDATE CENSUS RACE QUESTION

A notable example of how Americans fall through the cracks in census data-gathering caught my eye recently. It appeared on the black-oriented TheRoot.com website under this intriguing headline: "I found one drop; can I be black now?"

The "one drop" is a reference to the old oddly American racial rule that one drop of "black blood" in your veins makes you black. As a full-fledged black American, I wondered who is so eager to join the club?

The answer turned out to be a white woman who had written to The Root's "Race Manners" advice column. Through genealogical records she uncovered an African-American ancestor who long ago had passed for white. Now faced with census forms, among other documents that ask us Americans for our race, she was wondering which box to check.

"Do I check both, and come across as a liar to those who don't know my history?" she asked. "Or do I check just white, and feel like a self-loathing racist?"

I sympathize with the woman's confusion. In changing times, government forms are often the last to catch up.

It has only been since 2000, for example, that mixed-race people are allowed to check more than one racial box on the U.S. census. And that's just one area of government forms not keeping up with America's changing demographics.

On question No. 9 in the 2010 form, for example, you can check "white" or "black, African-American or Negro" or "American Indian or Alaska Native." Then there are 11 other choices that are ethnic nationalities in Asia and the Pacific Islands.

Hispanics are mentioned in a separate question, clearly as an ethnic group, apparently in response to the confusion in 2000 that the Census Bureau says resulted in about 43 percent of Hispanics failing to specify a race. Some even wrote in "I am Hispanic."

Even so, the new form leaves out mention of the entire Arab world, among other significant regions, leaving those individuals to check some other group's box or write something in the catchall box labeled "some other race."

More extensive questions of ethnicity and ancestry have been asked since 2000 by another set of longer forms, the American Community Survey. Unlike the 10-year census, the survey is conducted among a sample of 250,000 people every month.

That's a good model, some experts, say, for how the 10-year census could give a more complete and realistic picture of America's changing demographic landscape.

"We shouldn't be governing in the 21st century by a race classification given us by a German doctor in 1776," former Census Director Kenneth Prewitt wrote to me in an email.

He was referring to the German medical scientist Johann Blumenbach, whose 1776 book, "On the Natural Varieties of Mankind," established the familiar but woefully inadequate five-race model we know so well today: "Caucasian, Mongolian (Asian), Malay (Pacific Islanders), American Indian and Negro."

That was too simplistic then, let alone now. Yet we still tend to stick with it officially, in our daily conversations—and even in a popular children's song about how God loves all the little children in the world. ("Red and yellow, black and white/They're all precious in his sight ...")

In a book to be released in June, titled "What is Your Race? The Census and Our Flawed Efforts to Classify Americans," Prewitt, now a public affairs professor at Columbia University, calls for an overhaul of census race questions.

It's not enough just to count noses, he argues. We know, for example, that income gaps have been growing since 1960 between Americans of all races who have schooling beyond a high school diploma and those who don't. Yet, our focus on racial differences too often gets in the way of what we should be learning about class barriers.

Prewitt lays out a bold plan for phasing out questions about race while phasing in new questions aimed at measuring differences in income, education and upward mobility and social assimilation—key questions in determining how well our fabled American melting pot is working.

Whether Prewitt's scheme is widely embraced, it's worth talking about. Americans are changing too much for us to squeeze ourselves into the old boxes.

FEBRUARY 1, 2012

GINGRICH'S SECRET LOVE AFFAIR WITH SAUL ALINSKY'S TACTICS
Activism Model Works Both Ways

Saul Alinsky is a name most people don't know, so why does Newt Gingrich drop Alinsky's name at every opportunity without explaining who he is? Because it is not what the Republican presidential candidate says that counts; it is what his audiences feel when he says it.

"Saul Alinsky radicalism is at the heart of (President Barack) Obama," the Republican presidential candidate said on CNN last weekend.

"I believe in the Constitution; I believe in the Federalist Papers," the former speaker of the House told a Jacksonville, Fla., audience Monday. "Obama believes in Saul Alinsky and secular European socialist bureaucracy."

Can you feel it? Talking about the late, great Chicago-based community organizer this way is a "dog whistle," in political lingo. It is heard in special ways by those who are tuned in to the conservative blogosphere, which can't seem to get enough of Alinsky, especially when it enables bloggers to link words like "radical" and "socialist" to the former Chicago community organizer now sitting in the White House.

Having covered some of the Chicago community groups that Alinsky helped launch, I find Gingrich's demonization to be ironic. In many ways, the Georgia Republican has more in common with the Alinsky model of activism than Obama does.

For example, one of the most memorable rules in Alinsky's popular "Rules for Radicals: A Pragmatic Primer for Realistic Radicals" instructs: "Pick the target, freeze it, personalize it, and polarize it." Watching Gingrich go after the media in debates by personalizing figures like CNN's John King and Fox's Juan Williams made me wonder whether Gingrich was following Alinsky's gospel.

Unfortunately, for Gingrich, the tactic flopped when he tried to go after CNN's Wolf Blitzer in the first Florida debate. "Blitz" remained unshaken and Gingrich lost the night. Gingrich should have followed another Alinsky rule: "A tactic that drags on too long becomes a drag."

Obama, by contrast, only reluctantly turned to a personalizing and polarizing populism in recent months, after almost three years of fierce obstruction by congressional Republicans. Many Obama supporters urged him to get more Alinsky-tough—like Gingrich.

In fact, quite a number of conservative-thought leaders hate Alinsky but love his books. His advice shows how to get results, regardless of whether you're a lefty or righty.

"The best way to describe Alinsky is a 'pragmatic populist,'" Sanford D. Horwitt, author of "Let Them Call Me Rebel: Saul Alinsky, His Life and Legacy" told me in a telephone interview. "Alinsky had no patience for rigid ideologues."

As a result, the "father of community organizing," as he is widely known, may be more passionately popular on the right these days than he is on the left.

For example, Dick Armey's FreedomWorks, a conservative advocacy organization that assists tea-party groups, has distributed Alinsky's books in training sessions. William F. Buckley Jr., the late conservative icon, described Alinsky as "very close to being an organizational genius."

The sincerest form of flattery may come from conservative adaptations of Alinsky's model like David Kahane's "Rules for Radical Conservatives" and the very similarly titled Michael Patrick Leahy's "Rules for Conservative Radicals."

By contrast, the left-progressive Occupy Wall Street movement could use more Alinsky advice, in my view. Alinsky insisted, first and foremost, that organizers have a clear agenda and a plan for achieving it before beginning their protest.

The occupiers have neither, which makes me wonder how they would know victory if they achieved it.

Yet, as much as the right begrudgingly admires Alinsky, conservative political correctness prevents many from admitting it. It's easier to police their ranks by pinning on a soft-on-Alinsky label. Sarah Palin, for example, recently accused Gingrich's Republican critics of practicing "Alinsky tactics at their worst." Hardly. But she probably hasn't read much of the real Saul.

In rebuttal, we have Philip Klein at the Washington Examiner labeling Gingrich a "Saul Alinsky Republican," citing the Newtster's John King attack. As Texas Gov. Rick Perry might say, "Oops!"

I'm changing my view of Gingrich's Alinsky obsession. It might be the result of love more than hate. After all, they have so much in common.

JUNE 8, 2011

SHE'S JUST NOT THAT INTO YOU. REALLY.

An Australian demographer has found a malady that makes some middle-aged men think they are more attractive to women than they actually are.

He calls it "hotness delusion syndrome."

I don't know if it's true, but it may help us to answer some bizarre questions on the recent political scene. Among them: Why would Rep. Anthony Weiner send photos of himself via Twitter to young women, giving new meaning to the congressional term "distinguished member"?

The New York Democrat's woes involve "sexting," the text-messaging version of phone sex. He sent what he called "inappropriate" messages to six young women. These famously included a photo of his crotch bulging in underwear that he sent by Twitter to a female college student in Seattle, who he says he knew only by their exchanges of tweets.

There were also photos of him flexing his arms and bare chest that he sent to women he said he knew by Twitter, before and since his marriage last summer to Huma Abedin, an aide to Secretary of State Hillary Clinton.

His macho-man photos are haunting not only for their goofiness but also because they so closely mimic the bare-chested self-portrait that brought an abrupt end to the political career of U.S. Rep. Christopher Lee this year.

Lee, a New York Republican and married father, posted his "macho" photo on Craigslist, passing himself off as a divorced lobbyist to an anonymous woman who was seeking a date. If anyone should have learned from Lee's experience, it is Weiner.

Yet they were hardly the first prominent men to be tangled in allegations of reckless sexting. A more aggravated level of lewdness was claimed against retired pro football quarterback Brett Favre last year in an investigation of photos of his private parts he allegedly sent to Jenn Sterger, 26, a sidelines reporter for the New York Jets.

In the pop music world, rap music star Kanye West is alleged by RadarOnline.com to have sent photos of his family jewels to several women via MySpace. Fortunately for him, the social standard for rap stars is such that the photos actually may enhance his career.

The larger question is why this online age seems to turn otherwise sensible men into the cyber-equivalent of Dominique Strauss-Kahn, the former International Monetary Fund chief and one-time French presidential hopeful, who New York police say sexually assaulted a hotel maid.

We already know how the empowering anonymity of the Internet can make otherwise civil souls turn the online world into what Australian ethicist Clive Hamilton denounced as a "belligerent brutopia." I find evidence of that on a daily basis in emails.

A further clue into the dark reaches of the hyper-masculine cyber-soul might be found in the malady hotness delusion syndrome that Australian demographer Bernard Salt found in men in their 40s who think they are super-attractive to women.

A shortage of eligible middle-aged bachelors in Australia is causing some single guys to overestimate how desirable they are to the opposite sex, says Salt, author of "The Big Tilt: What Happens When Boomers Bust and Xers and Ys Inherit the Earth."

I suspect a version of this malady may be showing up on this side of the Pacific, especially in men who think sane women can't wait to see twittered photos of their naughty bits.

Powerful Washington men may be particularly susceptible to delusions of their own hotness as they hear more respect and admiration than they experienced on, say, the high school debate team.

Wherever they may be, Salt advises men in their 40s to look in the mirror before they get too full of themselves and "discount their hotness by the proportion by which there are more women than men."

Otherwise, fellas, you could be in for the rude revelation that that certain someone is not nearly as into you as you might have thought.

JULY 28, 1999

A $200 BRIBE FOR NO BABIES: WILL THIS SOLVE ONE PROBLEM CAUSED BY DRUG ADDICTION?

Coming soon, perhaps to a birth-control clinic near you: A $200 bribe for you to get yourself sterilized, either temporarily or permanently.

Of course, there is a catch. To qualify for this program, you must be a drug addict or in recovery.

A cash-for-sterilization offer begun by an organization called CRACK (Children Requiring a Caring Kommunity), was founded two years ago in Anaheim and has opened its first national expansion office in Chicago.

CRACK also has put up billboards in Florida and Minnesota with a toll-free hot line and this straightforward offer: "If you are addicted to drugs, get birth control. Get $200 cash. Stop the cycle of addicted newborns now!"

This sort of thing can catch on. Other states may follow. There are a lot of people around who, like CRACK's founder Barbara Harris, want to do something drastic about the thousands of babies born every year to drug-addicted parents.

There is nothing new about states offering birth control to low-income women as part of their health coverage. But just because it is offered does not mean people are going to take advantage of it, especially when their lives already are disorganized by drug addiction. For them, Harris merely is adding $200 worth of inducement.

Her offer is open to men and women. So far 57 women and zero men have taken her up on it, according to CRACK figures.

Hey, guys, what's going on? Shy?

Of course, there also are a lot of people who are just as troubled by the notion of paying potential parents to get themselves sterilized as they are by the crack babies such parents sometimes produce.

"Coercing women into sterilization by exploiting the condition of their addiction is just plain wrong," one Chicago-area Planned Parenthood official said.

Talk radio was even more agitated. The most common word I heard to describe the program on one black-oriented talk radio station in Washington, D.C., was "genocidal."

"White America realizes they are about to lose their majority," one African-American male observed, implying that conspiratorial efforts to thin our ranks are on the upswing.

Thank you, Louis Farrakhan.

As an African-American I have long had my antennae out for conspiracies against the race. Heaven knows American history is full of them. But my racial antennae aren't twitching much at this CRACK program. Compared to the damage crack cocaine has disproportionately done to black and Latino Americans, Harris' bribe-for-no-babies plan pales.

Besides, if she is a racist, she's an exceptionally clever one. A white Anaheim PTA parent, Harris is raising four black children she adopted as crack-addicted babies from the same mother. She also has led a local anti-discrimination program, according to her web page, which has the memorable addresses: "www.cracksterilization.com" and "www.cashfor-birthcontrol.com".

No, Harris appears to be just one of many angry Americans who has held trembling drug-addicted babies in her arms and become outraged enough to want to do something about it. Exploiting? If so, crack addiction is worse exploitation. Considering the human misery that birth control avoids in such instances, two hundred bucks sounds like a bargain.

Of course, the drug user might just use the cash bribe to buy more drugs. Harris realizes that, she said, but adds that at least the drug dealer has a "choice," which is more than crack babies have.

She makes a good point. In fact, the biggest problem I have with Harris' scheme is not that it does so much but that it accomplishes so little.

Like community programs to "buy back" handguns, CRACK is too modest to make more than a dent in a very big social problem.

The best you can say is that it gets a message out, a message that brings public attention back to an issue and a class of people too few of us want to think very much about.

Sadly, programs that bribe drug addicts to sterilize themselves signal a form of social surrender, not unlike needle-exchange programs that provide addicts with free needles to avoid HIV infection. In a society unwilling to pay for adequate drug-treatment programs, it is reasoned, at least we can offer clean needles.

Unfortunately, poor addicts who seek drug treatment find themselves facing waiting lists several months long, precisely because politicians have been more eager to build jails than drug treatment facilities.

In that sense, Barbara Harris is a modern-day missionary. She may not offer spiritual salvation, but at least she offers money. If government won't spend enough time or money to deal with the roots of our national drug addictions, frustrated citizens like Harris inevitably will come along to deal with its least fortunate end products.

JULY 4, 1990

LIBERALS MOUNTING OWN HATEFUL ASSAULT ON FIRST AMENDMENT

If you are the sort of person who thinks the First Amendment is under assault only from conservative bluenoses who can't stomach Robert Mapplethorpe, raunchy rap lyrics or flag-burners, guess again.

A number of legal scholars in traditionally liberal-progressive bastions are burrowing into America's free-speech doctrine with all the vigor of W.C. Fields' legendary last-minute perusal of the Bible as he lay on his deathbed, "Looking for loopholes, m'boy, looking for loopholes."

Unlike the anti-porn or pro-flag crusaders, the new-wave censors are calling for speech limits to protect the sensibilities of women and minorities from "hateful speech" or "verbal assaults," whether on campus or in the woman-bashing work of such entertainers as 2 Live Crew or Andrew Dice Clay.

Legal scholars are deeply divided over new campus codes to restrict speech offensive to women and minorities and some feminists are pushing anti-pornography laws, calling porn a violation of women's rights.

In one such exercise, titled "Why Protect Racial Speech?" in the spring edition of the Yale Law Report, associate Yale law Prof. Ruth Wedgwood writes, "We should not turn so casually from the relationship between epithetical speech and society's obligation to protect its members from justified fear of physical harm."

Unlike government, which has a superiority of force with which to defend itself, Wedgwood writes, "minority groups lack the same capacity for physical self-help and may suffer palpable and justifiable fear at even 'abstract' suggestions of intimations that they should be harmed."

She goes on to say that "such speech causes a real harm, destroying a citizen's sense of physical security."

The New York Times recently quoted Mary Ellen Gale, a professor at the Whittier College of Law in California and a former president of the Southern California affiliate of the American Civil Liberties Union, as saying the notion that everybody should have a chance at speaking and being listened to is a nice ideal but "we live in a real world, not an idealized marketplace of ideas."

Beware those who disparage the free marketplace of ideas.

Like Wedgwood, Gale suggests that someone who is the target of racist speech on campus is frightened into silence and no longer able to participate as well in university life.

Yet the censoring of "hateful" speech may be more insidious than the censoring of pornographic speech because, as difficult as porn may be to define, "hateful" is even more difficult to define and, because it describes ideas, it is more subject to mischief.

Do we really want to let our politicians decide what ideas we shall be allowed to see or hear? Or would we rather decide for ourselves?

Perhaps you thought the guarantee of free speech even when it is abusive of a minority group was settled in 1978 when the Supreme Court said neo-Nazis could march in the Chicago suburb of Skokie, even though its population includes a number of Holocaust survivors.

Guess again. As with almost all matters of law, legal scholars have refused to let it rest. Heaven protect us from those who would protect us.

The most troubling question is this: How do you ban speech so offensive as to be called "hateful" without restricting all speech that offends someone?

How do you write a law that will keep, say, former Klansman David Duke off campus, to save minority students from offense, without also keeping Muslim Minister Louis Farrakhan off campus to protect Jewish students from similar offense, an action that would in itself offend quite a few black students?

That's the problem with opening loopholes in the First Amendment. Where does it end? And who decides for you what is obscene or what is "hateful"?

It is particularly troubling that the censorship of "hateful speech" is most furiously pursued on the nation's campuses, ironically a traditional bastion for free expression. What does this say about the state of debate in the land of the free? How long can ideas be aired freely in an atmosphere chilled by benighted efforts to protect the feelings of various groups?

Perhaps it reveals an unhealthy insecurity felt by some that the power of sensible ideas cannot withstand an assault by the outrageous, even though sensible ideas have withstood such assaults throughout this nation's history.

And, as an African-American who attended a predominantly white university and heard quite a bit of what now might be called "hateful speech" long before these new protective rules came along, I have to wonder why we are so eager to "protect" each other from problems that should be a matter of personal responsiblity.

As a society, we can censure without censoring. To censor a remark or idea is to glorify it by exalting its status to that of something dangerous. To censure it is to cast it out of our households and send clear signals to our children and everyone else that such material is unacceptable in respectable society.

Once we hand that responsibility over to politicians, we may gain a little peace but, in the long run, we risk much more.

NOVEMBER 7, 1993

COLOR IS FADING IN MAYORAL RACES

Some people incorrectly think I don't like Rush Limbaugh, just because I view him and Pat Buchanan as the Beavis and Butt-head of American political discourse.

Not true. I appreciate people who disregard "P.C.," not "political correctness," but rather what my friend Tom Kochman, a Chicago diversity consultant, calls the "politeness conspiracy." We too often want to raise burning questions about sensitive issues like race or gender, but don't, for fear of being considered impolite.

Not Rush. He speaks his mind and gets paid handsomely for it, I think partly because it is such a relief even for those of us who usually don't agree with him to hear candid views in these politically timid times.

So, to find out what members of his mammoth and predominantly young, white, male audience have on their narrow minds, I eagerly tuned in to catch his slant on last Tuesday's mayoral elections in New York City. That's the unlikely city in which the conservative Limbaugh lives, in about as much comfort, he says, as a monk assigned to Sodom.

Rush didn't disappoint me. In his unmitigated glee over Republican Rudolph Giuliani's victory, he lashed out at Rep. Charles Rangel, the Harlem Democrat, who blamed Mayor David Dinkins' loss on white reluctance to vote for blacks.

Sour grapes, said Rush of the remarks, which matched those President Clinton made earlier at a Dinkins campaign rally. Tingling with excitement, the man who calls himself blessed with "talent on loan from God" flashed a card on the screen that showed the racial breakdown of New York's 1989 mayoral race. Whites elected Dinkins with a whopping 30 percent of their vote, while Giuliani received a piddling 6 percent of the black vote, Limbaugh pointed out.

Triumphantly, Limbaugh challenged Rangel and, presumably, the president to take a few more lessons in math. That brought hoots of laughter and applause from his studio audience. Interestingly, I noticed Limbaugh did not ask how many votes anyone thought Giuliani would have gotten had he not been running against a black man.

Or whether white voters, faced with a mediocre incumbent and an untested, volatile challenger, might be less willing to accept mediocrity from a black incumbent than they would have been from one of his mediocre white predecessors.

Giuliani picked the right opponent at the right time. New Yorkers didn't really trust Giuliani, but they had gotten fed up, in many ways, with Dinkins. He failed to stop the hemorrhaging of jobs from New York City. He failed to reorganize his city's messy government. He failed to soothe growing concerns about crime and racial unrest, the "healing" on which he was elected.

So, you might say that New York voters took the advice given once by that great sage Mae West: When forced to choose between the lesser of two evils, pick the one you haven't tried before.

Limbaugh reported facts, but, as usual, only the facts that would help his punch line. No, race was not the only issue in New York, but it was an issue and that sorry development cannot be blamed on blacks alone.

The willingness of white voters to take a chance on a black challenger has made close races out of what should have been cakewalks in cities like New York, where Democrats outnumber Republicans 5-to-1, and Chicago, where the Democratic nomination had been tantamount to victory since the 1930s, until a black man won the party's primaries.

Interestingly, when polls showed Dinkins solidly ahead in his first campaign, he barely won the actual vote count. Some voters always lie to pollsters, but it is now an established fact that white voters lie more when race is involved, whether it is Douglas Wilder or David Duke. There's that "politeness conspiracy" at work again.

No matter how much we may try to hide it, race has been a significant, often crucial factor in elections throughout American history, even when opponents were of the same race, and we're not rid of it yet. Instead, we should deal with it-realistically.

New Yorkers, including Limbaugh, could learn from the model left behind by the late Mayor Harold Washington of Chicago. After squeaking through a minefield of race-baiting to win narrow victory in 1983, Washington, unlike Dinkins, didn't try to fool every one of his many, diverse constituencies. Instead, he firmly nudged some of his most ardent black supporters aside to devote his attention to assuring whites, Hispanics and liberal swing voters, as well as mainstream blacks, that he would address their most pressing community concerns.

The result is what New York author Jim Sleeper calls a "civic identity" or "Rainbow II," a new interracial coalition that expands the old rainbow of minorities, women, labor and the poor to embrace common middle-class concerns like crime, taxes, economic development and re-inventing government.

Rainbow II may lose a few of those who support Rainbow I, but versions of it already have helped black mayors win predominantly white cities like Minneapolis, Seattle and Kansas City. It helped Republican Richard Riordan beat Democrat Michael Woo in Los Angeles.

And, in two black-on-black contests, it helped Cleveland's Michael White and Detroit's Dennis Archer beat opponents who tried to paint them as sell-outs to whites and suburbanites.

Interracial cooperation, instead of confrontation, appears to be the wave of the future in big city politics. If so, it is a welcome wave. It might not make exciting talk radio, but it might save our cities.

NOVEMBER 21, 1999

MEET PAT'S NEW RETRO PAL

It is hard to think of a precedent for the odd alliance Pat Buchanan has made with Lenora Fulani, although the Hitler-Stalin pact to carve up Poland comes to mind.

Hitler and Stalin were political opposites. But they agreed for a time, at least, to work together out of their mutual interests, mainly to conquer and oppress their mutual neighbors.

So it is with Buchanan and Fulani. "In traditional political terms, Pat Buchanan stands for all the things that black progressives such as myself revile," Fulani told a news conference in Washington.

And the feeling is mutual, I am sure. In the annals of politics making strange bedfellows, the Buchanan-Fulani alliance almost breaks the bed.

Fulani, a psychologist, is boldly pro-choice, pro-feminist and a self-described "militant black nationalist, ... Marxist and social therapist."

Buchanan is, well, Buchanan, a self-described "paleo-conservative" who fled the Republican Party because, in his view, it was getting too liberal for him.

Yet, despite their differences, there they were, Pat and Lenora, standing side by side in front of the news cameras out of their mutual desire to stand in front of news cameras.

Buchanan hopes Fulani's endorsement will make him look less like a racist or anti-Semite, charges he frequently has heard, sometimes from prominent conservatives, because of some of his more controversial remarks. Now he can say that at least one of his best friends is black and a liberal too!

Before he decided to run for president for the third time, Buchanan was a nationally famous conservative columnist and commentator. He often has been called a racist—a charge he vigorously denies—because some of his less temperate remarks sound like code words for bigots.

For example, he has called for a moratorium on immigration, although he sees nothing wrong with the immigration that brought his own ancestors here from Europe.

He has called for an end to affirmative action, although he suggested in two columns over the past year that "it might be time for Euro-Americans to demand affirmative action" in Ivy League colleges, where he proposed "reserving 75 percent of their slots for non-Jewish whites."

Most recently he made news with a pro-isolationist book that suggests World War II could have been avoided had we only left Hitler alone to slug it out.

Now Buchanan needs some new buddies. When he joined the Reform Party, he called the Republicans and Democrats "two wings of the same bird of prey." Suddenly his former friends and colleagues on the Republican right were denouncing him in ways that questioned his very sanity. That's what he gets for biting the hands that have fed him since his days in the Nixon administration.

In the Reform Party, which has become a national homeless shelter for the politically odd, Buchanan has found a seemingly unnatural alliance with Fulani, a leader in the party's left wing.

Like the proverbial gal next door, she was available. Those of us who have been following left-progressive movements over the years have seen her move from one left-progressive party and movement to another, latching her little faction to other people's organizations the way a pilot fish latches on to sharks to feed and take a free ride.

Since she emerged in New York City's political scene in the early 1970s, she has tried with varying success to latch onto leaders and candidates as varied as Lyndon LaRouche, Jesse Jackson and Louis Farrakhan.

Now it is Buchanan's turn. Together this odd coupling embodies the old saw about how politics at their extreme left and right begin to come together and sound alike.

Buchanan and Fulani take that political paradox to a new height or, if you prefer, depth. They represent the last gasp of retro-politics, the politics of moving backward.

It is a politics that feeds off fear and anxiety, whether it is about immigrants taking jobs here or big corporations shipping jobs overseas.

It is a politics that views the economy as a limited pie to be fought over and carved up among interest groups, instead of an expanding organism of market forces that can grow large enough to feed everyone.

It is a politics that finds common cause between Buchanan's isolationism and Fulani's protectionism.

It is a politics whose time is not now. The most popular candidates of the Republican and Democratic Parties at present are men of moderation like George W. Bush, John McCain, Al Gore and Bill Bradley.

Each is gathering strength by trying to carve out new ideas in the moderate center of American politics. Each is thinking about how America can best prepare for a new century and a new world that will be smaller and more tolerant of diversity than any that have come before.

Buchanan and Fulani don't have time for that kind of future. They are too busy refighting old class and ethnic battles of the past. They belong together, happily moving backward, away from the rest of us.

JULY 17, 1991

THOMAS' PRAISE OF FARRAKHAN A TWO-EDGED SWORD

It didn't surprise me to hear that conservative Supreme Court nominee Clarence Thomas once professed great admiration for Black Muslim Minister Louis Farrakhan. In many ways, Farrakhan is the quintessential conservative. Just watch out for his snake oil.

Like Thomas, he stresses self-help as the proper road to black progress. He urges poor blacks to reject government welfare, promote the family, dress conservatively and abstain from drugs, alcohol and pork.

He encourages men to form neighborhood patrols to fight crime and encourages women to be fruitful, multiply and devote themselves to maintaining strong family life at home.

Like Thomas, Farrakhan doesn't like affirmative action. In fact, he goes even further, denouncing racial integration altogether as a liberal pipe dream.

This, too, is not all that far removed from Thomas' views. He was a black nationalist in college, a devoted fan of Malcolm X and, as he said in an insightful 1987 Atlantic magazine profile by Juan Williams: "I don't see how the civil-rights people today can claim Malcolm X as one of their own. Where does he say black people should go begging the Labor Department for jobs? He was hell on integrationists. Where does he say you should sacrifice your institutions to be next to white people?"

So far, so good. But, while much of what Farrakhan, with his uniquely soothing yet provocative oratory, says about self-improvement also has been said by other more conventional black leaders, Farrakhan's message is poisoned by troubling demagoguery, some of which comes straight out of the Twilight Zone.

Like his mentor, the late Elijah Muhammad, Farrakhan has professed the belief that the white race was created out of a "germ" by an evil wizard as punishment for the sins of the black race and that racial justice finally will come at Armageddon.

Few Farrakhan admirers I know will admit openly to believing any of that poppycock, but, like alcoholics who insist they are only "social drinkers," they find it easy to ignore the parts of Farrakhan's message that they don't like while they soak up the parts they do, even when the entire barrel is tainted with drops of poison.

That may be what happened to Clarence Thomas. In two 1983 speeches still on file at the Equal Employment Opportunity Commission, then-chairman Thomas praised Farrakhan as "a man I have admired for more than a decade."

An aide at the time has confirmed to reporters that Thomas delivered the Farrakhan tribute to Atlanta's Association of Black MBAs. The other, prepared for delivery at the Capital Press Club a few weeks earlier, reportedly was not delivered after Thomas decided to ad lib.

It is worth noting that this happened a year before Farrakhan's connections to Jesse Jackson's presidential campaign, his description of Adolf Hitler as "great ... wickedly great" and his referring to Zionism as a "dirty religion" brought him to the attention of mainstream media in 1984.

Nevertheless, among blacks Farrakhan's more controversial views were widely known, if not always acknowledged. In the late '60s, when Clarence Thomas was a self-professed black nationalist and Malcolm X fan in college, Farrakhan, a former calypso singer then called Louis X, already was moving rapidly into the prominence Malcolm X enjoyed as Elijah Muhammad's chief spokesman.

As early as 1972, Farrakhan was making anti-Semitic references to Jews' controlling the media, and the spurious forgery known as "The

Protocols of the Elders of Zion" was always available in the bookstore at his Harlem temple.

Perhaps, like many others, Thomas chose to borrow a bit from Farrakhan's appeal as a way of showing his black credentials to a black audience, rather than do the right thing, which would be to expose Farrakhan's snake oil.

Now it's time to play catch-up. In a prepared statement responding to the flap, Thomas said: "I repudiate the anti-Semitism of Louis Farrakhan or anyone else. While I support the concept of economic self-help, I have never tolerated bigotry of any kind."

Like Jesse Jackson, Thomas repudiated only some of the man's ideas, not the man. That did not sit well with some Jewish leaders. Abraham Foxman, national director of the Anti-Defamation League, said attempts to distinguish the messenger from the message "only legitimized Farrakhan's overall message of hate."

As Kingfish used to say on "Amos 'n' Andy," brother Clarence got a heap of 'splainin' to do. Unlike Kingfish, Thomas should get a chance to do his explaining in front of the Senate Judiciary Committee.

That's progress.

SEPTEMBER 4, 1985

THE CASE FOR "AMOS 'N' ANDY"

I have a confession to make: I like "Amos 'n' Andy."

Yes, I know I am not supposed to like that ancient television comedy about Amos, Andrew H. (for "Hogg") Brown, Kingfish, Lightnin' and the Mystic Knights of the Sea Lodge Hall.

After all, in the world of black entertainment, the names "Amos 'n' Andy" have taken negative connotations like those attached to poor old "Uncle Tom."

The popular television program that was made from an equally popular network radio was taken off the air in the late 1960s as a result of protests from the National Association for the Advancement of Colored People and other civil rights groups.

Former Ebony magazine reporter Donald Bogle expressed the prevailing wisdom of the show in his excellent book on Hollywood's historical stereotyping of blacks, "Toms, Coons, Mulattoes, Mammies &

Bucks." Its major flaw, Bogle writes, was in "depicting Negro professionals as just as idiotic as the servant figures of the Hollywood films."

But, to the best of my recollection, that assessment is not entirely fair. Amos, at least, was a level-headed cab driver who put his family responsibilities ahead of everything else and often had to bail Andy and Kingfish out of scrapes. In a world more perfect than ours, blacks would be no more offended by that than whites would be offended by "The Honeymooners."

It also gave some fine black actors work, even if it was not the kind of work they would have preferred. No blacks were allowed on network noncomedies until 1967 when Bill Cosby co-starred with Robert Culp in "I Spy."

Interestingly, since "Amos 'n' Andy" was censored, it has become a major hit in home videotape rentals and sales and I do not think all those customers are Klan members. "Amos 'n' Andy" is not "Birth of a Nation."

Although the network stations are too nervous to think about it, there has been talk among the independents and cable stations of bringing the show back. While I will not actively campaign for it, I will not exactly lose sleep over it if it happens.

To me, the most objectionable aspect of the show was not its depiction of black life but that it was the only depiction of black life available on prime-time television. Sure, we could laugh at the antics of white people in comedies like "The Honeymooners" in the 1950s, but we could also see the seriousness of white people's lives with "Playhouse 90" or "The Armstrong Circle Theater."

Today we have a choice of black roles on television, although our choices remain ridiculously limited. Where are the depictions of the black experience that produced such fine works as "A Soldier's Story" or "The Color Purple" in other media?

Too many television programmers believe the public will not accept serious black programs. These are some of the same people who thought the public would never accept a comedy about a mobile Korean War surgical hospital. Nevertheless, "M+A+S+H" was a hit.

Yet we have made progress. Cosby was on Newsweek's cover last week because his upper-class Huxtable family has become a number-one hit. As a comedy success for more than two decades without using race as material for his act, Cosby criticized young comics who do use it.

"'Saturday Night Live' is one of the biggest offenders," he said. "You don't see a black person there unless they give you their signature that they are black, and therefore that's what's funny. The joke will be on his or her color, you see."

He has a point. But to be fair to Richard Pryor and Eddie Murphy, I do not think they are making fun of their color as much as they are making fun of those on both sides of the color line who make a big deal about color.

Every ethnic group produces its own set of comedians because we need to laugh at ourselves once in a while.

"Amos 'n' Andy," for better or worse, is part of our American heritage. When we can feel secure enough about ourselves to enjoy the program in its proper historical context, we can say we have made real progress.

CHAPTER SEVENTEEN

MARRIAGE SLIPS OUT OF STYLE?

While culture warriors debate why marriage has been in decline, particularly in low-income black households since the early 1960s, marriage continues to decline—in low-income households of all races.

The columns in this chapter mark various points in the development of that trend and the debate—from the conservative welfare issues of the 1980s to the more recent focus on "income inequality" across racial lines by conservative think tanks as well as liberals.

FEBRUARY 7, 2001

WHEN MARRIAGE GOES OUT OF STYLE

British anti-abortion groups are outraged that teenage girls as young as 16 now can buy emergency contraceptive pills, "ECPs," in pharmacies without a prescription. ECPs, a morning-after pill, are intended to prevent pregnancy within 72 hours after intercourse. Britain is following France, which has been allowing such sales for almost two years. Last year France upped the ante by allowing school nurses to dispense the pills in high schools and junior high schools.

Could we Yanks be next? So far, news items like this have stirred barely a ripple on this side of the Atlantic. Yet both illustrate a growing and, in many ways, baffling new concern throughout the industrialized world: a soaring percentage of babies born to unwed parents.

Americans seem to have become remarkably accustomed to such news. Many of us breathed a sigh of relief when the U.S. Department of Health and Human Services announced that, among other happy developments in the prosperous 1990s, out-of-wedlock teen pregnancies declined.

But as one expert, former Sen. Daniel P. Moynihan, pointed out, the "rate" of out-of-wedlock pregnancies declined but the "ratio" hasn't. In other words, the total number of pregnancies per 100,000 people has declined in America, but the percentage of births that are out of wedlock has climbed. And, contrary to popular mythology, out-of-wedlock births have not just climbed for minorities. That myth is based largely on widespread misunderstanding of research Moynihan pioneered.

The New York Democrat became famous in the mid-1960s for his then-controversial findings as head of the Labor Department's policy research that the percentage of African-American babies born out of wedlock had surged to 25 percent and still was growing. By the end of the 1990s, it had grown to an even more startling 70 percent, a point at which Moynihan said it quite likely will level off for the foreseeable future.

Meanwhile, white America's out-of-wedlock birth ratios are following the same pattern set earlier by blacks. By the end of the '90s, out-of-wedlock births among whites had soared past the 25-percent rate that alarmed Moynihan when it showed up among blacks in the 1960s.

Marriage, in other words, seems to be going out of style among parents throughout the industrialized world.

To illustrate this trend in a September speech to the American Political Science Association, Moynihan reported that out-of-wedlock births have soared in the following countries between 1960 and 2000:
  • United States: From 5 percent to 33 percent (as of 2000)
  • Canada: From 4 percent to 31 percent (as of 1996)
  • United Kingdom: From 5 percent to 38 percent (as of 1998)
  • France: From 6 percent to 36 percent (as of 1994)
The big question, then, is not whether, but why marriage is going out of style? Some European officials have cited a lack of consistently good sex education for teenagers. That undoubtedly plays a role.

Moynihan, in his new position as a senior public policy scholar at the Woodrow Wilson International Center for Scholars, told me that he suspects out-of-wedlock births increase as the penalties for such behavior shrink.

He also noted that he has not seen a similar decline in respect for marriage in the less-developed world. He recalled marveling in India, where he was ambassador from 1973 to 1975, at men who slept on the streets of poverty-gripped Calcutta so they could save money for their daughters' dowries. It was a matter not only of love but necessity, Moynihan allowed, since a son-in-law was expected to help take care of his in-laws in their old age.

"As we succeeded in stabilizing an industrial economy, the consequences of what had previously been irresponsible and ruinous behavior receded," he said, in his characteristically scholarly style.

Maybe. In Scandinavia, conservatives often note, where very liberal governments offer the most generous cradle-to-grave social services on the planet, out-of wedlock birth rates have soared past 50 percent. Yet if the remedy is to cut off support to such families, it could create more problems than it solves.

Or maybe the customs and consequences that we associate with marriage are changing in unexpected ways. Some new research indicates that, in many households, an out-of-wedlock child is not necessarily a fatherless or abandoned child. Many fathers are present, supportive and nurturing of their children, despite the absence of marriage licenses. Unfortunately these fathers tend to fade away statistically as the child moves into the teen years when the guidance of a responsible father often is most valuable.

What is to be done about out-of-wedlock births as a serious social problem? I think we have to recognize countless single parents—mostly moms—do heroically wonderful jobs of raising their children, but most children tend to do better with two parents at home.

We also need to recognize that single parents are not necessarily bad parents. We need to do more studies to find out what works.

It's not just a black problem. It is not even just an American problem. The decline of marriage is a world problem looking for some world-class remedies.

JUNE 3, 2001

TWO-PARENT HOMES ARE DISAPPEARING

Sometimes government forms just don't give you enough room to say what you really want to say.

When the census form or tax form asks for marital status, I look for a box that says, "Married, and proud of it."

Or, "Married, and let me tell you, it hasn't always been easy all of these years, but we've stuck to it and...."

But, no. Uncle Sam doesn't care. You only get a few little boxes to describe your life to the government. As a result, you get a lot of statistics that tell you about changes in our population and precious little explanation for why the change is happening.

One thing we do see in the latest population figures is a decline in the percentage of "married households." For the first time, people who live alone—one-fourth of the adult population—outnumber married couples with children.

At the same time, single parenting is growing. In fact, married households would be dropping even faster across this country were it not for the contributions of one group in particular: recent immigrants.

One recent Washington Post analysis found that traditional American two-parent families are increasingly new immigrants, particularly Asian and Hispanic.

Two-parent families increasingly are found in the parts of the country that are attracting the largest numbers of immigrants, particularly the West, which has a fourth of the nation's population, the Post found. The Midwest, which received the fewest immigrants, ended the decade with a larger overall population but a net loss of 30,000 married couples with children.

That trend confirms recent findings by former Sen. Daniel P. Moynihan, a leading expert on family structure. By the end of the '90s, out-of-wedlock births among whites in America had soared past the 25 percent rate that alarmed Moynihan when he reported it among blacks in the 1960s. By the end of the 1990s, it had leveled off at 70 percent among blacks, yet still rises among whites.

Now a senior public policy scholar at the Washington-based Woodrow Wilson International Center for Scholars, the New York Democrat finds marriage rates are dropping among parents throughout the industrialized world.

At a record 33 percent, America's out-of-wedlock birth rates actually are lower than those of the United Kingdom, France and Scandinavia and about the same as Canada's.

This alarms politicians. Tucked deep in President Bush's 2002 budget is $60 billion for grants to "promote responsible fatherhood," promote "successful parenting" and "strengthen marriage" with faith-based and other more conventional programs.

I favor programs that help parents get married and stay married, if the programs will help reduce poverty. But even $60 billion may not be enough money to put more than a dent in the out-of-wedlock childbirth ratios that have been bubbling upward in all income groups and across racial lines.

Maybe the question we should be asking is, what do immigrants, often arriving here from underdeveloped countries, know that we in the sophisticated, modernized industrialized countries do not?

One thing that parents in less affluent societies have more of is need—often quite desperate need. In poor communities here or abroad, people turn to each other for survival because they have to.

As economies and government support to the needy become stronger, Moynihan has observed, the consequences of irresponsible behavior decline. Families become more mobile. Communities break apart. So do many homes.

So, instead of teaching the industrialized world about the virtue of marriage, new immigrants may find marriages breaking down in the next generation as their children become more Americanized.

To reverse that trend will require a social sea change. Marriage will have to become chic again, according to my friend Iris Krasnow, a former UPI reporter who left journalism to raise four children.

Married 13 years, she interviewed 300 people for her new book, "Surrendering to Marriage: Husbands, Wives and Other Imperfections."

"I've learned four things," she told me. "Marriage can be hell. The grass is not greener (with someone else). No one is perfect—including you! And you might as well love the one you're with, especially if you have children."

Love the one you're with? Sounds like an old rock tune. Of course, not everyone can dance to it. Some marriages are better off divorced.

But she's right about the grass not always being greener, especially for the kids.

FEBRUARY 6, 2013

FAMILY BREAKDOWN HAS GONE BIRACIAL

I know from past experience that I'm going to upset some folks by saying this, so brace yourselves: Marriage is very important and beneficial to the raising of children, but there's little evidence that it fights crime.

I bring this up in response to the sincere, well-meaning readers who say we won't be able to do anything—anything—about urban violence until we reverse the decline of marriage in African-American households.

I'm as troubled as any concerned black parent about the rise in out-of-wedlock births in black America since the 1950s. But I am even more troubled when I hear people who should know better try to lay every social problem, including the nation's current gun-violence debate, at the feet of single-parenting—as if nothing else mattered.

Heather Mac Donald, a writer-analyst at the conservative Manhattan Institute, helped set this tone in a widely circulated 2010 City Magazine essay on black-on-black violence in Roseland and Altgeld Gardens, the Chicago areas where Obama famously worked for four years as a community organizer.

Her conclusion: Obama and "decades of failed social policy" in crime-plagued, low-income areas on the city's Far South Side "ignored the primary cause of their escalating dysfunction: the disappearance of the black two-parent family."

For those who read down far enough, she does mention that Obama is aware of the decline of marriage in African-American households. She quotes his call for cultural change in his widely covered Father's Day speech in Chicago during his 2008 presidential campaign.

"If we are honest with ourselves, we'll admit that ... too many fathers (are) missing from too many lives and too many homes," he said then. "We know the statistics—that children who grow up without a father are five times more likely to live in poverty and commit crime; nine times more likely to drop out of school and 20 times more likely to end up in prison."

That's the speech, you may recall, that upset the Rev. Jesse Jackson as too condescending, although most black voters didn't seem to mind.

Mac Donald wants more than that. She dismissed Obama's "bromides about school spending, preschool programs, visiting nurses, global warming, sexism, racial division and income inequality." Such spending will be wasted, she said, until poor black Chicagoans curb unwed pregnancies and stop the "culture of illegitimacy."

I believe quite the opposite, that we can't expect to see much of a turnaround in out-of-wedlock births as long as we have rising educational and income inequality—and not just in black America.

A variety of sociologists and economists on the ideological left, right and nonpartisan middle have found downward mobility to be a shared experience across racial lines for many working-class and middle-class Americans, especially since the Great Recession.

As a headline on an article by Isabel Sawhill, an expert on domestic poverty and federal fiscal policy at the Brookings Institution, in the latest Washington Monthly put it: "Family Breakdown Is Now Biracial."

She writes that Daniel Patrick Moynihan's controversial 1965 report, "The Negro Family: The Case for National Action," "looks remarkably similar to a profile of the average white family today," with the sharpest declines in marriage rates occurring among the least educated of both races.

Marriage, in a sense, has become a new symbol of status, especially for the college-educated. "The group for whom marriage has largely disappeared now includes not just unskilled blacks but unskilled whites as well," Sawhill writes. "Indeed, for younger women without a college degree, unwed childbearing is the new normal."

Sawhill does not cheer this development, which she and other experts following in Moynihan's path have found to be a pattern throughout the developed world.

If the rise in out-of-wedlock births was tied that closely to crime and violence, I think we would see a more consistent pattern connecting them. Instead, we see crime going sharply up and down in various cities and across the country, while unwed child-rearing steadily climbs.

A development this huge calls for more than a simple one-size-fits-all analysis. I'm not saying that government programs provide all the answers, but we're only beginning to ask the right questions.

MAY 9, 2010

MARRIAGE ON A TIGHTROPE

Motherhood no longer appears to be what it used to be.

Compared to 20 years ago, today's mothers of newborns are older, more educated, less often white, more often Hispanic—and less often married.

A record 41 percent of American births in 2008 were to single mothers, according to a new Pew Research Center study of census and other data released in time for Mother's Day. That's an increase from 28 percent in 1990.

Is marriage over? Not quite. But the report did find an increase in unmarried women in their childbearing years over the last two decades and, judging by the numbers, the idea of marriage as a precursor to parenting in America appears to be suffering setbacks.

That does not bode well for the kids. Traditional marriage is better for kids emotionally, academically and economically, as President Barack Obama, who barely knew his own dad, wrote in "The Audacity of Hope," his 2006 memoir. Children "living with single mothers are five times more likely to be poor than children in two-parent households," he wrote. "... And the evidence suggests that on average, children who live with their biological mother and father do better than those who live in stepfamilies or with cohabiting partners."

Although the unmarried-mother share of births increased most sharply for whites and Hispanics, the Pew study found, the highest share is black women. That trend was forecast 45 years ago this past March in "The Negro Family: The Case for National Action," a landmark report by a young White House appointee named Daniel Patrick Moynihan. He warned that a disintegration of the black family threatened to undermine President Lyndon B. Johnson's war on poverty. Black out-of-wedlock birthrates had soared since World War II to 25 percent, compared to 7 percent for whites. Black out-of-wedlock birthrates have since soared to about 67 percent by 1990 and 72 percent today, according to the Pew study, compared to 53 percent of children born to Hispanic women, 29 percent of children born to white women and 17 percent of children born to Asian women.

Although Moynihan, who later became a Democratic senator from New York, subtitled his report, "A Call for National Action," it has led instead to an abundance of new arguments and excuses for inaction. Liberals tend to accuse conservatives of "blaming the victim" and conservatives accuse liberals of dodging "personal responsibility" and promoting dependency on hardworking taxpayers.

In fact, both sides are right. It is hard to promote marriage as a solution to social problems when the decline of marriage is itself the result of many social, economic, historical and personal problems, including poverty, crime, high incarnation rates and a widespread erosion among too many youths that personal responsibility does any good.

That's why the one silver lining in the report is in its confirmation of a health trend that delights social scientists, even if they are unable to completely explain it: a decline since the early 1990s in teen pregnancy rates in all racial and ethnic groups, even as each group had a higher share of new mothers aged 35 or older.

After disturbing surges in the 1980s, teen birth rates and pregnancy rates are down to their lowest level in 20 years. Various experts are not sure why, except two reasons show up in other studies: Fewer teens are having sex or more of them are using contraceptives. The reasons vary from widespread fear of AIDS and other sexually transmitted diseases to a rise in conservative attitudes toward casual sex.

Reasons for changed attitudes vary. A 2008 study by the Guttmacher Institute, founded by Planned Parenthood but often quoted by both sides of the abortion debate, found that abstinence education programs have helped reduce teen pregnancy rates but so has education in contraceptives and STDs.

Regardless of the reason, we should take good news wherever we can find it—and try to encourage more of it. Finding the answers to these encouraging trends among teenagers might lead us to positive cultural changes among older groups, particularly unmarried fathers who, as Beyonce sings in her popular tune, need to "put a ring on it."

OCTOBER 31, 1993

COMING SOON: THE NEW UNDERCLASS

Quick. What kind of picture comes to mind when you hear the following words: "Poverty." "Welfare mothers." "Teen pregnancy." "Crime." "Underclass."

If an image of poor black people comes to mind, consider yourself fully indoctrinated by unfortunate modern-day stereotypes that distort the real nature and extent of poverty in America.

It was not always thus. In the 1960s, when news cameras followed John and Robert Kennedy into rural Appalachia, the face of poverty presented to the public was white.

And a funny thing happened: The sight of suffering white families spurred white America in those times, which admittedly were more prosperous than today's era of economic uncertainty, to fund the most ambitious war on poverty America has ever seen.

The white poor remain among us, but today's face of poverty conveyed by the media tends to be that of a violent, young, urban black male, reared, we are led to presume, by a young, single welfare mom.

The response from Americans who don't look like them (and from more than a few who do) has been less compassionate than fearful, angry, suspicious, resentful and contemptuous. Today we are less inclined to buy a government prescription than to buy a gun.

Liberals dislike this development and so, it turns out, do conservatives like Charles Murray, whose 1984 book "Losing Ground" helped fuel the Reagan-era assault on welfare programs as allegedly being more of a cause than cure of social problems.

While white Americans have incorrectly put a black face on poverty and pushed it to the margins of their thinking, a new white "underclass" is gaining visibility.

Out-of-wedlock births have grown fast enough among poor whites, Murray writes under the eye-grabbing headline "The Coming White Underclass," in last Friday's Wall Street Journal, to touch the threshold Daniel P. Moynihan detected in 1965 when he was simultaneously praised and attacked nationwide for calling it a dangerous pathology among poor blacks.

Since Moynihan stirred controversy with his report, black out-of-wedlock births have grown from less than 30 percent to more than 60 percent of all black births in America.

"But the black story, however dismaying, is old news," writes Murray, now a fellow at the conservative American Enterprise Institute. "The new trend that threatens the U.S. is white illegitimacy. Matters have not yet quite gotten out of hand, but they are on the brink. If we want to act, now is the time."

The 1991 census shows births to single white women have risen to 22 percent of all white births, says Murray. But, even more startling, 44 percent of births to white women who were below the poverty line were out-of-wedlock, he says.

Murray reminds his readers of something too many Americans too often forget: a larger percentage of blacks are poor, but in raw numbers poor whites have more people in poverty, more out-of-wedlock children, more women on welfare, more unemployed men and more arrests for serious crimes.

"Yet whites have not had an 'underclass' as such," Murray writes, "... Instead, whites have had 'white trash' concentrated in a few streets on the outskirts of town, sometimes a Skid Row of unattached white men in the large cities. But these scatterings have seldom been large enough to make up a neighborhood. An underclass needs a critical mass, and white America has not had one."

Or maybe whites have not had an underclass "as such" because most Americans have refused to see it.

I agree with Murray's data, but, I differ sharply on his diagnosis and prescriptions. Despite connections he admits are "murky," he blames today's "underclass" on social programs that he alleges, encouraged out-of-wedlock births.

I agree with the University of Chicago's William Julius Wilson that rising out-of-wedlock births are a symptom of deeper problems, like structural changes in the economy that have removed the low-skilled, high wage jobs.

Those jobs brought black families (like mine) from the rural south to big industrial cities and supported the social fabric of black communities. When they went, so did "marriageable men," Wilson writes. Welfare moved in and the fabric frayed.

Since Murray blames the problem on out-of-wedlock births, he would "solve" it by starving today's welfare moms into more acceptable behavior. Remove welfare supports, he says, and they would have to find help with family, boyfriends or foundations, or the state would put their kids in foster homes. He is not kidding.

I favor less draconian measures. There's probably nothing wrong with the underclass that jobs and, wherever necessary, a reinfusion of the work ethic and family values wouldn't fix.

Most Americans will agree, I suspect, once they find that a problem they thought belonged to somebody else has arrived at their doorsteps.

CHAPTER EIGHTEEN

WOOING WOMEN'S VOTES

While everyone expected Obama to bring Democrats a bonus in black votes, the gender gap of female voters, especially unmarried white women, in their favor was a gift from the GOP. This chapter revisits some of the issues that alienated leading conservatives like Rush Limbaugh and left Mitt Romney, judging by his comments, still largely clueless after his defeat.

JANUARY 29, 2014

RIGHT WING'S CRINGE-WORTHY CONVERSATIONS

Male lawmakers should not even vote on abortion.

That was Alan Simpson's position before the Wyoming Republican retired from the Senate—and it still is.

Abortion is a "terrible" and "hideous thing," as I recently heard him reiterate in a seminar on the federal budget at Harvard University's Shorenstein Center. "But it's a deeply intimate and personal thing. ... Men legislators shouldn't even vote on it."

No, Simpson has not "drunk the liberal Kool-Aid," as the stridently right-wing RINO-hunting (Republican in Name Only) thought police might put it. He simply understands how easy it is for us guys to sound unintentionally and arrogantly clueless, as any seasoned divorce lawyer can tell you, when we try to expound on what women really want or need.

That bracing reality comes to mind amid the fallout over former Arkansas Gov. Mike Huckabee's recent remarks about birth control and women's libidos. The message he was trying to deliver was not quite what a lot of us heard.

"If the Democrats want to insult the women of America by making them believe that they are helpless without Uncle Sugar coming in," Huckabee told the Republican National Committee's winter meeting in Washington, D.C., "and providing for them a prescription each month for birth control because they cannot control their libido or their reproductive system without the help of the government, then so be it."

Uh, hey, Mike, you do know that the rest of America can hear you, right?

Having met Huckabee, a Fox News host and ordained Southern Baptist minister, I'm sure he meant well. But with that one long "libido" sentence, his speech against the Democrats' allegation of a GOP "war on women" quickly turned into yet another fire for party leaders to put out.

Republican National Committee Chair Reince Priebus rebuked Huckabee's comments. "You know, you have to accept the political world we live in, in the sense that you cannot offer up words like 'libido'—wherever that came from—you don't offer up these sorts of lobs and set-up passes and serves that allow the Democrats to spike the ball," Priebus told NBC's Chuck Todd on Monday.

Priebus' response illustrates the GOP's current challenges with gender and diversity.

Almost a year after the RNC's post-election "autopsy" report called for outreach to persuadable moderates on issues like women's health, the right wing's culture warriors are still preaching mostly to the converted.

"The Republican Party needs to stop talking to itself," the report advised. "We have become expert in how to provide ideological reinforcement to like-minded people, but devastatingly we have lost the ability to be persuasive with, or welcoming to, those who do not agree with us on every issue."

Yet, that message had not quite reached another possible 2016 Republican presidential contender, Sen. Rand Paul of Kentucky. He offered his own cheerfully tone-deaf reaction Sunday to Huckabee's speech. "This whole sort of war on women thing, I'm scratching my head because, if there was a war on women, I think they won," he said on NBC's "Meet the Press." "You know, the women in my family are incredibly successful."

He went on to talk about how successful the women in his fortunate family have been. "I think some of the victimology and all of this other stuff is trumped up," he concluded.

That reminds me of conservatives who dismiss the concerns of African-Americans with, "Hey, you've got a black president. What more do you need?"

I actually don't rejoice in the sound of Republicans continuing to provide more cross-cultural cluelessness for Democrats, late-night comedians and others to mock. I miss the days when both parties competed for the votes of women and people of color.

Instead, today's polarized politics and energized social-media environment sheds more heat than light.

GOP leaders who care about winning elections, not just firing up the base, have been promoting training sessions to help candidates communicate better with women voters. I wish them success. But the first step to winning someone's vote is to show that you really care about earning it.

JANUARY 15, 2012

REPRODUCTIVE FREEDOM?

Caution: This presidential campaign endangers reproductive health. Women's rights to contraception and other reproductive health services seem to face even more than the usual threats from the 2012 Republican presidential candidates. All of which raises new questions about whose freedoms today's conservatives really want to defend.

And that ratchets up pressure on President Barack Obama at a time when his administration is expected to announce soon how a "conscience clause" might apply to the Affordable Care Act. Such a provision would allow religious organizations to deny insurance coverage for employees' contraceptive and other reproductive health needs.

Yet, timely as it is, the issue of contraception was not welcome in the recent Republican presidential debate on ABC. Host George Stephanopoulos was booed by the largely Republican audience when he pressed former Massachusetts Gov. Mitt Romney on whether he agreed with former Sen. Rick Santorum that states have the right to ban contraception, even though Santorum was not recommending that states do that.

Santorum believes the U.S. Supreme Court was wrong when it decided in the 1965 Griswold v. Connecticut decision that a right to privacy justified overturning a state ban on contraceptives. Romney tried to dismiss the question as an "unusual topic" since "no state wants to" ban contraception. As Stephanopoulos persisted, Romney called the question "a silly thing." Some audience members cheered Romney and booed Stephanopoulos.

But none of the candidates is calling for an outright ban on contraceptives. Instead they would chip away at women's access, especially if it receives federal funding.

They would deny funding to family-planning initiatives and organizations. They would legislate away health insurance coverage of birth control. They would block federal Food and Drug Administration approval for almost any new contraceptive, especially if it suggests to anti-abortion activists the remotest possibility that it would stop a fertilized egg from developing.

For example, Stephanopoulos could have questioned Romney about how the economic platform on his website promises to "eliminate Title X family planning programs benefiting abortion groups like Planned Parenthood."

Created in 1970 during the Nixon years, the program does provide funds to abortion providers, such as Planned Parenthood, but federal law bars the program from covering abortion procedures. Its other health services, like birth control, sexually transmitted disease screenings and cervical cancer exams, have earned praise across party lines. Yet two Republican budget proposals in the past year would have zeroed them out.

Even libertarian Rep. Ron Paul of Texas, fierce defender of individual liberties on most issues, manages to make an interesting exception. He recently joined four other GOP candidates in signing a Personhood USA pledge saying that life begins at conception. However, he did accompany it with a "signing statement" saying he would limit enforcement of said personhood to the states, not the federal government.

Although Texas Gov. Rick Perry used to say he would allow an abortion in cases of rape, incest or when the life of the woman is endangered, he conveniently went through a "transformation" just before the Iowa caucuses. He announced in December that he now opposes abortion in all cases, except when the life of the woman is endangered. Still he maintained opposition to the defunding of clinics that provide birth control.

The question is hardly academic to the many Americans who rely on contraceptives to prevent unintended pregnancies and sexually transmitted diseases. The Alan Guttmacher Institute, whose findings are quoted by both sides of the abortion debate, estimates that without contraception funding from Medicaid or Title X, the number of abortions in the United States would be almost two-thirds higher and the number of unintended pregnancies among poor women would nearly double.

All of which raises the significance of the conscience-clause debate. One of the cornerstones of the Affordable Care Act that Republicans call "Obamacare" is its expansion of access to insurance coverage for everyone who needs it. Every expansion of exceptions to health care providers would allow private religious beliefs to trump otherwise evidence-based practices in public health.

The birth-control debate is about rights, quite obviously, but it also concerns the ability of any civilization, country or community to fight poverty and advance itself. Around the world and throughout the centuries we have ample evidence that statistics of education, health and optimism are tied to the empowerment of women. That's why sensible conservatives, as opposed to the radical right, understand that "freedom" is something more than a slogan to be limited to guys only.

APRIL 11, 2012

LISTEN UP, ROMNEY

Mitt Romney is trying to talk his way out of his gender gap, but take it from me, women like guys who listen. My wife told me that.

Since Ann and Mitt Romney's long marriage appears to be quite strong, he probably knows the value of being a good listener. Unfortunately, his speaking style doesn't display much of it on the campaign trail.

Listening matters. As important as policy may be, voters tend to choose the candidate they think is "on my side." They want someone who connects with them, who conveys an understanding of their hopes and dreams.

That's why recent presidents like George W. Bush and Bill Clinton, whatever else you may think of them, always seemed to have their big ears on when talking to people. Listening leads to a level of connection and understanding that voters, among others, appreciate.

By that standard, I used to think Romney, the seasoned businessman and former Massachusetts governor, might well have an advantage. President Barack Obama looks by contrast like a loner who has to remind himself to look less professorial and more warm and fuzzy.

Yet it is Romney who has habitually stepped on his own campaign victories with gaffes and a persistent awkwardness about his wealth and political beliefs.

Unlike Bush's folksy "I hear you" or Clinton's empathetic "I feel your pain," Romney's delivery tends to sound about as engaging as a CEO's annual report to stockholders.

I believe that helps explain why a new ABC News/Washington Post poll, which asks which man "better understands the economic problems people in this country are having," gives the edge to Obama (49 percent) over Romney (37 percent).

Among women, Obama scores 20 points over Romney on this empathy question, up 3 percentage points since a February survey. That tends to match the widening gender gap between the two candidates in other recent polls.

The partisan gender gap is not new. Men have been voting mostly Republican and women mostly Democratic for more than 30 years. But the gap suddenly widened in the past couple of months.

A Pew Research Center poll has Romney trailing Obama by 20 points among female voters for the second month in a row—and virtually tied among men.

And the latest Gallup/USA Today poll found Romney trailing the president by 9 points among women in battleground states in March—and by a ratio of 2-to-1 among women under age 50—after a virtual tie a month earlier.

Why? Conventional wisdom blames a string of debates and controversies about birth control and related social issues of particular importance to women. In fact, these issues have often crowded out the economic issues on which Obama is more vulnerable.

As Romney looks increasingly like he will be the Grand Old Party's nominee, he faces the same challenge that dogged Sen. John McCain four years ago: How do you hold on to the party's skeptical conservative base while reaching out to attract swing voters and close the gender gap? McCain answered that challenge by choosing Sarah Palin as his running mate. That didn't work out so great. McCain lost the election, but the pantheon of TV punditry gained a new right-wing superstar.

Romney's awkwardness about equity for women showed itself when a reporter asked for his thoughts at the all-male Augusta National Golf Club. Obama had just called for the club, home of the Masters golf tournament, to accept women as members.

Romney agreed, but with an awkward response so loaded with qualifying "ifs" that it sounded like an insurance contract: "Certainly if I were a member, if I could run Augusta, which isn't likely to happen, of course I'd have women into Augusta," he said. I think that was a "yes."

Romney often sounds like he could use what President George H.W. Bush used to call "the vision thing." It calls for more than balanced budgets. It begins with a strong inner desire to repair the nation's divisions and revive our sense of shared values and common purpose. Women appreciate that. Men do too.

FEBRUARY 26, 2012

HOW SEX HIJACKED ELECTION TALK

How has an election year that was supposed to be all about economic recovery suddenly become all about sex? Critics blame the media. They have a point. The media keep reporting what the candidates are saying.

When you have made social issues like abortion, gay marriage and reproductive rights your central issues, you should not be shocked that media cover them. Yet, when you look at the extreme positions into which social conservatives have pushed the Republican Party, it's not hard to see why their candidates would like to change the subject.

That became harder to do as this year's most decisive issue, the sluggish economy, has shown signs of improvement. Promising news like Friday's report that consumer confidence was up for the sixth straight month takes at least some of the steam out of Republican anger over President Barack Obama's handling of the economy.

What's troubling for many Republicans is how social issues of gay rights and reproductive rights have sprung up into the news at a time when public opinion, particularly among independent voters, is moving away from conservative positions on those old culture war issues. Even Rick Santorum, the former Pennsylvania senator whose rise to the top tier of Republican presidential candidates has come largely on the shoulders of social conservatives, was sounding like a flip-flopper in the Arizona presidential debate on the issue of contraceptives.

Before the debate, he had said that as president, he would talk about "the dangers of contraception in this country." He also gave a lawyerly response to the question of whether he thought states had the right to ban contraceptives. That response gave listeners the impression that he wanted states to do that—and that he, as president, might ban contraceptives too.

He has vehemently denied that, pointing out that, although he personally disapproves of contraceptives, he has voted in favor of them for others. As a firm supporter of access to contraceptives, as polls show most Americans are by a wide margin, I nevertheless will allow the former senator to have it both ways on that issue. By the same logic, I forgive liberal Democrats who deplore abortion personally but defend the right of others to choose.

I was further encouraged by Santorum's professed support for Title X, the federal program that provides contraceptive services for low-income women. In past statements and in his 2006 book "It Takes a Family," Santorum touts his support for Title X.

This record offered him a convenient defense when he was embarrassed by his own mega-donor Foster Friess, who notoriously suggested in a television interview that women practice birth control by holding an aspirin between their knees. If Friess never heard about political correctness before he told that old wheeze of a joke, he knows about it now.

But days after Santorum cited his support for Title X in a CBS interview and again on Fox News, he stated flatly at the presidential debate in Mesa, Ariz., that he was against it.

In response to his rival Rep. Ron Paul of Texas, Santorum said, "As Congressman Paul knows, I opposed Title X funding. I've always opposed Title X funding, but it's included in a large appropriation bill that includes a whole host of other things, including ..."

He was interrupted at that point by booing from the crowd and by front-runner Mitt Romney as the former senator tried to explain that he opposed Title X and only voted for it as part of larger pieces of legislation.

"I think I was making it clear that," he sputtered somewhat defensively, "while I have a personal moral objection to it; even though I don't support it, that I voted for bills that included it. And I made it very clear in subsequent interviews that I don't—I don't support that."

More booing. In moments like that, Santorum's reputation for consistency was shattered up against the pragmatic realities of compromises that are a part of legislating.

Unfortunately for him, they are the sort of retreats from principles and ideological purity that his party's populist tea-party wing regularly condemns.

As long as the party's right wing seeks perfection in mere mortal politicians, its members will be disappointed, especially when they're talking about matters as touchy as sex.

MARCH 7, 2012

COULD THIS BE THE END OF LIMBAUGH?

Americans praise civility, but we constantly reward rudeness. That annoying fact of life helps explain why the blessings that Rush Limbaugh brought to the Republican base recently turned into a curse.

The switch happened abruptly as the conservative radio icon came under attack from all sides for calling a female law student a "slut" and a "prostitute," among other insults in three days of on-air rants. Limbaugh finally apologized over the weekend, as several of his sponsors were reported to be withdrawing their advertising.

Now we know which Speech Police even Limbaugh respects. Sponsors rule.

Slower to respond were the Republican Party's leading presidential candidates. Politics makes strange ironies. Four years ago Democratic presidential candidate Barack Obama wrestled his way out from under the burden of his Chicago pastor, the Rev. Jeremiah Wright Jr., and his intemperate remarks. Now President Obama gets to watch his Republican rivals try to evade Limbaugh's rantings.

Obama publicly broke all ties to the unrepentant Rev. Wright and suffered not a bit with his base. The Republican presidential wanna-bes are not that lucky. Their attempts to distance themselves from Limbaugh's vile language without losing his supporters come off like profiles in cowardice.

GOP front-runner Mitt Romney, approached by a reporter, said Limbaugh's language was "not the language I would have used," then tried to change the subject to the economy before scurrying off.

Rick Santorum, Romney's closest challenger, said on CNN that Limbaugh was "being absurd, but that's, you know, an entertainer can be absurd." That's how Limbaugh excuses himself too. He says he's an "entertainer" whenever people who disagree with him take him seriously. Yet he seldom objects when his conservative fan base circles the wagons around him like a messiah.

Master spinner Newt Gingrich on NBC's "Meet the Press" called it "appropriate for Limbaugh to apologize and I'm glad he apologized." Then, with a "but," the former House speaker managed to blame the dust-up on his pet target du jour, the "elite media."

"I am astonished at the desperation of the elite media to avoid rising gas prices" and several other issues "to suddenly decide that Rush Limbaugh is the great national crisis of this week." Never mind that, if any media worker qualifies as an "elite," it is Limbaugh.

But let's hear it for Rep. Ron Paul, the Grand Old Party's only presidential hopeful to question the sincerity of Limbaugh's expressed contrition over his "very crude" language. "I don't think he's very apologetic," Paul told the CBS program "Face the Nation." "He's doing it because some people were taking their advertisements off his program. It was his bottom line that he was concerned about."

No wonder so many independent voters appreciate Paul's candor. And no wonder he hasn't got a prayer of being nominated by either of the two major parties.

Helping to confirm Paul's suspicions the next day, Limbaugh's lengthy on-air apology managed to blame his favorite whipping boys and girls, the political left.

He just couldn't help himself, he said: "Against my own instincts, against my own knowledge, against everything I know to be right and wrong, I descended to their level when I used those words to describe Sandra Fluke," the law student.

Ah, well, he's just an "entertainer," right?

Last May, MSNBC suspended host Ed Schultz for a week after he described conservative radio host Laura Ingraham as a "right-wing slut," a remark for which he later apologized. But Limbaugh's syndicator, Premiere Networks, a subsidiary of Clear Channel, said it would not suspend Limbaugh, despite his breathtaking assault against a private citizen whose only crime, after all, was to testify before a congressional committee hearing in support of mandatory health insurance for contraception.

But don't kid yourself into thinking this is the end of King Rushbo's reign. Like a radio shock jock, he'll probably benefit from his recent negative publicity, as long as his ratings hold up.

The Republican candidates may not get off that easily. Limbaugh has distracted voters from issues like the economy and religious freedom, on which President Obama is vulnerable, to contraception, an issue that gives credence to the Democrats' charge of a GOP war against women. With friends like Limbaugh, Republicans don't need Democrats.

NOVEMBER 18, 2012

ROMNEY'S "GIFTS" GAFFE

Mitt Romney finally has it figured out. He knows why he lost. Guess what? It was all President Barack Obama's fault.

Of course, that's not exactly the way Romney puts it. He puts it in a way that sounds even sillier than that. Or perhaps, depending on your worldview, more tragic.

In a 20-minute afternoon conference call with his major donors and fundraisers eight days after Election Day, Romney blamed his loss on Obama's showering groups with what Romney called "gifts" to various groups of voters, "especially the African-American community, the Hispanic community and young people."

Zounds! As we used to say back in the day when most people received their news on newsprint, stop the presses!

As the sly prefect in the movie "Casablanca" might say, I am shocked, shocked. Thanks to the former Republican presidential candidate, I now realize that Obama openly and shamelessly—Gasp!—offered programs and policies to America's voters that actually would help them to improve their lives. Those Chicago guys will stop at nothing.

"In each case, they were very generous in what they gave to those groups," Romney said.

A simple question came to my mind upon hearing this news about gifts: Where's mine?

Romney was proud to contrast Obama's so-called gift-giving strategy with his own tight-fisted talk about "big issues for the whole country: military strategy, foreign policy, a strong economy, creating jobs and so forth."

"With regards to the young people, for instance, a forgiveness of college loan interest was a big gift," said Romney, who probably never had to take out a college loan in his life.

"Free contraceptives were very big with young, college-aged women," he said. Sounds like he's been listening too much to Rush Limbaugh, the conservative radio talk show host who called law student Sandra Fluke a "slut" and "prostitute" for advocating government-funded contraceptives. Republicans fume at Democrats for suggesting the Grand Old Party is waging a "war against women," although it's not hard to see where the Dems get that idea.

In that light, I congratulate Ohio state Sen. Nina Turner, a Cleveland Democrat, for introducing a bill in April that would require men to visit a sex therapist before getting a prescription for erectile dysfunction drugs like Viagra. What's good for the gander should be good for the goose.

"And then, finally," said Romney, "Obamacare also made a difference for them, because as you know, anybody now 26 years of age and younger was now going to be part of their parents' plan, and that was a big gift to young people." And, I would add, to many of their parents.

That President Obama sure is a clever fellow, giving so many Americans what they want. I wonder why that notion apparently didn't appeal to Romney? Oh, right. It did.

He promised seniors, for example, that he'd restore President Obama's $716 billion in Medicare cuts, despite his passionate pleas for cuts in soaring budget deficits. He also promised that, no matter what measures, he wouldn't touch Medicare and Social Security spending for at least a decade.

Romney looked like Santa Claus to upper-income earners with his promises to protect them from Obama's proposed income tax hikes. He also promised Wall Street that he would roll back the Dodd-Frank financial regulations that were legislated to rein in the abuses that led to the 2008 financial crash.

Yet, on the campaign trail, Romney referred to none of these offerings as gifts. Now his post-mortem sour grapes sent even his fellow Republicans, like Louisiana Gov. Bobby Jindal and Wisconsin Gov. Scott Walker, fast-walking away from him. Wise move, gentlemen.

Romney's remarks echo his earlier secretly recorded comments to donors last year in Boca Raton, Fla., about the "47 percent of Americans" who "don't pay taxes," refuse to take responsibility for their lives and will support Obama no matter what. "I'll never convince them that they should take personal responsibility and care for their lives," he said. What is it about talking to donors that brings out Romney's inner upper-class twit?

"My job is not to worry about those people," he said. That's OK. I don't think they're too worried about him, either.

CHAPTER NINETEEN

HISTORY ISN'T EVEN PAST

Black liberals and white conservatives, in my experience, share a peculiar amnesia in common: We forget everything but the grudges. This chapter's columns revisit that notion in today's squabbles over the display of the Confederate flag, the usefulness (or not) of apologies for historic transgressions and where we go from here in achieving "the promised land" prophesied by Martin Luther King Jr.

APRIL 11, 2010

IT'S NOT HATE, IT'S HATEFUL HISTORY

Brag Bowling and I have a lot in common. We both care a lot about history. We just happen to come down on opposite sides of the Civil War. Sort of.

Bowling is the commander of the Virginia Division of The Sons of Confederate Veterans, an organization dedicated to the proposition that the South is getting a raw deal in a lot of history books and in the public's memory about the war.

I gave him a call after Virginia's Gov. Bob McDonnell backpedaled a bit on a proclamation he signed at the urging of Bowling's organization to designate April as Confederate History Month in Virginia.

The proclamation threw McDonnell into a hot mess, particularly with his African-American constituents, and raised questions about his viability as a rising national star because the proclamation omitted any mention of a prominent cause of that war: slavery.

Worse, when reporters asked him about the omission, he dug himself deeper. There were "any number of aspects to that conflict between the states," he said, but "I focused on the ones I thought were most significant for Virginia."

Is slavery not "significant"?

It just so happened that my wife and I recently spent a weekend in Charlottesville to see Thomas Jefferson's home at Monticello, an intellectual Disneyland for history buffs. With knowledgeable tour guides, we took a mental trip back in time to get into the lives and the heads of Jefferson and Sally Hemings, among other people Jefferson owned as property.

We also discussed horrifying examples of how, as Chief Justice Roger B. Taney declared in the Dred Scott decision, slaves "had no rights which the white man was bound to respect." Cleverness, good fortune and the mercies of one's master were a slave's only protections from assault, abuse or separation from the rest of one's family. These are not insignificant aspects of history.

After McDonnell's idea of significance failed to go down well with such prominent black supporters as BET co-founder Sheila Johnson, who had endorsed him, and former Gov. L. Douglas Wilder, a Democrat who refrained from endorsing his opponent, McDonnell acknowledged his "mistake."

He added a paragraph to describe slavery as an "evil and inhumane practice," which now annoys Bowling, who calls the addition inaccurate. "Virginia did not leave the Union to defend slavery," he said. "Virginia seceded after President Abraham Lincoln called up troops to invade the lower South. Virginia was solidly pro-Union but refused this intrusion on their sovereignty. It had nothing to do with slavery."

But Virginia did join the Confederacy, I reminded Bowling. What, I asked, about Confederate Vice President Alexander H. Stephens' declaration in his historic 1861 speech that the breakaway government's "cornerstone rests upon the great truth that the negro is not equal to the white man; that slavery subordination to the superior race is his natural and normal condition?" Bowling admitted he had not read the entire speech. I strongly advised him to do so and we will talk again. He said he looked forward to it. So do I.

I'm not mad at him. Our brief yet cordial conversation offered a reason why McDonnell as a savvy Southerner should have known better than fall into this stew. He stumbled into a second Civil War, a continuing clash between the dueling memories of African-Americans and "Southern heritage" whites.

As a descendant of the Confederacy, Bowling has a lot in common with me, a descendant of Southern slavery. The Sons of Confederate Veterans are spiritual descendants of the "Lost Cause," a post-bellum movement that sprung up after the war to justify the Confederate cause as noble, chivalrous, militarily clever and only incidentally tied to slavery.

Both of us agree that too many people oversimplify the causes of the Civil War as either all about slavery or nothing to do with slavery. The truth of history is always more complicated and too many people don't take history seriously enough.

We are bound by a shared heritage. Each of us wants our side of history to be known and told "accurately." Neither of us wants to be told that our ancestors' suffering, struggles or hardship count for nothing.

JUNE 26, 2005

APOLOGIES ARE ALL ABOUT THE FUTURE
More than 4,700 Lynchings Occurred between 1882 and 1968, and the Senate Finally Comes to Grips with America's Troubled Racial Past

"The past is never dead," William Faulkner once wrote. "It's not even past." Senate leaders found that out the hard way when they decided to take up a piece of long-unfinished business, a Senate apology for failing to outlaw lynching.

Even in this enlightened era of Oprah and Obama, the dawn of America's most tolerant, egalitarian multiracial and multicultural century, even the august Senate has no easy time coming to grips with its troubled racial past.

The resolution, sponsored by Democrat Mary Landrieu of Louisiana and Republican George Allen of Virginia, apologizes to "the victims of lynching and the descendants of those victims for the failure of the Senate to enact anti-lynching legislation."

More than 4,700 lynchings occurred between 1882 and 1968, mostly of African-American men, according to Alabama's Tuskegee University, which has been documenting the mob murders for more than a century. Nearly 200 bills to ban the practice were introduced by 1950. Seven presidents asked Congress to make lynching a federal crime. The House of Representatives agreed three times to do so, but powerful Southern lawmakers, using the filibuster, killed each measure in the Senate.

This time a nice, robust bipartisan passage should have been easy. Majority Leader Bill Frist of Tennessee certainly must have thought so before he and other Republican leaders let the matter reach the floor. Who, after all, would want to be perceived as soft on lynching?

But, alas, high expectations turned victory into a disappointment. Frist opted for a voice vote instead of a roll-call vote, which would have put each senator's vote on record. Now, attention has zeroed in on the 8 senators who have not signed on as co-sponsors. News media eyes quickly turned to Trent Lott and Thad Cochran, the delegation from Mississippi, which led the nation in lynchings and has the highest proportion of blacks in its population. Lott, who lost his majority leadership after appearing to praise the late South Carolina Sen. Strom Thurmond's years as a leading obstacle to civil rights reforms, was not returning reporters' phone calls on the matter.

Cochran told The Clarion-Ledger in Jackson, Miss., that he didn't feel he should apologize for Senate actions that occurred before his time, "But I deplore and regret that lynchings occurred and that those committing them were not punished."

Yet, the newspaper noted, he previously co-sponsored measures "apologizing for the U.S. government's mistreatment of American Indians and Japanese-Americans," which also happened before his time. An apology dealing specifically with Senate actions apparently struck too close to home—a tipping point, as an old Southern fable goes, where the Senate had "stopped preachin' and gone to meddlin'."

That's a blemish on the Grand Old Party's racial image at a time when its chairman, Ken Mehlman, has been touring the country's black churches and historically black colleges to expand the party's black vote.

Allen and Landrieu said they were moved to action by a powerful book, "Without Sanctuary: Lynching Photography in America," edited by James Allen, who collected the photos, and published them in 2000 in conjunction with a traveling exhibit. Most of the photos come from postcards.

Hard as it may be for today's generations to believe, postcards of lynchings often were sold door-to-door and sent to friends and relatives until 1908, when the postmaster general forbade sending them through the mail. "This is the barbecue we had last night," reads a nicely scripted message on the back of one photo of a burned body.

When I wrote about Allen and his photo collection in 2000, I noticed how remarkably unashamed the white citizens in the photos appeared to be. "One can see faces quite plainly," I wrote. "No Ku Klux Klan masks here."

Women and children were included, even encouraged, to attend. Lynchings were big community events—as thrilling for participants as a carnival, a street fair or a church picnic. It is not hard to imagine the constituent pressures on the South's senators and congressmen, all of whom were Democrats back then, to beat back federal encroachments on their "state's rights."

Today one can properly question the value of apologies that do not lead to any particular action. But, as Abraham Foxman, national director of the Anti-Defamation League, which was founded after the lynching of Leo Frank, a Jewish businessman in Marietta, Ga., in 1915, has said, apologies are important in the healing of a nation.

Faulkner was right. Those who think the past dies by itself will be disappointed. Apologies are more than the closing of an old chapter. They are the beginning of a new one.

MARCH 11, 1998

REVISITING KERNER: A HALF–RIGHT PREDICTION

Thirty years after the historic Kerner Commission predicted a deepening racial divide in America, an offshoot group is lamenting how true that prediction turned out to be.

That's a mistake, in my humble view. I think the group should be celebrating how wrong the prediction turned out to be.

The Kerner Riot Commission was created by President Lyndon B. Johnson and headed by former Illinois Gov. Otto Kerner during a period when the nation was having about 100 civil disturbances a year. The commission famously predicted that "Our nation is moving toward two societies, one black, one white—separate and unequal."

The latest follow-up comes from the Milton S. Eisenhower Foundation, a private-sector project which includes some Kerner veterans and was formed to continue the commission's work.

This month, the foundation released its latest report and, like its predecessors, the report argues that the racial gap is not only real but getting worse.

Reaction to the report from blacks and whites across the nation has been a huge, collective yawn.

The reaction has mostly fallen into two major camps. There are those who say they don't believe it and those who say they knew it all along.

I fall into a third camp. It is the realistic camp. It is the camp that says we are doing better and worse at the same time. So we should celebrate our successes and learn from our mistakes.

Not everybody wants to hear this. It is easier for many of my friends, particularly the liberal black ones, to argue that we haven't made any progress, so they can more easily justify aggressive race-specific (meaning blacks only) remedies.

And it is easier for many of my other friends, particularly the conservative white ones, to argue that we blacks have made all the progress that anything but our own bootstraps can help us make, which absolves them of any responsibility.

The Eisenhower group pretty much falls into that first liberal group. Its last report was released five years ago, a year after the 1992 Los Angeles riots. We Americans felt pretty divided during those days of Rodney King and Reginald Denny, for good reason.

But take a closer look. Unlike the riots in the 1960s, black people did not make up the majority of the arrests made during the Los Angeles riots, and many black-owned businesses were burned right along with white- and Asian-owned businesses.

What's that about one divide? Obviously we have several. Some are racial, but most are economic.

On this question, even the Kerner veterans practice a bait-and-switch technique. The foundation's report announces a racial divide but speaks mostly of a class divide. In a very quick paragraph, it acknowledges the tremendous economic and political progress the new black middle class has made, then it goes on for the rest of its 200 pages to report what most of us already know, that the plight of today's black poor is actually worse than it was 30 years ago.

Obviously, we have become more than two nations.

Economically, the gap between poor blacks and better-off blacks has been widening faster than the gap between poor and better-off whites.

Politically, the Democrat Party has become blacker over the past 30 years, while the Republican Party has become the white-flight party. Yet, during the same period, black mayors and other black elected officials have grown from near-zero to several thousand. Black political clout has grown. The next challenge is for blacks to be properly represented in both major parties.

Socially, over the past 30 years whites have de-tribalized in many ways, welcoming such black icons as Oprah Winfrey, Bill Cosby and Colin Powell into their hearts. At the same time, many blacks have re-tribalized, looking inward to strengthen black institutions and offer aid and counseling to those underprivileged African-Americans whom the civil rights revolution left behind.

Discrimination still dogs the black middle class, but, most of it is a minor nuisance compared to the oppression so many of us have overcome.

The biggest divide in this nation today is between the movers and shakers and those who get moved and shaken. Over the last 30 years, many of us have begun to move from the underclass to the upperclass. More will follow. The biggest defining economic difference is education. The better educated we are, as African-Americans, the more choices we have for better income and living standards.

In this regard, the new Kerner follow-up report is right on target. It advises us to invest more heavily in programs that work, like Head Start, Job Corps and enriched after-school programs.

But we also need something the report, which is heavily focused on government action, fails to address. We need a spiritual revival. Those of us who escaped poverty kept going in our relentless pursuit of education and success because our families and communities infused us with a re-lentless optimism. We had hope. We need to spread it around.

APRIL 2, 2008

PROMISED LAND: ARE WE THERE?

Words do matter. Forty years ago Rev. Martin Luther King Jr. ended a rally speech in Memphis on a note that was eerily prophetic, since it would turn out to be his final speech.

"Like anybody, I would like to live a long life," he said, speaking without notes to the church rally on April 3, 1968. "Longevity has its place. But I'm not concerned about that now. I just want to do God's will. And he's allowed me to go up to the mountain. And I've looked over. And I've seen the promised land. I may not get there with you. But I want you to know tonight, that we, as a people, will get to the promised land."

King was assassinated the next day.

Which leaves a probing question for us black Americans 40 years after King's prophetic speech. Have we reached the promised land?

The answer is: It depends.

We, as a people, have reached the promised land, if you believe the old James Brown song of the late 1960s: "I don't want nobody/to give me nothing/just open up the door, I'll get it myself." How far has the door opened up?

It's obvious that black multimillionaires like Oprah Winfrey and Black Entertainment Television founder Robert Johnson have made it, thanks partly to hard-won opportunities that the civil rights movement opened up.

Yet, how you feel about how well black America is doing can be a defining issue as to where you stand along the nation's black-white, rich-poor cultural divide.

A young community organizer discovered that in 1985 on Chicago's South Side, where he came to work for a church-based group seeking to improve living conditions in high-crime, low-income neighborhoods.

One day, the 24-year-old activist, a biracial Ivy League graduate, was trying to make a point to a prominent black pastor. Black problems were becoming more economic than racial, the organizer said. The minister wasn't buying it.

"Cops don't check my bank account when they pull me over and make me spread-eagle against the car," the pastor said. "These miseducated brothers, like that sociologist at the University of Chicago, talking about 'the declining significance of race.' Now, what country is he living in?"

The allegedly "miseducated" black scholar was William Julius Wilson. His 1978 book, "The Declining Significance of Race," was changing the national conversation about where black America was headed. It analyzed the impact of shifting economic forces affecting Americans of all races and called for economic remedies over race-specific ones.

But the pastor was a proponent of black liberation theology who responded to every one of the younger man's class-based views with race-based answers. Even the growing black middle class brought no comfort. "Life's not safe for a black man in this country, Barack," the pastor said. "Never has been. Probably never will be."

Yes, the young organizer back then was Barack Obama, who's now seeking the Democratic nomination for president. It was his first encounter with Rev. Jeremiah Wright Jr. of Chicago's Trinity United Church of Christ, as recounted in Obama's 1995 memoir, "Dreams from My Father."

The sharp contrast between their views takes on new significance, now that inflammatory snippets from Wright's sermons have turned Obama's 20-year membership in Wright's church into a political embarrassment. In a landmark Philadelphia speech Obama denounced Wright's remarks, but not Wright, and called for a new conversation on race.

Obama pointed out that the basis of black rage is real, but race relations in America are not static. America already has progressed enough to enable him to be the Democratic front-runner for president. I'm sure King would agree.

At the time of his death, King was helping black Memphis garbage workers organize for better working conditions and the same respect that the city afforded white workers. In the wake of the 1964 Civil Rights Act and the 1965 Voting Rights Act, King was expanding his focus from fighting racism to fighting poverty.

Since then, black America reduced its poverty rate to about 24 percent by the mid-1990s from more than 50 percent in the '60s. Progress is being made by Americans of all races. But not even a black president could do everything that needs to be done.

The biblical promised land, it's important to remember, was not a place to relax. It was a place to work, provide for your family and achieve economic independence.

In that sense, I don't think we African-Americans have reached the promised land. We're only beginning to see it from here.

CHAPTER TWENTY

GETTING PERSONAL

DECEMBER 29, 2010

A STUTTER UNFIT FOR A KING
Learning How to Subdue the Beast

At last somebody has made an epic triumphant movie about a heroism with which I am personally familiar: that of a recovering stutterer.

In "The King's Speech," actor Colin Firth gives an Oscar-worthy portrayal of the inconsolable despair behind the stiff upper lip of Britain's stuffy King George VI, the royal family's second banana who never aspired to be king, but fate had other plans.

In 1937 his older brother, King Edward VIII, gave up the throne to marry his divorced American lover, Wallis Simpson. The young Duke of York had to step up despite his debilitating stammer, as the English prefer to call it, a condition that severely threatened his ability to perform one of the most important duties left for a British royal, rallying his country on the brink of a world war.

As an adult, the aspiring king did what I and many of this country's estimated 3 million stutterers have done, he sought therapy. In his case, the therapeutic Yoda for the royal Jedi was Lionel Logue, whom actor

Geoffrey Rush turns into a scene-stealing force, trying—when he is allowed—to break down the royal inhibitions and build a necessary level of trust between the aspiring king and his commoner therapist.

"The movie helps to demystify stuttering," said Atlanta lawyer Adam Marlowe, 31, in a telephone interview. Marlowe is remarkable for containing his own stuttering well enough to become a successful litigator, a job for which effective talking is essential.

After a stuttering eruption caused an unusually "bad meeting" one day in New York City, where he was living at the time, Marlowe decided to seek help at the American Institute for Stuttering, a nonprofit organization of which—full disclosure—I happen to be a board member. There he received much of what is depicted in the movie, treatment that probed the underlying emotions, memories, anxieties and attitudes that undercut his ability to control his own voice.

"A lot of people want some quick cure, a mechanical technique or a magic pill that will make everything fine," he recalled. "In reality what really helped me was what you saw in the movie, a long-term therapy, working on your voice and your breathing but also on how you view yourself as a stutterer in the world."

In my case, I thank the public school system in my hometown, Middletown, Ohio, for providing me with a parade of encouraging speech pathologists in grade school. I also thank my high school's speech and debate club and supportive grown-ups like Fred Ross, a local attorney and family friend who patiently coached me through what Marlowe might call a "bad speech" in a contest at the local Optimists Club when I was 14.

After sympathetic applause from the crowd, I slumped off toward a corner where my coach was waiting with a big smile on his face. "When are we going to start working on next year?" Fred asked. With his encouragement I came back the next year and stunned the crowd with a near-flawless performance that, in a moment suitable for a Walt Disney film, took home the second-place trophy. It was better than first-place, as far as I was concerned. I've hardly stopped talking since.

Every stuttering kid needs optimistic support like that. I was reminded of that night as I watched Colin Firth's young prince in the film's opening scenes. He faces a microphone that looks as large as the U.S. Capitol Building to stutter his way through a speech that is being broadcast to the entire British Empire. During the real-life 1925 speech, which he failed to complete, the future king's hesitation lasted over a minute in several cases, according to Mark Logue, the therapist's grandson and co-writer of the movie, in an interview with NPR host Diane Rehm.

The prince went to Lionel Logue a year later because, as his grandson recalls, "by that stage he was pretty desperate." But, as history shows, he persevered. He beat what I call "the beast."

This is a film intended to make everyone feel good about his own potential. Most important to me is the message it sends to concerned parents like mine were. On film and in real life, King George VI never completely cured his stuttering. None of us do. Like reformed alcoholics, we are constantly recovering, learning how to subdue the beast so it does not stop us from pursuing greater things.

JUNE 23, 2004

FREEDOM SUMMER OF '64
I Was 16 Years Old, Angry at America's Homegrown Apartheid and Delighted to Rub Up against a Small Part of History

Some people say unsolved civil rights-era murder cases should be left alone. The quest for long-delayed justice, they say, is not worth the re-opening of those old social wounds. For others among us, those wounds never healed.

Forty years have passed, for example, since Freedom Summer, but I still vividly remember the massive project to register blacks in the South to vote. The Constitution had granted African-Americans the right to vote almost 100 years earlier, but that radical notion had not taken hold in the South.

Among the black folks willing to risk their lives to change that were a young mom and dad who showed up, tired but determined, with their teenage daughter at my family's doorstep in Middletown, Ohio.

They had driven all the way from rural Mississippi to help train young volunteer civil rights workers at nearby Western College for Women, which is now part of the Miami University campus in Oxford, Ohio, before the volunteers left for the South.

A local minister had asked my parents if they could make a bedroom in our large house available to the family. We understood. If you were black in those days, you could not routinely check into the first hotel or motel you came across. You either slept in your car, more often than not, or drove all night until you reached your destination.

I was 16 years old then, angry at America's homegrown apartheid and delighted to help host our visitors. Thanks to my parents' hospitality, I rubbed up against a small part of history.

Word came on June 21, 1964, that three of the volunteers who trained at Western College were killed on a remote country road in Neshoba County, Miss., where they had gone to investigate the burning of Mt. Zion Methodist Church, a black church. By the time their bodies were discovered buried in an earthen dam more than a month later, the youthful faces of Michael Schwerner, 24, and Andrew Goodman, 20, two white men from New York City, and James Chaney, 21, a black man from Meridian, Miss., had become part of our national memory.

Federal agents identified a local "klavern" of Ku Klux Klansmen as the killers who chased down the civil rights workers late at night, shot Schwerner and Goodman in the chest and beat Chaney to death. It was Schwerner, despised by the Klan for his effective organizing work, the Klansmen were really after, investigators said. Chaney and Goodman were apparently killed because they were witnesses.

Three years later, seven alleged members of the Ku Klux Klan were convicted of federal conspiracy charges, but none served more than six years in prison. Eight others were acquitted, and three others were freed after mistrials. The state never brought murder charges in the killings, which were chronicled in the film "Mississippi Burning"—with way too much Hollywood license.

Four decades later, a lot has changed in the South. Blacks vote, hold public office and have a better than even chance of being judged for the content of their character, not just the color of their skin.

And now a multiracial coalition that includes Mississippi's Atty. Gen. Jim Hood and Gov. Haley Barbour is pushing for a new federal murder investigation in the deaths of Schwerner, Goodman and Chaney.

It would be the latest in a series of seemingly cold civil rights cases to be reopened. The U.S. Justice Department recently opened a new investigation into the 1955 lynching of Chicago teen Emmett Till in Money, Miss. In 1994, Byron de la Beckwith was convicted in Jackson, Miss., and sentenced to life in prison for the 1963 killing of civil rights leader Medgar Evers.

Twelve of the original Neshoba County defendants are still alive, including Edgar Ray Killen, the alleged leader of the klavern and an ordained Baptist minister. Since the state never filed murder charges, all could be charged with murder now without violating their protection from double jeopardy.

Some people say such cases should be left alone, that we're better off trying to forget such episodes, turn the page and move on. I say we should never forget.

We need to remember Schwerner, Goodman and Chaney as symbols of hope. Those two Northern Jewish men and one Southern black man offer us Americans a powerful vision of intergroup respect, cooperation and mutual sacrifice in our increasingly diverse nation.

We need to remember, contrary to "Mississippi Burning," how black folks in Mississippi, and certainly not J. Edgar Hoover's FBI, took the lead in winning freedom for black Mississippians.

When Americans of all colors consider whether it's worth it to get up off our comfy couches on Election Day and leave our cozy homes to go and vote, we should remember what Schwerner, Goodman and Chaney did to help all Americans to vote.

In short, as old-school civil rights leaders used to say, we need to remember Schwerner, Goodman and Chaney as a reminder that freedom is not free.

SEPTEMBER 4, 2013

HIGH SCHOOL NEWSPAPER INK DRYING UP

I was thumbing through my Class of 1965 high school yearbook a few years ago when I was stopped dead cold by an autograph left by one of my teachers: "Dear Clarence: All I ask is that you mention my name when you win your first Pulitzer Prize. Don't forget. Mary Kindell."

I was stunned. It was 1989. I had just won a Pulitzer Prize for commentary. While I was getting over the shock, reporters were calling with the usual reporter questions: "How'd you get started?" "Who was your inspiration?" etc., etc.

That's why I was thumbing through my yearbook, to refresh my memory. It's embarrassing to blow facts, especially the facts of your own life.

My life in journalism began at my high school student newspaper under Mrs. Kindell's supervision at Middletown High School in Middletown, Ohio, where she also taught a one-credit-hour journalism class.

My initial media goals were modest. I didn't have much of a social life. Journalism, a field that compensates articulate nosiness, was a good way for me to meet people. Mrs. Kindell encouraged me to pursue my media interests and, just as important, helped pacify my alarmed parents, who wanted me to be a doctor.

I put down my yearbook and called Mrs. K. She didn't sound surprised to hear what she had written. "I always knew you could do it," she said.

I thought she probably issued that challenge to all of her young aspiring journalists, I said. Maybe, she responded, "but you're the only one who has taken me up on it."

I apologize to Mrs. K for tooting my own horn with this anecdote. She encouraged modesty and humility in her aspiring "journos." Put the story first, she instructed us, not your egos.

But I have a couple of good reasons for this deep dive into my anecdotage. For one, Mrs. Kindell turned 99 recently and deserves this shout-out: Happy birthday, Mrs. K!

At an August reception with four birthday cakes in her honor at Middletown's First Presbyterian Church, she told me she feels fine. Her only complaint was a persistent numbness in her hands that makes it hard to type or use the telephone, a poignantly cruel twist, in my view, for someone who helped to improve my skills on typewriters and telephones.

My other justification for these memories is to sound an alarm for the endangered state of high school journalism. Opportunities for today's aspiring or potential high school journalists to receive on-the-job learning like that offered by Mrs. K are slim and getting slimmer.

Even in New York, the media capital, only 1 in 8 public high schools have a student newspaper, The New York Times reported in May, and many publish only a few times a year.

Nationally, about two-thirds of public high schools have newspapers, according to a 2011 media study by the Center for Scholastic Journalism at Kent State University. But whether on paper or online, student newspapers tend to be absent from lower-income schools and lower-income students.

That's sad because, as Robert Fulghum titled his best-seller, "All I Really Need to Know I Learned in Kindergarten," I often feel as though I learned all I really needed to know about journalism in high school.

Newspapers of all sorts have been battered for decades by television and widespread illiteracy.

With the explosion of Internet traffic, too few youngsters are learning good news literacy. As Mrs. Kindell taught, you need to be a good reporter before you start giving your opinion. Today's world of blogging and tweeting encourages the opposite. Too bad we don't have more Mrs. Kindells to go around.

CHAPTER TWENTY-ONE

WINNERS OF THE 1989 PULITZER PRIZE FOR COMMENTARY

JUNE 26, 1988

THE PEOPLE'S REPUBLIC OF CHICAGO

If you ever needed an example of how politics can be, in the words of Ambrose Bierce, a strife of interests masquerading as a contest of principles, just look at the fight some Chicago aldermen are waging with the American Civil Liberties Union.

The ACLU has filed a $100,000 federal civil rights lawsuit on behalf of an art student whose controversial painting of the late Mayor Harold Washington was seized from display at a student exhibit in the School of the Art Institute of Chicago by nine aldermen and various police officers on May 11.

The suspect painting, a thoroughly tasteless rendering of Washington in women's underwear, was eventually released from custody after apparently being roughed up (a hole was slashed across its face) and is still at large. So, unfortunately, are the aldermen.

Artist David K. Nelson, 23, says he meant no harm, that he was moved to make "an anti-deistic statement" when he saw a poster that portrayed Washington as something of a deity. Oh, really?

Nelson showed a reckless disregard for taste and civility in a town treacherously polarized along racial lines. Washington's memory is so highly regarded by blacks here that an attack on him is interpreted by many as an attack on the black community. If Nelson did not know that, he is more than a fun-loving goof. He's pretty stupid.

But even if Nelson were a fire-breathing racist, he deserves to win this case. His right to free expression deserves to be protected as much as the Picasso statue at the Daley Civic Center should be protected from the likes of one former alderman who once called for replacing it with a statue of ex-Cub Ernie Banks.

Attacks on anyone's civil rights, no matter how loathsome that person's expressions may be, can come back to bite you. One extreme example, Ald. Robert Shaw, who seldom lets facts get in the way of a narrow pitch to his constituency, accused ACLU lawyers of always taking "the white side" in black-white disputes. Say, what? Where was he during the ACLU's countless cases of defending the rights of minorities, like its victory for Dick Gregory's campaign to march through the late Mayor Richard J. Daley's all-white Bridgeport neighborhood in 1969?

And how about Ald. Bobby Rush, who as a Black Panther leader in the turmoil of Chicago in the '60s was helped many times by the ACLU? Now, as a party named in the Art Institute suit, Rush called the suit "frivolous and impetuous" and accused the ACLU of having political or publicity-seeking motives.

Well, as a black Chicagoan who has waited all of his adult life to see black political empowerment in a city where old power elites had held blacks back for decades, I am thoroughly disappointed by this episode. After seeing, under Harold Washington, a black leadership emerge as the very embodiment of Rev. Martin Luther King Jr.'s progressive dream, I have watched it deteriorate since his death in November to the likes of Idi Amin or "Baby Doc" Duvalier. Welcome to the People's Republic of Chicago.

Of course, with the 20th anniversary of Chicago's disastrous 1968 Democratic convention approaching, it is sobering to note how, at their worst, the city's emerging black political powers are only repeating the flagrant disregard for civil liberties their predecessors sometimes showed.

It is ironic to see aldermanic storm troopers, some of them lukewarm in their support for Washington during his life, become thundering zealots after his death, threatening the Art Institute with physical harm and compelling the police to order the painting imprisoned to avoid a riot. Sorry. Court precedents that support the duty of the police to control the mob, not the person whose expression is inciting it, run long and deep.

But the bigger irony is that Washington was a bold supporter of civil liberties. He probably would have laughed the painting off. "We're not in the business of censorship," he said when his aldermanic enemies bashed his administrator for a black poet's controversial poem on the city Department of Fine Arts' novel "Dial-A-Poem" service. "If you scratch one word, where does it stop?"

I am sure Washington would have had the good sense to have avoided making a major issue out of a silly drawing. Such good sense would have denied it the publicity it has enjoyed as it is flashed constantly on the local evening news as this issue drags on.

Frankly, I wonder how the aldermen found out about the painting. They are less likely to be associated with the fine arts than with, say, crayons and coloring books. Perhaps the artist told them. Maybe Nelson wanted what in the '60s we used to call a "happening" and today is called a media event. Whether that is what he wanted, it is precisely what he got.

"In the city of Chicago, the liberty of free expression is gravely ill," civil libertarian Nat Hentoff wrote in New York's Village Voice. So, it appears, is the sobering influence of good leadership.

JUNE 19, 1988

TAWANA BRAWLEY, TWICE A VICTIM

When elephants fight, according to an ancient proverb of the East African Kikuyu people, it is the grass that suffers. So it is with the peculiar case of Tawana Brawley, a black schoolgirl who, whether or not she was the victim of a racially motivated abduction and rape as she says, appears to have become lost in the struggle between her "friends."

Last November, police found Brawley, then 15, of Wappinger Falls, N.Y., smeared with dog excrement and wrapped in a garbage bag, racial epithets written on her body in charcoal. She said she had been sexually abused over four days by six white men, one of whom showed a police-type badge and holster.

The case shocked the nation. Bill Cosby and a black publisher offered a $25,000 reward. Boxer Mike Tyson offered to pay for her college education. Black leaders challenged politicians and the media to explain why the bizarre case was not receiving more attention. That is not its problem today.

It has received the world as an audience via the media, including "Donahue" and "Nightline," with one question constantly raised: Can a black get justice in America's criminal justice system? Unfortunately, the case has turned into too much of a media circus and a mud-wrestling match for political opportunists to be a good one on which to judge that question.

The Brawley family brought in three controversial heat-seeking black activists, Rev. Al Sharpton and lawyers Alton Maddox Jr. and C. Vernon Mason, all of New York City and all of whom achieved national fame for forcing the Howard Beach case to a special prosecutor. In that case, one black man was killed and another badly beaten by white youths in Queens.

Brawley's hive of advisers pressured Gov. Mario Cuomo to appoint New York State Atty. Gen. Robert Abrams as special prosecutor in her case. Then they added to its bizarre nature with their bizarre behavior. Dissatisfied with Abrams because he has never tried a criminal case, they have refused to let her or her family cooperate with police or talk to reporters.

They are not impressed with the teams of seasoned prosecutors Abrams has under his command and the resources the state of New York has committed to Brawley's case.

Instead, they have accused the state of a cover-up in which they also suggested, while offering no evidence, that the Mafia, the Ku Klux Klan and the Irish Republican Army are involved.

Unfortunately for Brawley's hive of advisers, her story has fallen apart. Medical tests showed no evidence of injury, sexual assault or lack of food. Police and reporters have found nothing to back up her account but quite a bit that contradicts it.

For example, some of her school chums and neighbors saw her at a party and elsewhere in the housing complex where she formerly lived during the four days she was missing and presumably held captive. Two neighbors say they called police after seeing her acting strangely and crawling into a garbage bag. Other witnesses say they heard voices and activity in the Brawleys' former apartment, then supposedly empty. Police later found dog feces and discarded charcoal in the courtyard and some of Brawley's clothing in the apartment.

Then last week Perry McKinnon, a private investigator and former aide to Sharpton, said on TV that Brawley's advisers had doubted her story all along but were keeping the charade going to enhance their own stature and fundraising abilities. "There was no case, only a media show," he told WCBS- TV.

Sharpton and the lawyers called McKinnon a liar, but their credibility, already shaken, is crumbling. Abrams has subpoenaed McKinnon and the advisers may be on the verge of becoming defendants.

Sharpton, Mason and Maddox are men who would be "King"—Martin Luther King. They look more like clowns. As a black American, I see no reason to laugh. If they have been using Brawley's misfortune to squeeze an unsuspecting public of money and support under false pretenses, the joke may be on me.

And what about the central question: What really happened to Tawana Brawley?

Whatever happened, her misfortune has been compounded by sharpies like Sharpton and the rest who have not allowed her to go before a grand jury and let justice take its course. They are elephants of activism wrestling with elephants of the state while Brawley and the rest of us down here in the grass try to keep our heads down.

JANUARY 20, 1988

THANKS FOR BEING HONEST, JIMMY "THE GREEK"—TOO HONEST

Thank you, Jimmy "the Greek" Snyder. Your remarks about black athletes help confirm what many of us have been saying about the entertainment industry known as professional sports.

Patterns of racial discrimination run so deeply through professional sports, as through the rest of our society, that even a savvy 70-year-old oddsmaker like yourself can lose track of what is acceptable and what is just plain goofy to say on television.

You goofed after being asked by a TV reporter in a Washington restaurant for your comments on black athletes as part of a story observing Rev. Martin Luther King Jr.'s birthday.

Most folks know how to finesse such moments, even to the point of outright hypocrisy. President Reagan, who fought King while the civil rights leader was alive, lavishes him with tributes now that he is dead—even while opposing reforms King's movement brought about.

But you didn't play that game, Jimmy. You said what was on your mind and your mind had some pretty oddball notions about black athletes: "They've got everything. If they take over coaching like everybody wants them to, there's not going to be anything left for the white people. ...I mean, all the players are black; I mean, the only thing that the whites control is the coaching jobs."

Yeah, you really stepped in it with that, Jimmy.

"The black is a better athlete to begin with," you said. "Because he's been bred to be that way, because of his high thighs and big thighs that go up into his back and they can jump higher and run faster because of their bigger thighs, you see..."

"This goes back all the way to the Civil War when...the slave owner would breed his big black to his big woman so that he could have a big black kid..."

I believe you when you say you were trying to praise, not demean, black athletes. You just had a peculiar way of doing it that reminded everyone of how a seemingly intelligent guy like you can harbor some pretty ridiculous notions about race.

It also reminded a lot of us how often the sentiments you expressed must be passed around in backrooms and boardrooms, in and out of sports.

Your "big thighs" sentiments were essentially like those of sports broadcasters who, in the heat of play-by-play analysis, attribute skill in white players to "intelligence" but in black players to "natural" talent. And although your remark, perhaps offered in jest, that "there's not going to be anything left for the white people" was compared to last year's gaffe by former Los Angeles Dodgers vice president Al Campanis when he said blacks do not have the "necessities" to manage, it differs little from positions respected conservatives offer in complete seriousness.

"What a court adds to one person's constitutional rights, it subtracts from the rights of others," said Judge Robert Bork. Was he not saying, in effect, that if we continue to give rights to blacks and other minorities there will not be anything left for whites?

Sen. Paul Simon thought so. When he asked the judge to clarify his statement before the Senate Judiciary Committee, Bork did not back down. "I think it's a matter of plain arithmetic," he said.

When Bork says it he gets praise from conservatives and begrudging admiration from moderates. When you say it, Jimmy, you get the ax.

Sometimes it is not what you say but how you say it. Your mistake was to articulate your sentiments in the words of common folk.

Of course, there is another way of looking at it that could have kept you out of trouble. As Simon told Bork, "I have long thought it to be fundamental in our society that when you expand the liberty of any of us, you expand the liberty of all of us."

Judge Anthony M. Kennedy, no liberal, agreed. "Our constitutional history is replete with examples," said the current Supreme Court nominee. "As a result, all of our freedoms have been enhanced."

I hope your experience has taught some folks a valuable lesson, Jimmy. You do not have to show the race hatred of a Ku Klux Klansman or the racial fear of Bernhard Goetz to be a racist. You can have many black friends and still qualify, just by showing the racial ignorance of, say, an Al Campanis.

Now, like him, you're the fall guy. Some of us are willing to forgive you, Jimmy. The entertainment industry known as professional sports won't.

APRIL 6, 1988

DR. KING'S LEGACY: THE WAY IS CLEAR, THE WILL IS UNCERTAIN

It is always dangerous to play the game of "What if...?" But I cannot help but think Rev. Martin Luther King Jr., who was assassinated 20 years ago this month, would be amused to see what some people have done to his memory.

I think he would be amused to see his status exalted in some quarters to that of a saint. Ol' "Doc," as his associates called him, didn't even want long eulogies at his funeral. He said he just wanted somebody to say that "Dr. King tried to love somebody." He wanted to be remembered only as "a drum major for justice."

But if Dr. King would be amused by what others have done to his memory, he would be thoroughly bemused to see what has happened to his movement.

The broad coalition of students, laborers, sharecroppers, politicians, clergy and ethnic leaders he pulled together has split many separate ways. The moral clarity of his campaign against America's legal apartheid has become so muddled that even conservatives like Ronald Reagan, who opposed both the Civil Rights Act of 1964 and the Voting Rights Act of 1965, speak as if they know more about the civil rights movement than those who led it.

In fact, that's the justification Mr. Reagan has used to battle affirmative action and other modest efforts designed to open opportunities for women and minorities; he labels them "preferential treatment."

Maybe. No fair-minded person is comfortable with the idea of quotas.

But conservatives do not do Dr. King justice if they think "affirmative action" is an idea that popped up after his death. As he pointed out during the last Sunday sermon of his life, the first people to benefit from preferential treatment were not black. They were the people who settled the West and the Midwest in the years after the Civil War under an act of Congress that gave away millions of acres of land to encourge expansion and settlement of the Western frontier and, as he said, "to undergird its white peasants from Europe with an economic floor."

"But not only did (the government) give the land, it built land-grant colleges to teach them how to farm. Not only that, it provided county agents to further their expertise in farming. Not only that, as the years unfolded it provided low interest rates so that they could mechanize their farms. And to this day thousands of these very persons are receiving millions of dollars in federal subsidies every year not to farm. And these are so often the very people who tell Negros that they must lift themselves by their own bootstraps."

At the same time, Dr. King noted, the Emancipation Proclamation freed the slaves without so much as a pot to put their porridge in.

"It's all right to tell a man to lift himself by his own bootstraps, but it is cruel jest to say to a bootless man that he ought to lift himself by his own bootstraps," he said.

Twenty years after Dr. King's death, most black Americans are enjoying the benefits of his work, in one way or another. Legal segregation is a thing of the past, blacks are in positions of visibility and authority that would have been hard to imagine 20 years ago and, depending on whose statistics you believe, a half to two-thirds of black Americans can be called "middle class."

But that leaves about 30 percent of black America still living under poverty, with life worse in many ways. When opportunities opened up, the most upwardly mobile blacks were the first to leave urban ghettos, leaving the hard-core unemployed more socially isolated than ever. With street gangs, drug dealers, teen pregnancy and inferior schools, many are locked into a seemingly permanent "underclass."

The biggest problems facing black Americans today are economic. They are not likely to be solved with civil rights remedies, but they could be relieved with public and private action to encourage economic re-development and rebirth in our inner city ghettos, just as government incentives played a key role in helping pioneers develop the Old West.

American ingenuity is expected to create millions of new private sector jobs by the end of this century. Yet millions of our young people will not be able to fill those jobs unless we reform our schools, break the welfare cycle and encourage new businesses to open in the communities of the people who need them most, especially when they can be owned and managed by some of those same people.

The government has no more land to give away, but it can invest in a new generation of urban pioneers. As Dr. King once said, "We now have the techniques and resources to get rid of poverty. The real question is whether we have the will."

FEBRUARY 24, 1988

A BREACH IN TV'S CYCLE OF IGNORANCE ABOUT BLACK LIFE

Long before "The Cosby Show" made its debut in the fall of 1983, Bill Cosby had to argue with writers, producers and network executives who questioned whether the program's middle-class Huxtable family was "typical" of black family life.

And after it hit the air, some critics ridiculed it as "a white show." One New York City critic went so far as to say Cosby was "so white he didn't even qualify to be an Uncle Tom."

This was foolish talk, of course. The middle-class Huxtables represent values to be found in far more black American households than the goofy clowns Hollywood usually passes off as typical black folks.

And Cosby got the last laugh. Black and white households across the nation welcomed the program as a respite from the narrow view of black family life put forth by such past efforts as "Amos 'n' Andy," "Beulah," "Amen" and "The Jeffersons." Now in its fourth season, "Cosby" remains firmly perched at the top of the ratings and in the nation's hearts.

Still, it is curious that the skeptics, almost all of them white, are so firmly convinced they know more about black life than the black people who live it.

"Whenever someone starts talking about a 'typical' black family," said Dr. Alvin Poussaint, an associate dean at Harvard Medical School and a consultant to the program, "I ask them where they got their image of black family life. Usually it turns out that they got it from watching television." Speaking as part of a panel discussion I moderated last week at the University of Illinois at Chicago, Poussaint asked the members of the predominately black audience to imagine what they would do if they were asked to write a story about life in an Asian-American household.

The statement brought a laugh. Except for the few Asian-American students in attendance, none of us claimed to have the background (the "cultural context," as Poussaint calls it) to know enough about Asian-American home life—at least not without doing a lot of research.

Yet the entertainment industry known as prime-time television routinely allows writers from middle-class and suburban white backgrounds to create inner-city minority characters without bothering to find out how minorities really think or behave. The results often are a perpetuation of stereotypes from the "Amos 'n' Andy" days that are so removed from everyday reality that they harm the view whites have of minorities and the view minorities have of themselves.

And the more they are shown, the more they are believed. That's how institutional racism works. It is not the racism that wears white sheets or burns crosses. In all likelihood, the writers, producers and other creative types mean no harm. This is not the racism of hate or fear. It is the racism of habit. It is the racism of ignorance that feeds upon itself and becomes institutionalized into a tradition that over time allows myth to be mistaken for truth.

Cosby, to his credit, has tried to break that cycle of ignorance. Unlike "All in the Family," which Cosby felt only made viewers more comfortable with their prejudices, he vowed to avoid drawing cheap laughs from race, sex, obesity or old age. He hired Poussaint to help screen out subtle stereotypical images and to insert subtle but positive information about black American life.

As a result, a girlfriend of young Theo Huxtable was rewritten so she would admire his scholarship as much as his basketball skills. A Norman Mailer novel assigned to Theo as homework was changed to "Invisible Man," a classic by black writer Ralph Ellison. Mentions of institutions like Harvard or Yale were changed to prominent black universities like Howard, Morehouse or Central State.

Poussaint has been criticized by some as sort of an in-house censor. That's a bum rap. As a consultant, he helps keep the show honest, but he does not have the final word. If real doctors can consult "St. Elsewhere" and real lawyers can consult "L.A. Law," it only makes sense to give real black people a voice in shows about blacks. Better yet, we should look forward to the day when real black people have more of a voice in all areas of management.

Of course, the industry's copycat syndrome is not limited to matters of race. New ideas always have a tough time in television, at least until they make their first $1 million in profits.

But perhaps the success of "The Cosby Show" will open enough minds to make it easier for television to show a little more authentic black life in dramatic shows as well as in comedies.

The media, like other industries, only hurt themselves by remaining too firmly rooted in their misguided past. We need to wake up. It's not just a good deed. It's good business.

MAY 4, 1988

THE MAYOR STANDS BY HIS MAN— AND LOOKS LIKE A HEEL

It is an enduring curiosity of politics that so many leaders are brought down not by the exposure of their foolish acts but by foolish attempts to downplay their significance.

President Richard Nixon might have completed his time in office had his administration dealt in a straightforward manner with the Watergate affair, instead of dismissing it as a "third-rate burglary."

Jesse Jackson's presidential campaign was ruined four years ago not so much by the report that he had called Jews "Hymies" and New York City "Hymietown" as by his clumsy attempts to deny it for almost two weeks before he finally apologized.

Now here in Chicago, a town whose politics have never been for the squeamish, acting Mayor Eugene Sawyer is in danger of being brought down by foolish attempts to downplay his association with a key adviser whose fanatical views make Louis Farrakhan and Lyndon LaRouche sound like George Bush.

The top aide, Steve Cokely, has become famous in recent days for saying, in taped lectures for followers of Nation of Islam leader Farrakhan, that he believes Jews are part of an international conspiracy to rule the world, a conspiracy that includes Jewish doctors who are injecting AIDS into black children.

In his tapes, sold by Farrakhan followers, Cokely shows himself to be an equal-opportunity bigot.

He criticizes Jesse Jackson and the late Mayor Harold Washington for their association with Jews and recounts a speech he gave to students at Xavier University in Cincinnati in which he covered a crucifix with some of his literature and called it a "symbol of white supremacy."

Sawyer should have expected trouble when, as an alderman, he hired Cokely in 1985 after his previous employer, former Ald. Marian Humes, fired Cokely for criticizing Columbus Day as a "racist holiday."

Of course, Sawyer jettisoned this loony right away, right? Wrong. Instead, he said he was asking Cokely to "tone down" his rhetoric, said that he was "reviewing" the situation, cited his own support for Jewish causes and called for sympathy for Cokely's need to have a job.

Okay. But does he have to have a $35,568 job as a "coordinator of special projects"?

Even if Sawyer's "review" leads to Cokely's removal, the damage of the delay will have been done.

Of course, Cokely then resigned swiftly to save his boss further embarrassment, right? Wrong. Cokely was about as enthusiastic about leaving as Ed Meese or Manuel Noriega—and twice as embarrassing. All he did was say he was sorry if his statements had offended anyone.

Of course, Chicago's black leadership, which has been so forthright in criticizing Al Campanis, Earl Butz, Jimmy "the Greek" Snyder and every other white person who has said anything even mildly racist, immediately called for this embarrassment to resign, right? Wrong.

Remember, this is Chicago, the only town that associates St. Valentine's Day with a massacre, a town whose resentments run deeper than its deep-dish pizza.

City Hall insiders say Sawyer is afraid of black backlash. Ever since a coalition of white ethnic aldermen—fierce foes of Harold Washington-and a few black alderman voted Sawyer into the mayor's seat in an all-night city council session last November, he has been trying his best to endear himself to Washington supporters, who view him with obvious skepticism.

Insiders say Sawyer is trying to buy time before edging Cokely into a less sensitive position. But Sawyer's failure to dismiss Cokely immediately only aggravates public outrage and exposes the deadly indecisiveness Sawyer showed on his historic election night, when he wavered so much over whether to accept the draft of a mostly white group that he appeared to faint from the strain.

Interestingly, Sawyer's black critics have been taking heat from Sawyer's white supporters of a sort that may be about to end. Washington's foes, who always tried to paint Washington's battle against Chicago's old-time political machine as a simple battle of black vs. white, have been pushing Sawyer as a great healer ever since they put him in power. What's the matter, they would say to Sawyer's critics, can't you deal with a black mayor who gets along with white people?

Well, Sawyer's not getting along with white people so well these days. With his reluctance to offend even the most fanatical segments of his city's black community, Sawyer looks less like a healer than a heel.

It must be comforting for traditionalists to note that business goes on as usual in Chicago, a city never mistaken for a haven of brotherly love.

MAY 25, 1988

IN HENRY HORNER OR WINNETKA, NOBODY GETS USED TO KILLING

A Winnetka woman who happens to be a friend of mine was still dealing with the shock of last Friday when she said something remarkably revealing about the way we all relate to tragedy.

As most of the nation must know by now, a wacky woman named Laurie A. Dann went berserk with a gun in Hubbard Woods Elementary School in north suburban Winnetka, killing an 8-year-old boy and wounding five other children and a college student before killing herself.

It was a tremendous shock, especially for a peaceful upper-class suburb that had only two homicides recorded in the previous 30 years.

In fact, the shock was worse for Winnetka than for those who live in some of the more violent neighborhoods of Chicago, my friend said, because at least the people who live in crime-ridden urban neighborhoods "are more used to it."

Maybe. But as one who has spent quite a bit of time in high-crime neighborhoods and has known quite a few of their residents, I have yet to meet any I would say was "used to it." I don't think anyone ever gets "used to it."

Yet I am sure that's the reaction of quite a few folks. It may explain the extraordinary amount of concern that was expressed for the emotional well-being of Winnetka's children immediately after the tragedy.

The very next day, hundreds of students, parents teachers and professional counselors poured into Hubbard Woods School, just to figure out how to reassure their children and themselves that their lives could go on, in spite of the violence and tragedy Laurie Dann brought into their lives.

There was concern that the children of Winnetka would have post-trauma stress-a difficulty sleeping at night, an inordinate fear of strangers or just a burning desire to talk it out. The coping process, as it is called, had begun.

But that's not all. Gov. James Thompson called for increased school security and there were other calls for tighter gun control laws, to keep firearms out of the hands of wacky folks like Laurie Dann.

Those are just a few of the things that happen when horror comes to one of America's wealthiest suburbs.

Two days later and miles away from Laurie Dann's shooting spree, a 9-year-old boy named Alonzo Campbell was shot and critically wounded in the crossfire of someone else's dispute while walking down the street in his neighborhood, the Henry Horner Homes public housing project.

A reporter for this newspaper tells me that when she went to the hospital to write Campbell's story, she was the only reporter there. Small wonder. It is much bigger news when children are shot in Hubbard Woods than in Henry Horner.

Horner's 6,400 residents, stacked by government policy into 10-story high-rises that stretch along seven blocks of Chicago's economically devastated West Side, are constantly terrorized by powerful gangs engaged in wars over drugs and other vices.

Children in Henry Horner Homes know stray bullets sometimes can smash through apartment windows. They learn early to do the low crawl home to avoid gunfire. One murdered boy was left sitting up in an elevator as a warning to others.

Lafeyette Wilson, a 12-year-old Henry Horner resident, has seen at least two young gunshot victims die and knows about others. In the fall, the apartment next door was firebombed.

Now his mother worries that he is becoming "unusually withdrawn." She has told Alex Kotlowitz, a Wall Street Journal reporter who befriended the family, that the child has "a lot of hate built up inside him."

It does not take a visitor to Henry Horner long to notice how children who grow up in such an environment do not remain children for long.

"A couple of weeks ago, I was standing around with some of the kids on a basketball court when somebody lit a firecracker," Kotlowitz said. "Big deal, you know? ... But the kids ran for cover. They didn't hesitate. They just disappeared."

The governor has not called for a crackdown on anything in Henry Horner. Neither has the mayor or any of the presidential candidates. Henry Horner residents may not have grown completely "used to" their violence, but it looks as if most of the rest of us have.

I do not wish to diminish Winnetka's tragedy. But in sharing the pain of those made victims by a tragedy that is not likely to happen in Winnetka again soon, is it not an appropriate time to consider those for whom senseless violence is a far more frequent occurrence?

If you want to appreciate the joys wealth can bring, consider the misery that comes with poverty.

If you want to appreciate the American dream, consider our national nightmare.

If you want to know how lucky you are, consider those who are less fortunate. It might even help you sleep better at night.

JUNE 15, 1988

A DEPLORABLE EFFORT TO HELP DENTISTS SHUN AIDS VICTIMS

A Chicago man notified his dentist of 10 years that he had the AIDS virus. For his courtesy, he was told never to come back to the dentist's office. The patient has sued. Now the Illinois General Assembly, in the apparent belief that no good deed should go unpunished, is considering a bill that would make such discriminatory conduct legal for all the state's dentists.

By allowing dentists to refer any "person with an infectious disease within 10 working days to another dentist" with "facilities or training equal to or better than the referring dentist," the law would free dentists to dump patients on other dentists, not because the patient needs special care but because the first dentist does not want to be bothered.

In a sense, the sponsors of this deplorable legislation, which whisked through a committee by a 13-4 vote after only a few minutes of testimony were allowed, are the moral equivalent of the vandals who burned an Acadia, Fla., family out of their home simply because their three hemophiliac children have the AIDS virus. What looks at first glance like a nice way to protect dentists from possible exposure to a deadly virus is really a reckless response to a serious public health dilemma, a feeble attempt to separate the feared from the fearful without educating anyone.

Although it violates ethical standards established by national medical societies that call for disciplinary action against medical personnel who refuse to treat AIDS victims, the proposed law has the backing of the Illinois State Dental Society, which argues that dentists do not want any government telling them whom they should treat.

Although that response sounds reasonable at first, it raises the wrong question. Since authorities believe as many as 1.5 million people are infected with the AIDS virus and that more than 90 percent do not know it yet, all dentists, as well as other medical workers, should be following the guidelines established by the federal Centers for Disease Control with all patients, rather than depending on the patients to tell them they have the virus- especially when states are considering legislation that will make AIDS victims even less likely to reveal their condition.

That means dentists should wear surgical gloves and masks when working in contact with body fluids. Unfortunately, many dentists would rather not bother to "glove up," whether for reasons of vanity, convenience or fear of unsettling patient confidence. That, in itself, is a shame, since the risk of catching herpes, hepatitis or a similar communicable disease probably is greater than that of catching AIDS. Of course, a dentist has as much right to behave foolishly as anyone else. Even so, legislation designed to help him or her discriminate will hardly help.

Besides, the legislation itself could be life-threatening to patients. The 10-working-day limit, dangerous for most patients who have, say, a gum infection, could be fatal to someone whose immune system already has been thrown haywire by AIDS.

Then there are those within the profession who think dentistry is demeaned by laws that allow dentists to cop out on their fellow medical professionals, like surgeons and paramedics who face greater daily risk of AIDS exposure.

"The medical community is going to say once again that dentists are not really doctors," said Dr. John Davis, dentistry specialist at the University of Chicago's Zoller Clinic. "Or that we are not really ethical. That bothers me as a professional."

"A soldier can't decide in the heat of battle that it's too cold, there's too many bullets and I want to go home," said Dr. Stuart Levin, infectious disease expert at Rush-Presbyterian–St. Luke's Medical Center. "To do so would be a dereliction of duty, a cowardly act. If a dentist does not want to act as a professional, he should not expect to be called 'doctor.'"

Sadly, now that the public has more education and fewer irrational fears than ever about AIDS, legislation to protect discrimination against its victims revives the notion that carriers of the virus or victims of the full-blown disease should be regarded as civilly as lepers in the Middle Ages.

And that poses long-term danger. Even the Reagan administration, as hard- nosed as they come about protecting the rights of majorities against aggressive civil libertarians, has come around to the position that it is better to encourage those who are in high-risk lifestyles (particularly the three H's: homosexuals, hemophiliacs and hypodermic needle-using drug addicts) to be tested and, if found "positive," to be candid with those who should know about their condition.

If patients with AIDS know it could result in the loss of their chosen health care provider, they simply will be less candid with their dentists and with anyone else who has a need to know. Unless politicians begin to show some responsible leadership on this issue, the battle against AIDS, as one expert put it, will be won in the laboratories but lost in the streets.

OCTOBER 19, 1988

SOME VICTIMS DON'T ELICIT THE SYMPATHY OF CONSERVATIVES

When George Bush and other great conservative thinkers chastise liberals for caring more about criminals than their victims, I wish they showed a little more care for victims like Brenda Patterson of Winston-Salem, N.C.

She may not be a victim of violence, but she is a victim as surely as if she had been bopped on the head by a purse snatcher.

Her troubles began when she was hired as a teller and filing clerk at the local McClean Credit Union in 1972, she says. That was when her supervisor told Patterson, who is black, that she would be working with all white women and "they probably wouldn't like her."

She soon found herself loaded down with the work of three or four people, more work than anyone else in her job category. When others went on vacation, she was ordered to take care of their work as well as her own. But when she went on vacation, her work piled up until she returned.

She also was the only worker in her job category who was assigned to clean and dust. When she complained, her supervisor told her that—get this!—"blacks are known to work slower than whites by nature."

All of the above and more are alleged in racial-harassment charges she filed against her employer after she was laid off in 1982, and she has witnesses ready to back up her testimony.

Yet the case has found its way to the Supreme Court, hung up on what conservative hardliners in other circumstances might call "technicalities." In hearing Patterson's case, the Supreme Court has decided to hear re-argument of Runyon v. McCrary, the landmark 1976 decision under which Patterson filed. That move comes as a shock, particularly to the civil rights community. It appears to confirm fears that the Reagan-era court is prepared not just to maintain the status quo on civil rights reforms but to turn the clock back.

The high court decided in Runyon that the family of a black child who had been denied admission to a private school because of his color was entitled to damages under the 1866 Civil Rights Act, a law passed just after the Civil War to protect former slaves from contracts intended to bind them back into the conditions of slavery under the Southern "Black Codes."

The Reagan Justice Department decided to stay out of it, but other conservatives, including the Washington Legal Foundation, which was founded as an ideologically conservative version of the American Civil Liberties Union, vigorously jumped in on the side of Patterson's employer.

They argue that the original 1866 law was intended to provide only what it says, that all people shall have the same right "to make and enforce contracts" as whites.

Paul Kamenar, the foundation's executive legal director, argued that the high court is "usurping Congress by continuing with the fiction that Congress had abolished all discrimination in private" back in 1866. To dig this up like some sort of archeological find, he says, makes redundant all the actions taken by the civil rights movement in the 1960s and '70s.

That's persuasive, but not convincing. No civil rights law passed before or since has the broad scope or offers the same range of penalties and remedies as Runyon v. McCrary. No other law offers as much ammunition against discrimination by private schools, shops, insurance companies, business contactors and employers with fewer than 15 workers.

Patterson, who originally filed her complaint with the Equal Employment Opportunity Commission, turned to Runyon after she found that EEOC procedures would not entitle her to a jury trial or to damages.

Conservatives say they are tough on crime, but when it comes to defending the rights of those accused of violating civil rights laws, they can turn soft as oatmeal.

After all, this is not a case of affirmative action or so-called "reverse discrimination." Patterson's allegations describe straight, old-fashioned racism with uncommon clarity. If civil rights laws have no teeth in a case like hers, what does?

Fortunately, Justice Antonin Scalia, who may be the court's most respected conservative voice, has offered a ray of hope that reason will prevail. The Supreme Court knew about its "redundancy" when it decided Runyon 12 years ago, he said as he intensely questioned Roger S. Kaplan, the credit union's counsel. So why should the court disregard its own precedent in this case? Scalia asked.

When Kaplan responded that a decision such as Runyon "intrudes on Congress," Scalia shot back, "If that's all you have, Mr. Kaplan, I'm afraid that's nothing."

Agreed. Thank you, Justice Scalia. Everyone is entitled to her day in court. Maybe someday Brenda Patterson will have hers.

DECEMBER 21, 1988

MAYBE WE SHOULD PAY CONGRESSMEN ACCORDING TO MERIT

Poor Congress. Once again our lawmakers have been backed into a corner and forced to deal with one of the most difficult, agonizing, hand-wringing, teeth-gnashing decisions they ever have to face: their own pay.

Otherwise brave and courageous members of Congress want to run and hide in a closet when questions of their own pay come up. It's not that they don't want the money. Like every other working stiff, they do.

But unlike other working stiffs, they also have to answer to constituents back home. Most, it appears, are scared witless that, no matter how modest the increase may be, it will come back to haunt them in their next election bid.

So how do they do it without touching off a voter backlash? At present, rather than take the heat, they pass the buck.

They pass it to a presidential Commission on Executive, Legislative and Judicial Salaries. If the commission calls for a raise and the President approves it and Congress fails to vote it down in 30 days, it automatically goes into effect. Call it "dynamic inaction."

The commission recently suggested a 50 percent increase for consideration by the President. If he approves it in his budget message to Congress on Jan. 9, it would boost their current $89,500 to (ring the cash register) $135,000. But there's a catch: The lawmakers would have to give up their honorariums, the lucrative fees they receive for speeches and other public appearances. House members can keep up to 30 percent of their salary ($25,850) and senators can keep up to 40 percent ($35,800). The rest they donate to charity.

But even with that giveback, they're still catching heat. Ralph Nader, for example, calls it "a shameless salary grab."

Of course, Nader, by his own accounting, takes in $200,000 a year in speaker's fees, not including his book royalties. But at least he has to sing for his supper. Members of Congress, if their new increase goes through, will sing less yet make more. No wonder they want to hide rather than go on the record with a vote.

Obviously, Congress would ease public resentment if it would just go a little further. Lawmakers should go ahead and vote themselves a pay increase, but base it on performance.

In every other sector of our society, pay somehow is related to merit. It may seem a bit outlandish to pay $1 million to a basketball player to play a kid's game, but we also know he would not be earning that much unless he was worth much more in revenues to the team owner. The same is true of million-dollar TV news anchors and movie stars.

Not so in Congress. Members of Congress are paid the same, rain or shine, whether or not unemployment, inflation, the deficit and international drug trafficking are running amok and the country is sinking into pestilence and despair.

Consider, then, the possibilities of a merit system that would reward senators and congressmen for their performance, not their bulljive.

If Congress housed the homeless, balanced the budget, put a serious dent in drug traffic and actually passed rules and regulations that they had to follow like everyone else, they would get their pay raise.

Of course, if they dragged their heels and failed, they would have to give it back. After all, a true merit system also has to have its demerits.

Imagine a system that would penalize congressmen who are linked to misconduct, conflicts of interest and other appearances of impropriety. We could save a lot of money if we paid politicians according to their honesty and candor. Lots of money.

And how about attendance? When I watch C-SPAN, what are all those empty seats I see most of the time? Where are all our lawmakers anyway? Out getting coffee? Many of us who live and work in the real world get docked if our bosses don't know where we are. The same should be true of Congress.

For that matter, we could use a little less abuse of franking privileges that allow senators and representatives to use the mails free. I get enough junk mail as it is.

Yes, I am beginning to like this idea of a merit system for congressional pay. The possibilities seem endless, even if the probability does not.

Congressmen and senators don't mind putting our money where their mouths are. Maybe when it's their money that hangs in the balance, they would mind their mouths more often.

Of course, you may ask, isn't merit what elections are supposed to be about? Sure. Maybe that says something about why so many senators and congressmen are so sheepish about asking for a raise.

INDEX

O

Q. & A. WITH CLARENCE PAGE

You've been writing your column for three decades now. How much has your perspective evolved over the years?

I used to be troubled by negative mail. Then I learned to stop taking it personally. When a person who castigates me like pond scum one week praises me as a national hero after I've written something with which they agree, I realize that it is my opinion that they are responding to, not to me. Let 'em vent. It's cheaper than therapy.

What do you think gives your column such a broad appeal?

I'm pleased when readers say, "I don't agree with you much, but I appreciate knowing where you stand." I think when people turn to the opinion pages of their newspaper, they expect to read some opinions—strong, clearly defined, and offering enough information and insight to help them form an opinion of their own, whether they agree with mine or not. I try to include a few laughs where appropriate, too.

There's so much information exploding all around us every day through different media, I'm delighted to hear a reader say they liked a column so much they pinned it to the door of their refrigerator. That's great. That's the place for the most important messages in many family's households—like mine. I call it the Refrigerator Pulitzer. Every columnist wants to connect with their readers with that deep degree of passion.

You've garnered a reputation as an unbiased critic unafraid to strike at either side of the aisle. How do you maintain this balance in your writing and TV appearances?

I try to set my moral compass to what's best for America's families, not what's best for a particular political party or interest group. That can be tough sometimes, not when I'm criticized by the relentless grumps but when I am criticized by someone from my own opinion tribe who says, "I thought you were on our side." I assure them, "I am on your side, even when I offer bitter medicine. It may be hard to swallow but it's good for you."

My perspective hasn't changed much, but the world has. I've always portrayed myself as a good Midwestern, middle-of-the-road voice for the sensible center. I am amused when people paint me as a hard-core liberal or hard-core conservative, based on the same column!

But as true right-wingers have gotten a stronger voice in Congress and the media, I am often viewed as a liberal simply because I don't call myself a conservative. I still defend a lot of conservative ideas when I think they offer a reasonable alternative to what liberals are offering. But I have learned better than to expect many conservatives to give me credit for that.

How has your identity as an African American informed the politics of your column?

It's interesting to me that I and every other black columnist I know get occasional complaints from conservatives that we write about race "all the time." I don't write about race all the time, but the very fact that so many people seem to see race in my columns tell me just how intensely feelings about race, among other tribal considerations, inform everybody's politics—whether they want to acknowledge it publicly or not. As an African American who grew up in the last days of Jim Crow segregation and the hard-won victories of the civil rights revolution, I write about racial issues more often than most white columnists do. But when I write about climate change, mortgage defaults, student loans, the obesity epidemic, the future of public education, are those racial issues? Maybe not on the surface, but my experience informs my awareness of how differently those issues play out in white communities compared to communities of color.

Similarly, growing up in a black, low-income community but attending integrated schools helps me to understand that you don't have to be black to be poor in America. In fact, white poor outnumber black and Hispanic poor, even though a lower percentage of whites are in poverty. Yet you'd hardly know that from the coverage that poverty usually receives in daily news reports. As a result, I can't mention that fact on a radio program, for example, without hearing from some white person who wants to know my source for that, as if they can't believe it. My source is the Census Bureau. But growing up black in America has made me more sensitive to the value of facts against a flood of rumors and the importance of empathizing with disadvantaged people, regardless of their race, ethnicity, gender, or other background.

Have you found it difficult to try to keep ahead of the curve after over thirty years in journalism?
It is rather unsettling to have your world shaken up as much as the world of media has been rattled in recent years. I thought, for example, that I would never squeeze my bulging imagination into the tight little girdle of Twitter. But, counseled by my millennial-generation son, I love it now. It's not only fun but an easy way to direct people to my column to get a longer read. Of course, my growing appreciation for Twitter means that my son and his crowd are doing what they did when us boomers took over Facebook. They're moving onto something newer that I don't understand—like Instagram.

But what I find reassuring is that the fundamentals of journalism remain in place. Whatever the medium of conveyance might be, people still want reliable news and opinions. They've only got so much time to spend with their media, so we in the media still have to compete for their valuable time and loyalty. Even though the competition grows increasingly fierce, I find it's invigorating. It keeps me young—maybe young enough to figure out Instagram.

Who are the journalists you most enjoy reading today?

I'm surprised and saddened by how many of them are dead. Mike Royko, Molly Ivins, James Baldwin, Louis Grizzard, Art Buchwald and Erma Bombeck are a few of the columnists that excited and amazed me over the years with their fresh points of view, lively wit, and most significantly, their ear for the language, issues, and attitudes of the people and communities that nurtured them. Reading Royko you could almost hear the voices of the Eastern European men in his father's tavern hashing out the issues of the day over shots and beers. Reading Baldwin's essays you can hear the voice of a black kid who grew up with more religion than money in the Harlem ghetto of his time, trying to hash out the ethical contradictions of the world around him. Voices as old as Damon Runyon and Frederick Douglass that shaped my own approach to writing still amaze me with how robustly they live long after their creators are gone.

Among the living, I'd say I admire David Brooks for his tireless search for new ideas regardless of the politics involved, Nicholas Kristof for calling attention to stories the rest of media ignore too often (like the kidnapped Nigerian schoolgirls), Kathleen Parker as a witty outside-NYC counterpoint to Maureen Dowd—whom I also love to read—and my Pulitzer-winning pal Leonard Pitts who has breathed new life into the column-writing trade at a time when his voice is very much needed. This is, of course, not a complete list.

ABOUT THE AUTHOR

Clarence Page, the 1989 Pulitzer Prize winner for Commentary, is a columnist syndicated nationally by Tribune Media Services and a member of the Chicago Tribune's editorial board. Page also has been a regular contributor of essays to "The NewsHour" with Jim Lehrer and a regular panelist on "The McLaughlin Group," NBC's "The Chris Matthews Show," ABC's "Nightline" and BET's "Lead Story" news panel programs.

Page's other honors include lifetime achievement awards from the National Society of Newspaper Columnists, the Chicago Headline Club and the National Association of Black Journalists. He received a 1980 Illinois UPI awards for community service for an investigative series titled "The Black Tax" and the Edward Scott Beck Award for overseas reporting in 1976.

Page was a reporter, producer and community affairs director at WBBM-TV from 1980 to 1984. Before that, he was a reporter and assistant city editor for the Chicago Tribune, during which he participated in a 1972 Task Force series on vote fraud, which also won a Pulitzer Prize.

His book "Showing My Color: Impolite Essays on Race and Identity" was published in 1996 by HarperCollins.

Born in Dayton, Ohio, he grew up in Middletown. He began his journalism career as a freelance writer and photographer for the Middletown Journal and Cincinnati Enquirer at the age of 17. He graduated from Ohio University with a bachelor's of science in journalism in 1969. Forty-five years later, his alma mater inducted him into its Journalism Hall of Fame.

He also has received honorary degrees from Columbia College in Chicago, Lake Forest College, the Chicago Theological Seminary and the John Marshall School of Law, among others.

Page is married, has one son, and lives in the suburbs of Washington, D.C.